Dougie Young

i

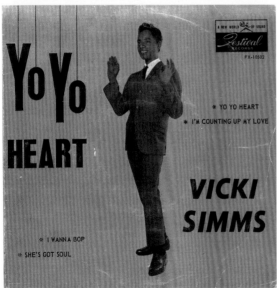

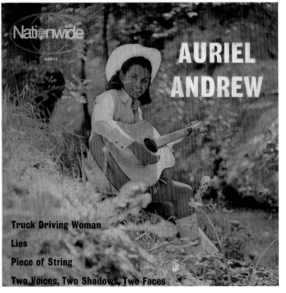

JIMMY LITTLE
on Festival Records

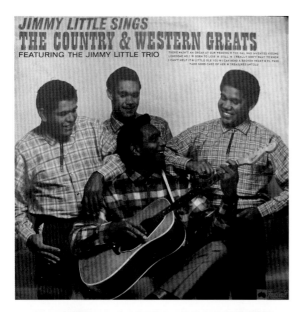

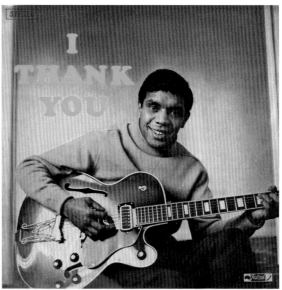

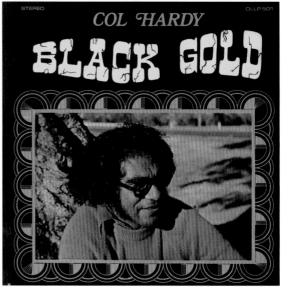

Live in Alice Springs: (top) Mac Silva on the traps with the Country Outcasts, 1975; (below) the Warrabrai Country Bluegrass Band, 1978

Herb Laughton in Alice, CAAMA cassette cover; artwork by Redback Grafix

Isaac Yamma, CAAMA cassette cover; artwork by Redback Grafix

Roger Knox on bass

(Above) Darwin's Mills Sisters; (below) Wilga Williams

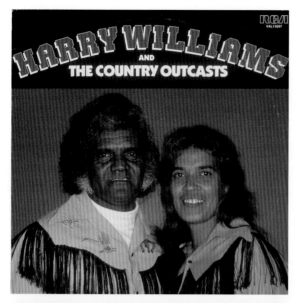

(Above) Bobby McLeod singing on ABC TV'S 7:30 Report, *1988*
(Below) Roger Knox and Euraba Band, Buddy Knox at far left

Kev Carmody on stage at the QSong concert, Brisbane, 2010

On NITV (National Indigenous Television network): (above) the reformed Mop and the Drop-Outs at the Woodford Folk Festival in 2011; (below) Troy Cassar-Daley and Warren H. Williams at the Tamworth Country Music Festival, 2011

Archie Roach and Ruby Hunter; painting by Jandamurra Cadd

In the quarter century since Australia's Bicentennial celebration of 1988, Aboriginal people have come to occupy a more visible and prestigious role in their country's culture, even as their communities continue to suffer levels of discrimination and neglect that are little short of genocidal. But long before Aboriginal painters, singers, dancers, actors and directors received acclaim both locally and internationally, it was country music that first gave the original Australians a voice in modern Australia.

Black skin and country music might seem unlikely bedfellows to some, but country has always offered an outlet for the disenfranchised, and Aboriginal country music has a long and rich history. Its earliest and best-known star is certainly JIMMY LITTLE, but he's far from an isolated figure: DOUGIE YOUNG, HARRY AND WILGA WILLIAMS, AURIEL ANDREW, VIC SIMMS, BOB RANDALL, BOBBY MCLEOD and ISAAC YAMMA, for example, all played crucial parts in the evolution of the music, and the tradition was carried forward into the new century by the likes of ROGER KNOX, TROY CASSAR-DALEY, KEV CARMODY, ARCHIE ROACH and RUBY HUNTER.

These are Australia's 'sorrow songs' – part honky tonk, part bush ballad, and all Aboriginal. They told black stories in a way white Australians could also understand, because a love of country music was something they shared, if not always willingly. Aboriginal country not only gave a sense of community – and solace – to its own dispossessed people, it also offered the possibility of common ground – before there was anything else – in a divided country.

In the years since BURIED COUNTRY was initially published in 2000, it has been recognised as a groundbreaking work of cultural history and restitution, drawing on the author's in-person interviews and extensive research. The major figures in Aboriginal country are profiled in depth in its sixteen chapters, while many more are covered in its many sidebars, which also offer detailed analysis of the origins and context of the music. This new edition is expanded and fully updated, lavishly illustrated with rare photographs and memorabilia (including a new set of colour plates), and features a complete discography and index.

PRAISE FOR **BURIED COUNTRY**

Buried Country traces new pathways into the songlines
of a hidden and resonant Australian musical history.

Sophie Best, THE AGE

Buried Country is a great book. I despise terms such as
'important book', so I'll just call it a necessary book.

Paul Toohey

An overdue antidote to non-Aboriginal ignorance of the indigenous
tradition. Walker is an astute observer and interpreter of popular
roots culture . . . The reader is drawn in like a moth to the light as he
illuminates the link between country music and Aboriginal identity.

Robin Ryan, AUSTRALIAN JOURNAL OF INDIGENOUS EDUCATION

Walker's book is an act of restitution, making visible part
of our musical history that has long been submerged.

RHYTHMS

A zestful ramble through this large and little known territory. There
are so many compelling personalities and riveting stories in this
book [but] although many are deeply tragic, somehow the book
and the voices speaking within it remain remarkably buoyant.

Peter Doyle, HQ

Challenges the secularist cultural relativism of the assumed readership.

Graeme Smith, CENTRE FOR STUDIES IN AUSTRALIAN MUSIC

Greil Marcus's *Invisible Republic* explored a 'weird, old America' which
was reflected in its dusty folk songs and hillbilly tunes. With *Buried
Country*, urban cowboy Clinton Walker has done a far better job.

Jeff Apter, ROLLING STONE

PRAISE FOR **BURIED COUNTRY**

A vast underground river of passionate music that is mostly unheard by white Australia. Clinton Walker's captivating book gathers all these winding tributaries and brings them to the surface for the first time.

Noel Mengle, COURIER MAIL

Eminently readable, revealing and intriguing, [this] book should prove an eye opener for those who think of Aboriginal music purely in terms of Yothu Yindi.

Fred Dellar, MOJO

An absorbing and at times bleak account of Aboriginal country music . . . Walker wisely allows his subjects' first hand reminiscences to carry the narrative . . . Compulsively readable.

Stephen Cummings, THE AGE

Moving and timely in the extreme, it is an education and a real pleasure.

Jason Blake, ROLLING STONE

Buried Country is a powerful collection of resources. Every school, every library, should have these resources.

McKenzie Wark, THE AUSTRALIAN

If the chardonnay set stopped playing their copies of *The Buena Vista Social Club* long enough, they might find something happening in their own back yard of at least the same interest and of inestimably more relevance to where this country has been and where it is headed.

Keith Glass, THE HERALD-SUN

A vivid and intriguing look at this genre, even if you usually only listen to country music under the threat of death.

Shane Danielson, THE AUSTRALIAN

Purfleet backyard band: Robin Pacey, Fred Dumas, Joe Simon

Buried Country

THE STORY OF
ABORIGINAL COUNTRY MUSIC

Clinton Walker

VERSE CHORUS PRESS   ★   PORTLAND   MELBOURNE   LONDON

Verse Chorus Press
PO Box 14806, Portland OR 97293
info@versechorus.com

The original edition of this book was published in 2000 by Pluto Press (Australia). This expanded and completely revised edition first published in 2014 by Verse Chorus Press.

Front cover photograph: Jimmy Little. Courtesy, Jimmy Little.

Back cover photographs: (*from top left to bottom right*) Ali Mills, Auriel Andrew, Bobby McLeod, Bob Randall, Col Hardy, Dempsey Knight, Gus Williams, Wilga Williams, Lionel Rose, Roger Knox, Troy Cassar-Daley, Kev Carmody. Photos of Bobby McLeod and Bob Randall by Clinton Walker; other images courtesy of Skinnyfish Music, Opal Records, Hadley Records, Festival Records, Liberation Music, *Rolling Stone*, and Heather Perryman.

Design and layout by Louise Cornwall

The author and the publishers wish to thank all those who supplied photographs and gave permission to reproduce copyright material in this book. Every effort has been made to contact all copyright holders, and the publishers welcome communication from any copyright owners from whom permission was inadvertently not obtained. In such cases, we will be pleased to obtain appropriate permission and provide suitable acknowledgment in future editions.

Printed in China by C&C Offset Printing

Library of Congress Cataloging-in-Publication Data

Walker, Clinton, 1957-
  Buried country : the story of aboriginal country music / Clinton Walker. – Expanded and completely revised edition.
     pages cm
  "The original edition of this book was published in 2000 by Pluto Press (Australia)."
  Includes index.
  ISBN 978-1-891241-38-3 (pbk.) – ISBN 978-1-891241-97-0 (ebook)
  1. Country musicians–Australia–Biography. 2. Country music–Australia–History and criticism. 3. Aboriginal Australians–Music–History and criticism. 4. Aboriginal Australians–Biography. I. Title.
ML394.W35 2014
781.642089'9915–dc23
                    2014005224

CONTENTS

FOREWORD
by Paul Kelly

The music was, and is, always there — around the campfires, in the schoolhalls and the sideshow tents, on the ovals and beaches and under the corrugated iron roofs of open-sided sheds, in the footy clubs and pubs and churches. The music told yarns, fuelled the good times, lifted the soul and eased the pain. The end of a cigarette glows in the dark outside a backstage door. Smoke curls from under a bridge at the edge of town.

The music is a river. The mainstream rolls relentlessly on, picking up flotsam and jetsam and strewing debris along its edges while the source stays hidden, hard to get to, and the springs, creeks, feeder streams and tributaries often remain unnamed and forgotten. Songwriters and singers, like the river, simply pick things up and pass them on. Some get known locally, some further afield, but everything comes from somewhere. The local feeds the general and the many make the one.

Clinton Walker stepped into the river and went upstream and underground. He wandered up dry creekbeds and heartbreaking gullies. The tracks criss-crossed and disappeared then reappeared again. He followed the songlines and came back with this report of everyday heroism and sudden beauty.

*The Kelly Gang, fronted by Ella Kelly,
at the Tamworth Festival, 1987*

INTRODUCTION

Long before it was commonplace for Aboriginal dance companies to tour the world, or for acrylic 'dot paintings' to sell for astronomical sums (even though most of the money *still* doesn't get back to the artists), the only black Australians white Australians were aware of were either boxers or hillbilly singers – or both, in the case of Lionel Rose, world bantamweight champion and owner of numerous gold records, including a number one single.

Before indigenous Australians became known as novelists and poets, theatre producers and Hollywood movie stars, it was country music that gave them a voice in modern Australia. Country music and black skin may seem an unlikely combination to some; but like the majority of Aboriginal people, I've never seen black country music as anything bizarre, nor interpreted it as a symptom of the decline of traditional society. After all, archetypically white country music and black jazz and blues all developed in the United States from the same source, the violent meeting of Africa and Europe in the antebellum Deep South, and only added richness to the new world as a whole. *Buried Country* is about a similar culture clash – the lives in which two cultures intersected, and what grew out of that: flowers in the dustbin of history.

Telling black stories in a way white as well as black could understand, Aboriginal country music was not only a salve for its own downtrodden people, it established some common ground between black and white Australia. In today's globalized digital music market it is sadly a tradition if not in decline then certainly under siege, but Aboriginal country music continues to sustain many pockets of life, especially throughout regional Australia, and its history and legacy still informs much of the black music created in this country. It's all storytelling, after all, whether it takes the form of the plaintive warblings of acoustic guitar–toting singer-songwriters or the angry raps of urban MCs, and it wouldn't have matured the way it has without Koori country having first blazed a trail.

Once Captain James Cook 'discovered' the east coast of Australia in 1770 and the first British penal colony was established in 1788 at Port Jackson, the site of present-day Sydney, the Aboriginal civilization that dates back tens of thousands of years was rapidly destroyed. As the frontier expanded inexorably, Aboriginal people were rounded up and often massacred, much like Native Americans in the USA. The survivors were herded onto reserves run by the government or into missions run by churches. In the newly federated nation of the early twentieth century, where the 'White Australia' policy was a bipartisan article of faith, mixed-blood children were taken from their families and put into orphanages, or foster homes, or servitude – these were the 'stolen generations'. The practice continued in some states until the 1970s, displacing between 60,000 and 100,000 innocent Australians. And despite a succession of apparent victories – from the 1967 referendum that granted citizenship to Aborigines in what was their own land to the High Court's 1992 Mabo decision, which overturned the myth of *terra nullius* on which modern Australia was founded – to this day there is still no treaty between black and white Australia, and black Australians still suffer discrimination that amounts to genocide.

In his brilliant book *Black Talk*, African-American jazz musician Ben Sidran argued that "any examination of black culture in America is necessarily an examination of the relationship between black and white Americans. This relationship . . . has shaped the cultural evolution of all Americans." This is just as true of black and white Australians.

I first heard the term 'jumping fences' in Alice Springs in 1999. It refers to interracial sex, but could also serve to describe the way modern, especially post-modern, music has developed: purism is an outmoded idea, and the only way to progress – the only way to survive! – lies in cross-pollination and hybrid offspring. This is not meant as a metaphor for assimilation, the weasel word used to describe Australian government policy on Aborigines before being superseded by 'reconciliation'– rather, it is the reason why popular music remains a flourishing art form.

THROUGH A SERIES OF SIXTEEN extended profiles, accompanied by a string of interlocking sidebars, *Buried Country* describes the emergence of Aboriginal performers in modern Australian music and the parallel development of a unique tradition or genre that spanned the period from between the wars to the 1990s, when there was a palpable changing of the guard and a whole new wave of Aboriginal music broke through with more success than ever before.

An era was symbolically closing at the beginning of the 90s, when pioneers Dougie Young, Harry Williams and Isaac Yamma all died. Remarkably, given that the average life expectancy of Aboriginal Australians is criminally short, these three were the only major characters in this story who were no longer alive when the first edition of *Buried Country* was published in 2000. That another half dozen have died since then, including Jimmy Little, makes me sad indeed, but I am also glad that I committed to seeking them out so many years ago, and taking down their words when I could.

The new era that dawned in the 90s was marked by the rise of digitisation and globalisation; by the success of Yothu Yindi, with their classic 'Treaty' 12-inch remix, and dancefloor diva Christine Anu; and by the emergence of a new generation of potent folk-country singer-songwriters such as Kev Carmody, Archie Roach and the late Ruby Hunter. This consolidation provided the springboard for indigenous music to leap so confidently into the twenty-first century, in which Geoffrey Gurrumul Yunupingu and Jessica Mauboy can top the Australian charts and also look to move onto the international stage.

BEFORE AND AFTER WORLD WAR TWO, Australian Aboriginal people took to hillbilly music for a number of very good reasons. Apart from anything else, given that most Aborigines still live outside Australia's major cities, it was about all they ever heard. Certainly, the only live music they experienced – apart from what they made themselves – was in the form of touring country shows by the likes of Tex Morton, Buddy Williams and Slim Dusty.

Secondly, they could relate to it. Not only did Aborigines share many of country's roots (gospel music, minstrelsy, bush bands, ballads), they were attracted because country songs are story songs, and that was what songs did in traditional Aboriginal society – they told stories. Aboriginal culture was predominantly oral, so it latched onto an oral aspect of the whitefellas' predominantly written culture. The potency of singing was enormous to Aboriginal people; in fact, as the phrase 'No songs, no laws' suggests, singing could kill – and it can still heal. Country music was music of the land, as well, so it told the types of stories they could relate to. They found familiar its tales of horses and love gone wrong, of dead dogs and drinking.

Thirdly, country music is guitar-based: it is therefore portable and, in one sense, easy to play. Easy to play competently enough to get by, that is; like all music, however simple, at its best it is highly sophisticated.

Fourth, given the importance of mimicry in Aboriginal culture (much traditional music and dance is based on imitating animals), it seems only natural that black Australians would throw the white man's songs back at him.

Finally, there was the more intangible appeal of country's loping rhythms and mournful melodies – it radiated a sadness, a sense of loss that Aboriginal people identified with absolutely. "Because we had so much loss," as Bob Randall has said, "country music gave us something we could gain."

AS A MUSIC WRITER AND WHITEFELLA, it was the passion I had for rock'n'roll that led me inevitably to its roots in country music, as well as jazz and blues. If country was part of my own white trash heritage, jazz and blues introduced me to African-American culture. I grew up in Melbourne in the 1960s, and like everybody else I saw Jimmy Little sing 'Royal Telephone' on *Bandstand*. Even better than that, I cheered on our hometown hero Lionel Rose as he made the transition from the ring to the stage.

I first encountered Aboriginal music first-hand in Sydney in the 1980s, when the Warumpi Band, Coloured Stone and Roger Knox somehow penetrated Darlinghurst's inner sanctum of indie rock, where the likes of Nick Cave and the Go-Betweeens ruled. I can still remember the first time I heard Warumpi's 1983 debut single 'Jailanguru Pakarnu'. It was the freshest blast of roots country-rock I'd ever heard – rockabilly by any other name. Not only did I become a fan of the band, it provided my point of introduction to Aboriginal Australia. I know music can build bridges, because it's done it for me.

My friends and I made the trek to Tamworth, Australia's Nashville, a few times in the 80s. We always made sure we caught Roger Knox and his band Euraba, because to us – a mob of would-be urban cowboys with our own self-described 'country-grunge' band – Roger was an unsung black superstar, and his visits to Sydney were all too infrequent. The fact that Roger has remained a largely unsung black superstar is one of the main reasons I wrote this book in the first place, and why this new edition, which will be published in America and Europe as well as Australia, is coming out now: because the story obviously still needs to be told.

After working in the late 80s on a special called *Sing It in the Music* for what was then the Aboriginal Program Unit of ABC-TV, Australia's national broadcaster, I became more and more aware that there was a whole rich history that was in danger of disappearing without being adequately recorded. The whitefella has always had a tendency to write things down, but it's incredible that a phenomenon of the magnitude and distinction of Aboriginal country music was overlooked for so long. Except that, as American writer Mike Davis points out in *City of Quartz*: "'corporate multiculturalism' is an attitude that patronizes imported diversity while ignoring its own backyard." He's talking about arts funding in Los Angeles, but his characterisation applies equally well to the (high) arts industries in Australia; so perhaps it's not so incredible that Aboriginal country was largely ignored by the guardians of Australian culture for so long.

Compounding the problem is this music's perennial status as the poor cousin in relation to supposedly more legitimate arts. As sociologist/philosopher Pierre Bourdieu has put it, "Nothing more clearly affirms one's class than tastes in music": the ruling class and its cultural gatekeepers hate popular music, *especially* country music. When *Buried Country* was first published, there were already something like seventy books in the bibliography of Aboriginal art and painting, but only one on contemporary Aboriginal music – and this with regard to a culture that has always been predominantly oral, not visual. So I set myself the task of trying to get this story down, little knowing what a Pandora's box I was opening, how little I actually knew, and how deeply I would get drawn in.

I could never have gotten it *all* down, of course. In *The Devil's Music,* Giles Oakley rejected the idea that W.C. Handy could be called the 'father of the blues', given that "hundreds of nameless and forgotten singers and musicians, cotton-pickers, levee camp, saw-mill and turpentine camp workers, roustabouts and farm hands, were singing and playing the blues, alone or in groups, at work or at their ease" – and all these scatterlings contributed something to the evolution of the genre. But just as surely as Handy, Robert Johnson and Howlin' Wolf are seminal to the story of the blues, the great black stars of Australian country music ultimately presented themselves, and they are the subjects of the sixteen chapters that form the spine of this book.

In the (pre-Internet) mid-90s, when I was starting my research in earnest, Paul Toohey, a fine writer, told me after he was unable to help me find a rare story on Isaac Yamma he'd once read somewhere, "It's all oral." I ended up finding a lot more documentation than I expected, but it was as disparately located as the musicians themselves, and in the end, of course, it didn't remotely compare with actually going out and meeting these characters in their own country.

It was only after I was able to parlay the book publication into an accompanying documentary film that I was able to complete my research, when I went out on the road to do the shoot with director Andy Nehl and cinematographer Warwick Thornton in 1999. I couldn't help feeling a bit like John Lomax and those other musicologists who went to the Deep South in the 1950s and rediscovered – alive! – long lost bluesmen like Skip James.

Getting to know the cast of characters of *Buried Country* personally was a rare privilege, and I use that clichéd phrase here because I know that for once it's justified.

What was extraordinary, to start with, was that even though indigenous Australians die appallingly young, so many of the people I was looking for were still alive in their fifties and sixties. It became a matter of even greater urgency, then, to get their stories down.

In order to retain as much of the original book's integrity as possible, I have resisted the temptation, for this new edition, to tamper even with the chapters about those who've subsequently died – not only Jimmy Little, but also Bobby McLeod, Lionel Rose, Gus Williams, Herb Laughton and more. I thought it better to keep them alive on the page – the way I first rendered them, encountered them – rather than impose a change of tense that would have distorted the whole shape of the narrative. Naturally, I've corrected the mistakes I found, to my consternation, all through the first edition, but apart from doing that, and filling in a few hitherto grey areas as a result of everything I've learnt over the intervening decade, I have not really revised any of my analyses or critical judgements. The book remains largely as it was first written, from the vantage point of the turn into a new century.

There are more than a few new illustrations, though – including, I'm delighted to say, a section of colour plates. And there is one new chapter. This chapter, now the second-to-last, is an expanded version of what was formerly a sidebar with the same title, 'New Corridos'; it's about the wave of artists such as Kev Carmody, Archie Roach, Ruby Hunter and Tiddas who made their presence felt in the 1990s. When I first started researching *Buried Country* in those years, this phenomenon was still in the process of establishing itself. At the time, I was so consumed by the past that I paid insufficient attention to the present. The clarity brought by more than a decade of hindsight means I'm better able now to appreciate these artists' place in the bigger story; I can see how their divergence from the country tradition – in which their roots were nevertheless firmly planted – contributed to its revitalisation, and how their work represents as much as anything a resolution of the bigger story, rather than the long-rumoured death of the tradition.

I have also added an afterword. If country music is still, as it always used to claim, the biggest music in the world, there's no doubt that it's no longer quite so big, as younger audiences turn increasingly to other genres, and these last few pages discuss the way the tradition is indeed under siege, yet still alive. And kicking. What is Dan Sultan, after all, but an alt-country-soul singer? And a deadly one at that!

Unless otherwise indicated, all quotes derive from interviews I conducted personally. Detailed acknowledgments and sources are listed in the endnotes.

This guitar kills racists: Billy Craigie at the Tents, early 1970s

ULTIMATELY, BURIED COUNTRY IS A TESTAMENT to its gallery of amazing characters – to their talent, determination, grace and generosity of spirit. It was such a pleasure to be greeted, every time, with such openness and enthusiasm. I was moved and humbled by the way people could sit there and talk with humour, dignity and courage, over and above any bitterness or anger, of being stolen as a child, institutionalised and beaten; of being forcibly disconnected from their homelands and spirituality, of being slapped down by bigotry every day of their lives. Or about being raised in an alien religion, or being forced into virtual slave labour, or being prone to alcoholism; about being harassed by police and all the other authorities, and doing hard time in jail; about pervasive ill-health and death, which still steals far too many, far too young.

Aboriginal people have survived by holding fast to a sense of community, to extended family ties, if not to their stolen land. For Aboriginal musicians, this is their strength, even as it sometimes also works against them. For most musicians, life is led on the road, touring, playing to the people, but for Aborigines freedom of movement was long severely restricted – in Queensland until as recently as the mid-70s. The very Aboriginal concept of collective ownership and responsibility further discourages self-promotion. Songs are handed down and shared around – only for the common good, not commercial gain.

The record business in turn hasn't exactly come to Aboriginal music's party, at least not until very recently. Forces other than racism may well lie behind this, though – the music industry is an equal-opportunity exploiter, and it probably just couldn't see a buck in it.

Whatever the reasons, the recorded legacy of Aboriginal performers is slim. But music exists as a living, breathing entity before a recording freezes it in time, and the vinyl signposts that exist, which are admittedly one of my few yardsticks, merely point to the bigger story – the lives of the people out of which this music arose. So what I've tried to do in this book is capture those lives, the lives behind the songs, and I'd like to hope that my subjects' voices rise off the page rather than my own, because it's their stories that are important.

Unidentified singer, probably Vincent Quayle, at the 1976 National Aboriginal Country Music Festival, Canberra

The music began in captivity: and is, still, absolutely, created in captivity. So much for the European vanity: which imagines that with the single word, *history*, it controls the *past*, defines the *present*: and, therefore, cannot but suppose that the *future* will prove to be as willing to be brought into captivity as the slaves they imagine themselves to have discovered, as the *nigger* they had no choice but to invent.

James Baldwin, "Of the Sorrow Songs"

LITTLE BY LITTLE

★ Jimmy Little ★

JIMMY Little has an almost regal presence. Perched on an old kitchen chair under a shady tree in his overgrown backyard in Sydney's inner west, he offers white-sliced sandwiches from a Tupperware container and a choice of soft drinks from a cooler underfoot. Planes thunder overhead.

"Here I am," he says softly, intently, "looking out in my semi-retiring years in quiet suburbia – at the pulse of what's going on in the world – and we come from the river, and went to mission schools and mission churches . . . It's wonderful to reflect on one's own good fortune. I've been divorced from the hardship and heartache. I look back on my life and think, boy, I had smooth sailing. When I look at my fellow artists, I travelled the same path, but . . ."

Born in 1937 at Cummeragunja, near Echuca on the Murray River, which forms the border between New South Wales and Victoria, James Oswald Little carried on the daring spirit of the place. Cummera was one of the oldest missions in the country, producing two of the great pioneer fighters for Aboriginal rights, Pastor Doug Nicholls and William Cooper; it was always a community in the vanguard, a veritable Aboriginal Athens. Jimmy Little went on to become Australia's first black pop star. In the late 50s the only other Aborigines as well known as Jimmy were artist Albert Namatjira and singer/activist Harold Blair, and maybe a few boxers.

"This is where" – now Jimmy leans forward, as if to share a secret he's only just discovered himself – "I don't want to sound like I'm blowing my own trumpet, but I realize I'm unique, one of a kind, as the first commercial Aboriginal artist." Surprise lights up his face.

"Still current," he adds. "I could easily have been described as being novel in the beginning, a token, but I believe my staying power, my endurance, has finally convinced them I'm not. I'm not seasonal."

There were times along the way when Jimmy contemplated becoming a preacher like Pastor Doug. Indeed, he has an aura of serenity, warmth, and self-control – not to mention a tendency to get cosmic. He was strongly committed to the temperance movement during the 60s. But Jimmy was chosen to do something other than dedicate his life to religion. He was chosen to sing. It was perhaps not so much that he wanted a career in music as it was pre-ordained. His father, Jimmy Little Snr, was an entertainer, a song-and-dance man as well as a religious man, and Jimmy followed in his footsteps. It is the tribal way.

Jimmy Little is pure voice. He can sing anything. That's what everyone's always said. And though he may never have written many songs himself, who has ever complained of Sinatra (or Elvis, or Normie Rowe) that he didn't write his own material? When Marj, Jimmy's wife of forty years, talks of her husband and his artistry, it is in terms of singer's singers like Sinatra, Charlie Rich, Tony Bennett.

To this day Jimmy can reinvigorate every song he sings with his extraordinarily bold less-is-more approach. He can pare a song down to next to nothing, and it will still be more potent than any fully blown arrangement. Even near-acapella, Jimmy's sound is at once epic and intimate, delicate. Listen to him sing the Reels' 'Quasimodo's Dream' on his 1999 comeback album *Messenger*: when he takes it all down to a tense and breathy silence, it is a most powerful moment.

"He would sing so softly, but so strong, I was afraid to touch my guitar," says Kenny Kitching, one of Australia's leading pedal-steel guitarists, who worked with Jimmy in two separate stints in the late 50s and early 70s. "A lot of jobs he would do, he'd go out on stage and there might be an eight-piece band there, and he'd turn around to them, off mic, very politely, and say, Look, I only need piano and bass, all you other guys can have a break, go and have a drink. And then he'd turn around and tune his guitar and he'd have the crowd eating out of his hands."

In the early 50s, when Jimmy first came to Sydney, he was a hillbilly singer. It was only when he left EMI Records in 1958 and joined the Festival label that he steered in a more polished pop direction, balancing 'evergreen' Irish songs with country-gospel, and soon struck all-consuming success.

In 1963, just before the Beatles swept the world, Jimmy released a rousing version of the country-gospel standard 'Royal Telephone'. It was the year's top-selling Australian record, reaching number three in the national charts, and at the time the third-biggest Australian record ever. *Everybody's* magazine, the bible of the teen scene, named Jimmy Australian Pop Star of the Year in 1964.

If this was a peak for Jimmy, and for Aboriginal Australia, he rode out the British Invasion the same way most artists of his generation did, by keeping a loyal audience in the clubs. His sound was 'countrypolitan', to use the awkward Nashville term of the day – a hillbilly ballad base with pop trimmings. After an enormously successful comeback in the late 90s, Jimmy Little was acknowledged as the elder statesman of Aboriginal music and an iconic figure in Australian music generally – above all a much-loved Australian. But he didn't come by this status without tribulation. There was even a period, in the militant 70s, when Jimmy lost his Aboriginal audience. He was seen as part of the old guard, too polite (he wasn't called 'Gentleman Jim' for nothing). He was called other, less flattering names too. With typical grace, Jimmy continued to work with the Foundation for Aboriginal Affairs in Redfern, while at the same time playing almost exclusively to white audiences in the clubs.

"I don't want to be a leader," he said in 1979. "I just want to express myself and contribute to the happiness of everyone who comes in contact with me."

But maybe Jimmy had to accept he was a leader of sorts whether he liked it or not – and eventually, of course, he did. Yet he wears that with humility. He is a beautiful and generous man whose pride, though understated, runs deep.

Jimmy Little Snr (centre front) with the Wallaga Lake Gumleaf Band and Vaudeville, 1930s

"I never try to sell myself as a recording or television star," he told *Pix* in 1962 as he approached his breakthrough. "To me, it is far more important to be a success as a human being than an entertainer. More than anything, I want to show my people that it is possible for them to succeed in many of the fields which they have come to regard as exclusively the white man's domain."

"HE STARTED LIFE AS A PICCANINNY in a blackfellows camp in Echuca," *Pix* itself said. "He was the oldest of five piccaninnies and his father was the local balladist and dancer. At 14 he started work as a casual labourer and later earned thirty shillings a week as a bean picker."

Jimmy Little Snr was himself an Aboriginal legend, a Yuin man from the NSW south coast who met Jimmy's mother at Cummera during the Depression. Jimmy's father used to tag along with the Wallaga Lake Gumleaf Band – one of the first touring Aboriginal acts, which formed a union with Cummera's vaudeville troupe in the 1920s – and he was one of a number of Yuin men who resettled at Cummera and married.

Jimmy fondly remembers growing up during the war years. It was difficult, but at least his mother was still alive at the time. Cummera itself, though, was by then in decay.

Founded originally in 1874 by Wesleyan Methodist Daniel Matthews as the Maloga Mission Station, Cummeragunja sits on the NSW side of the Murray, opposite the Victorian township of Barmah, 20 miles upriver from Echuca. By the 1930s – by which time NSW's original Aboriginal population of around 60,000 had withered to 11,000, and Victoria's from 15,000 to only a couple of thousand – the Depression was motivating widespread political

★ *Songs of the Lord* ★

Gospel music is one of the principal building blocks of contemporary pop, a common source for both white country and black soul. Just as similarly displaced African Americans found solace, even joy, in the faith and music of a new religion, many Aboriginal people, under the mission system, also embraced Christianity and its rituals and songs. There's almost no Aboriginal country singer who didn't start out in a church choir.

For many, the term gospel conjures up images of the classic black American solo or small group form – Sam Cooke, Mahalia Jackson, the Staples Singers – funky, call-and-response stuff that grew out of field hollers and work songs as much as hymns (and, in its fusion with secular blues, spawned soul music). Aboriginal gospel started out traditionally, in the 1800s. By the 1950s, choirs from isolated outback missions in central Australia, like Hermannsburg and Ernabella, were celebrated in the south. In 1967, the Hermannsburg Choir, originally founded in the 1880s, released an album recorded at the Bethlehem Lutheran Church in Adelaide. Around the same time, albums appeared by the Ernabella Aboriginal Choir (*Singing Walkabout*, EMI) and the Elcho Island Junior Choir (W&G Records).

As country music took over as the voice of black Australia, Aboriginal gospel fused with it. Everybody knows the adage about both kinds of music, country *and* western; well, country-gospel is the real marriage made in heaven. Jimmy Little's 1963 hit 'Royal Telephone' was merely the breakthrough; Aboriginal country-gospel would continue to grow and thrive until the 1990s, while Jimmy himself cut a string of gospel albums parallel to his more usual country-pop releases.

In 1964, the Sydney branch of Dutch major label Philips released a gospel album by Torres Strait Islander duo the Assang Brothers, or 'George and Ken' as they were billed on the record; 'George' was, of course, the singer who had enjoyed an early rock'n'roll success in the 50s under the stage name Vic Sabrino. *Just a Closer Walk* was a vibrant collection of mostly well-known spirituals, not so much hot gospel as something a little cooler, more country ballad–style, and more Islander with its balmy, saltwater lilt.

Western Australia, 1960s

In the 80s, cassette technology boosted Aboriginal country-gospel as it did so many other genres. When Pope John Paul II toured Australia in 1986, he was treated to a special concert in Alice Springs that was recorded for release on cassette by CAAMA; its mix of country, gospel and country-gospel was a natural fit. Singers like Darwin's Robyn Green and Western Australian Josie Boyle led the way, followed by others all round the country, like Trevor Adamson, Steve and Carol Yarran, Leon 'Tex' Kinkaid, Mick Thaiday, Ken McKenzie ('the Christian Bushman'), Sharon Mann and Tim Edwards.

The country influence on gospel has faded since the 90s, but it's still alive, most notably in the work of Harold Dalywaters, from the Top End, a policeman and recovering alcoholic who's recently cut three CDs. When Cyril Green (born Cyril Peters), the original guitarist in the Jimmy Little Trio, recently released a belated solo album, it was a country-gospel set called *Privileged Life*. Some of the choirs are still singing out too: Hermannsburg, Ernabella and Areyonga. But young black Australians nowadays, even in the remote outback, are more likely to tune in to soul, hip-hop and R&B than country music, and this shift is reflected in more recent gospel recordings by singers like Lexine Solomon, Elverina Murgha-Johnson and Georgia Corowa.

●●●

activism. Increasingly wised-up Aboriginal people, supported by white radicals, started making a noise. Jimmy was just a toddler in February 1939 when the people of Cummera walked off the reserve in protest at deteriorating conditions and management. Encouraged by the presence of Doug Nicholls, the people crossed the river into Victoria. Jack Patten, president of the NSW Aborigines Progressive Association, was arrested. As Mavis Thorpe Clark wrote in *Pastor Doug*: "They moved from the Murray to other river banks on the edges of towns where there was some prospect of obtaining at least casual work. Their humpies jostled the shanties of unemployed whites around Mooroopna and Shepparton."

After Australia got involved in the Second World War in 1939, the protesters returned to Cummera. Then, just after the war ended, Jimmy's mother suddenly died. Jimmy still seems saddened.

"Mum was the baby of eight girls and four boys. She met Dad when she was 15; she had me when she was 17. She died when she was 29 . . . When the heart of your home is removed – whether it's Mum or Dad, or both of them – it must turn your world upside down. I felt there was a void, an emptiness – but there was also a challenge."

"NOW," SAYS JIMMY, DRAWING A BREATH, "going back to my grandparents, on both sides, that was back in a tribal existence. With each family in the clan, the natural skills are passed on, the sons would carry on the father's trade. The storytellers, in dance and song, would carry on the trade, the medicine people would carry on their trade." He continues:

In my grandfather's day, he saw new people come into the country. This is colonisation. So they knew they couldn't continue, that those lines wouldn't be passed on, and the children had to be prepared: develop – instead of me playing the didgeridoo, I'm playing another wood instrument, the guitar.

See now, my grandfather, he had to get a line of work. His skills from tribal days – tracking the animals. So he was employed by the police force, tracking human beings. So we were told as children, keep the skills sharp. Apply them to the new trade. My dad, he worked in a timber mill, fruit picking, peas and beans and corn. He liked to be outdoors, not cooped up inside. He was a freedom man. We all loved freedom.

Music was an automatic family thing. Mum and Dad were vaudevillians. They used to arrange entertainment at the various Aboriginal mission settlements, and my father would also organise teams of our people to give concerts throughout the district to raise funds for the mission. My uncles were vaudevillians, and that's how I got started.

All the seminal early Aboriginal pop influences course through Jimmy Little's veins. He heard new music on the wireless and at the pictures (hillbillies, Hollywood cowboys, Broadway musicals) and he took it all in, but his deepest roots, in vaudeville and gospel, explain much about him.

Jimmy learnt his fundamental lessons in a very old world. Vaudeville, or music hall, was the dominant popular entertainment in Australia, as it was around the globe, until the 1930s, when radio and film started to supplant it, and it had offered a vehicle for Aboriginal people to express themselves.

Vaudeville's roots could be traced back, in part, to nineteenth-century 'nigger minstrel' shows, which themselves grew out of the 'plantation melodies' and spirituals of African-American slaves in the antebellum Deep South. These were root forms, of course, that not only struck a real chord with Aboriginal people in Australia, but also fed directly into country music.

It's almost uncanny the way the minstrel tradition took particular hold among Aborigines in a part of Australia that could be compared to the Mississippi Delta – the Riverina, where the Murray meets the Darling. "Back in the Maloga days," said Mavis Thorpe Clark in *Pastor Doug*, "the Aboriginal people were drawn to Negro spirituals. For fifty years these songs flowed with the waters of the Murray." The Fisk Jubilee Singers, the original African-American minstrel vocal group, paid a special visit to Maloga while on tour in Australia in 1886, and this obviously planted some important seeds.

Jimmy Little Snr was one of a generation of Aboriginal song-and-dance men who commanded a vast range of tunes, from spirituals to songs by Stephen 'Camptown Races' Foster; he also sang some of his own compositions. In the 20s and especially the 30s, touring

Aboriginal vaudeville troupes, or concert parties, most often including a gumleaf orchestra, were common along the eastern seaboard, from the Coorong in South Australia where the Murray meets the sea – where musicians like Tom Lyons, Isaac Hunter and Annie Koolmatrie plied their trade – to Kuranda near Cairns in far north Queensland.

Individual Aborigines first made an impression on white Australia as members of circuses, boxing tents and rodeos. The next step was obviously the (barely more legitimate) stage. In the 20s the combined Wallaga Lake/Cummera band and vaudeville (whose eminence was rivalled only by the gumleaf orchestra from Lake Tyers, in Gippsland) embarked on an ad hoc tour as they walked the almost 700 km from Wallaga, on the NSW south coast, to perform at the Palais Royal in Melbourne.

In 1932 the Wallaga Lake mob marched to the tune of its own singing gumleaves at the opening of the Sydney Harbour Bridge, and the following year appeared in the early Australian feature film *The Squatter's Daughter*. It was after this that Jimmy's father moved to Cummera and married Frances McGee. Touring was made a little easier by the fact that Cummera's boss, Pastor Atkinson, had a car, a 1929 Chevrolet.

"What work we got was enough," Jimmy remembers, "but there was times when it was hard to work. We had to raise money for the elderly, and we had to raise money for the young. So we'd go out and entertain white audiences – two ways – by playing competition football, and cricket – sport of any description – the mission would go into town and play the town. That was daytime entertainment. At night, the sun would go down and the footlights would go up. So the sporting people were the roadies for the showpeople then! And the entertainer would have his stage and his theatre."

Jimmy is beaming now. "My father was a dancer, in terms of traditional dance and show business, vaudevillian dancing, and he was a comedian, a natural comedian and storyteller. As a boy in the audience, I'm watching Dad on stage with a lantern and a little fan, and some crepe paper and this was fire, on stage with all the lights out and they're dancing around the fire . . . I would see him add charcoal colouring . . . like that Al Jolson thing? Blackface, what did they call them? Minstrels. So Dad saw the minstrels, and related, I can do that, I'll do that. He'd come out and do that. Mum would come out in a lovely evening gown, and she'd yodel in a clear voice, sing Swiss yodelling songs."

Jimmy smiles wistfully. After his mother died he was moved with his four younger siblings – Fred, Colin, Betty and Monica – to live at Worrigee, near Nowra, Wallaga Lake, with his Aunty Jane Hickey, his father's sister.

Jimmy would go out working with his father, who lived in nearby Moruya. Then for some reason, as if by divine intervention, he had an epiphany: He realised that even if he was black, he was as good as anybody. "Not better," he stresses, "as good as." He was barely a teenager – it was 1950 – but he decided at that moment to dedicate himself to a career in music.

"Jim went away on his ambition," Aunty Jane told *Women's Weekly* in 1966. "Self-taught in everything, he was. Then I paid for him to learn his singing – I wanted him to take singing with a piano, but the teacher said he was determined to sing with a guitar."

"I had to be disciplined because I was the eldest," Jimmy says. "I set the example all the other kids saw. I saw an opportunity to ease my own aching pain of losing Mum – I felt drawn to a magnet, to experience life musically. I realised, gee, what Mum and Dad were doing, in the vaudeville show, I can do that – then I wanted to make records. So Dad bought me a guitar. I had all my relatives around me, so I had all the teachers I needed – all the records I listened to . . . Radio, pre-television, was another wonderful teacher. I'd go to the movies, all the musicals, see all the classics. To me it was so inviting: I can do that . . . I realised, if I can – I didn't think commercially then, but I'm using these words now – if I can capitalise commercially on a homegrown ability, I could take what I felt was a gift and expand it through an audience, and that audience would be my extended family."

"My dad, seeing what my skills were, he told me, follow your dream. He told me how to follow my dream by supporting me, buying me a guitar. He taught me the appreciation of an audience. He taught me to be uncomplicated and simple but sincere. He taught me manners, appreciation, he taught me what people may say are basics. He said, son, you will never be lost, even when I'm gone." (Jimmy's father went on to live to a relatively old age, remarrying, working as a truck driver and, curiously, joining the conservative Liberal Party.)

"I felt I needed to express my love of life, and what blessings I had, even though my family had been disrupted," says Jimmy. "I was reaching out for affection, appreciation, or understanding. All these emotions made me look a little harder at myself, analyse what the future might hold."

"I HAD A DREAM AS A LITTLE BOY," Jimmy told new teen mag *Young Modern* in 1963. "After my father bought me my first guitar I formed a particular love for that instrument. I began to play it and it came quite easily, in a natural way." Jimmy's brilliance as a nylon-string finger-picker, jazzy like Willie Nelson, was a sadly underexploited aspect of his talent.
"I tried to get on the road and tour with these travelling shows . . . You see, all the country guys, they were touring all over Australia. Rodeos, all that. Well, I was listening to them on radio going, I want to do that, I want to do that."

In the early 50s, Australia was still a predominantly rural society, enjoying the postwar reconstruction boom. Aboriginal people only got the crumbs. The White Australia policy of successive governments functioned as a form of apartheid, relegating them to the fringes of society.

Koories in NSW and Victoria were further displaced from the land into an urban environment. For Jimmy Little, Sydney – which might as well have been Hollywood – was only a couple of hours away on the train. His ticket was a foothold in a country music scene that was itself exploding.

At a time before radio was syndicated and homogenised as it is now, regional stations all over Australia sprang directly out of local interests and, just as in America during the 30s, live broadcasts of music were their bread and butter. As a result of this, along with the postwar arrival of multinational recording companies (which ended EMI's effective monopoly), country music enjoyed a phenomenal boom, becoming arguably the first example of a truly Australian popular culture.

★ Bronco Billy ★

Who was the first Aboriginal hillbilly singer? Was it Billy Bargo? Born Albert Wilson around 1904 on Palm Island in Queensland, Billy Bargo won two national rodeo titles (in 1941, for saddle bronc riding and roping); he was also a 'Whipcracker and Yodeller', as he was billed when he appeared at the first Corroboree season at the Olympia in Melbourne in 1949. He was the classic singing cowboy.

Bargo Bill, as he was sometimes also known, toured as part of Tex Morton's Wild West Rodeo Circus before WWII, and legend says he used to fill in on radio for Tex when Tex was indisposed (too drunk to sing) – and nobody could tell the difference! According to the Australian Stockman's Hall of Fame, Billy Bargo was on a par with other Aboriginal rodeo champions like Jack 'Coolibah' Watson and Alex Haydon, "a highly respected competitor, a first-class horseman and [he] had a host of friends"; however, "little is recorded of his career."

After polling the highest number of votes ever on the national radio show *Australia's Amateur Hour* when he sang Carson Robinson's 'Bridle on the Wall', Bill went to Melbourne to perform as part of yodelling cowgirl June Holm's wartime concert party. He became a member of 3DB's *The Hillbilly Club* alongside Holm, Smoky Dawson and Sister Dorrie. By the end of the war, he was "the hero of the youngsters" in Melbourne, fronting his own Wild West Show & Variety. In 1947, British Pathé shot a newsreel of him whipcracking a cigarette out of the mouth of his pardner Dan Dare.

By 1952 though, the original Aboriginal hillbilly had fled Melbourne to avoid bigamy charges, and when he died in 1962, he was working as a lift-driver in Auckland, New Zealand. On his death certificate it says, "Marital Status: Never Married." He left no recordings for posterity.

●●●

It was during these years that Americans like Jim Reeves, Hank Williams and Patsy Cline were redefining hillbilly music as a pop form. In Australia, Buddy Williams and Slim Dusty led a similar charge for the bush ballad. Beyond EMI, record companies like Philips and new local labels Rodeo and Festival were establishing their offices and studios in Sydney, and a circuit of country gigs was developing in the western suburbs, where many erstwhile farming families were beginning to relocate.

In 1952 guitar-picker Pat Ware, himself still quite young at the time, saw the 15-year-old Jimmy Little perform at a show in Nowra. Jimmy was entering every talent quest he could – it was a way you might get 'discovered', and certainly a means of gaining valuable experience. A picture in his amazing two-foot-thick scrapbook, taken in a Nowra hall in 1952, shows him in his full cowboy outfit alongside no less than six men in drag, several hula dancers, a magician and a several other artistes. Pat Ware was immediately impressed by the enormous natural talent, confidence and charisma that this shy, pretty black kid possessed.

Born in England and raised in Berrima, not far from Nowra, Pat Ware was based in Sydney, where he was one of the most in-demand session musicians in town. Ware had played sessions with Slim Dusty, among others, before he threw himself behind Jimmy, urging him to come to Sydney. This Jimmy did first in 1953, when he was 16, to compete in Terry Dear's *National Amateur Hour*. Smitten with Hank Snow, he sang a yodelling version of 'Till the End of the World'. Although he didn't win and went back home, he finished second and was encouraged nonetheless.

"Pat said, Oh, why don't you move up here to Sydney, we'll work up a duo," Jimmy recalls. "I came back and forward for twelve months. I'd come up for a weekend, do some radio shows, meet people . . ."

Jimmy arrived in Sydney to stay in March 1955. He had just turned 18. He got a job in a timber mill, which he held down for the next five years, and soon after that, at a football club social, he met the woman he would marry three years later, a beautiful young Koori lass from Walgett called Marj Peters.

"We got a bass player, on the old double bass, and that was my trio," Jimmy says. "Myself on rhythm guitar. A lot of pieces were missing. One of my guitarist friends, Ken, he used to make his own electric guitars – now you just buy what you want."

Pat Ware's mate Al Neaves had one of the first reel-to-reel recorders in town (he went on to become a respected name in Australian studios), so Jimmy didn't cut an acetate, as was the practice of the day, but rather made what was one of Australia's first demo tapes. This alone was sufficient to convince the all-powerful agent/promoter Ted Quigg to take on the trio. Quigg was a pioneer whose clients included, at various times, Frank Ifield, Slim Dusty and Reg Lindsay; he and Jimmy became like family.

"I took it slowly," says Jimmy. "Get a residency here, a spot there, try to build on that. And it happened . . . There was a ready market out there for a new country singer. Every month I'd go out on the harbour, on this cruise, in this country show. A three-decker boat – it's not here anymore, they sold it to Japan and it got wrecked on the way. Every Wednesday, once a month, there was this big country spectacular. So that was another showcase."

By December 1955 *Spurs* magazine, the journal of Australian country music, reported on the impact Jimmy was making, especially as a result of his appearances on the fabled *Kalang* showboat. He had appeared on *Melody Trail* on 2KY with the McKean Sisters, and on Reg Lindsay's *Harmony Homestead* on 2SM. These were choice spots. The record companies could no longer ignore him. Ron Wills, who would go on to produce 'A Pub with No Beer', signed Jimmy to EMI.

> The deal with EMI was the new voice, the new sound. They said, you do an overseas hit song, a cover version, but on the B-side, you can do one of your own. We thought, alright, so that's what we did. For twelve or eighteen months.
>
> The radio stations were playing all their material – we had to sing what the radio was playing. Australian artists, the radio didn't play a lot of our stuff. Only a few artists were fortunate enough to make their own image.

Jimmy went out to EMI's original Australian studio and pressing plant at Homebush in western Sydney and cut four sides, which were released simultaneously as two Regal-Zonophone 78s in August 1956. Credited to 'Jimmy Little with Pat Ware and Alby Horton', the A-sides were country standards, 'Mysteries of Life' and 'Stolen Moments'; they were backed with two songs co-written by Jimmy and Pat Ware, 'Heartbreak Waltz' and 'Someday You're Gonna Call Me'. 'Mysteries of Life', legend has it, sold 1,300 copies in a week, which made it a smash. Jimmy recalled:

> This was on the threshold of ten o'clock closing. Pubs opened up, and they put on live entertainment. That became my employment. The hotels had what I'd call the mums and dads. The teenagers who didn't go with mum and dad to the hotel, they went to the dances. So here I was, singing to their mums and dads at the hotels, and then going across the road to sing at a dance, to the people my age. Then the clubs came along to compete with the hotels.

Poker machines were legalised in NSW in clubs – football clubs, bowls clubs and the like – in 1956, and this underwrote their expansion. Again, this was an adult audience listening to a teenage crooner.

> Imagine this now: there were 3,500 licensed clubs in New South Wales. That's not counting the hotels. So that's the kind of opportunity I had, that's how I got all this experience. And exposure.
>
> When I did a gig by myself, I was well equipped, self-sufficient, I could just sit on my stool and play guitar, I'd do the evergreens, I did the Western hits, movie themes, like Johnny Mathis had one called 'A Certain Smile', I did that. So I was able to play these songs, there was a jazz style about my guitar playing, after listening for all those years, soaking things up like a sponge. I'd do the Aussie bush ballads. When I was on a rock show I'd do rockabilly, or I'd be the Sam Cooke.

Jimmy at eighteen in 1955, just before leaving Nowra for Sydney

Kenny Kitching sometimes augmented the trio in those days, when, along with Ned Kelly's, it was one of the only working country *groups* in Sydney (most performers merely sang in front of the house band or piano player). "Jimmy just had that charisma, magnetism, that people loved," Kitching says:

> I was fortunate in those days, I was the only steel guitarist around. I'd heard all those Hank Williams records and I wondered how they got that lovely sound, and then I got into Hawaiian music and I built my own guitars.
>
> Jimmy was just on the scene. And he was just such a gentleman. He was a Jim Reeves freak, they were the only records he had!

After four more Regal-Zonophone singles, Jimmy was promoted to EMI's more prestigious Columbia imprint, and released two further singles in the new 45rpm format. These discs were remarkable for the original songs featured: the first, 'Frances Claire' (backing up 'Waitin' for You'), was inspired by the birth of his daughter; the second, 'Give the Coloured Lad a Chance' (backing up 'Oh, Lonely Heart'), was written by his father. Released in 1958, these were the first songs written as well as recorded by an Aborigine.

Just as Elvis himself had only his father Vernon to share his success with, Jimmy Little too was perhaps driven to achieve something for his dear departed mother. In the face of all that, the explosive lyrical content of 'Give the Coloured Lad a Chance', the first Aboriginal protest song to be recorded, was almost secondary.

"I ARRIVED ON THE SCENE at the same time as Col Joye, Johnny O'Keefe, Lucky Starr and Judy Stone," Jimmy told *Woman's Day* on the occasion of his twenty-first anniversary in show business, in October 1975. "The big difference was that they were all rockers and I chose to stick to the gentler song that told a story. Deep down, you know, I'm a real country boy."

In 1959 Jimmy left EMI and joined Festival, where he would step up to a new level. "I could have stayed with EMI, but they wanted me to stay hillbilly, and Festival, Ken Taylor and Hal Saunders, had this go-ahead to sign up all the young pop artists. Including me."

In retrospect, Jimmy was forsaking an extraordinary privilege – being allowed to record his own songs, with his own band – but he wanted to go where the action was, to get with the younger pop set, so he threw himself at the mercy of Ken Taylor. Thus his original partnership with Pat Ware dissolved. Ware was at once more of a purist and an innovator; he went on to enjoy a long career in country music as a guitar hero, songwriter and broadcaster.

Unsurprisingly, it was the new, locally owned major Festival Records, with Taylor as A&R manager, that jumped quicker than the multinationals, even long-established EMI, to collar

Jimmy's first recording session at EMI's old Homebush studios in 1956: bandleader Herbie Marks on piano-accordian, Pat Ware on guitar at back right

the local rock'n'roll uprising. Taylor added Jimmy to his already stellar roster as a dark-skinned balladeer with a proven track record and the willingness to expand on it.

Ken Taylor was a stiff-upper-lip autocrat who found rock'n'roll vulgar but wasn't above trying to make a quid out of it. Success bred success, and he ruled Festival the way studio bosses once ruled Hollywood. Johnny O'Keefe tended to run his own show, but beyond that, whether you were black or white, Col Joye, Digby Richards or Jimmy Little, you did as Ken Taylor decided.

> Festival signed me up as modern country, but they allowed me to sing evergreen ballads, and the more they heard me the more they let me go. They said, Oh, you've got a pretty big repertoire, you've proved you've got an audience out there, what do you want to sing? I was singing 'Danny Boy', I was doing songs like 'Maggie', these Irish ballads, it was all because of my voice; no-one was doing that, I had a market to myself.

Jimmy's first release for Festival was an EP called *Ballads with a Beat*, which included his orthodox reading of 'Danny Boy' – and it went top ten. This was followed by a successful cover of Marty Robbins's contemporaneous hit gunfighter ballad, 'El Paso'. Ken Taylor shaped Jimmy's image around his velvet voice, and to his and Jimmy's credit it was never less than dignified. Sincerity was the keynote, a persona that was soft, sometimes too sweet, and certainly not strongly or assertively Aboriginal. "It saddens me," Taylor wrote in his 1970 memoir *Rock Generation*, "that a performer like Jimmy should ever come face to face with the racial problem – but not when one lives in a city where a hotel manager once cancelled accommodation for Ella Fitzgerald when he found out she was coloured!"

Taylor and Ted Quigg both claimed to be occasionally frustrated by Jimmy no-showing – which they put down, as was the custom of the day, to the Aboriginal habit of 'going walkabout'. In fact, no-showing is one of country music's great traditions, from George Jones on down, and Jimmy was still only a kid, after all, even though he had a wife and baby daughter, and he was black in the big city and surrounded by all the brightest lights.

As late as 1962 Jimmy was still talking about becoming a man of the cloth. It is indeed noteworthy that Jimmy's marriage survived over fifty years of fast-lane show business. His faith is his ballast. In 1959, after appearing on Roy Acuff's 'Grand Ole Opry' tour of Australia, he took time off from music to make his acting debut in *Shadow of the Boomerang*, a feature film produced by American evangelist Billy Graham and shot just outside Sydney. *Man against God in a powerful story of raw human emotions that spans two continents*, went the blurb. Ken Taylor was asked to provide a song for Jimmy to sing in the film – on 24 hours' notice. He remembered:

> Hal Saunders and I studied the briefing: Jimmy was to be posed sitting in the Australian counterpart of an American bunkhouse – a modern young man, dreamily strumming on a guitar and singing quietly to himself of his ancestors . . . a young

man in conflict, torn between the ways of his fathers and the new 'mod' culture that now enveloped him. The song, we were told, should reflect all this. But that's all we were told. A title occured to me almost at once, 'Shadow of the Boomerang'.

'Shadow of the Boomerang' superseded the film's working title, and the song became Jimmy's fourth Festival single, released around the same time the film premiered in New York, in October 1960. It is another unrecognised classic, passed over in its day in favour of Jimmy's less controversial material.

"They were love songs I did," Jimmy says. "Because I came from that era, and they [Festival] recognised me as a romantic sort of singer, they allowed me not to do story or comedy songs, they allowed me to sing love songs. Or semi-religious songs."

At a time when LP records were the hot new hi-fi format and expensive for producers and consumers alike, Jimmy was privileged, again, in getting to record them at all, let alone so many. Following his first, *You'll Never Walk Alone*, he released *Sing to Glory* and *Tree in the Meadow* – titles that give a fair indication of their mostly gospel content. Jimmy would go on to release 26 albums for Festival over the next two decades, although more than half of these were budget repackaging jobs and compilations that recycled the same stock of material.

When music first appeared on Australian television, then in its infancy, Jimmy was there too. He became a member of the *Bandstand* family, one of Col Joye's clean-cut crew. For white Australia, he was perhaps the model modern Aborigine – clean, well spoken, knew his place, didn't drink, had a good woman and healthy children and, perhaps most importantly of all, earned his own keep and didn't whinge. This, short of genocide, might have been the sum total of middle Australia's idea of assimilation. A number of reports in the early 60s emphasised, as if surprised that such success was possible, how much Jimmy earned (considerably more than most white wage slaves), and how seemingly 'normal' he and his family were, living in suburban Sydney and going about their business without causing major disruptions, as if they were aliens.

"The test was never dollars and cents," Jimmy says now, "although I knew that was part of the package. As artists, we do what we want to do, and we satisfy ourselves. Please the public. I wanted to come off a show and move back into the comfort zone of Jimmy Little the person, and I had a partner from day one on whom I could vent my feelings, my anger, fears, talk about life. I had this wonderful friend in my wife who was very stabilising. I wasn't alone out there."

"Proud of his ancestry, Jimmy is a three-quarter caste," *TV Times* asserted in February 1962. "Unlike many Aboriginals, he doesn't stress the white blood in him, but neither does he make special capital of being Aboriginal."

America may have been simmering on the brink of outright domestic race war to parallel the escalating conflict in Vietnam, but in Australia, its distant colonial cousin, the civil rights and anti-war movements trailed a few years behind. About as high profile as Aboriginal culture got in the early 60s was the All-Coloured Revue, almost a throwback sort of show but the first of its kind, put on by Jimmy and Ted Quigg and starring the cream of contemporary black Australian talent.

The show premiered at Auburn Town Hall in Sydney in September 1962. It was so successful that in mid-1963 it went out on the road. The show starred Jimmy as compere and featured artist; the house band was sometimes the Opals, sometimes Col Joye guitarist Dave Bridge's Quartet. The Opals were a mixed country band from Penrith, led by guitarist George Fisher and incorporating Col Hardy, an exciting new Aboriginal country singer from Walgett, plus Jimmy's brother Freddie Little, a railway worker who some still say was a better singer than his big brother.

In the program notes, Ted Quigg, who himself adopted an Aboriginal boy, wrote: "My idea for presenting this show to you is to introduce these young true Australian coloured people. I wish to show that they can take their part in our world and do what they wish in whatever profession they choose – even in the tough one of an entertainer . . . I also wish to show that these young coloured people can hold their own with the best of us, if given the one thing they ask for – the opportunity – which I feel has been proved by our star, Jimmy Little. Jimmy is one of our greatest entertainers and I am very definite in saying, the finest gentleman I have met in the business during my 33 years."

IN DECEMBER 1963 DJ BOB ROGERS wrote in *Teenagers' Weekly*: "A few weeks ago I reported that gospel music had failed to catch on in Australia. Today, one of the top songs around the country is an old gospel tune. Such is the uncertainty of the music world, where anything can happen. However, it is not the wild sound of 'pop' gospel, which as I predicted did not take off in Australia, but a sincere ballad with a religious feeling called 'Royal Telephone'."

Jimmy's version of the song followed its successful American revival by Burl Ives, which had been a hit in Perth and was pushed along in Australia by the concurrent launching (by the

Jimmy on the road with Col Joye, early 60s

Seventh Day Adventists) of Dial-A-Prayer. It was kept out of the number one spot on the 2UE Top 40 of 22 November 1963 (the day US President Kennedy was assassinated) by the Crystals' 'Then He Kissed Me'.

Of the remaining eight records in that week's top ten, four were surf songs. Elvis's 'Bossa Nova Baby' was at 16, and the Beatles' first Australian hit, 'She Loves You', at 23. Yet even as the full impact of Beatlemania hit Australia in 1964, Jimmy hung on to win *Everybody's* local Pop Star of the Year award ahead of Billy Thorpe, the Delltones, Little Pattie and Jimmy Hannan. Jimmy was on top of the world, but it was a world that was obviously, even then, very rapidly changing.

As late as 1974, Jimmy was able to say to *TV Times*, "Being an Aboriginal has been a definite advantage. I think people are intrigued to see an Aboriginal singer who can play guitar and speak good English. It's unique to the average Australian."

Jimmy was perhaps crucially aware that too much, too soon would only have the effect of scaring whites off. At the same time, even as he trod softly, he never backed down or allowed himself to be shamed. Ken Taylor recalls:

> I saw him almost blow up on a television program one night when, as a member of a panel, he debated the question of colour prejudice in Australia. But he quickly replaced a flash of anger with his usual quiet smile. It was the only time in his life, I would think, that he was ever caught off guard, but it reflected a deep hurt somewhere inside him. I should state that Jimmy is not really a good example of anti-Aboriginal discrimination. He doesn't, in fact, permit himself these days to mix socially very much with whites. The moment he finishes his recording sessions or public engagements he seems to disappear – sometimes completely overlooking the next booking made for him by a harassed manager.

Jimmy was leading something of a double life, maybe even a triple life. He was a pop star in the white world, he was his own man at home, and he was another Jimmy Little out among his own people, the Aboriginal community in Sydney, and in Redfern particularly.

To this day Jimmy will brush off politics much like Elvis famously did. Jimmy is naturally retiring, diffident. This is not to say that his feelings don't run deep. But it was never Jimmy's nature or style to preach fire and brimstone. He was a conciliator who paved the way for reconciliation. First of all, he had to learn to accept the mantle of public Aborigine, when there were very few such figures and it was hard not to feel like a bird in a cage. Jimmy just managed the best he could. When the groundbreaking Foundation for Aboriginal Affairs opened in Redfern in 1965, he became a fixture there, along with other musicians like Col Hardy and his Festival labelmate Candy Williams.

In 1963 *Young Modern* ran a report entitled 'Racial Harmony? The keys are black and white':

With pricklings of guilt in our own conscience (national section of that complicated apparatus), we thought we'd like to take a look into the mind of an ordinary, well-adjusted, well-educated young Australian on this subject of race prejudice – not a religious leader, not a politician, not a union member, not a 'do-gooder'. Just an honest young Australian, making his way in life.

It wasn't easy at first to persuade JIMMY LITTLE, famous Australian ballad singer, to be in it.

He was afraid that readers might think he was seeking publicity for publicity's sake . . . that he was trying to cash in on the colour question for his own personal benefit.

Jimmy told *Young Modern*:

I realised that people had clung too long to their old ways and customs for modern, changing life. I felt that if I could communicate between the two peoples in friendship and understanding, I could perhaps set a small example for my own people and the world around us.

I think the worst thing is that word 'black', not because it designates a colour, but because it implies something inferior or contemptible. The word black is used to discredit an Australian, and it hurts.

Prejudice is more overt, of course, in country towns than it is in cities, where the attitude is more cosmopolitan. I have never been refused accommodation, or had business people rude to me, although I realise that may be partly due to the fact that I am a name in the entertainment world. Sometimes I encounter slight shock, as people think, Gee, I did not know he was dark. But usually a show of quiet independence, in a nice way, is ample to ensure politeness and even friendliness.

There is NO reason why an Aborigine cannot excel in any field for which he has training or talent, IF HE REALLY TRIES. I know much has been made of the damage which alcohol has done to talented Aborignies. But alcohol has been a problem in the lives of talented people of other races.

On a piano there are a number of white notes and a number of black notes. On either alone, you can play assorted tunes, but you can only achieve full harmony if you use both black and white.

THE FOLLOW-UP TO 'ROYAL TELEPHONE' was a single called 'One Road', written by the young Bee Gees, with whom Jimmy had already often shared a stage. When it came out, in February 1964, Jimmy told the *Telegraph*, "The current surfing music craze doesn't worry me. I have been singing for ten years now and have been through them all – jive, rock, twist."

'One Road' was not a hit though, and it signalled the immediate end of Jimmy's Top 40 career. Like everyone else, he was blown off the charts by the Beatles and all that came in their wake. But that doesn't mean he didn't continue to thrive throughout the 60s. Again like so many of his contemporaries, the first-generation rock'n'rollers, he gradually drifted back to where it all began, where they all began – country music. Jimmy worked constantly, and continued to record regularly.

He was the complete pro, "a pleasant, poised young man," as he was typically, somewhat paternalistically, praised by *Young Modern*, "immaculately neat and well-dressed . . ."

"The private person was a family man by the time I was getting fairly good money," he says. "I made small fortunes. What I'd call small fortunes. Bulk money would come in, record royalties, or I'd do a tour, so there'd be a lot of money there . . . But most of the money went back into me. I saw myself as a product, so I had to maintain the product, so it was always extra shoes, new cufflinks. Things the private person didn't need."

As a Christian and non-drinker, calm and collected even in the heady climate of show business, Jimmy was the subject of a 1966 cover story for the Australasian Temperance Society magazine, *Alert*. He said: "Regardless of race, colour or creed, liquor is unnecessary and a dangerous enjoyment. A purpose for living is the answer to most people's problems, especially the Aboriginal liquor problem. I have always recognised someone greater than myself. They need a spiritual experience, otherwise the pressures and difficulties of life will overcome them."

Festival tried to cast Jimmy in a different light. On 1967's *Ballads with Strings*, he was the lounge singer. Again, it was not much of a stretch, given how much he'd always adored Nat King Cole. On *New Songs from Jimmy*, also in 1967, he was the senior interpreter, tackling material by Australia's top young songwriters like Barry Gibb, Lorna Barry and Gary Shearston. But it was his country side that was most successful. After playing out the gospel card with 1964's *Onward Christian Soldiers*, Jimmy premiered a new act, his new band, on *Jimmy Little Sings: The Country and Western Greats*. It was another modest first that Jimmy was even then shy of drawing attention to – Australia's first all-black recording band. Naturally they were all relatives: on drums, Doug Peters; guitar, leader Cyril Peters; bass, Neville Thorn.

Jimmy promoted the first all-Aboriginal country show in 1965, at Anzac House in Sydney. At the same time, with white Australia beginning to find some sympathy for the Aboriginal plight, he played before 3,000 people as part of a protest in Sydney's Martin Place.

"I am very aware of the fact that I am not a fullblood Aboriginal and am not a real part of the old culture," Jimmy told the *Northern Territory News*. "Sometimes I wish I was. In travelling around I have come to realise how little we know of the original culture. Sometimes I wish I knew more of my forefathers and understood what they did and believed in. Today, young boys and girls with our racial background in Sydney and other big centres don't find time to look back. They look forward and they see opportunities there."

Jimmy too suffered from the loss of culture as well as family. In trying to negotiate a sustainable path for himself, he became confused, as anyone would. But he was never less than pragmatic: "I would like to see the Aboriginal race retain an identity and not be swallowed whole. I would like to see them part of the whole community but retaining the best of their own culture. But the full opportunities for education and jobs must be there too."

AS THE 60s TURNED INTO THE 70s, and Reg Lindsay followed up his 'Jungles of Vietnam' with a cover of John Stewart's 'Armstrong' (a country song that celebrated the recent moon landing), and while Australia's formerly placid streets were being torn apart by student demonstrations, Jimmy released with some fanfare a single called 'Goodbye Old Rolf', a dead dog song in country music's grand tradition of dead dog songs.

Of course, Jimmy had previously recorded 'Old Shep', so 'Goodbye Old Rolf' was no great stretch. And this was perhaps Jimmy's problem in the 70s – he wasn't stretching himself – and yet he still filled houses wherever his name was on the marquee!

His 1969 album *I Can't Stop Loving You* was a refreshing return to a simple country sound, thankfully devoid of Ken Taylor's preferred Mitch Miller-like string and choral arrangements, with the spotlight on Jimmy's delightful guitar-playing – and also that of George Fisher, former leader of the Opals. Now Jimmy was playing off songs like 'Gentle on My Mind' with 'Love Me Tender', or the Mills Brothers' 'One Dozen Roses'.

His official bio of May 1970 stated: "Jimmy sings everything from showstoppers to simple C&W ballads in a manner which captures audiences of all ages." He was trying to be all things to all people, not to offend anyone. He might have done better had he considered a more

Live in the late 50s: (left) with a pick-up pub combo plus Kenny Kitching on steel guitar, and (right) with Candy Williams on guitar

challenging repertoire. But maybe he was under Festival's yoke. Why didn't Festival play up one of his own rare compositions – like 'Blacktracker', which he gave to Col Hardy, who recorded it in 1978? Were they scared of spoiling Jimmy's wholesome image? Was Jimmy?

Jimmy says now:

There's an argument for, as an artist . . . Tell the audience, this is me, my life, take it or leave it, I think it's good, it's worked for me all this time. If it's not your vibe, well, that's cool, but give me a chance to perform it. There's an argument for that too. But you can be a little bit flexible: I'll please them for a while, I'll please myself later . . .

The hook in every song, for me, is imagining the writers, their joy and pleasure, imagining them coming up with a line or a phrase or a chorus that has never been done before. And the melody's got to be right. It can have great lyrics, but the melody, if the tune is a tug of war and it should be another way, and if the beat is too hard or too slow – so those three things: the words, about the subject, has got be blended and closely related to the melody and then those two combined sitting on the rails, the bed of a beautiful rhythm. These are the three things I look for. The key word is balance. Blend.

The second Jimmy Little Trio: (left to right) Cyril Peters, Jimmy, Neville Thorn, Doug Peters. State Theatre Sydney, Central Methodist Mission National Aboriginal Day Show, July 1964

A report in the *Central Coast Express* on an appearance Jimmy made at the Gosford Leagues Club in 1972 read: "As usual, Jimmy was just great. He came on stage in an immaculate white suit with lilac shirt and white tie, looking very mod. Backed by his own quartet, he went into a very smooth act indeed. His repertoire included his very famous 'Royal Telephone' but Jimmy has now added 'Sin to Tell a Lie', 'Four in the Morning' and a terrific rendition of 'Daddy, Don't You Walk So Fast' – this last number bringing a great ovation.

"With this kind of very polished performance, Jimmy and this troupe can go on forever, giving people what they obviously want without resorting to all sorts of noisy gimmicks."

IN 1972 ABORIGINAL PROTESTERS pitched the Tent Embassy on the lawns in front of Parliament House in Canberra. Jimmy, whose current album was *Winterwood,* a more sombre offering, was completing a two-year stint as chairman of the Foundation for Aboriginal Affairs. It was too little, too late for the more militant faction. By 1975 the Foundation had folded, superseded by the first wave of Aboriginal legal and health services, and also theatres. Jimmy continued to work the clubs.

Jimmy never claimed to be more than a simple song-and-dance man, like his father. "I just love it all," he says, "and so I just pick my songs, my program for the shows in advance. This show's going to be that kind of audience. I'll package it up for them. Whatever it is, I dress for the occasion. I might wear a tux at the Hilton, and I'll be doing whatever a Hilton audience wants. If I go down to the Three Bells in Woolloomooloo [a legendary rock'n'roll bloodhouse that Jimmy played in the 50s], I'll look at the audience and go . . ." – now Jimmy giggles impishly – "Oh, they wanna hear this! . . . I can look at an audience, throw a few things at them and see what the reaction is, or get the next book out . . ."

"I don't get involved in politics. I keep right away. I leave that to the politicians to debate. They don't need a ballad singer to put his two cents' worth in. I don't see people with hate, no matter what they say. I see people who have been hurt, who are rising out of a life that they see has betrayed them and finding a vehicle out. I don't condemn, who am I to prejudge anybody?"

When Jimmy went back into the top ten with 'Baby Blue' in the spring of 1974, for the first time since 'Royal Telephone', he said he hoped the record would get him "out of the rut I feel I've gotten into over the past few years." But like the hits enjoyed by many of Jimmy's old Festival labelmates who all seemed to be making comebacks at the same time, mostly with country songs – Col Joye's 'Heaven is my Woman's Love', Judy Stone's 'Would You Lay with Me', even Digby Richards's 'People Call Me Country' – 'Baby Blue' would turn out to be an Indian summer.

Within a few years, Johnny O'Keefe, the leader of the pack, would be dead. His era had ended long before. Jimmy Little, like the rest of them, would not bother the charts again, at least not until his more recent rebirth. But even if a simple song-and-dance man was enough for his club audiences, Jimmy lost something else. *TV Times* reported in 1974, "Little admits he is not as popular with his own people as he would like to be."

★ *Lone Voice* ★

Harold Blair wasn't the first Aborigine to release a record – Sydney ballad duo Olive & Eva claimed that distinction in 1955 with 'Old Rugged Hills'/'Rhythm of the Corroboree' – but he was Australia's first black music star, an operatic tenor whose fame rivalled even Albert Namatjira's. Born in Cherbourg in south-central Queensland in 1925, Blair travelled to New York after the Second World War to further his studies. But even though Australia's 'high culture' vultures sniffed at his voice, Blair went on to become a sort of Australian Paul Robeson during the folk boom – a black concert hall singer who recorded folkloric and spiritual material and was a stalwart of the civil rights movement.

In 1956 Melbourne independent label Score Records released what it trumpeted as 'the first original recording of Aboriginal songs' – Blair's recorded debut, singing material such as 'Jabbin, Jabbin' (from Lethbridge's famous *Australian Aboriginal Songs*, published by Allan & Co. in 1937). He followed this in the early 60s with a 3-track single for Crest Records featuring choral gospel standards such as 'How Great Thou Art' and 'I'll Walk with God'. Around the same time he played the title role in a stage revival of *Uncle Tom's Cabin*. Blair also composed a signature song, 'O Land of Mine', which he dedicated to the time "when my people shall be free," but it went unreleased. He died in Melbourne in 1976, aged 51.

●●●

Jim Martin (bass), Cyril Peters (guitar), Jimmy, Doug Peters (drums), Kenny Kitching (steel guitar), 1970s

After a protest record like Vic Simms's album *The Loner* had been released in 1973, and acts like the Kooriers and the Country Outcasts arrived on the scene, it no longer seemed to be enough for Jimmy just to sing. His songs had to *say* something.

"I fail to get half the Aboriginal population of any town I play," Jimmy told *TV Times*. "They won't come down to see the show and there's a big 'why' there."

One reason was that most clubs wouldn't admit Aboriginal patrons. Jimmy went on: "When an Aboriginal makes it in the white man's world I think the Aboriginal community feels rejected. They feel you've disassociated yourself from them by taking up the white man's way of life. I have the same background as most Aboriginals. I went to mission school and all that, but I chose to do what I'm doing, and I've gotten out of touch to some extent because I went my own way. But I've never lost my pride."

Jimmy continued to work the clubs. After 1975's *All for Love*, he released *Travelling Minstrel Man* in 1976. In 1978 he released the double-set *An Evening with Jimmy Little: Live at the Opera House*. It didn't exactly turn out to be his *Hot August Night*; in fact, it turned out to be his last album before Festival finally let him go.

In 1983, he recorded the single 'Beautiful Woman', a reggae track produced by Beach Boy alumnus Ricky Fataar that even Jimmy himself conceded, in retrospect, was a song too late. It was his last release for Festival after nearly a quarter of a century. And then, just as he had before, Jimmy quietly slipped away.

THE MUSIC INDUSTRY IN AUSTRALIA changed dramatically in the 1980s, becoming much more corporatised. That there was no longer a place in it for Jimmy Little still seems extraordinary.

Jimmy bowed out gracefully, as he would, vowing to make the most of the opportunity to spend more time with his family – now he and Marj were raising their young grandson too, James III – get back in touch with his roots, and pass something on. Inevitably he was reinvigorated by the experience, and this eventually launched him into another new public life in the 1990s, in which his legend was finally cemented, with starring roles on stage and screen and then a triumphant return to recording too.

> Sometimes you've got to take the reins. My destiny says I've got to go there, within a certain time frame. I always felt in control even though I was under management to Channel 7, EMI, Festival, agents, whoever. I had agreements on the dotted line but ultimately it was me saying, now this is what we'll set up, this will be beneficial in the long term and short term . . . It was always up to me to say yes or no.
> Maybe destiny just had all of this in store for me and it was just up to me to be mindful of it and play according to the rules. I think in lots of ways what I've done was pre-ordained, it was just the degree of my decisions. But it's all the same really.

Posing for a photographer with a guitar on his front verandah, sitting on another old kitchen chair, Jimmy can sing almost any oldie you call for. He can bring a smile to your face or a tear to your eye in an instant. Just how many songs does he know?

"Well, you forget a lot. But if you add it up over the years, there's gotta be a few hundred there. I can get the book out, and I think, gee, I haven't played that one for a couple of years – but then it all comes back. I'm getting too old to learn too many new songs, though!"

(Left) Jimmy at a Festival Records function in the mid-70s, with other legends of this generation – Johnny O'Keefe, Judy Stone, Festival sales manager Roy Atkinson, Heather McKean and her husband Reg Lindsay, and Col Joye; (right) with fans, early 70s

Jimmy will never stop singing. He's the son of a songman, after all. But he knows that as the world keeps on changing, the bloodlines have to keep adjusting, whether anyone likes it or not.

The next generation . . . In my case, my wife and I taught our daughter and our grandson: Get ready for the world of technology. My daughter is a scriptwriter and author, a speaker at university, we prepared her for that. And our son, he's hittin' a baseball out of the park down there in Redfern!

Both our children were born in the heart of Sydney, one in Paddington, one in Balmain. This is how much things have changed. They're urban kids. Now where are our children's children going to be? Growing up in New York or growing up in London? Japan? That's typical of lots of cultures and generations. Greeks, Italians. That's why I relate to all the nations, we're all the human family, gone out, in our time . . .

It's just important what you do is solid ground, a base to work from.

◖◖◖

Herb Laughton at the country club in Alice Springs, May 1978

BEYOND THE BUNGALOW

★ Herb Laughton ★

The irony is beyond cruel. The old telegraph station on the north edge of Alice Springs, where Herbie Laughton now reposes recounting his life story, where he grew up as a stolen child, is today a tourist trap. In the soft late afternoon light, as the shadows grow longer over the dry waterhole and the sky starts to glow, it almost seems idyllic. The huge peppercorn tree which yielded the bush tucker sweet that was the closest thing Herb ever had to a lollie when he was a kid is still flowering.

Inside the main stone building, a dozen illustrated panels hung along the walls tell the story of Alice Springs and of the construction and life of the old telegraph line, the 'singing string', for which this facility was originally built as a relay station. Tourists can easily overlook the solitary, reluctant panel that plays down the site's involvement in barbarism even as it refers to it – the place's notorious years as a 'half-caste home' during the 1930s, when it became known as the Bungalow. It was part of one of the greatest shame jobs ever perpetuated, a genocidal assault on mixed-blood children who were among the first of the stolen generations.

Born in Alice in 1927 to a white father and a half-caste mother (who herself had been taken from her Arrernte mother), Herbie Laughton was stolen when he was two. He is sometimes close to tears and other times erupts in incredulous laughter as he recounts his story. For a long time he kept it all bottled up inside, releasing the anguish and frustration only partially in his music. He is the acknowledged grandfather of country music in the Northern Territory, but even this success could not compensate for a lost past, or place. Eventually, in the late 80s, Herb attempted suicide.

He survived that suicide attempt – survival, indeed, seems to be one of his talents – and in the intervening decade much of the dark weight of his memories seems to have lifted from his shoulders. Because he's started to talk about it.

Herb always had an outlet in music, but even there he avoided what was too painful. 'Old Bungalow Days', for example, written in 1978, is poignantly nostalgic, seeking out only the positives in his memory, as if attempting to override the absolute awfulness of it. Instead of bemoaning the monstrous cruelty and alienation, the fear and hunger, 'Old Bungalow Days' celebrates the kinship that was forged between the kids. The song is an extraordinary triumph of the generosity of Herb's spirit, avoiding anger, blame or bitterness.

But as significant as it was to write a song like 'Old Bungalow Days' – and to finally record it for the first time, along with a dozen or so others, in the early 80s – it wasn't enough to ease the despair in Herb's heart that within a few years would lead him to try and kill himself.

"In my way," Herb says, trying to get hold of what he's trying to say with his hands, "I'm trying to express myself through my life, what the misshape I had through my life was like, you know, the thing that I just can't seem to . . . fit in. Every time I try and do something . . . achieve something, nothing happens, you know. I wasn't getting no recognition. It was hard speaking to people until just recently, after I wrote this song 'Trust in the Lord'. That's when I ended up in the hospital for six weeks, when my memory was gone."

It wasn't just, as the song's title suggests, that Herb found God in a hospital in Alice after being discovered half-dead and delirious in the desert. There is too much Aboriginal spirituality in him to give himself over completely to Christianity, after all. While 'Trust in the Lord' uses standard 'I saw the light' imagery, it wasn't so much that Herb had visions of angels as that he outed personal demons.

Herb's path to self-destruction was triggered by a visit to the local video store. "Nowhere to turn, I had no way to see," he sings, "In this sad world of sin and poverty."

They just opened the video shop out at the old racecourse, north of Alice. And I said, I don't watch television. And they said, Oh it's a must, just get this one. So I did go over where you get video tapes, and they had these little boys, they only about twelve, and they putting up this porno and talking filthy, dirty and that. And I said, what if my children do that, my grandchildren, what's this world coming to? So I lied down and I couldn't go to sleep. I lay there awake all night, half dozing, half awake, and I got up at seven o'clock in the morning, jumped in my Toyota heading for work, because I never miss work, and that was me last thoughts. They found me just when the sun going down out the side of Hermannsburg. They come down to investigate and they found me with me wrists cut here, and I'm talking in a daze, you know, and they took me straight to Ward One.

I was there for six weeks, and only because I had a Christian doctor, who used to look after Mum and Dad when I met them, you see. He found out that I was in hospital so he come and took over, and he understood, you know, what I went through. I had to go back right to my childhood days, right far as I can remember, and I told all the story, I had to go all through that. He said, Oh, you had a terrible life, that's why you broke, you've kept all this sadness in you. Wouldn't talk to anybody. He said, your best medicine from now on is to talk to people. He said, now you've got to keep singing songs, writing songs and that, talking to people and like now, nowadays you couldn't stop me talking . . .

Herb laughs. It's true. He swats at the flies and gazes around the old Bungalow. The memories flood in and he no longer holds them back. "I just keep talking and talking because I find it a lot better when I talk, you know, it's all out of me. Before, I kept that inside me. I just burst."

"The path of life my saviour declared for me," Herb sings on 'Trust in the Lord', leaning against a sliprail, "I now believe in life's eternity."

"FIRST OF ALL," SAYS HERB, leaning into his yarn with the ease of an experienced bush storyteller, "I was born the seventh of February, 1927, and I was taken away from my mother. They snatched me away from my mother's breast and put me in an institution, and I grew up there. They took my mother away first. She only had me . . . my eldest brother's a policeman's son, and I'm a miner's son. My poor mother was only about 16, 17. They kept us and she had to go off for work as cheap labour. I grew up like that."

Central Australia was opened up, and turned upside down, when the telegraph line went through in 1870.

> I suppose you read about that Stuart that supposedly blazed a trail from Adelaide up to Darwin for the old telegraph line, to get communication from England, the news and all that? Well, after Stuart the linesmen came and put up all these poles, then these booster stations. And then the railway come through [in 1928]. Now all the while this was happening these European men, who were working on the line, were getting Aboriginal girls in the family way, see. This scandal was going on, so the government decided to pull out any part-Aboriginal kids and then put 'em in institutions. That's what they done.
>
> They sent us out to Jay Creek there, out west. We were there and then they shifted us into here, this old telegraph station, what we call the old Bungalow. That was round about 1932.
>
> I grew up here. I didn't have the love of a mother or brother or sister. These children didn't even know their names or where they come from. [They'd] just snatched them and given them a name.
>
> Being here, that was the saddest days of my life. But in that old Bungalow song I didn't put all of this in. In that song I just wanted to bring the happiness and the way I felt when I come down, down the old waterhole here, reminiscing.
>
> Most of all, my song tells you a story of my life, like what I went through . . . I went to work from when I was 12 to 28 years of age, and I had nobody my age to talk to. You wouldn't get me talkin' like this! I didn't know my mother until I was 28, and then at that time I only met her for about two days. And then from there, after I got married, years after, I met my mother again. I only lived with them for about five years before she passed away, but I found out she went through a hell of a lot more than I did, you know. And for about five years she gave me all the love I never had.
>
> I was home one day and I got to real thinking. See, I was getting letters and phone calls from the children that grew up at my time and they still searching for their mothers and that, you see, and I got my own problems and that. I was really upset and I'm thinking about my childhood friends and that, you know, so

HERBIE
LAUGHTON

At the old telegraph station, 'the Bungalow', in the early 1930s

I grabbed the guitar, just out the blue, and I went across to the old waterhole. I sat down there, then I shut me eyes, you know, and I could hear, I could almost hear these children swimming, and I heard my name being called, you see. And I'm there, tears coming down from me eyes because I was really upset because me and the missus wasn't getting on and my children were growing up as strangers because I was working out on the roads all the time, and then, blowing through the gum trees, I got this tune sound real nice. I just grabbed a pen and that . . . Well, that song is a funny song. It was the happier days of my life, yet it was the saddest days of my life – it's a mixed-up song, you know.

Then later on we got into this reunion, like Bungalow reunion, but a lot of those girls and boys of my time, they were all passed on, you know, dead and gone, most of them.

IT DOESN'T MATTER HOW MUCH SMALLER the world keeps getting, Alice Springs, deep in the heart of Australia's red centre, is still a long, long way from most everything else. Alice has been much romanticised. It rests uneasily, has always been beset by tension between black and white.

Traditional Aboriginal culture was almost completely killed off in the south-east, where the frontier first ploughed its furrow. In the centre and the western desert, with its vastness and inhospitability to white settlement, Aboriginal people sidestepped the white man for much longer. But between the missions and the cattle stations, most Aboriginal people were eventually tethered to the white man.

After federation in 1901, the problem for Aborigines was that they were still not recognised; they were dismissed as a state responsibility. In 1911 the Commonwealth took over running the Northern Territory from the South Australian government, and it was then that the campaign of rounding up half-castes began.

Driven by the first Commonwealth Chief Protector of Aborigines, Dr Herbert Basedow, the first stolen generation went to institutions in Darwin, at the Kahlin Compound, and in Alice Springs, at Stuart Town. The Alice Springs 'half-caste institution' shifted base several times, first from Stuart Town out to Jay Creek in 1928, and then back closer to town, to the old telegraph station, in 1933 – but it always kept the same name, the Bungalow.

At least Herb Laughton was still in his mother's country. Other kids were completely displaced. Herb knew who his grandmother was, and she sometimes smuggled food in to him. Herb was at the old telegraph station until 1940, when he turned 12, and only now can he articulate the downside, which was most of the experience.

When I was two years of age, they had this massacre up here at Coniston. There was this dingo shooter, a whitefella, and he ran away with this young Aboriginal fella's wife. Shot through, so this young Aboriginal fella killed him, speared him. What did the police patrol do? Killed them all.

Our first superintendent, can't think of his name. When you get so old, your memory . . . You've got to think back real hard . . . Mr Freeman, Freeman his name was. He used to be drunk all the time and he used to be real cruel, he used to set his dog onto us and everything.

When I was six years old, we were starvin', and the superintendent he had this shed, with wire fences, and in the middle they had all these benches with their tinned stuff like jam and whatever, and I was doing this shanghai and I hit this tin of jam, knocked it on the ground and run off down the creek with it. Next minute I get pulled by the ear, this superintendent, he's kicking me up the arse all the way back. I had to bend over a stool, and he got this cat-o'-nine-tails and he was floggin' me. And then from there I was put inside a dungeon, they used to have cellars in those days for cool rooms, so he locked me in there for three days and two nights. I was cryin' there, I was only six years old. My brother sneaked out from the dormitory and said, don't cry. When I heard this story about the massacre, these big kids talkin', oh, if they catch you doin' something wrong, they're going to shoot all of us, in my mind when they locked me in there, that was my fear, they're going to shoot everybody and I'm going to be locked in here and nobody's going to let me out. I'll die in there. This was my fear all the time. But I lived through it.

AFTER WORLD WAR TWO BROKE OUT in 1939, the Bungalow was closed and its inmates transported elsewhere. Herbie, at 12, was old enough to be sent out on station work. (After

★ Claypan Dancing ★

In the south-east of the Australian continent, convicts, turnkeys, soldiers, sailors and settlers introduced Anglo-Celtic folk music even before the church arrived on the scene with its musical traditions.

Aborigines picked up instruments, licks and songs off the white man, and an image emerges of the claypan dance as the original corroboree substitute: in a dry riverbed at dusk, people would gather to drink and dance and sing. It is a tradition that survives to this day.

If twentieth century popular music was the result of a collision of European and African cultures in the rural Deep South of America, the clearest point of intersection was formed by what were called string bands, in which poor whites and black slaves played and danced alongside one other. This multiracial source subsequently split into blues and country, the two apparently different-coloured sides of the same coin. Aborigines picked up the same range of instruments from white bush bands in Australia – not just stringed instruments (fiddle, banjo, mandolin, autoharp, tea-chest bass) but also piano accordion and harmonica – and from the end of the nineteenth century, black musicians and bands were spreading throughout the country.

One of the many accounts of this music comes from Margaret Tucker, who grew up at Cummeragunja during the First World War. In her 1977 autobiography, *If Everyone Cared*, she remembered the 'shotgun weddings':

> After the feast was over, believe it or not, a violin and a concertina would come to light. There were old Uncle Jack Ingram and old Uncle Billy Redmond, a Victorian from Healsville. He played concertina and my! he was wonderful with that instrument. One of the Coopers played the violin. The rollicking dance tunes from that little Aboriginal three-man band, and others playing gum leaves, was something to remember.
>
> Those Aboriginal musicians were asked to play for white men's socials and dances. You may think it is strange our Aboriginal people picking up the white people's instruments and playing their music, when their own singing and harmonising was natural. Now white youths are playing the didgeridoo.

The best musicians were known as 'kings'. In the 1920s, when Aboriginal buskers entertained passengers on the Melbourne-Sydney train when it stopped at Yass Junction, at a certain point they would step aside saying, Make way for the king! – and then the top fiddler would take his bow.

String band from Purfleet (Sunrise Station) near Taree, NSW, around 1909, with Bert Marr (fiddle), Fred Dumas (accordion), Bob Bungie (banjo), Lena Bungie and Harriet Neville (vocals) and Hazel Bungie (autoharp)

During the 1930s, saltwater string band music exploded in the Top End as a result of the musical currents that flowed with the ocean between Torres Strait in the east and Broome in the west. Darwin, located between them, was a magnet and a melting pot. The Cubillo family, who had arrived from the Philippines aboard pearling luggers in the late 1800s, led their rondello ensembles and guitar orchestras for decades. Jaffa Ah Mat was a songman from Thursday Island in the Torres Strait, author of 'Old TI' (aka 'TI, My Beautiful Home'); in Darwin in the early 30s he joined the band led by the Malayan Pon brothers, Jacob and Herman. In 1934, Darwin Aborigine Val McGuinness, who Ah Mat taught to play mandolin, also joined the band. He would go on to become a towering figure in Top End music, and the saltwater sound was always destined to cross over with country, if only because of the way Hawaiian steel guitars so informed hillbilly music.

With the outbreak of war, McGuinness moved to north Queensland, where he found work and started a family. There, in a perfect illustration of how the songlines feed back on themselves, he taught the young Seaman Dan his first chords on guitar. Towards the end of the 50s, McGuinness moved back to Darwin, and with his sons and his young nieces the Mills sisters looking on, he played places like the famous Sunshine Club. Kathy Mills told Philip Hayward: "When they first started, they played a type of old ballroom dancing music adapted for Aboriginal people but the Torres Strait musicians brought in different rhythms and bar chords and that

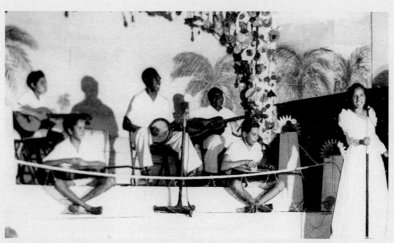

How guitars took over: Post-war concert party from Cherbourg, with Sally Anderson fronting Jack O'Chin's band of two guitars, two lap steel guitars and a banjo

South Seas beat – and that changed it and we made that style our own here."

At around the same time, at the other end of the continent, in Tasmania, yet another, somewhat less balmy variation on the string band tradition was emerging. The only indigenous string-band music released on vinyl, the EP *Cape Barren Island Dance Music*, came out of Tasmania in the late 70s, when Norm Brown and Elvin Beeton overdubbed guitar and spoons accompaniment onto tapes of fiddle solos by the late Les Brown. Les Brown was a blackfella who grew up on Bass Strait's isolated, windswept Cape Barren Island, where many Tasmanian Aborigines were shunted, and there, playing everything from fiddle to the church organ, he developed a

Servicemen swapping licks in Darwin, 1941

sort of Antarctic bluegrass sound. In 1967 he was recorded on cassette playing at parties at Ulverstone, and these tapes formed the basis of the EP, and then more. In the late 90s, songman Ronnie Summers, who grew up on Cape Barren at the feet of the master, formed a band called the Island Coes to pay tribute to his heritage, and in 2000, the Coes released the marvellous CD *Born on Old Cape Barren*, which contains as many great old-timey country tunes as songs adapted from tapes of Les Brown.

A similar act of restitution took place in the Top End. Following a musical play about the Cubillo family, *Keep Him in My Heart*, that was staged in Darwin in 1993 and based on field recordings that scientist/folklorist Jeff Corfield made of Val McGuinness just before he died in 1988, those same tapes – which included McGuinness's legendary version of 'Waltzing Matilda', 'Watjim Bat Matilda' – were further channelled in 2002 into the Darwin Festival show *String Bands and Shake Hands*, which starred Kath Mills and her daughters the Mills Sisters, along with the by-now-famous Seaman Dan, author of 'TI Blues'. Leading Mills Sister Alyson, who would go on to score a turntable hit with her ukulele-driven "real Kriol" version of 'Watjim Bat Matilda', told Corfield: "It's not as if it's just the past we're talking about. Mum has got 29 grandchildren, after all, spread all over Darwin and Australia. This music's also about the present."

●●●

the war a new home was opened in Alice Springs at St Mary's, and the practice of stealing children continued, although it was no longer explicitly government policy.)

Herb ran away from his first station job because he wanted to try and find his mother. He ended up back in Alice, working at the airstrip. By 1942 he had shot through again, heading south, carrying his swag and a guitar, still looking for his mother.

"I went down south, and during the war they wouldn't let you get on the train and come back unless you got a pass from the government that showed you had a job and accommodation. So I left my job not thinking, told my girlfriend I was going for two weeks but I was stuck down in South Australia jumping trains for three years."

Herbie didn't cop it as bad as some because he could pass for white, and that made for easier passage.

"When I was 18 I went to Gawler to join the army. I was dressed up in ringer's clothes. They said, No, we're not takin' no more recruits off the land." Herbie became a drifter, roaming the country in search of his mother or a way back home. He found neither. It was this experience, however, that inspired him to write his first song, 'Old MacDonnell Ranges', on the seventh day of the seventh month of 1947, according to his own handwritten songbook.

"I never got no recognition, you know. We started country right through the Northern Territory," Herb asserts now. "Now I got a CD out, I might get more recognition."

I mean, I'm the daddy of country music in the Northern Territory. There was no music up here in them days when I started playing. There was only two fellas in Darwin, Herman Pon and Jacob Pon, they used to play Hawaiian style, mandolin and that. I used to be doin' country, yodelling, I did a lot of that.

I was just on my own, I wasn't playing for money or anything, I just used to give concerts, a lot of old Hank Williams songs, and Buddy's songs, I think Slim must have started after that . . . Country music has changed over the years. Old Hank Williams . . . Jimmie Rodgers was the first one in America when he started with the blues and that . . . old Negroes started that goin'. With Jimmie Rodgers, he created this type of music, country music. Americans used to call it hillbilly. Here, Buddy Williams, Tex Morton and then Slim, they sorta created this country ballad, genuine like Australian, Australian country, which is based on folk songs, telling stories about station life, life on the land . . .

'Red River Valley', all these old Gene Autry songs, I'd bring them up. But if I get up and sing a Hank Williams song, I sing it Herbie Laughton style; if I sing a Slim Dusty song, I sing it Herbie Laughton style. You've got to be yourself if you want to people to take to you.

Herb was inspired to take up music at a young age.

I was still in the old telegraph station when Tex Morton come through there in the 30s. He was goin' up to Darwin, and he wrote that song 'Fanny Bay Blues' [a tribute to the Darwin jail, recorded in 1937] and he come over to our institution and played his guitar and mouth organ, and I got induced, I'd like to play like that.

Years after, around about the bombing of Darwin [1942], a fella came down, a Filipino bloke, he was going to Adelaide, and he had an old Gibson guitar, and he was broke, so he asked me to buy this guitar. I said, Jeez, and I jumped at it, I couldn't play it or nothing. I said, I'll teach myself to play this bloody thing. So I started.

I was just going along and there was a Buddy Williams show, so I said to Buddy, could you show me three chords? So he showed me them and I got it in my memory, and I was right then, I was just teachin' myself.

I used to mimic Tex Morton all the time, just walkin' around, you know. When I got to know Buddy and that, that sort of pushed me a bit more.

I went working out of Broken Hill with a shearin' mob, travellin' round, and all the time I was a young fella trying to get back home, you know. Every time I jumped a train they'd put me off at the next station. This went on for three years. I found out my mother was at a little town called Emery Bridge and I went down there but she'd already come back to the Territory, see. And here am I, stuck down there. So there was a train coming in, pulling in, and I thought, should I give it one more go? It was an army train, and I'm lookin' and there's my uncle and he said, What the blinkin' hell you doin' here? One of his soldier mates said, don't you worry young fella, you get your gear and we'll fix you up. This bloke made some room and said, when the conductor comes you duck in there and hide. And that's how I got back.

I was singin' 'Old MacDonnell Ranges' on the train for 'em there, see. That was the first one I wrote.

AT THE END OF THE WAR, when Herb finally got back on the Ghan, the train to the Alice (he wrote a song about that later too), Slim Dusty and Hank Williams were only just getting their start in music as well.

Herb Laughton moved around all through the Territory, from the centre to the top end, Alice to Darwin. He was a lost soul, basically, heartbroken after a failed romance, always in search of his mother and the next meal. He survived because of his strong back, his kindness and his wits, which included his ability to turn a tune.

I went up to Darwin in 1947 and I was workin' on the roads when they were first building the roads up there, and then I got a job with old Freddie Bush, who had a boat. How I got on there, they smuggled me, I got drunk one night and went to a party, I was playin' my guitar and all that and I got paralytic drunk, the first time, and the next thing in the morning I find myself rockin' and rollin' on the sea!

We were takin' the groceries and mail and all that up to the islands, to Croker Island, and we'd bring back the pearl shells. That's when I saw Bobby Randall's mob, they were only little fellas then, we did a concert there.

Bob Randall, like Herb, was a stolen child from Alice Springs, who was growing up in the unfamiliar saltwater country of Arnhem Land. He too would become a great songwriter.

"I haven't seen Bobby now for ages," says Herb.

> But he's writing and singing good songs. There's one good song he made, 'Brown Skin Baby' I think, it's nice. Aboriginal people, see, through their old ways, before whitefella ever got to Australia, when they learnt something, they didn't have books to write in, so they kept it in there [he points to his head]. This is old times, before alcohol come along.
>
> Aboriginal people, before Europeans got here, they were storytellers. Now country music, every song you sing tells a story.
>
> That's what their old ancestors were like, they'd tell Dreamtime stories. Then when they heard country music, it was just like their old ancestors telling stories the whitefella way. That's what country is. It tells a story and that.

Herb also used to ship out to the leper colony on Channel Island and entertain the sufferers there (after an epidemic in the 1930s, leprosy was one of numerous whitefella diseases, including VD and TB, that killed off Aboriginal people in the Top End). "And Wednesdays, I used to go into the Darwin Hospital and everyone would sing along."

When Herb experienced his first tropical cyclone he decided he'd had enough of Darwin and he returned to the familiar desert country of Alice Springs.

> Down the Gap here in Alice there used to be old Aboriginal cottages, the first housing the Aboriginal people had, you know, and I used to give concerts down there, just myself and that, free concerts, and people used to come, all the old families used to come down, sit down and listen to the singing, you know. I used to sing all these old ballads.

Herb even got a little group of his own going, the Central Arunda Band, with Ernest Perkins (brother of Charlie Perkins, famed Aboriginal activist) on harp, Cyril Hampton on string bass and Billy Wilson on lead guitar. But he found trying to keep it together was more trouble than it was worth. Too much drinking and carrying-on generally. Herb let the band go. He was old-fashioned. Like his idol Buddy Williams – and unlike Slim Dusty, who made the transition to having an electric backing band – Herb preferred to remain a solo act.

And then all of a sudden the very desert itself reared up and bit Herb like a poisonous snake. Swallowing mouthfuls of red dust on top of a bacterial throat infection gave Herb quinsy, a now-rare illness akin to acute tonsillitis.

Fever quickly developed. Herb was rushed to hospital, the agony in his head and throat intense. When the abscesses on his tonsils burst, he felt considerable pain relief but at the same time there was a considerable discharge. Herb had a head full of pus and plastic tubing, a literal taste of death.

All this perhaps explains why, after 'Old MacDonnell Ranges', even though Herb's songbook contains seventeen more entries (and he says he's written more than that), his second original composition, 'My Desert Rose', does not appear until some eighteen years later! Because when he came out of hospital six months after the quinsy first attacked him, Herb no longer had command of the instrument that in many ways made his life bearable, virtually his sole validation: Herb lost his voice. Or rather, it was stolen from him.

How cruel could the world be? First they took him from his mother, now they've taken away his song, his only means of communication with the world. It was a sudden and tragic end to a promising start in country music.

In 1955 Herb joined the roads department in Alice Springs, his first ever paid job and the only one he held till his retirement 38 years later, in 1993. He got married and had seven kids before he and his wife separated. And he stopped singing.

BUILDING ROADS IS A TOUGH JOB, a job traditionally imposed on African-American chain-gangs in America's Deep South. Herb took it in his stride.

It is testament to his strength of will, though, that Herb's singing career can now be seen as having two distinct phases – before and after the quinsy. Even though he had to spend 20 years in the wilderness, Herb would reclaim his voice and return to writing and performing. It wasn't so much that he couldn't quit music, perhaps, as music refused to quit him.

After he wrote 'My Desert Rose' on the first day of 1965, the floodgates opened, and by the end of the 70s Herb had produced a string of Territory country classics, from 'Arunta Man's Dream' and 'Ghan to the Alice' to 'My Finke River Home', 'Storm in My Heart' (boosted by a version by his friend Gus Williams) and 'Alice Springs Waltz'.

Says Bob Randall: "Herb started it all off, with the songs he composed. He had his own style, and they're very good story songs, in the country style. His contribution is enormous."

"When I was working on the road," says Herb, "I was in charge of the gang and I used to get the men working and of course I had my old guitar there, so I'd go out with the truck, I'd go out to the scrub and I'd be practising, practising, singing, and in time I could just start singing again. I tried to yodel, but I could never yodel again. I put that down to all the nerves, you know, damaged down there, when they shoved this tube down me throat to keep me alive."

OLD McDONNELL RANGE'S   Key of D

COMPOSED BY H. LAUGHTON
YEAR 7-7-1947

TACK ME BACK, OER THE OLD, McDONNELL RANGE'S
WHERE OFTEN TIMES, IN THOUGHTS I LONG TO ROAM
TACK ME BACK, OER THE OLD, McDONNELL, RANGE'S
TO MY N.T. OLD ALICE SPRINGS, HOME
— CHORUS —
BY THE COTTAGE'S, BACK, TO OLD HEAVITREE, GAP
ONCE MORE, THERE MY SWEET-HEART, TO SEE
TAKE ME BACK, OER, THE OLD, McDONNELL RANGE'S
TO MY N.T. OLD ALICE SPRINGS HOME.
— music played —
LET ME GAZE, AT THE BEAUTIFULL, SCENERY
OF THE RANGE'S, AROUND, MY HOME TOWN
AWAY, IN THE HEART OF, AUSTRALIA
TO THE N.T. OLD ALICE IM BOUND
— CHORUS —
BY THE COTTAGE'S BACK, TO OLD, HEAVITREE GAP
ONCE MORE, THERE MY SWEET-HEART, TO SEE
TAKE ME BACK, OER THE OLD, McDONNELL RANGE'S
TO MY N.T. OLD ALICE-SPRINGS HOME
— MUSIC —
NOW YOU SAY, YOU, MISTRUSTED, ME DARLING
WHEN YOU SAID, THAT MY LOVE, WAS UNTRUE
AS I ROMED, OER THE WIDE, OPEN SPACES
BUT MY THOUGHTS, THEY WERE, ALWAYS OF YOU
— CHORUS —
BY THE COTTAGE'S BACK, TO OLD HEAVITREES, GAP
THAT IS WHERE, I AM LONGING, NOW TO ROAM
TAKE ME BACK, TO THE OLD McDONNELL RANGE'S
AND MY N.T. OLD ALICE SPRINGS HOME

"In the evenings they said, Come on, sing us a few songs. We'd sit around and we'd sing a few songs and that's how I kept me music going, you know. Those fellas that worked there used to sort of get me going, which is good because I never neglected my music, you know. If I'm in a tent or a caravan later on, I'd sit down, and I'd pick out a few little tunes with good words to it, yeah."

It was desert country icon Gus Williams who, sometime during the 60s, encouraged Herb to take the first step back on stage. "Gus came to me," remembers Herb.

> He reckoned that when he was a little bloke he used to come and hear me singing down here at the Gap. He said, you inspired me, come back and write more songs, come with us tourin'. In the couple of years after that I started singing a little bit and Gus had a band going and he said, what about coming now? I said, all right, yeah, I'll come. I sort of got back, I said, this is not bad. People clapping while I'm singing, so I'm not too bad. So that's how I'm going now all the time.
>
> We played at the youth centre, me and old Gus. His son Warren, he was only a little fella then, playing drums. We were doing tours to all these settlements and that, and I got back to writin' songs. Gus had a nice young daughter who was a real good singer but she passed away. One evening we had to play on the oval there because we had too many people – it wasn't only Aboriginal people, it was just packed – we couldn't fit 'em in the hall. I felt real proud over there.

It was always a disappointment to Herb that his children didn't follow in their father's footsteps the way Gus Williams's and Isaac Yamma's boys did: Warren Williams and Frank Yamma are now pillars of central Australian music. One of Herb's sons, Gerry, was a member of Amunda in Adelaide in the late 80s, but he dropped out of music after that.

By the beginning of the 80s, with the formation of CAAMA (Central Australian Aboriginal Media Association), Alice Springs was enjoying its own version of the Harlem Renaissance. Herb Laughton was one of its elders. He was integral to the annual Aboriginal country music festival run by Gus Williams at Ali-Curung.

"Mothers and fathers and all the relations came down, oh, the atmosphere was really good. Kids would be singing all the old Australian songs. My niece, she won a trophy. It make you feel real proud when you got young kids following your footsteps."

Herb was inspired to write more specifically Aboriginal songs like 'His Ancient Race' and 'Old Aboriginal Stockman'. In 1983, CAAMA released a debut album by Herb, some 35 years after he wrote his first country song.

Herb recalls: "Philip Battye and Philip Macumba, when they first got going, they asked me what I thought of Aboriginal media. I said, that'd be good, and they asked me if they could record my songs and use them, and I said, Yeah, I'll be in that. So they ran off 150 tapes or something and I said, I don't want anything for it as long as you get this up and running."

Listening to that dusty old cassette, which was Herb's sole release up until 1998, that's how it sounds: dusty. And Herb's music remains unchanged to this day – almost a missing

At the Warrabri Aboriginal Country Music Festival, 1980, with Gus Williams's Warrabri Country Bluegrass Band

link between the 30s and the 70s, between black and white, between Buddy Williams and Isaac Yamma.

Herb himself can leap across several decades – or lives – in a single breath:

> Buddy Williams did a few of my songs, and before he died, he asked me for some more songs, he asked me to send him some . . . I knew Buddy for years, see, on and off. One day he come here and played at the youth centre, and I said, Buddy, can I sing a couple of my songs? So I got up there and sang a couple of my songs, and he got to like me, and he said, Look, have you got any songs I could record? So I give him 'MacDonnell Ranges' and 'Ghan to the Alice', about three or four of these songs. He wanted more, I said, no, not yet, next time . . .

Herb wrote all the standard types of country songs, the lovesick song, the homesick song, the work song, the train song, the gospel song. The big leap he took, apart from introducing Aboriginal songs into the genre, was to inject romantic love into his songs, in other words, to inject the love song into Australian country music generally. Love is a theme conspicuously absent in Australian country, bush ballads and folk songs. The reason usually given for this is that the pioneers were men without women. At least, without white women. But even when the sexual balance of the population started to even up, and even though love songs or love-lost songs are at the core of American country music, Australian country maintained its reserve – certainly, Tex, Buddy, Slim and most of their progeny are not known for their songs about women. Horses, sure. Trucks, dogs, drinking, the weather – the same. Other blokes,

★ Jabbi-Jabbi Songs ★

Wendy Lowenstein records Paddy Rowe in Broome, 1969

In 1969 *Australian Tradition*, the journal of local folk culture, ran a cover story on Broome elder Paddy Rowe, proclaiming his 'jabbi-jabbi' songs the traditional Aboriginal equivalent of British broadsides. Long before that, though, Aboriginal music was already developing its own modern form of gossip song – which is where it overlaps with traditional Australian folk music.

Early Australian bush balladry naturally reflected the lives of the pioneers, and it fed directly into country music. The white man's use of Aboriginal women for sex, for example, was a common enough theme in nineteenth-century Australian songs. In 'The Old Bullock Dray', a white stockman takes a gin for his wife. Interracial violence was not portrayed – only in occasional songs from the Deep North do 'ferocious blacks' appear.

Aboriginal people adapted songs like 'Black Velvet' and made them their own; the single greatest Aboriginal folk song is 'Jackie-Jackie', which became a country standard too. Echoing the term jabbi-jabbi – which of course echoes the English word jabber, meaning to talk gibberish – and not to be confused with 'Jabbin Jabbin', the Queensland dawn song that was famously transcribed by H.O. Lethbridge in his 1937 collection *Australian Aboriginal Songs* and has since been sung by Harold Blair, Lionel Long, Diana Trask, Sean & Sonja and Maroochy, 'Jackie-Jackie' is Australia's 'Stagger Lee', and has had more owners than an old Holden. Most often it fires off from the shanty tune 'Johnny Todd', and just as the original Jackie-Jackie was the only survivor of explorer Edmund Kennedy's ill-fated 1848 expedition to Cape York Peninsula, the song's anti-hero has the last laugh too. It was the first gentle stroke of cultural payback, and has been sung by everyone from Harry Williams to Chad Morgan.

Some of the jabbi-jabbi songlines live on to this day, not least of all in Broome, where Scotty Martin has picked up where Paddy Rowe left off and recently released an album, *Jadmi Junba*.

their mates —no worries. But women, apart from mothers? As Buddy Williams put it in 1953, 'I'd Rather Have a Pony Than a Girl'.

But with Herb Laughton, even when he was wandering there was always a sweetheart at home. The theme is present from his very first song on. Try as Herb might, he is refreshingly incapable of quite constructing a cliché. He keeps reshuffling the deck and mixing metaphors. His songs all blend into one, yet there are strange turns throughout them all.

Herb wrote specifically Aboriginal songs as soon as anyone, starting with 'Arunta Man's Dream' in 1969. And regardless of their subject, there is great Aboriginality in the detail of all his songs. But he musters even more power when he puts together a song like 'Old Aboriginal Stockman', which paints a portrait of one of his uncles at a point way past his usefulness. Written in 1984, 'Old Aboriginal Stockman' is the perfect companion piece to Ernie Bridge's 'Helicopter Ringer', a song written a few years earlier about the reason why men like Herb's uncle were now redundant. Herb's 'Old Aboriginal Stockman' has already been covered by Gus Williams and Broken Hill's Bluey Matthews; it was also considered for inclusion on Slim Dusty's landmark hundredth album, though it didn't eventually make the cut.

Rather than stepping things up after the release of his 1983 CAAMA cassette, though, Herb seemed to drop off. Bands like Warumpi and Coloured Stone were clearly the wave of the future; old acoustic solo country singers were a thing of the past. Only Isaac Yamma bridged the gulf. Herb consequently got caught up in a cycle of depression. As his kids got older, they lost interest in music and drifted away. Even his nephew, Gus's son Warren Williams – the one among them all who showed the most promise, and in whom Herb took so much pride – seemed to be letting it slip through his fingers. Herb wrote 'Your Careless Ways' in an attempt to warn him off the grog. Herb's world seemed to be unravelling.

It was at this point that Herb went into the video store that night and fell into the depression that drove him to end it all. When he came to, in the hospital, he felt as if he was drowning in a sea of antipathy. Or was it just a flashback to the time he was drowning in a pool of pus and vomit? There was no way, it seemed, he was going to get out of this world alive.

But then he was thrown a line, and he clutched at it. He pulled himself back into the land of the living, and at the end of the line was a Bible. That was fine by Herb. He knew the Bible – only now he knew just how powerful it really was.

When Herb got out of hospital he started to talk openly about his life. He started to purge some of the sadness.

HERB LAUGHTON IS STILL ALONE IN THE WORLD – he lives by himself in a small, tidy unit in Alice. Who would presume to imagine what goes through his heart and mind on those long days in the twilight of his life? Herb is a man who has endured pain deliberately and savagely inflicted by other men, yet he is a beautiful, gentle man who would not wish ill on a living soul. This spirit that lives through his music is something that deeply enriches the Australian country canon.

Because of his upbringing, Herb still can't be convinced that anyone cares for him. He is still reaching out to be wanted. On the verandah at his front door he's placed an old jam

Left to right: Stan Coster, Herb Laughton, Rocky Page, Brian Young

tin, which he leaves stocked with lollies for the local kids. A note sits beside it, offering the sweets, signed, "I am truly your friend, Herbie Laughton."

"I was very touched when Buddy passed away," he says wistfully.

Because I was planning on giving him some songs, but I was too late . . . When Buddy asked me for some songs, I had a feeling he had Aboriginal blood in him, I had this feeling all the time. And the last time, he said, Come on, mate, have you got any more songs I can record?

The only way I could get him to admit it . . . I said, Buddy, look . . . my songs, I'd like some Aboriginal people to do. And he said, What the bloody hell do you think I am? So I said, I knew it all along.

He said, I wouldn't have got anywhere if they knew.

Herb still plays to tourists at various spots around town, the Araluen Arts Centre, other places. "I love it, it's my hobby," he beams. But sadly, his songwriting has ground to a halt. Could it be that since he's started talking so much, he's got nothing left to say in song?

I give up writing songs a while ago because my family, my sons and daughter, they had no push, no inspiration, I thought, Why I am writing these songs?

Now when you get around about 70, 80 and that, well, you know all that feeling or inspiration, all that's sort of gone out of you, you know. You haven't got, like when you're playing sports, you're up in your prime, and you know, right there, you're going good, but nothing's happening for you. Same happened to me when I was writing songs and that, singing and that, and I had my voice and all that, before that quinsy thing, well, that's the time I would have been really into it. I would have been recording, I would have been up now with my own group but after that long spell . . . then the second time, well, that sort of knocked a lot out of me, you see, and I just can't get back. But I still sing a few songs and that.

Me and Gus, we stick to the old country, but we're not knockin' the young fellas, they've got their type of music.

I don't know who is running CAAMA and that now though, but instead of having a gospel session or country music session they only get this one type of music now, they do the rock and the heavy metal. You get this feedback from people, Where's all the country songs, where's these gospel songs you used to sing and all that, you know? But you don't get that no more.

In 1997 Herb and Gus were invited to appear at the Stockman's Hall of Fame in Longreach. Gus was still pretty active then. He's ten years younger than Herb, after all.

"It was really good," says Herb.

We went to Camooweal and then to Longreach. And while we were playing there, just over in the stockyard, all the equipment came in a big truck from Brisbane, because Gina Jeffries was going to play there too, so Gus and I had to play that morning. It was bloody hot too, and the ringers, they're right in front of us showing all these tourists how we used to do it in the old days, brandin' and cuttin' out – it brought back memories to me really! – and I got on stage and I thought, I better sing 'Leave 'Em in the Longyard'. I was singin' all these old songs. I got a real kick out of that.

We went back to the caravan park and a lot of the tourists came with us, they didn't stay to see Gina Jeffries, they came with us and I just sat around with these Aboriginal blokes and they could pick out all these old Elvis Presley songs, and we had the whole caravan park there, saying, sing this one, sing this one!

We didn't get paid for it, but I felt really good.

When Herb set off for Tamworth in 1998, it may have been the last great mission of his life. He was going to cut an album, a proper CD, at Lindsay Butler's, a real recording studio.

As the distillation of a life lived long and very hard, the album is a small token indeed, maybe a dozen songs, Herb's greatest hits. Lindsay Butler shows them the respect and kindness they deserve, and the result is affectionate and sprightly.

It may not even be Herb's words so much as his singing itself that carries the weight, shows the scars. His voice is ragged, cracked and faded. Like it's been knocked down and walked over. Like Herb has. It is weak and tired, an old man's last reaching out . . . but it is triumphant, and in a strangely distant sort of way, it stings.

❡❡❡

The Pitt Sisters appearing on Australia's Amateur Hour *with host Terry Dear: (left to right) Dear, Heather, Dulcie (later Georgia Lee), Sophie, and Wally Pitt.*

DEEP NORTH BLUES

★ The Pitt Dynasty, the Assang Brothers ★ and Other Queensland Blackbirds

Country music developed naturally in Australia in the 1930s, and we took keenly to jazz too – but we almost seemed to bypass the blues. Even though it was one of the building blocks of jazz and rock, blues remained ghettoised 'race' music, even in America, until well after the Second World War (as opposed to jazz, which became the dominant American pop form in the 30s in the shape of – mostly white – swing big bands). Not much blues reached Australia, in fact, because local record companies couldn't see a market for it. It's largely because they didn't hear much blues or R&B – and their successors, soul and funk – that Aboriginal people have not identified strongly with these black American genres, even though it was all music born of a similar sense of displacement, loss and sorrow.

Aborigines didn't identify much with jazz either, because in Australia jazz was a sophisticated urban phenomenon. Most black Australians still live in the bush, and it's only relatively recently that anyone in the bush, black or white, started listening to much music beyond Slim Dusty. Yet jazz and blues did have an impact. Indeed, if black Australia has a popular music tradition other than country (prior to the emergence of outback settlement bands in the 80s, at least), if there is a flipside, as they used to say in the record business, then it consists mainly of women, mainly from the Deep North, mainly singing jazz and blues. This alternative lineage developed during WWII and is still alive today. In fact, with the decline of the country tradition in the 90s and the growth of dance music, rooted in soul and funk, it has even gained the ascendency now. Just as Ben Sidran can say that any examination of black America is necessarily also an examination of white America, perhaps only an examination of the Deep North Blues, the counterpoint to the long-dominant country tradition, can cast that dominant tradition into the sharpest relief.

COMPARISONS BETWEEN AUSTRALIA'S DEEP NORTH and the American Deep South are inevitable, not only because of the redneck racism and steamy heat they have in common but also because they are both musical melting pots. From the Top End around Darwin through the Torres Strait Islands to the east and down south to the canefields of tropical Queensland, the Deep North region was built to a large extent on slavery. Pacific Islanders were 'blackbirded' to work on the mainland, or plied the seas on pearl luggers. The musical tradition of the Deep North therefore differs from that in other parts of the continent, as Russell Ward explained in *The Australian Tradition*: "The influences which have shaped their songs and dances have come from the islands to the east, as well as from New Guinea, and they disparage the Aborigines' dances, which they refer to as 'shake-a-leg'."

During the Second World War, Australia as a whole was opened up by the influx of all things American. Music was naturally prominent again, especially among African-American servicemen, most of whom were stationed in the Deep North, out of greater white Australia's view. It was the meeting there of black Australians with black Americans that generated sparks and started a tradition that produced the first, and still some of the biggest, names in indigenous jazz and blues – not just Georgia Lee but the whole dynasty she spearheaded, her sister Heather Pitt and Heather's daughters Wilma Reading and Heathermae Reading; plus other Queenslanders like Candy Devine, Cheryl Bracken, Syvanna Doolan, and eventually also Marlene Cummins, Christine Anu and others; even a couple of men, George Assang (aka Vic Sabrino) and Johnny Nicol.

Georgia Lee, born Dulcie Pitt in Cairns in 1922, was as good and as successful an Australian jazz vocalist as any in the 1950s. She played all the top spots, with all the top bands, and for a few years in the mid-50s she worked overseas, in Britain. "I sang blues and jazz, and also a lot of our own Torres Strait songs," she told ABC-TV show *Blackout* in 1992. She even managed to record an album, *Georgia Lee Sings the Blues Down Under*, which was probably only the third album cut by an Australian woman. Released in 1962, it was certainly the first album by an indigenous Australian, and – most importantly – it remains an extraordinary album, although one which was barely recognised as such until as recently as 2009, when it was re-released on CD and belatedly added to the National Film & Sound Archive's Registry of seminal Australian recordings.

Women have long received short shrift in Australian music. For black women, the situation has been even worse. And that took its toll. They certainly faced a much harder road than the one suggested by the recent feel-good feature film *The Sapphires*, an only notionally true story about an Aboriginal girl group that toured Vietnam in the 60s during the war there.

On the other hand, singing was one of the rare roles in which white Australians could accept black women at all, once the likes of Bessie Smith, Ivy Anderson and Billie Holiday had established the archetypes.

When the full force of the Pitt dynasty hit the south in the 1960s, there were even more black women vying for the available nightclub engagements and TV spots, let alone recording dates. There was Sydney's own Bettie Fisher, as well as Christine Asleh and Lorna Beulah. Cheryl Bracken, the sister of singing boxer George Bracken, came down to Sydney from Palm Island; Syvanna Doolan also started out in Queensland, before she too came south. Live music was booming in Sydney in the 60s, with the liberalization (and corruption) of licensing laws. There were plenty of hot Maori chicks on the circuit too, performing with showbands, women like Joy Yates and Inez Amaya, and there were always American performers coming and going, as the war in Vietnam escalated and more GIs spent their R&R in Australia.

Some of these women worked quite successfully on and off the club circuit. The most successful, Wilma Reading, achieved that status by going overseas. If they recorded anything at all, most of them didn't do so until much later. After *Georgia Lee Sings the Blues Down Under* in 1962, it was a full decade before an indigenous woman returned to vinyl, when Auriel Andrew released her debut EP on an Adelaide label in 1970. The Aboriginal women who followed Auriel into recording studios in the 70s were nearly all country singers like her, overshadowing, for the meantime at least, jazz, blues and soul divas such as Syvanna Doolan.

Roberta Sykes, after learning drums, once won a Brisbane talent quest to sing on TV's *Bandstand*. In the 60s she was a go-go dancer in Sydney nightclubs. But as she wrote in her autobiography *Snake Dancing*, in words that surely express what many of her peers must have felt:

> Despite my own shaky survival on stage, I had witnessed the racism and sexism which permeated that area of work, and did not feel that I wanted to continue in that direction. Audiences wanted to watch me because of my 'exotic' looks . . . but no-one wanted to hear what I was thinking.
>
> To me, dancing was a physical expression of my emotions, of my pain, as well as a means to release the tension created by my pain, but it was a way of maintaining, not progressing. I felt the need to go forward, but to where?

THE DAUGHTER OF A JAMAICAN FATHER and a Creole mother of mixed Indian, Aboriginal, Islander and Scottish descent, Dulcie Pitt grew up in far north Queensland during the Depression. Her father was a well-known local figure, and she was one of seven siblings who were the first black students at Parramatta State School in Cairns. Music was a constant soundtrack to her life. There was singing in church and singing under the mango trees and frangipanis. The rhythms of the Islands were pervasive, but there were also new influences arriving all the time via radio, records and Hollywood movies.

As the Pacific war theatre heated up in 1942, Australia became the base for tens of thousands of American troops. Allied GHQ was located in Brisbane from mid-1942, and large numbers of US troops were stationed in the Deep North, including most of the black GIs, who filled service rather than combat roles, staffing and guarding supply warehouses and fuel depots in port cities from Brisbane north to Townsville, Cairns and Darwin. And the Yanks – like all the region's previous migrants – brought their music with them. Heather Pitt told *Blackout*, "I never knew about jazz [growing up], because up in the north all we ever heard about was palm trees and grass skirts, but I was very fortunate to have met jazz musicians coming up to Cairns, and it was through them that I learnt all this music."

The American military took music so seriously as a morale-builder that it issued its own records, called V-Discs, and promoted its own bands made up of some of peacetime's swingingest cats. Glenn Miller is perhaps the best-known enlisted man; his plane famously disappeared without trace over the Atlantic.

★ *White Business* ★

If music in traditional Aboriginal society was an integral part of everyday life – communal property with a noble, often sacred purpose – in the modern West it became a business. Whitefellas' first response to Aboriginal music was to pin it under glass. The next step was to sell it. One of the first pieces of music of any description published in Australia, in 1834, was John Lhotsky's 'A Song of the Women of the Menero Tribe'.

Individual ownership and commercial application, which were alien concepts to Aborigines, characterised musical endeavour in the colonies from the first, and for a long time in this environment, Australia's black music was white. The stock in trade of music publishers and record companies is exploitation. In the 1920s, music hall duo Vaude & Verne had a hit with 'My Little Lubra', a sort of local variation on the 'coon song'.

The first Aboriginal songbook was published in 1937 by Allan & Co., and it was these charts, which had been transcribed by anthropologist Dr H. O. Lethbridge, that Harold Blair used when he recorded his 1956 EP, *Australian Aboriginal Songs*.

The 1940s' Jindyworobak movement in music, art and poetry sought to incorporate Aboriginal influences, but it was a concert-hall conceit, and today even such 'hits' as John Antill's *Corroboree* sound ill-conceived and unconnected.

Following the arrival of the vinyl LP in the 50s, with its high fidelity and longer form, all sorts of traditional and folk music forms were absorbed by the exotica boom, and Aboriginal music was no exception – labels all round the world released albums of field recordings made by anthropologists and ethnomusicologists such as Richard Moyle, A.P. Elkin, Jeremy Beckett, R.M. Berndt and Catherine Ellis.

It wasn't till the 60s, with modern jazzmen like John Sangster and composers like George Dreyfus and Peter Sculthorpe, that Aboriginal music was more effectively integrated into a fruitful fusion. More often,

though, Aboriginal motifs were simply appropriated as cover art or gimmick. Johnny O'Keefe's unsuccessful campaign to launch himself in the US pitched him as the 'Boomerang Boy'. Boomerang songs became virtually a genre in their own right, in fact: Terry and the Teenbeats' late-50s single 'Boomerang Baby' ("Come on back to me" was the refrain, of course) became one of Australia's rare rockabilly classics. The title was so good that songwriter Charles Marawood used it again in the 60s for a single by Tony Cole and the Crestaires. The genre even travelled overseas. American songwriter Lonnie Coleman's 'Boom Boom Boomerang' was a 1955 hit for hillbilly duo Tom Tall & Ginny Wright; that title, too, was deemed so good it was used again, in 1961, on a fine doo-wop side by Johnnie Shepherd; it's a wonder neither of these discs was much of a hit in Australia. Ahead of his 1955 tour of Australia, English bandleader Ted Heath cut an EP called *Australian Suite* containing a track called 'Boomerang' (alongside 'Dance of the Dingoes' and others).

In the wake of Rolf Harris's 1960 novelty smash 'Tie Me Kangaroo Down, Sport', English comedian Charlie Drake's worldwide 1961 hit 'My Boomerang Won't Come Back' was nowhere near the last gasp of the notorious 'coon song' tradition. In 1967, local doo-wop group the Delltones released 'I'm a Boomerang Bender'. As recently as 2010, Ali Mills, of Darwin's Mills Sisters, included a version of 'Alabama Coon' on her debut solo album. Rolf Harris went on to score another hit in 1962 with 'Sun Arise', a song co-written with TV naturalist Harry Butler in an attempt to emulate traditional Aboriginal music; it was eventually covered by shock rocker Alice Cooper, of all people. In 2008, in the UK's *Daily Mail*, Rolf Harris apologised for racist references in 'Tie Me Kangaroo Down, Sport', only to proceed to tell poverty-stricken Aboriginal people to "get up off your arse and clean up the streets your bloody self."

The war provided a lot of work for musicians, Australians as well as Americans. The Australian services ran touring concert parties, and with so many men mobilised, the pubs, clubs and mess halls were jumping to the sound of hot bands and vocal groups.

In Brisbane and Sydney, African-American servicemen were restricted to areas where local blacks already congregated. In Sydney, after a few dances at suburban Campsie, the Manzil Room was opened in Kings Cross, and the Booker T. Washington Club in inner-city Surry Hills. The bands were white (made up of locals), but as Andrew Bisset put it in *Black Roots, White Flowers*, "the girls were nearly all coloured . . . either Islanders, Maoris or Aboriginals." In the Queensland capital, Aborigines organised dances at the Protestant Alliance Hall in Red Hill before a 'negro club' was opened in South Brisbane.

The 'negro-only' North American Services Club was opened on Flinders Street in Townsville in 1942, with segregated brothels close by. Music was everywhere. Artie Shaw's Navy Band visited in 1943, jamming with Graeme Bell in Mackay. The US Army Base Section 2 Band operated out of Queensland, while Bob Crosby's Marine Band was offshore in the Pacific islands.

Bob Lyons, who led the US Services Pacific Band, was in Cairns when he reputedly 'discovered' vocal trio the Pitt Sisters, or Harmony Sisters, made up of Dulcie, Heather and Sophie Pitt, with their brother Walter on guitar. This was a time when groups like the Andrews Sisters, the Ink Spots and the Mills Brothers had much more appeal than solo singers – they displayed no small amount of Islands influence, too – and Lyons encouraged the Pitts to take the plunge. They had already competed quite successfully on Terry Dear's radio *Australia's Amateur Hour* when it was broadcast from Cairns, and in 1944 the group – minus Sophie, who got married instead – headed to Sydney, where they played concerts for the Red Cross and then got booked into the Tivoli.

By 1946, with the war over, Wally Pitt had had enough. He lived out his retirement on the NSW south coast, and was reluctant to talk about the past. It's been and gone, he said on the phone. Two years was enough for him. Struck paternalism everywhere we went, he said, as if we weren't intelligent enough to look after ourselves. He wasn't bitter though, not at all. Wonderful memories he had, wonderful people he met – there's no people like show people, he said – but those days are been and gone. Well, he said, that was an interesting talk, and he hung up the phone to go to bed.

When Wally decided to pack it in, the girls faced a fork in the road. Heather headed home, where she already had a family to raise. Dulcie was the most ambitious, and she reinvented herself as Georgia Lee.

After V-Day a great weight was lifted off everyone's shoulders. People could get on with their lives again, they had everything to celebrate, and so it was still a great time to be a musician. Traditional jazz boomed as dance music in all the big cities, and the ballrooms, town halls, nightclubs and sly grog joints were all still jumping.

When she was first in Sydney, Georgia Lee sang with Graeme Bell's Jazz Band and the Port Jackson Jazz Band, both legendary acts. Graeme Bell billed his hot new discovery as 'Beauty in Sepia', a 'Jamaican Blues Singer'. When Jim Somerville left the Port Jackson Jazz

Band in 1948 to form the Jazz Rebels with Doc Willis, Wally Johnson, Merv Acheson and Len Evans, Lee went with him. She sang further with George Trevare's band and Jack Brokensha's modern band.

Every night in Sydney after the Trocadero Ballroom closed, much of its 3,000-capacity audience went on to Kings Cross, to sophisticated late-night clubs like the Café Society and gangster Abe Saffron's Roosevelt ('the Boozy Roozy', which began life during the war as a US officers' club). There they continued dancing, drinking and making whoopie into the early hours. Georgia Lee was a star of this scene, its resident 'dusky bombshell'. She was a fully paid-up member of Kings Cross bohemia, sketched for a portrait by artist Donald Friend, who wrote in his diary that she was like "Hollywood's ideal of the Island belle."

In 1949, Lee left Sydney for even more fashionable Melbourne, to take up an offer to sing with Ossie Fletcher's smart outfit at Claridge's. She stayed for a record eight-month stand. At the same time, she was recording her first radio sessions with Graeme Bell's band. During winter 1949, she cut seven sides with Bell: 'Basin Street Blues', 'Mean to Me', 'Nobody Knows You', 'It Had to be You', 'Careless Love Blues', 'One and Two Blues' and 'Tuxedo Junction', only two of which ever saw release. In December she cut four more sides with Bell: 'You Made Me Love You', 'Sleepy Time Gal', 'I'll See You in my Dreams' and 'Time on my Hands', none of which were released.

Because Bell was a 'traddie', as the practitioners of traditional (New Orleans or 'Dixieland') jazz came to be known, his music was barely touched by more recent developments like the big band sound, let alone the emerging modernism of bop. So the material Georgia Lee recorded with him, rather than trying to keep pace with contemporaries like Billie Holiday, Ella Fitzgerald or Dinah Washington, harks back to classic blues as defined in the 20s by innovators like Ma Rainey and Bessie Smith – much the same sort of material Les Welch was performing in Sydney at around the same time with other black female singers such as Georgina de Leon and Nellie Small.

Georgia Lee left Claridge's towards the end of 1950 to go over to Ciro's, where she stayed for more than two years. Guitarist Bruce Clarke also went over to Ciro's from Claridge's, and in 1951 he produced a session with Lee for Melbourne label Jazzart Records, which was owned by Bob Clemens, who also booked Lee into his Downbeat Club. Clarke cut two sides with Lee as vocalist with his Quintones, 'St Louis Blues' and 'Blue Moon'.

★ THE MELB

S ON THE ICE
te With The Crowd

...cording to Ray Dèan, maestro down at St. Moritz
x and violin there 6 nights and Saturday afternoons
uld know. As a matter of interest, Ray Dean has
pular Ice Palais began as such, which, I think, was
leader was drummer Ray Graves—incidentally, Ray
or a season or two before Ray Dean became maestro the leader
le.

eader in Melbourne
n quiet, unassuming
's no doubt about his
patrons and his men,
nave been with him for

inds, 2½ years; trumpet,
ut the same I think; Max
otling his sax and clarinet
and still is, so there you see
is firmly entrenched in a very
b, as playing at an ice palais
tability on account of the various
music required, particularly when
comes to their annual extravaganza, viz.,
their Ice Revue, which usually lasts for a
week. I'll be seeing this popular quintette
again in the near future.

Dusky Bombshell, Georgia Lee
Last issue Nellie Small was chief fem
vocal news. This month, charming Georgia
Lee gets the limelight, mainly thru' the
reception she received at the recent Celeb-
rity Jazz Concert in the Melbourne Town
Hall, when she appeared on the bill with
Graeme Bell and Co. and other star jazzists.

● Georgia Lee.
Georgia was, I believe, born in Cairns
(Q.) 27 years ago. Her mother being of
Indian, Aboriginal and Scotch descent, her
father Jamaican. After schooling at Cairns,

From Music Maker *magazine, June 1949*

"The work she did at Ciro's – and it was *the* nightclub, very Hollywood – she was probably at her peak then," said Clarke. "We used to sit next to each other on the bandstand. She was very glamorous, always well-dressed, very popular, very good. She used to do 'Stormy Weather', Lena Horne sort of stuff like that."

Also in 1951 Lee appeared in the special 'Aboriginal Moomba' show staged in Melbourne as part of Victoria's centenary celebrations. Organised by what was then the Australian Aborigines' League under the leadership of Pastor Doug Nicholls and fellow Cummera man Bill Onus, the Moomba show was a groundbreaking event, and Georgia Lee was central to its success. Bill Onus had previously staged a 'Corroboree season' at Wirth's Olympia Circus on the banks of the Yarra in 1949, showcasing black acts like vaudeville duo Jacky and Jemmy ('The Brown Boys of Mirth and Melody'), baritone Edgar Box, Margaret Tucker ('Princess Lilardia, singer of charming Aboriginal lullabies'), yodeller Billy Bargo, Ted 'Chook' Mullett's Gum Leaf Band and George Hill ('Blind Aboriginal Instrumentalist'), plus tap and traditional dancing. Now Onus collaborated with a white producer/director and writer to put on 'Out of the Dark: An Aboriginal Moomba' at the Princess Theatre. Thirteen traditional dancers were flown in from Cherbourg in southeast Queensland: after Nicholls delivered the prologue, leading roles were taken by Harold Blair, Onus himself and Georgia Lee, supported by the Williams brothers, Joyce Taylor, Alan and Joan Saunders and others.

It was a high note on which to leave Melbourne, which Lee did in 1953. She had connected with powerful English agent Harold Fielding and was heading for London – overland. Her first port of call was Ceylon, where she played for a few months with Max Wildman's Quintette before moving on to Europe. Her first gig in London, in October 1953, was at the famous Astor Theatre, where she was introduced as West Indian, from Trinidad, even though she sang a set of Torres Strait songs. "I was indignant," she told the *Women's Weekly*. "I wanted to be known for what I am – an Aboriginal girl. I'm proud of it!" She impressed important personages such as bandleader Ted Heath, and landed the plum spot of featured vocalist with Geraldo's orchestra. Geraldo's outfit played strict-tempo big-band dance music, so-called 'sweet music' – hardly jazz, but staple fodder for the British; they did weekly BBC radio broadcasts and routinely toured the country. Lee was a convincing chanteuse who attracted attention in her own right.

It was news in Australia when she knocked back a significant sum to stay on with Geraldo in the UK into 1955. "It's not money I want most," she told one newspaper, "it is to reach the top so that any success I have will reflect credit on my people and give the world a better understanding of them." In reality, she was homesick and in poor health. Before leaving London in 1957, she worked with Ray Ellington (the black English bandleader who played a lot with the Goons, no relation to the Duke), and song-and-patter group the Dominoes.

When she arrived back in Australia she was snapped up by entrepreneur Lee Gordon to support Nat 'King' Cole on his 1957 Australian tour. After this, at least according to the unsigned liner notes on her 1962 album, she suffered a nervous breakdown, possibly not her first: "Being in constant demand throughout Australia meant extensive touring and irregular hours. The strain was too much."

Georgia Lee with Nat King Cole on tour in Australia, 1957

Recalled Bruce Clarke, "She was very quiet, always very dignified, but she had to be . . . there was always blokes chasing after her because she was such a good sort. I didn't know anything about her until we were on the same stage. She never actually said she was Aboriginal. You almost got the impression she was Jamaican or something like that. She only told us later she was Aboriginal."

After recovering from her breakdown, and surviving the invasion of Australia by a white American gospel singer also called Georgia Lee, who came to shoot the movie *Shadow of the Boomerang* with Jimmy Little, the erstwhile Dulcie Pitt threw herself back into the fray. She was joined now by her sister Heather, who had worked her way south with her new husband/manager/ drummer Jack Flower and her daughters Wilma Reading and Heathermae Reading.

Wilma Reading was discovered singing in a coffee shop in Brisbane, the Primitif, following a softball carnival in the late 50s. Bandleader Lali Hegi was so impressed by the teenager that he offered her the vocal gig with his 17-piece orchestra on the spot. She convinced her parents in Cairns to let her do it, and moved to Brisbane. She then moved on to Sydney, where in 1960 she debuted at Sammy Lee's legendary nightclub The Latin Quarter, where gangsters, molls and the slumming upper classes caroused and hot music went down. With her stunning looks and voice, she was an overnight sensation. Festival Records stepped in and signed her to its prestigious Rex subsidiary, and she recorded three terrific singles for that label in 1960/61, the first a version of 'Nature Boy', the second 'In My Little Corner of the World'/'If I Were a Bell' (from *Guys and Dolls*) and finally 'That's How I Go for You,' a classic R&B raver written by Festival in-house man Franz Conde.

When Wilma's mother Heather debuted on Graham Kennedy's top TV show *In Melbourne Tonight*, in March 1960, she was described as 'misty voiced'. Heather settled in Sydney and started singing around the folk clubs and coffee shops as a duo with her brother Wally (briefly out of retirement) backing her on guitar. She appeared at the Troubadour alongside sojourning black American singer-guitarist Brother John Sellers and solo Aboriginal folk-country-bluesman Black Allan Barker.

Candy Devine had by now arrived on the Sydney scene too. Born Faye Guivarra in Innisfail, north Queensland, Candy had studied piano and cello at the Conservatorium in Brisbane, but forsook a career as teacher to go into show business. She sang jazz and blues

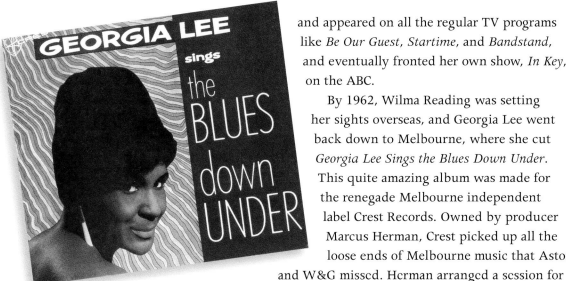

and appeared on all the regular TV programs like *Be Our Guest*, *Startime*, and *Bandstand*, and eventually fronted her own show, *In Key*, on the ABC.

By 1962, Wilma Reading was setting her sights overseas, and Georgia Lee went back down to Melbourne, where she cut *Georgia Lee Sings the Blues Down Under*. This quite amazing album was made for the renegade Melbourne independent label Crest Records. Owned by producer Marcus Herman, Crest picked up all the loose ends of Melbourne music that Astor and W&G missed. Herman arranged a session for Lee that reiterated the singer's affinity for classic blues with backing from a traditional jazz line-up. "She was just the best around at that sort of thing," he said.

Lee probably enjoyed a considerable privilege in even getting to release an album. This was a time, after all, when the 7-inch single was pop's coin of the realm, and only the biggest stars, invariably men, got to cut albums. Other Australian women of the same era – from Wilma Reading to Diana Trask, Helen Reddy and Olivia Newton-John – had to go overseas to find lasting success. Prior to *Georgia Lee Sings the Blues Down Under*, only two other women had released albums in Australia, Pilita Corrales and Noeline Batley – and Pilita was a Filipina interloper! (The sensational Diana Trask released two albums in 1961, *Diana Trask* and *Diana Trask on TV*, but both were conceived and recorded in the US, where Trask was now based.)

Georgia Lee had already been around the block, not just once but a couple of times, by the time the album was released, so it has to be regarded as a kind of swan song. Side A, dubbed 'On the Hot Side', featured uptempo versions of standards like 'Careless Love' and 'Basin Street Blues', plus the original 'Yarra Yarra Blues', written by Melbourne musician/impresario Bob 'King' Crawford. Side B, 'The Cool Side', offered ballads like 'Blues in the Night' and 'Nobody Knows the Trouble I've Seen', plus a second Crawford original, 'Down Under Blues'. As the album proves, Lee was a singer akin to Nina Simone: she didn't let her obvious familiarity with the mannerisms of the theatrical stage take anything away from the more spontaneous earthiness required by a 'soul' music like the blues.

As the album's liner notes concluded: "Georgia Lee is at home in any medium. Nightclubbing adults or jazz concert youngsters equally 'dig' Georgia's rich ballad voice which has full flexibility for true jazz interpretations, trad or modern. Her improvisation and dignified quality are shown to advantage on this album: Georgia Lee, with a personality as warm as hometown Cairns, has 'arrived'."

AND WHAT DID GEORGIA LEE DO as soon as she'd finally 'arrived'? After appearing in an ABC teleplay, *Burst of Summer*, she disappeared again.

Hype aside, she remained unseen for all of the 1960s. An EP of 'Island songs' that Crest Records had promised failed to materialise. "Georgia became severely depressed," Marcus Herman told Jordie Kilbey; she was "not up to the stresses of recording again."

Lee's sister Heather Pitt meantime powered through the 60s and into the 70s. She played a residency at the Texas Tavern in Kings Cross in Sydney for the best part of its infamous existence, from the late 60s to the late 70s – the Vietnam era, when visiting American servicemen on R&R leave demanded only the funkiest. She was the star of the Red Garter room, where jazz and blues was the fare (as opposed to the country music of the Barn room, where Nev Nichols and his Country Playboys ruled the roost). Heather recorded an EP with the Red Garter band which contained songs as disparate as 'Tie Me Kangaroo Down, Sport', 'Waltzing Matilda', 'Bill Bailey' and Woody Guthrie's 'This Land is My Land'. She also guested on an album, *Duke's Men*, by Doc Willis, who'd played with her sister Dulcie twenty years earlier, singing songs like 'Mood Indigo' and 'It's a Sin to Tell a Lie'.

Heather's other daughter, Heathermae Reading, was by now getting into the act too. After playing the Texas Tavern herself, she toured Vietnam and Thailand as singer in a band called the Sounds of Lawrence. Back in Australia, she appeared alongside Jimmy Little, Vic Simms and Auriel Andrew at a special indigenous show in the opening week at the Sydney Opera House in 1973. She went on to become a regular on variety television, sometimes crossing paths with her mother on the same shows,

Top: Heathermae Reading at the Central Coast Leagues Club in Gosford in the mid-70s; (above) Georgia Lee's comeback as Australia's Queen of Jazz, 1977

and then she too headed overseas. Basing herself in Holland, she cut a couple of disco-soul singles for the legendary Atlantic label, and in 1976 was the official Dutch entrant in the World Popular Song Festival in Tokyo, where she fared even less well than Australia's entrant, Marty Rhone. She later returned home and resumed working on the club circuit.

Georgia Lee made a comeback in 1975 as part of old ally Graeme Bell's Scott Joplin tribute at the Opera Theatre in Melbourne. *The Sting* was the current hit movie, its soundtrack reviving Joplin's turn-of-the-century ragtime classics. Bob 'King' Crawford was running Melbourne's Free Entertainment in the Parks program, and he gave a gig to Lee, who was by now a member of the Baha'i faith. In 1977, after Frank Traynor and Graeme Bell had claimed the title King of Jazz in 1975 and 1976 respectively, Lee was crowned that year's Queen of Jazz. It was a small token (the award was a short-lived contrivance) at the end of an extraordinary career. The following year, Crawford put together a Sixth Annual Australian History of Jazz show at the Myer Music Bowl, at which Lee appeared alongside all the old stagers like Bell, Traynor, Bruce Clarke, Bob Barnard, Smacka Fitzgibbon and Judy Jacques. After she passed her sceptre to that year's monarch of jazz, she once again faded from the scene, and this time she did not return.

Heather Pitt, after appearing on the ABC TV show and album *Dr Jazz* in 1977, joined her sister in retirement back in Cairns, where she died in 1995. Dulcie, Georgia Lee, would live another fifteen years; she died in 2010 at the age of 89.

WILMA READING FLEW THE HIGHEST, completing a mission her aunt couldn't quite pull off. She went overseas and she made it, "a three-octave vocal wonder export from the fifth continent Australia," as one blurb read, "who has conquered the international show business world from Las Vegas to London".

Wilma said: "When I got the chance to go overseas I took it, because we as Australian artists were never put at the top of the bill, it was always American artists, or English artists . . . All they [Australian record companies] were doing was copying the overseas hits. They didn't give the writers a chance in those days."

Today, Wilma Reading is still a striking-looking woman. In 2003, after the death of her husband, she too returned home to live in Cairns. Her CV reads amazingly: a 33-date one-woman tour of Russia with the Moscow Symphony Orchestra is not untypical.

Wilma Reading at the outset of her career

When Wilma first left Australia, she was spotted by talent scouts at her first international engagement at the Goodwood Hotel in Singapore and booked into the Tokyo Hilton. There, she was spotted by the American agency ABC, and booked into the Las Vegas Riviera. By 1965, she was on the cover of black American magazine *Jet*, celebrating her latest engagement as vocalist with the Duke Ellington Orchestra for a season at the Copacabana in New York. No singer could covet a gig more than playing with the Duke – to ride on the rhythm of the finest big band in history, your voice nestling alongside solos by Johnny Hodges and Paul Gonsalves. Wilma Reading was only 25 and she'd already reached the top of the mountain. Her aunt had

Wilma in the 70s

had to content herself with *Ray* Ellington!

When she moved on to London, Wilma was hired by Harold Fielding, the same agent who discovered her Aunt Dulcie, to replace Cleo Laine in his West End production of *Showboat*. Wilma went on to become a regular on British TV, appearing on all the top variety shows, like *Morecambe and Wise* and *The Two Ronnies*; she also starred in three BBC specials of her own. She was the supper club diva par excellence, while remaining all but unknown in her home country. She cut two albums and several singles for the English Pye label, and one album for the Dutch NCR label. These recordings reveal a singer of extraordinary range, control and sensuality. After singing the title song for the 1974 Omar Sharif-Julie Andrews film *The Tamarind Seed*, she went on to play a starring role in the 1979 blaxploitation disaster flick

Pacific Inferno. When she toured Russia in the 80s, flexidiscs flooded onto the black market. She was in Berlin when the wall fell, and sang as part of the re-unification celebrations.

Since returning to Cairns, Wilma has recorded a fourth album, *Now You See Me,* which puts her love of jazz alongside her Islander roots, and has taken up teaching music at a local college. Hers is a rare success story amid more widespread obscurity.

INDIGENOUS AUSTRALIAN MEN are less common in jazz and blues than the women. But like so many of the women, the two most prominent, George Assang (aka Vic Sabrino) and Johnny Nicol, hail from the Deep North. There is also singer Liz Cavanagh's uncle, Ray Cassady, a jazz guitarist from Ingham, mid-way between Cairns and Townsville.

George Assang was born on Thursday Island in 1927 and had Aboriginal, European, Islander and Asian blood. He was a vocalist who went by the stage name Vic Sabrino for most of the 50s, and was generally acknowledged to be about the only man in Australia at that time who could reasonably sing the blues. But in a journeyman career that spanned several decades Assang/Sabrino was in fact as much a genre-hopper as a label-hopper; though he certainly sang jazz and blues, he also sang country, pop, ballads, rock'n'roll, skiffle, gospel and folk – and it's by spreading himself thinly across all these genres that he's had an enormous impact on all Australian music. He died in 1997, but has received posthumous attention recently on the basis that, among his many firsts, he could be said to have cut Australia's first rock'n'roll record. Meaning that, at its very birth, overwhelmingly white Australian rock was, in fact, black!

"He was the only guy I knew who could silence a Sydney pub," said his one-time agent John Singer. "The only other guy was Harry Belafonte."

"We called him the Cairns Lair," said Graeme Bell, with whom Sabrino recorded, as did Georgia Lee. "He was a bit of gentleman larrikin, very well-spoken, like an actor. He did the club circuit, he was a very good guitarist too." In another life, he might have been a figure like

Vic Sabrino, 1950s and (right) George Assang, 1970s

Billy Eckstine, a deep baritone balladeer caught between two worlds, black and white, rock and pre-rock.

One of nine children, Assang moved with his family to Cairns in 1938, when he was eleven. He left school at 15 in 1942 and worked in the war effort. By this time he was already performing in his first band with two of his sisters and his brother Ken, who was barely into his teens. They played the same circuit in Cairns as the Pitt sisters.

After the war, George moved to Sydney, where he got a job as a panel beater. He was joined by Ken, and the duo started playing gigs as the Assang Brothers. George kept his day job, even became a union organiser, and though he would always continue to sing on and off with Ken, his breakthrough came as a soloist. Under his real name, he released his debut single, 'Daughter of Mona Lisa', on the Mercury label. Co-written by future Festival Records A&R Manager Ken Taylor and expatriate French bandleader and public relations man Red Perksey, the record was not a hit, but it established an important relationship between Assang, Taylor and Perksey.

When Perksey moved on to become Musical Director at Pacific Records, the forerunner to Australia's CBS operation, he took Assang with him. Somewhere along the way, Ken Taylor rechristened him Vic Sabrino. "I knew him even before he had this manager who gave him the name Vic Sabrino," remembered Graeme Bell. "He hated that name, so did I. It was just to give him another identity so his manager could sell him easier." As if he was some swarthy Italian stallion like Sinatra, or Dean Martin.

Vic Sabrino's first single for Pacific was another Taylor/Perksey composition, 'End of the Affair', a ballad written to cash in on the popularity of the 1955 film of the same name starring Deborah Kerr and Van Heflin. The song had already been covered once before, when Taylor recorded Sydney-based Jamaican-Australian jazz-blues singer Nellie Small singing it for Mercury. It was no more successful for Sabrino than it had been for Small.

Then rock'n'roll hit! The bastard offspring of hillbilly blues. In 1955, Red Perksey had Sabrino record a version of 'Rock Around the Clock' for Pacific. Bill Haley and his Comets had first recorded their version of the song, which was essentially a Western Swing number, in 1954, and though it was a minor hit in the US, that was nothing compared to what happened when the song was attached to the movie *Blackboard Jungle* and re-released in 1955. EMI Records in Australia, who owned the local option to license the disc, initially couldn't see any potential in it and refused to release it. Getting out the first version of a hot new song was of course a long tradition in the music business, especially in isolated Australia, so Red Perksey matched Sabrino with 'Rock Around the Clock' before it was otherwise available here. Perksey's own orchestra backed Sabrino on the track, and the recording was pretty good, definitely enhanced by Sabrino's burnished timbre. But as soon as Festival Records picked up EMI's lapsed local option on the Haley recording and released it in both the old 78 rpm format and the new 45 rpm format, that version set all-time Australian sales records.

Vic Sabrino released a few more rock'n'roll knockoffs for Pacific in 1956, including an Elvis twofer of 'Blue Suede Shoes'/'Heartbreak Hotel', then jumped ship to Festival. Ken Taylor had by now taken over at the new big local label and he was embarking on his ultimately successful

★ *Redfern Royalty* ★

Candy Williams at his uncle Major Murray's place in Redfern one Sunday night in the 50s

Candy Williams was the godfather of music in Redfern, Sydney's Aboriginal ghetto, sometimes called the Block. One of five famous brothers from Cowra in central NSW – his second single for Festival in 1960 was in fact a version of the Marty Robbins song 'Five Brothers' – Claude 'Candy' Williams was a wonderful "pop, country and western singer and comedian", as *Pix* put it in 1962.

Candy started out after WWII singing duets with his brother Harry, who would later lead the Country Outcasts, but he soon began to play an organisational role too. During the war, Bill Onus had put on weekly dances at Redfern's Railway Institute Hall, before he moved to Melbourne. In the 50s, Candy continued the tradition, becoming the ringleader of regular Redfern musical gatherings that shifted from house to hall before settling on a house in Lawson Street. "Those Sunday nights at Lawson Street were just great," recalls white songwriter Coral Dasey. "Claudie was there; it was his uncle's place. Jimmy Little used to show up, everyone would have a sing. Mainly we sang the country hits of the day; this was before Australian music became strong. There was a boxer, Teddy Rainbow, he used to do 'If I Ever Needed You'. His sister was Olive McGuinness and she sang as a duo called Olive & Eva with Eva Bell. They were marvellous singers, beautiful harmonies; they made a couple of recordings for Prestophone, a studio in George Street where Planet Hollywood is now."

Olive & Eva were the first Aborigines to release a commercial recording under their own name. They came from the same Eurambie mission at Cowra that the Williams boys hailed from, and in Sydney were virtually adopted by a white woman called Grace O'Clerkin, who was a great friend to the Aboriginal people. O'Clerkin taught the girls guitar, and wrote songs for them that suited their sweet ballad style. The four songs that made up their two Prestophone 78s in 1955 and 1956, 'Old Rugged Hills'/'Rhythm of the Corroboree' and 'When My Homeland is Calling'/'Maranoa Moon', became Aboriginal standards, sung by everybody from Harold Blair to Jimmy Little.

Candy and Col Hardy at the headquarters of the FAA, Sydney, mid-60s

In 1960, Candy signed a recording contract with Festival's prestigious new label, Rex Records. His first release was a duet with pop moppet Noeleen Batley, covering the American folk standard 'Tom Dooley'. 'Five Brothers', its follow-up, was a minor hit that got Candy on the TV shows of the day like *Bandstand*. His third and last single was a version of 'My Blue Heaven'. He was still playing around Redfern, at dances at McConnell's Gym, but when the Foundation for Aboriginal Affairs opened on George Street in Redfern in 1963, it ushered in a new era. At the FAA, Candy encouraged a new generation of talent, such as Col Hardy. At the same time, he was landing parts in television productions like the ABC's 1966 drama, *Wandjina*. In 1973, the Foundation moved to bigger premises, near Lawson Square. This was the era of Black Power on the Block. The first Aboriginal legal and medical services were located there, and also Bettie Fisher's Black Theatre, not to mention pubs like the Empress Hotel. Redfern's new house band the Silva Linings, led by drummer Mac Silva, played a blend of country, rock, pop and soul. Candy poached Mac to be part of an all-star line-up of the Country Outcasts that backed Harry and Wilga on a tour of the outback in 1975.

In 1976, despite deteriorating health due to diabetes, Candy was the driving force behind the first annual National Aboriginal Country Music Festival, held in Canberra. The festival was a wonderful blossoming, a moveable feast that took place every year for seven years until the final one in Townsville in 1982. When Candy died in 1983, the festival, and a significant part of Redfern, died with him.

●●●

quest to create a whole new constellation of modern Australian teen pop stars. But before he would first hit it big with Johnny O'Keefe and Col Joye in 1958 – long before he signed Jimmy Little – he experimented with two artists, Vic Sabrino and Ned Kelly. Kelly was a sort of rebel honky-tonk singer, a Hank Williams acolyte with a penchant for black guitarists, whom Taylor hoped he could tame into a pop star, in the same way he hoped to groom Vic Sabrino. In pursuit of a hit, Taylor sometimes recorded each of them performing the same songs.

In 1957, Sabrino released three Festival singles, 'Dust in the Sun', 'Hitch Hiking Heart' and 'Painted Doll'. All three were original Australian compositions, remarkably for that time: this was no small push. 'Dust in the Sun' was co-written by novelist D'Arcy Niland in collaboration with Leslie Raphael and designed to cash in on the current Australian film with the same title. Raphael had previously tried to cash in on Charles Chauvel's Aboriginal movie *Jedda* with a 1954 song, 'Dreamtime for Jedda', which was covered by country duo the LeGarde Twins among others, and he also collaborated with Niland, something of a folklorist himself, on some songs designed to cash in on the 1957 film version of Niland's own novel *The Shiralee*. The film *Dust in the Sun* was based on Jon Cleary's novel *Justin Bayard*, about a policeman in the outback and his Aboriginal prisoner (played by Robert Tudawali, who'd starred in *Jedda*); though the film was scored by Wilbur Sampson, Niland and Raphael composed a song with the same name, and it was released in two versions, one on the EMI label by the Horrie Dargie Quintet, the other by Vic Sabrino for Festival.

'Hitch Hiking Heart' was a Ken Taylor/Hal Saunders composition that Ned Kelly, obviously hip to some of the new teen strains, also cut for Festival. In Kelly's hands, with pedal steel and fiddle, it was pure, hard, honky-tonk. Sabrino's version, with horns and strings, remained country in all but its instrumentation; the same could also be said of its flipside, another country cover, 'Fraulein' (which, again, Ned Kelly also recorded). And all this happened quite a few years before Ray Charles released *Modern Sounds in Country and Western*! Additionally, Sabrino's version of 'Hitch Hiking Heart' can claim the distinction of being the first Australian recording of an Australian composition to be released in the US, where Decca put it out.

Sabrino's third Festival single in 1957 was 'Painted Doll', a rockaballad written and previously recorded, once again, by Ned Kelly. Backing Sabrino on his version was emigré American sax man Dave Owens with his band the Blue Boys, just before Owens put together the Dee Jays to back Johnny O'Keefe. The single was good, but within six months, once O'Keefe and the Dee Jays hit with 'The Wild One (Real Wild Child)', Ken Taylor had found his rock'n'roll star. Vic Sabrino and Ned Kelly both lost out as Taylor found other artists to follow in O'Keefe's footsteps, such as Col Joye and Digby Richards. Ned Kelly was so untameable that he was soon run out of Sydney show business altogether. Vic Sabrino, on the other hand, had a habit of always managing to land on his feet. His answer was to get another gig.

Sabrino was now hired by Graeme Bell to sing with the outfit EMI had asked Bell to put together, his Skiffle Gang. Skiffle was a sort of British equivalent to rockabilly, a pre-punk DIY form of folk-country-blues made on guitar, washboard and tea-chest bass. After Lonnie

Donegan had a hit in 1955 with his version of Leadbelly's 'Rock Island Line', skiffle became a whole movement, whose offspring included no less than the Beatles. It was easy enough for Graeme Bell – and Sabrino – to work with, because in many ways the skiffle repertoire was not very different to traditional jazz: songs like 'Sweet Georgia Brown', for example, which was one of the eight sides – virtually an album's worth of material – they cut for EMI in 1957. 'Skiffle Board Blues' and 'Come Skiffle Chicken' were Bell originals, but otherwise they covered traditional songs like 'John Henry' or 'Freight Train' (which was popularised around this time by Mike Seeger), the standard 'Gospel Train', and 'Don't You Rock Me, Daddy-O' and Woody Guthrie's 'Gamblin' Man', both of which had been hits for Lonnie Donegan. This was one of the ways in which jazz, blues, country and folk all crossed over with one another. The four 45s (credited to "Graeme Bell and his Skiffle Gang, with Vic Sabrino") were quite successful, with Vic's voice at its most comfortable on this material.

By now, though, the Sputnik was out of the bag; rock'n'roll was sweeping aside everything in its path. Vic Sabrino did not return to vinyl till 1964, after he changed his name back to George Assang and reunited with brother Ken to cut the gospel album *Just a Closer Walk* for Philips. Doubtless inspired by the success of Jimmy Little and his 1963 hit 'Royal Telephone', the album was moderately successful and the duo, as well as George as a soloist, were regulars on TV's *Bandstand* and *Sound of Music*.

In 1967, George and Ken joined forces with Kathleen McCormack, an Australian singer of Irish and Scottish ballads, and contrived to call themselves the Colonials, who cut another album for Philips. *Songs from Down Under* is another quite extraordinary entry in the Australian discography. Produced by Noel Gilmour, who'd worked with folkie Lionel Long on his double LP *The Bold Bushrangers*, the album's "basic conception . . . was to try and paint the widest possible musical picture of Australia," according to the liner notes. Amid the usual run of Australian folk standards like 'Botany Bay', 'Waltzing Matilda' and 'Wild Colonial Boy', there are two Maori songs, 'Pokare Kare' and 'Now is the Hour'; a Johnny Ashcroft/Hal Saunders song called 'Bush Fire'; and a Gary Shearston song, 'Bonnie Jess'. There's also a reworking of 'Dust in the Sun' with a full brass and strings arrangement, on which Ken takes the lead, and another number from Darcy Niland's 1966 book, *Travelling Songs of Old Australia*, called 'The Colour of My Nation': "I see the same stars all men see, and they are there for you and me . . . to black I turn for pride and consolation/Black is the birthright of my race, and the colour of my nation."

The album also contains the first recorded version of 'TI, My Beautiful Home' (aka 'Old TI'), the unofficial anthem of the Torres Strait Islands (the most important of which is Thursday Island, widely referred to as TI); it was a homecoming of sorts for the Assang brothers to sing it. According to Russell Ward, the song was written by Jaffa Ah Mat in the 1930s, long before Seaman Dan penned his 'TI Blues', although Ward acknowledges that "another well-known Island family, the Pitts, also claim to have contributed to it."

Both George and Ken, the album's liner notes concluded, "have travelled extensively throughout Australia, and have intimate knowledge of the places and subjects of which they sing," George in a voice "always full of expression."

By the end of the 60s though, George was starting to lose that "lustrous voice" of his because of emphysema, so from then on he concentrated on acting. In any case, by that time Philips had found Kamahl, the honey-and-dark-chocolate-timbred Sri Lankan crooner who from the late 60s to the early 80s reigned as Australia's biggest male solo star, virtually bankrolling the label with a string of no fewer than thirty hit albums. George Assang, meanwhile, scored guest-star roles in classic Australian TV shows like *Skippy* and *Spyforce*, and in 1971 landed a regular part in *Barrier Reef*. He appeared in all forty episodes of the show up to 1972, sometimes even croakily singing a song but more often emphasising his underrated guitar-playing. He was briefly married to glamorous actress Rowena Wallace. He guest-starred on sexy soap *Number 96* and on *Boney*, the TV series based on Arthur Upfield's novels about an outback Aboriginal detective. In 1973, he made his one movie, and what a movie it was . . . *And Millions Die!* was about Nazi war criminals on the run in Hong Kong; it starred Richard Basehart – and George Assang. It would make a great double feature at the drive-in with Wilma Reading's *Pacific Inferno*.

In 1979, Assang made his last recording, the first version committed to vinyl of a Bobby McLeod song that was then called 'Freedom Was a Common Thing' but later retitled 'Wayward Dreams' – it's one of the great songs in the Aboriginal canon. The track was included on an album sponsored by the trade union movement, *Flames of Discontent*.

Assang retired to Nowra on the NSW south coast – where Bobby McLeod came from and returned to – and there he died, aged 70, in 1997. His alter-ego Vic Sabrino was buried with him, along with any secrets they may have shared.

GUITARIST JOHNNY NICOL, FROM AYR in northern Queensland, is another figure who obscured his identity in order to advance in the music business – he presented himself as Maori after joining the Maori Troubadours in 1960. "I think like a lot of indigenous people," he said, "we went through the stage where we didn't really care to identify ourselves because of the prejudice, being afraid of rejection. It's strange, but it's a fact, Maoris were more accepted than Aboriginals. Now I'm proud of what I am."

Like George Assang and Georgia Lee, Nicol is of very mixed parentage, making distinctions of limited value anyway. The fact that he joined a band like the Maori Troubadours highlights the link between the 'blacker' music of indigenous North Queensland and that of New Zealand. The Troubadours were a showband led by the legendary Prince Tui Teka, one of a number of such groups that were active in Australia during the 1960s. Their typically Maori affinity with black American and Caribbean/Latin music was in line with Nicol's own tastes, and he spent a few years barnstorming with the band, playing the rural show circuit and clubs and pubs, and playing on the album *A Bit of This, A Bit of That* (Festival). Subsequently, in the mid-60s, Nicol went overseas, working his way from the Gold Coast to Las Vegas via Italy, and eventually landing a gig on cruise ships travelling between the Bahamas and Florida, where he picked up even more Caribbean influences.

Eventually Nicol returned to Australia and in 1972 he hosted his own ABC radio show. In 1974 he formed the Latin Soul Quintet, and when he released his first solo album, *Touch of Blue*, on Philips the following year, he was hailed as a new George Benson. And he thought George Benson was the new Johnny Nicol! Show business . . . "I had no great desire to be a star or anything like that," he said. "Playing guitar was just fun. All of a sudden you get a tap on the shoulder and a guy says, You want to join my show? The jackhammer seemed even heavier after that."

Despite going on to cut several more successful albums in the 80s, Johnny Nicol remains the invisible man of Australian jazz. This is perhaps because jazz purists look down on his calypso/bossa nova-influenced sound as middle-of-the-road supper-club fodder. But then, George Assang, Georgia Lee, Wilma Reading, Heather Pitt – none of them figure much in orthodox Australian jazz history either.

WITH THE EXCEPTION OF THE EXTRAORDINARY Pitt dynasty, indigenous women in Australian jazz and blues – such as Bettie Fisher, Syvanna Doolan, Marlene Cummins, Melbourne's Carole Fraser – have struggled to achieve enduring success. Judging by rare footage of *Bandstand* performances by some of these women, perhaps it was because they came on too strong: even singing Cole Porter, they were too raw, too soulful for a white audience that had been weaned on Doris Day and was happiest with a nice girl-next-door like, say, Judy Stone.

Johnny Nicol on guitar, Rex Hotel house band, Kings Cross, 1963

Candy Devine in Ireland in the mid-70s, with show band leader Dave Glover and US country star, Hank Locklin

Candy Devine went overseas, like Wilma Reading, and she too never looked back. She found herself playing a gig in Ireland and, as they say, never left. She'd sung a couple of important original Charles Marawood songs – 'Walk You High' and 'I Must Go' – in an Aboriginal-themed episode of *Skippy* in 1968, but these weren't released on record, and she wouldn't make it onto vinyl until Ireland's Spin label put out what is still her only album, *Candy Devine Sings*, in 1970. In 1976, she joined Belfast's new Downtown Radio and for four decades she was one of the station's star announcers; she returned to Brisbane when she retired in 2013.

Black women belting out the blues was not something Australian record companies ever really understood. And when the Beatles hit, regardless of the concurrent rise of Motown and Stax soul, of the Supremes and Aretha Franklin, Australia apparently wasn't interested in anything except the English boy bands. A group like the Sapphires were a typical flash in the pan. Women like Syvanna Doolan and Marlene Cummins – again, both from the Deep North – were only just survivors.

The biggest tragedy is the great – potentially even greater – voices that have been silenced, the careers that were snuffed out. Bettie Fisher, a jazz and blues singer from Sydney who was strong on the circuit and on TV around the late 50s/early 60s, is a prime example. (She should not be confused with the Betty Fisher from Darwin who, at the age of 14, won radio's *Amateur Hour* in 1946 singing the "plantation melody" 'My Curly-Headed Babby', but had any potential career or life in music snatched away by the authorities when she was forced to return to the mission.) The Koori Bettie Fisher was born at the Orient Point Mission near Berry on the south coast of NSW in 1941, and started singing semi-professionally in Sydney in the late 50s. She worked her way up to gigs with Graeme Bell and regular spots on TV shows like *Bandstand* and ABC-Brisbane's *Jazz Comes to Town*. When Jimmy Little mounted his All-Coloured Revue in 1962, Fisher was one of its star attractions, a gorgeous girl with a strong voice who was sometimes compared to Eartha Kitt. "The audience used to come along to look at the bunch of freaks," she once said, "and then they discovered the freaks could actually sing!"

Fisher was forced to retire from performing, however, after suffering a nervous breakdown in the late 60s. But like many an Aboriginal artist, she wanted to try and give something back, and in her capacity running Redfern's Black Theatre in the 70s, she worked to create opportunities for others that she had never enjoyed herself. She sometimes guest-sang with Redfern's country-rock house band Black Lace. And then she died, suddenly, aged 35, in

1976. The reason given was a heart attack. It is a common euphemism. What it really means is that she died of a broken heart, a heart so discouraged and walked-over that it could no longer continue to beat – and this malaise has struck an entire race of people. There are no recordings or footage of Bettie Fisher performing.

Possibly it gets back to what Roberta Sykes said in *Snake Dancing*, the same thing Syvanna Doolan blamed for her potential going largely unfulfilled. Doolan, the daughter of 'singing stockman' Fred Doolan, who grew up on Palm Island in Queensland's Deep North, complained bitterly that while white audiences were quite happy to listen to her sing, they didn't want to know about the reality of Aboriginal life in Australia.

Sibby Doolan is reputed to have once beaten Jamaican-American migrant Marcia Hines in a talent quest at the famed Whiskey-A-Go-Go in Kings Cross. But she was ever on the outer, and has left to posterity only one track recorded under her own name. Doolan started out singing blues and soul in Sydney clubs in the late 60s, and in the early 70s enjoyed some time in the sun, working with Bettie Fisher's Black Theatre in Redfern and sometimes singing with Black Lace, appearing in the play *The Cradle of Hercules* at the Sydney Opera House, supporting Sonny Terry and Brownie McGee at the Town Hall, singing at the Tent Embassy in Canberra and founding gospel choir the Mamma Hill Singers. By the late 70s she was back in the Deep North, living with her son in Townsville and fronting the Doolan family band Doctor Bones, which – in something of a genre-shift for Sibby – was a long-standing staple on the Queensland country music circuit.

By the early 90s, Sibby was back on the national stage, with a role in the touring production of Jimmy Chi's musical *Bran Nue Dae*, but it was her 1997 appearance on the ABC-TV show *Songlines* that must stand as her epitaph and greatest legacy. With Marlene Cummins's son, the brilliant Leroy Cummins, backing her on acoustic guitar, Sibby sang a song of her own called 'Sad Moon', and the song and its performance (included on the *Songlines* CD) are simply breathtaking, and give rise again to the question: how much more great music like this has gone lost? Sibby Doolan died, in Townsville, in 2013, aged 63.

Better late than never, then, that Marlene Cummins, after going back to Queensland to live and study in the 1980s, got her music going and eventually got into a studio and recorded, among other songs, her classic 'Pension Day Blues'; or that Carole Fraser finally got a couple of tracks out for posterity too, most notably her signature song 'Koori Woman', before she died. Or that Theresa Creed and Cindy Drummond eventually succeeded in releasing albums in the early 2000s. For all these women, their recorded debuts came after three or four decades in the game, when they were around 60!

The present-day inheritors of the Deep North Blues tradition, whether it's Christine Anu, Naomi Wenitong, Liz Cavanagh, Jessica Mauboy or Georgia Corowa, whether they play it straight or diverge into hip-hop or new urban R&B, are at least getting a rather earlier start.

❥❥❥

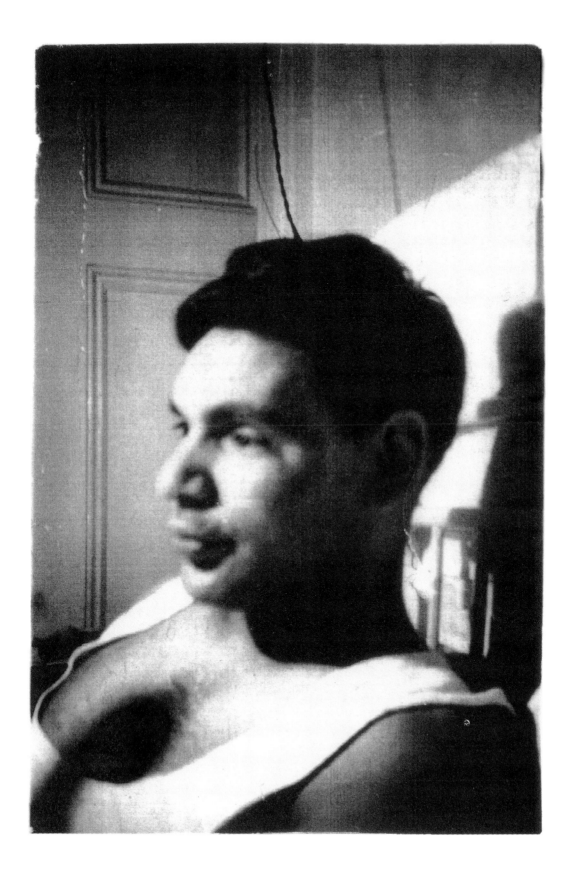

"I'M A BLUDGER, I'M A DRUNK, I'M A JAILBIRD"

★ Dougie Young and the ★ Troubadour Tradition

Dougie Young is the great phantom of Aboriginal country music, its first great anti-hero and, after Herb Laughton, its second great songwriter. His life story always had an element of myth to it: early accounts dated some of his songs to before he was born, and he was first reported dead in the late 70s, though he actually lived until 1991.

Born in the mid-1930s in Mitchell, near Cunnamulla in south-western Queensland, to a white father and Gurnu mother, Dougie Young was a troubadour, a modern-day rural songman. As shown by the quality of the work that fortune has left us, he was a brilliant talent despite the fact he barely attained a reputation outside his own stamping ground, the Darling River country of western NSW and Victoria.

Anthropologist Jeremy Beckett went to Wilcannia in the late 50s looking for remnants of traditional life. What he found, he later wrote, "was a lively community, with a lot of music and a lot of drinking." In 1964 Beckett made field recordings of Dougie Young singing eight of his songs, including the immortal 'The Land Where the Crow Flies Backwards'. These tapes were released as an EP in 1965 by Wattle Records, an independent label spawned by the folk revival.

By then, 'Where the Crow Flies Backwards' was already being covered by folkie Gary Shearston. In Dougie's first – and pivotal – encounter with the music business, he sold the song's copyright to Tasmanian singer Athol McCoy. He got paid, but for that tiny one-time payment he traded away the rights to his song's considerable future earnings. McCoy recorded the song himself for RCA in 1967; it has also been covered by Chad Morgan.

Dougie is comparable to Leadbelly in that he was an occasional convict co-opted by the folk movement; he updated the traditional Aboriginal gossip song in such a way that he established a new vernacular tradition. "I'm a bludger, I'm a drunk, I'm a jailbird," he told Kevin Gilbert in *Living Black*, his only interview for posterity. "I live it wild and free," he sang in his song 'I Don't Want Your Money'.

Dougie's notorious lifestyle, as depicted in his song 'Cut a Rug', simultaneously fuelled his music and cruelled his personal life. By the end of the 60s he had left his wife and family to live on the lam, and any glimmer of the success 'Crow' had hinted at seemed snuffed out. He was recorded for a second time in Walgett in 1969, but after that his output of songs slowed right down. He didn't cut his third and final session until a decade later, in 1979, when he was already very ill and only put down three songs.

All these recordings have been collected on a CD, *The Songs of Dougie Young*, released by the National Library in collaboration with AIATSIS (Australian Institute for Aboriginal and Torres Strait Islander Studies), and what an extraordinary document it is. It has the effect of transporting the listener back in time, having that same crackly ambience – that same dusty, faraway echo – that 1930s American field recordings of dustbowl balladeers and delta bluesmen have. Young plays the pick and strum, and though he's only an adequate guitarist at best, he can sell a song like a master. His has a bravura skill with words, and his tone is gorgeous. Even when he's acting as a sort of boundary rider of doom, he oozes a mischievousness and joy that is all too absent in most Australian country.

In the grand folk tradition, Dougie's tunes are mostly appropriated, redolent of Slim, or Chad Morgan or Jimmie Rodgers. Legend suggests Dougie used to deputise for Chad when the Sheik of Scrubby Creek was indisposed, and that makes sense. Dougie favours a bush ballad base but he sometimes swings to a bluesier American style as in 'Frankie and Jonesy', a rewrite of 'Frankie and Johnny'. The songs are almost all about drinking ("It was all comedy sort of stuff," says fellow Wilcannia singer Bill Riley, "I don't remember him writing any love songs"), and they are brilliant and hilarious, but at the same time tragic. This is Dougie Young's genius – his gift for social realism – the ability to wring the last black laugh out of the most despairing scenario.

THE LIFE OF DOUGIE YOUNG is contained in his songs. "He lived his music," says Bill Riley, who was a contemporary of Dougie's. "He wrote of his life and his mates." 'Halfcaste', written in the mid-60s, is a Red Foley-like oration set to the refrain from 'What a Friend We Have in Jesus', and is directly autobiographical: Dougie remembers living "on both sides of the track," growing up in Cunnamulla with Christianity, capital punishment and country music.

"I stand in the middle," Dougie told Kevin Gilbert. "I run the whitefellas down, now I'll run the blackfellas down."

'Where the Crow Flies Backwards' itself tells how, as a teenager after the war, Dougie packed his swag. He became a gun stockman who delighted in taunting authority – and in drinking. "Where the dear old Darlin's flowin', and the trees have lots of shade," he sings, "You'll find me 'neath the old gum tree, drinkin' goom and lemonade."

According to Bill Riley, Dougie "came to New South Wales in about '52." There he married Chrissie Johnson. "He got to love the Darling and after he settled in, started writing songs."

When riverboats were still steaming up and down the Darling, before the railway went through Menindee, Wilcannia was a thriving little town. After the war its population fell to 800, about half of which was Aboriginal. The government built two rows of houses. The climate of persecution was all-engulfing. People liked to drink, and when they drank they sang, and for that they went to jail.

"In those days," says Bill Riley, "Aboriginals weren't allowed to go in the pubs, they had no citizen rights. They had to get their grog and sneak around the back alleys, or down the river bank, and the coppers would chase them . . . It was a good atmosphere though. We used to go around sometimes at nine o'clock at night to start a claypan dance and sometimes they would go through to the early hours of the morning!"

Perhaps it was an echo of earlier times, of the halcyon days when Hero Black rode the riverboats, squeezing his accordion for a penny or just to pass the time. Hero or 'Paddy' Black got so famous he even went to Sydney to play at the NSW Sesquicentenary celebrations in 1938. All along the Darling you could sometimes still hear the ghostly strains of his best-loved tune, the 'Menindee Waltz'.

"Around the 50s and 60s," remembers Bill Riley, "guitar became more popular. In the earlier days it was all squeeze-boxes, button-accordions and harmonicas. Then, through their get-togethers, more Aboriginals learned to play the guitar."

Dougie first started mucking around on guitar as a teenager after the war. In 1957, by which time Dougie had written at least 'Cut a Rug' and 'Wilcannia Song', he had a riding accident that ended his working life. Now he was good for nothing *but* music. Plus maybe drinking.

'Cut a Rug' is, of course, one of the great drinking songs, which have been central to the country music tradition from 'What Made Milwaukee Famous' to Slim Dusty's 'Duncan'. 'Wilcannia Song' survives only as a lyric: in it, 'Youngie Doug', as he refers to himself, rues the time he serves in jail for drinking, but swears he's going to get straight back on it as soon as he gets out.

Unable to work even if there was work to be got – and it was in the 60s that rural Australia first started to feel the squeeze – Dougie escaped into alcohol. The fact that it was prohibited, and therefore dangerous, only heightened the excitement. Music went along with all that. Its release inspired celebration, and the cycle continued. Everyone would have a sing. "And if we wind up in the cells," as 'Wilcannia Song' put it, "Lord have mercy on our souls."

WHEN ANTHROPOLOGIST JEREMY BECKETT arrived from England and took up a post at Sydney University, he heard and became interested in Australian bush ballads. It is to his credit he saw something in Wilcannia because at that time, as he says, "Nobody had any interest in musicology, it wasn't on anyone's agenda. Certainly not this kind of music, anyway."

When Beckett first went to Wilcannia in 1958 he didn't encounter Dougie. He heard Dougie's songs sung by others, and he heard *about* Dougie, but he didn't see or hear or meet him. He did meet Fred Biggs on this trip, however. Biggs was well-known in the area, a singer who wrote his own songs – like traditional gossip songs, jabbi-jabbi songs – in (traditional) language. Beckett went back to Wilcannia later that year for an event Jack Quayle described in *Dawn* magazine: "The Wilcannia people made history recently when they produced their own real hillbilly show in the Wilcannia Memorial Hall. Many of the artists were at first very doubtful about appearing in public but as soon as they found how popular they were they had a world of confidence." Again, Dougie was not present.

Standards like 'Swanee River', 'Poor Dog Tray' and 'The Old Bullock Dray' were popular on the night but, as Quayle noted: "A number of the songs introduced in this show were composed by Wilcannia Aborigines. Bill Riley composed four and Doug Young and Babs Vincent, one each."

"We decided to get a concert group together," says Bill Riley, "my uncle Jack Quayle was the chief instigator of that, and he just rallied all the talent up and took a concert to the town hall in Broken Hill and it was a pretty big success. A lot of the people of Broken Hill reckon it was the best since Burl Ives! Jerry Beckett came along with his old reel-to-reel tape recorder and he got Freddy Murray, he's from Menindee, and myself. Doug Young was fairly new around Wilcannia then, he didn't get much of him at that time."

IT'S EASY TO REMEMBER DOUGIE YOUNG NOW, because he was eventually caught on tape – and that recorded legacy is quite enough on which to build a legend. But were there other troubadours like Dougie out there who simply were never 'discovered'? Certainly there were some.

Men like Fred Biggs and his counterparts around the country, such as Paddy Rowe, Cecil Taylor and Billy Redmond, who wrote and sang gossip songs in language, were clearly not going to penetrate the white world. But singers like Raymond Duncan from near Warwick in south-east Queensland, or Eric Craigie from Mooree, or Alby 'Bronco' Lovegrove in Perth, or Angus 'Hank' Williams from western Victoria, were writing their own country songs in English, in a similar way to Dougie Young and at around the same time, and their songs haven't survived in recorded form either, although some of Billy Redmond's songs are occasionally sung by surviving folk singers.

According to Roger Knox:

Nobody knows about these writers, these intelligent people, because they couldn't get out of their own community, and nobody would listen to them because they was talkin' truth and talkin' straight, talk about their struggle, talk about the odds they stood up against.

Clivie Kelly grew up trading licks along the Nulla Creek with a white farmboy called Gordon Kirkpatrick, who later changed his name to Slim Dusty, but Clivie Kelly could never presume to have any of the ambition that Slim took as his birthright. All he left behind was a single song, 'My Home in the Valley', which he never got to record, although it is still sometimes covered by other artists.

Aboriginal singers existed in a world untouched by the modern music industry, even as they were influenced by the recordings of others and by the wireless. The very nature of music had been changed by sound recording. As Evan Eisenberg wrote in *The Recording Angel: Explorations in Phonography*, before that time, "the musician sang for his supper. He did his work in the presence of his patrons – noblemen, peasants, festive clumps of peasantry – and, as he satisfied, he had his own needs met in return."

In fact it is quintessential to the Aboriginal music experience – and one reason it didn't break through sooner to a larger audience – that so much of it was for so long music exclusively of, by and for the Aboriginal community.

Might Dougie's Wilcannia contemporary Bill Riley still be an undiscovered gem then? Riley himself would modestly demur. "I was dedicated to my work in the bush," he says, "and so most of my entertaining was done around the local gymkhanas, rodeos. I never ever chased up a career in music." Besides, Riley adds, "It was when [Dougie] first starting writing his own songs that I got mixed up with him – and I knew I could never compete with songwriting like that!"

Bill Riley as pictured by Quadrant *in Wilcannia, 1958*

DOUGIE YOUNG'S ONLY REAL RIVAL as a recorded troubadour is Black Allan Barker, and again, not just because Black Al – who sometimes called himself Moarywaalla, sometimes even Allan Black – actually left a recorded legacy, but also because he crossed over into the white music world, if only to a very small degree.

Born at Marble Bar just south of Port Hedland in northwest Western Australia (the Kimberley) in 1942, Black Allan was a folk-country-bluesman who in the 60s was a doyen of the east coast coffeehouse circuit, an Australian Big Bill Broonzy or Lightnin' Hopkins. By the late 60s/early 70s, he'd become a curious incarnation of Aboriginal flower power.

"Black Allan is an example of a trendy contemporary Aboriginal," wrote Kevin Gilbert, again in 1978's *Living Black* – "moustachioed, guitar swinging and 'with it' in speech and dress. His ideas about alternative living, grass, geodesic domes and organic farming stand a little oddly alongside a need, expressed from the chambers of his soul, for something strong and beautiful and Aboriginal that he can refer back to as a point of security."

In Sydney in the early 60s, Barker was a regular on the burgeoning folk scene, often appearing at the famous Royal George Hotel, home to the Push (the bohemian demimonde that produced such figures as Robert Hughes and Germaine Greer), and at other venues

Folknik Allan, Wayside Chapel, Sydney, early 1960s

around Kings Cross like the Wayside Chapel, the Attic and the Troubadour. Another figure on this scene at much the same time was perhaps the only other man to even approach Aboriginal bush blues: his name was Frank Povah, who later played with Tasmanian Chris Cruise in the duo, Sweet Daddy Hambones. Like Black Allan, Povah hailed from north Western Australia; he was a folklorist, writer, editor and musician of mixed Aboriginal and European descent, who played ukulele and guitar from an early age and fused the influence of Broonzy, Leadbelly and Jelly Roll Morton with Australian bush balladry.

"In WA," he says, "I'd been playing pubs and coffee lounges since my late teens, in the 50s and early 60s. The Cross, Taylor Square, Darlo, was something else back then. It was a sort of hand-to-mouth existence but a hell of a lot of fun. The 'real' folkies – and no slur on them intended – got all the folk gigs and the rest of the world was more interested in rock and its variations than it was in old-time music."

Black Allan often appeared with the black American singer Brother John Sellers, who came to Australia with the Alvin Ailey dance troupe in 1962 and stayed on for an extended sojourn. As a direct link to the powerful American tradition, Sellers exerted no small influence in Australia, as did other African-American artists who toured here around the same time, like Odetta and Paul Robeson.

An article in Adelaide pop paper *Young Modern* in 1965 shone a spotlight on Allan. Under the headline 'Youthful Native Sings, Composes', it said:

> The long-haired, handsome lad with the wide, white smile received a boost to his career when he recently met up with visiting Negro folk/gospel/blues singer Brother John Sellers, in Sydney.
>
> Allan is 23, rather shy, but has a very pleasant voice. Not so long ago he was singing at a folk-song place in Sydney at only thirty shillings a night, but the right introductions and advice should help him to get places.
>
> Allan started singing at nine, mostly religious songs and hymns, in a Church of Christ mission hut in the middle of the desert, to the accompaniment of an old piano. However, around the campfires, he also listened to the traditional songs of his tribe, handed down from remote ancestors.

After Allan had heard recordings of Louis Armstrong, he thought about singing a lot. He went to Melbourne and heard other recordings – Billie Holiday and Big Bill Broonzy – and realised he had found what he wanted to do.

So here is a native Australian who plays guitar, sings folk and blues songs and songs he writes himself in two dialects – Nunoomda and Gurreeyurra – some sad, some romantic and gay. He lives in one of those terrace houses in Sydney's Paddington. People like Brother John believe that once he gets the right exposure, he'll be really on his way.

Well, he was going somewhere, sort of. By the end of the 60s, his hair had grown even longer, he'd traded his suit for a buckskin cowboy outfit, moved to Melbourne, Australia's new pop capital, and was sliding readily into the burgeoning psychedelic underground. He appeared at Australia's first-ever rock festival, Pilgrimage for Pop, at Ourimbah north of Sydney, in January 1970, alongside the cream of the acid blues bands, the reborn Billy Thorpe and the Aztecs, Max Merritt and the Meteors, and Wendy Saddington and Copperwine. Australian music enjoyed a great blues-driven renaissance in the early 70s (Billy Thorpe's transformation from clean-cut crooner in a suit to blood-curdling bluesman with pigtails wearing a civil war uniform was not dissimilar to Black Allan's), but Allan himself was obviously still too far-out for the record business.

Go-Set followed up Ourimbah with a short item on the Hendrix-like left-handed guitarist. "I started in 1962," Barker said, "when the blues here first began, before the other Aries people started doing it. Like Billy Thorpe, he's an Aries."

It may have actually been the dawning of the Age of Aquarius, but Allan didn't mind mixing metaphors: "Something else I'd like to say is, we're starting the 'M' club, only for people who have the 'M' sign written in the palm of their hand." He explained that 'M' stood for Mass, Mind, Mars, the Moon. He might have added Moarywaalla, or Music. No wonder interviewer Kevin Gilbert was confused. *Go-Set* went on quoting Barker:

Hippie Allan, 'Pilgrimage for Pop' festival, Ourimbah, NSW, 1970

I'm staying in Melbourne because Melbourne has the 'M' sign. No-one really knows what is happening except the 'M' people. It doesn't matter how old you are. There's a prediction that says that if the whites that think themselves better than the black people don't see what's happening, they will have to leave the country and the blacks and whites who get on will stay and groove.

Don't go against the sign of cool or you will destroy your own cool because the 'M' sign is an international super-cool thing. Peace, peace, peace, gods and goddesses, witches and warlocks. That's about all I've got to say except that I'd like to see white and black people together, that's all, and that Aboriginal law is better than white law.

But the 'M' revolution failed to materialise and Allan moved on from Melbourne, back to his home state of Western Australia. There, in the late 70s, he became involved in the founding of the Australian chapter of Greenpeace, after the group mounted its first action in this country, against the whaling station at Albany. Back in his very own country, the Kimberley, he was central to the famous 1979 protest against mining on Aboriginal land at Noonkanbah, north of Fitzroy Crossing.

Strangely, Kevin Gilbert seemed as determinedly uninterested in Black Allan's singing and songs as he was in Dougie Young's. "I used to be a muso and a hustler from the city," was all Gilbert reported Barker saying, "but I'm a tribal man, too. I went back when I was 33."

But Black Al never stopped singing, and it was in Port Hedland in the early 80s, when he was in his early forties, that he went into a recording studio for the first and only time, and cut the album *Fire Burnin'*. *Fire Burnin'*, the first all-original Aboriginal album since Vic Simms released *The Loner* a decade earlier, is another extraordinary document, and in so many ways, right down to Allan's trademark headband, it presaged the later arrival of Kev Carmody. Loaded with great songs like 'Take Me Back', 'Run Dingo, Run', 'Marble Bar Train Blues', 'Native Song' and 'Momma Blues', it is radical country blues, and it has a haunting, life-or-death quality.

With the cassette hot off the press, Allan journeyed south in 1983, to Lake Gnangara near Perth, for the eighth and last national Aboriginal country music festival. "They're singing the blues their way," the *West Australian* reported around his set. "But the songs he sang did not convey a peaceful theme." They did, however, win Allan the festival's songwriting award, much to his reported delight. *Fire Burnin'* made next to no impression outside Aboriginal hearing, however, maybe not even outside black Western Australia, and sadly it will have to stand alone as Allan's epitaph.

Barker continued his peripatetic ways into the 1990s. He was a common sight in Sydney in the 90s, busking in Central Station Tunnel, and then he moved on to the hippie capital of Nimbin, in NSW's Northern Rivers district, where he worked with Aboriginal kids. He was spotted busking at the Tamworth country music festival in 1994, now sporting a long white beard. He then went back to Hedland, where he ran a shelter for the homeless. He died, aged 61, in 2003.

WHITE ARTISTS ASPIRED TO MAKE IT, but black artists like Allan Barker and Dougie Young were trying first and foremost just to survive. Music was second nature to Dougie, yet even as it became what defined him, he came unstuck when he entertained ambitions for it and stepped outside his own world in that pursuit.

The ABC broadcast some of the material Jeremy Beckett had recorded on his initial trips to Wilcannia in 1958, but it was concerned about the portrayal of drinking, of 'negative stereotypes', and all copies of the tape seem to have been lost.

In the early 60s a battery-powered reel-to-reel tape machine came on the market, and it was with one of these that Beckett returned to Wilcannia in 1964, specifically to record Dougie. The resulting tape launched the Dougie Young legend.

Dougie was actually introduced to the world at large by Gary Shearston's version of 'Where the Crow Flies Backwards'. The profuse sleeve-notes gracing Shearston's *Australian Broadside* album from 1965 were by Edgar Waters, who ran Wattle Records:

> Dougie Young is an Aboriginal, like Kath Walker, and like her he grew up in Queensland. In almost every other way, the two are unlike. Dougie Young is what the anthropologists call a 'fringe dweller'; he lives today in the 'blackfellows' camp' outside Wilcannia in western New South Wales. He does not want to be assimilated into white Australian society; he just wants white Australians to stop pushing him around, and leave him and his people to live their lives in their own way. He does not wish to be known to a white audience as a poet; he just makes up songs to amuse his black friends in the hill-billy style which today is a common musical idiom of bush workers, white or black.

Dougie Young was thrust upon the world by a small conspiracy of believers. "He wasn't a strong personality," Jeremy Beckett remembers. "A very quiet bloke. Got things off his chest by singing. And he was alcoholic, fairly seriously."

Beckett reported at the time a rhyme he heard in Wilcannia that sang praise to the 'White Lady': "Beer is all froth and bubble/Whisky will make you moan/Plonk is another name for trouble/But the metho is out on its own."

Dougie's claim, made to Kevin Gilbert — "I've been in the fuckin' horrors and I've been in mental homes and come out four times" — is substantiated by his song 'Scobie's Dream', which is such a lurid description of the hallucinations that accompany the dry horrors, the DTs, it could only have been written by someone who knows them well. When Jeremy Beckett rounded Dougie up and sat him down in front of the microphone in 1964, he was sober, and an audience soon gathered. Eight songs went down. During 'Happy-Go-Lucky Darkie' you can hear a dog barking.

"I remember listening to one, 'Frankie and Jonesy'," says Beckett. "It's about chicken-duffing, and Frankie, who was the thief, was sitting there beside me, chuckling away!"

In January 1965 Beckett wrote an article for the *Australian* about Wilcannia, in which he noted: 'Dougie Young himself doesn't look like a national leader or coffee bar celebrity . . .

★ Freedom Writers ★

Gary Shearston sings 'We Are Going (To Freedom)' at FCAATSI conference in Canberra, 1967, as Faith Bandler listens on.

Like its American counterpart, the Australian folk revival of the 60s, which most successfully spawned the Seekers, was as much a political push as a musical movement. Aboriginal activist Charlie Perkins wrote of 1965's Freedom Ride, in which he led a busload of white students protesting racism throughout rural NSW: "Folk singers Gary Shearston and Jeannie Lewis helped tremendously in raising funds."

In turn, folk had a strong impact on Aboriginal people. Songs like 'Jabbin, Jabbin' and 'Jackie-Jackie' popped up all over the place. Gary Shearston covered Dougie Young's 'Where the Crow Flies Backwards' on his third album for CBS, 1965's *Australian Broadside*. Other songs did the rounds too. Lionel Long sang 'Jackie-Jackie', and also covered Gordon Tolman's 'Namatjira'; Gordon's own group, the Tolmen, cut it for RCA in 1963.

Gary Shearston was the closest Australia had to a Bob Dylan figure, and in 1965 he was commissioned by Aborigines to write 'a song of our own' to replace 'We Shall Overcome' and serve as a campaign theme in the lead-up to the landmark 1967 referendum. He took Kath Walker's famous poem 'We are Going' and made it more positive by adding the phrase 'to freedom' to its chorus. If the poll result is any measure, the song was successful, but its lifespan was as short as most advertising jingles.

Kath Walker, later known as Oodgeroo Noonuccal, had a number of her poems set to music. The best-known is 'No More Boomerang', which first appeared as a track on Phyl Lobl-nee-Vinnicombe's Aboriginal-themed EP *Dark Eyed Daughter* (W&G Records, 1968); it was subsequently adapted numerous times, most notably in the early 80s by Murri singer Les Collins.

Aboriginality has consistently remained a theme of right-on white Australian folk music, from Shirley Jacobs's 'Bush Girl' to the work of bands like Redgum and Goanna in the 80s. In 2003, Chloe and Jason Roweth's band Us & Them included versions of Clivie Kelly's 'My Home in the Valley' and Billy Redmond's 'Woodbine Hill' on their album *Better Than New*. As Gary Shearston himself said to Aborigines in 1965, "You are the people who know better than I can ever know what you want to say in songs."

●●●

when the tape recorder is going, he is more keen to get his friends singing or lead the children in "Sad Movies Always Make Me Cry" [a recent American country hit].'

In the same paper in July 1965, Beckett reviewed the EP that Wattle Records, Edgar Waters's label, had released featuring the material he himself had recorded, "a selection of six songs about Aboriginal life in the backblocks." Beckett showed understandable restraint: "At best [Young] achieves a pleasant, easy style somewhat reminiscent of Slim Dusty."

Mick Counihan was less equivocal in *Australian Tradition*: "The fact that these songs were written for the pleasure of the writer and his circle of friends, that they comment on his experiences, are unambitious and not stimulated by commercial ends, and that they are sung without pretension or gimmickry, makes them much more relevant to the traditions of folk music than most of the Australian folk record output."

Looking back, Jeremy Beckett reflects:

[Dougie] sold those two songs to Athol McCoy [in addition to 'Crow', McCoy bought 'Scobie's Dream', which he retitled 'Scobie's Hangover' for a 1968 B-side], and it was becoming apparent there was some kind of a prospect for him. But I don't think personally he had what was required – I mean, he was rather shy . . .

Dougie was 'discovered' somehow by the Mayoress of Willoughby. She must have gone up to Wilcannia or something, and so she invited him to Sydney to try and set up an audition for TV. He stayed for a while at Tranby [an Aboriginal college in Sydney], but for whatever reason, it never happened. Whether they didn't move on it or he got stage fright, I don't know. His marriage had already broken up by then, and he was on the grog. He just wasn't coping.

DOUGIE YOUNG REMAINS ELUSIVE. Until the first edition of this book appeared, only one photo of him had ever been published.

The interview Kevin Gilbert conducted with him is an hysterical and at times incoherent interpretation of Christianity that betrays alcoholic dementia. On the other hand, perhaps Dougie was not too far wrong in his belief that Australia was the first garden of Eden, for Jackie and Mary ahead of Adam and Eve. "They say drinkin' is a sin," he protested. "Drinkin' is not a sin because in the Last Supper Jesus Christ said, here's the bread, here's my body. Drink this wine, here's my blood."

Gilbert asks Dougie only a couple of questions about his music: first, simply, how did he come to write songs? "I never write," was the reply. He explained:

> I never take a pencil and never take a pen. I mean it's all in the mind. It's a funny thing because one night . . . I had me wife and family with me then . . . one night I started laughin'. My wife said, what's wrong with you? You in the horrors? I said, no, I composed a song. Course I've always played guitar. All the blackfellas around, they can all play the guitar and they said, we want some songs, see?
>
> Well, I composed these songs. And I said to him [Athol McCoy], You sell this song. Well, he did, and it's topped the bloody hit parade in country and western shows all over Australia. I never got nothin' out of it. Nor the others, neither. Well, it broke me up.

"He felt he was robbed," says Jeremy Beckett. "I found out that he did get paid. He didn't get a huge amount, but Athol McCoy paid him."

Dougie told Kevin Gilbert: "My wife said to me, don't give 'em no more songs. You don't sing no more. You finished. Well, it broke her fuckin' heart and it broke my heart. At the time we had about eight children, see? An' I knocked off."

IN 1969, AFTER HIS ABORTIVE STAY IN SYDNEY, Dougie recorded three songs in Walgett for Glen Vallance, a Canadian working for the Aboriginal Welfare Board. He went on to spend the 70s living in Balranald.

"I've never known Dougie to play in any pubs or clubs in Broken Hill," says Bill Riley, "but he's done over around Cobar, smaller towns, he travelled through Victoria, down around Hay, those places, he became a legend down around that way and his later years were spent around the edges of Victoria. I'm not even sure where he died, I think it was in Melbourne."

In 'Alf Kelly', from his last session in Sydney in 1979, Dougie pays tribute to family who looked after him at Balranald, and in 'Old Balranald Town', a superior rewrite of his own 'Old Wilcannia Town', which is itself reminiscent of 'A Pub with No Beer' or 'The Man from Snowy River', he describes a changing world:

> *All the boys knocked off drinkin', so the word's goin' round . . .*
> *There's no more claypan dances, all the accordions are still,*
> *They built a big brand new dance hall and the Board paid the bill,*
> *They hold big modern dances, and the music's so grand,*
> *Comes from one Seymour Weston, and his rock'n'roll band*

It was just a week after he'd been reported dead in 1979 that Dougie turned up in Sydney to prove those reports were, indeed, greatly exaggerated. It was then that he went into the studio for the third and last time. Even though Dougie was already quite ill by then, Anthony Wallis of the Aboriginal Artists Agency recorded 'Alf Kelly', 'Old Balranald Town' and 'Treaty', the last of these a non-narrative, politicised song, and as such not typical Dougie Young fare.

Jeremy Beckett was also on hand and recalls: "Certainly, by the time of those last recordings he was in bad shape. He had to be propped up and put in front of the microphone. The first time he gave us the slip. I went up to park the car, and when I came back he was gone. He was chain-smoking, he was very depressed. Whether he was on some sort of medication, I don't know, but I wouldn't be surprised. Some time after those recordings, he had a complete collapse, and he ended up in Adelaide Hospital or somewhere."

Prefiguring Yothu Yindi's hit of the same name, Dougie Young's last song, 'Treaty', finds some optimism only by avoiding the literal:

We are no longer now at war, the treaty has been signed
Let's communicate, don't hate, let's be lovin', good and kind

Dougie spent most of the 1980s in Melbourne, and then moved to Newcastle to live with one of his daughters. He was one of the great wordsmiths in all of Australian country music, a master of the tragi-comic and the Aboriginal songwriter who set the standard. When he died he was only in his late fifties, and it didn't even register a puff of smoke.

Says Jeremy Beckett: "Shortly before his death in 1991, he was reunited with his children in Wilcannia and travelled with them back to see his family in Cunnamulla. He didn't die in Wilcannia, as he said he would in 'Wilcannia Song', but his children made sure he was buried there."

ooo

Lionel Rose goes electric, at the inaugural National Aboriginal Country Music Festival in Canberra, 1976

TAKE A GLOVE, TAKE A GUITAR

★ Lionel Rose and the ★ Singing Fighters

The managers all stayed rich and fat
They bought him a guitar and cowboy hat
And then a second-rater knocked him flat
And the doctor said, Son, give the game away
Hungry fighter, give the game away

Ted Egan, 'The Hungry Fighter' (inspired by Aboriginal boxer Ron Richards)

There can't have been many Australians, regardless of race, creed, class or sex, who weren't tuned in to the radio that night in 1968 when Lionel Rose won the World Bantamweight title from Fighting Harada in Tokyo. Even little children were allowed to stay up late to listen. "All across Australia that night," said American magazine *Sports Illustrated*, naming Lionel its 'Boxer of the Year', "people clung to radios as if the ringside announcer were Winston Churchill." The *Times* in London declared, "Rose became the first aboriginal champion since Albert Namatjira!"

The Australian announcer that night was Ron Casey, Melbourne's doyen of sports reporters, and his call came in on a crackling signal live via satellite. There was Lionel Rose, this shy little black kid from back of Jackson's Track in Victoria, who had colour-blinded Australian sports fans and held the weight of a burgeoning country's hopes in his hands – and, when he won, showed the world what Australia was made of, the real Australia.

Lionel captured the public imagination at a time in the late 60s when the isolated and insular world of traditional Australia was starting to come apart. The Vietnam war was already dividing the country. Aboriginal people were pressing harder for their basic human rights. Prime Minister Harold Holt disappeared (while swimming off a beach south of Melbourne). At the same time, Cassius Clay was morphing into Muhammad Ali, becoming an inspiration for African Americans to rival Martin Luther King or James Brown. Lionel Rose was a black Australian hero who recalled a simpler time – such a nice lad, polite, modest, neat, good-looking. When university students asked him to lead a march in support of the Gurindji land claim, Lionel demurred, saying he would not take part "in any political movement either for or against the government." But Lionel's unspoken pride was enormous.

White Australians wanted to kiss and hug Lionel, and this was a considerable breakthrough, given how hard a time white Australia had learning to accept Aboriginal faces. Lionel came along and Australia just fell in love with him. He still carries the same aura. When he got back to Melbourne after winning the title, a quarter of a million people turned out on the streets to greet him. Could he ever have imagined he would scale such heights? And could he have envisaged the fall that would follow?

Lionel was barely twenty years old. He was the world champion, he was rich (relatively), he was black and he was beautiful. And yet aside from a taste for tobacco (Lionel smoked a pipe), his only indulgence this early in the piece was music. The drinking came later. Music was a constant in Lionel's life; only family and boxing were more important. He toted a guitar most places he went; he was starstruck when he met Slim Dusty. And when he went to LA to defend his title against Chucho Castillo, Elvis asked to meet *him*! (The King was fresh from his leather-clad 1968 comeback to the live stage, and Lionel was awe-struck: "I was blown out. He came across as a gentleman, an absolute gentleman.")

Early in 1969, with the champion's belt still in his possession, Lionel appeared on the TV variety show *Sunnyside Up*. Accompanying himself on guitar, he sang the old country standard 'Pick Me Up On Your Way Down'. Johnny Young, by now a producer as much as a pop star himself, saw Lionel's performance that night and gave him a ring. "I said, I'm a songwriter," Young later told the *Age*, "and I'd love to write you a song, what is it you want to say? He said, I just want to say, Thank you, I just want to say I appreciate it all."

"It was a sort of countrified song," Lionel remembers, "took all day to record. It was line by line, I didn't know what I was doing, I never been in a studio in my life."

Lionel finally lost his title on his fourth defence, to Ruben Olivares at the LA Forum in August 1969; by Christmas, his Festival Records single 'I Thank You' was on top of the charts. Today the song is virtually a national anthem to some, or a hymn. Belligerent Sydney newspaper columnist Mike Gibson may have protested, "Lionel can't sing and he knows it . . . [he] has a voice like a prairie dog with a thorn in its foot," but the record was the year's biggest local pop hit after Russell Morris's psychedelic opus 'The Real Thing' (which also happened to be written by Johnny Young), and it was the first number one single by a black Australian. Lionel received an MBE and was named 1969's Australian of the Year.

Going into 1970, DJs flipped 'I Thank You' over and started playing the B-side, 'Pick Me Up on Your Way Down', and the single was born again, ultimately staying on the charts for an extraordinary eight months and selling over 100,000 copies.

Lionel's hobby, which is what he's always considered his music, had become a phenomenon. But even as he carved out a music career that is far greater that most people realise – certainly much greater than just 'I Thank You' – it always remained a sideline. Lionel made a lot more money out of fighting. After he retired for the first time in 1970, he pursued music full-time before returning to the ring in 1975. During those years he cut two albums for Festival, the second of which, 1972's *Jackson's Track*, is a forgotten classic.

It is surprising that when Daryl Tonkin's book *Jackson's Track* was published in 1999, no one mentioned Lionel's album with the same title, especially since it is an unequivocally great record. Produced by Laurie Allen, veteran of 60s hit-makers Bobby & Laurie and subsequently a stalwart country outlaw, *Jackson's Track* is an autobiographical country concept album, a song-cycle that tells the story of a place and a life. But it fell on deaf ears – almost as if it was too good for Lionel to get credit for. So as Lionel prepared to make a comeback in the ring his music fell by the wayside.

'Pick Me Up on Your Way Down' turned out to be prescient. Lionel sang with limited technique but beautiful plaintiveness:

You may be their pride and joy
But they'll find another boy
And they'll take away your crown
Pick me up on your way down.

By 1976 his boxing comeback was over, ignominiously, and so was his marriage, but Lionel's real slide was only just beginning. In the late 70s, he seemed to spend more time in court than anywhere else, facing charges for drink-driving, stealing, assault and possession of amphetamines and marijuana.

In 1982, he declared bankruptcy. Subsequently he served ten days in jail and then suffered the first of a series of heart attacks that would have killed a lesser man. But Lionel Rose was already immortal, and he rebuilt his life on the temporal plane too.

He could never again return to the ring, but one of the beauties of country music, unlike rock or pop, is that it allows its artists to grow old gracefully – or even disgracefully, if they so desire. Singing is something Lionel can do, however informally, till the day he dies.

"Well, I can handle the pressure of a bloke out in front on points, that's my job," Lionel laughed.

Music was only for my enjoyment, and then when it became a professional thing, well . . . my musical talent is very, very limited. But you know, now it's different, I'm half-way to a hundred now. I've learnt a bit, so yeah, maybe do some [more singing] in the months and years to come.

Boxing was always first and foremost. But singing was something that used to relax me. It was a hobby too, you know. I come from a musical family, and when they sing, it's always there, every day. I got a couple of guitars upstairs now, you know. That's what it's all about, music's good for the soul.

Sharman troupe fighter Tiger Williams, the Black Bomber, shows Dave Sands how it's done with the gloves off

LIONEL ROSE WAS NEITHER THE FIRST nor the only singing Aboriginal boxer. There is a long tradition, in fact, and George Bracken, who held the Australian lightweight title in the late 50s, beat Lionel to the punch in getting onto vinyl first: he cut two rock'n'roll singles for W&G Records in Melbourne in the early 60s.

Long before Aborigines were commonplace in Australian sport, Aboriginal fighters were a staple of the Australian ring; their numbers were as disproportionate to Australians as a whole as the black prison population, if less unhappily so. Fighting in the tents was a way a blackfella could see the world, meet people, make a few quid . . . "Who'll take a glove?" the spruikers barked.

The best-known tent-fighting troupe was Jimmy Sharman's, and one Aborigine who travelled with it in the 40s was Tiger Williams, dubbed by Sharman 'the Black Bomber'. Williams would go out front in his green dressing grown and do the spruiking, playing guitar and singing and yodelling in the hillbilly style of Tex Morton and Buddy Williams.

Tent boxing largely died off in the 60s, although Queenslander Larry Dulhunty carried on for many years with a touring show that featured a bit of everything, including boxers and country music, with a strong Aboriginal presence. Among the fighters who passed through

Dulhunty's ranks in the 50s were Harry Grogan, a former Australian welterweight champion who sang of his Kuranda home, and Syd Santo, a heavyweight dubbed 'the Brown Bomber'. Hailing from the Atherton Tableland, which he once described as like a big paddock full of boxers and singers, Santo sang and yodelled Tex Morton-style; his signature song was 'The Big Rock Candy Mountain'.

As boxing's decline accelerated in the 70s, singing perhaps became a better option. Bobby McLeod, for one, gave up a promising future as a middleweight. Jim Ridgeway was another who had a number of successful amateur bouts before finding his voice as a country singer. Ridgeway, from Dubbo, teamed up with songwriter Joan Fairbridge in 1980 to produce the absolutely greatest one-off single in all Aboriginal country, 'Ticket to Nowhere'. A train song in the classic tradition, 'Ticket to Nowhere' encapsulated Aboriginal alienation:

> *Got a ticket to Nowhere, written on my face*
> *Going through Trouble, Sorrow and Disgrace*
> *Got a ticket to Nowhere, issued to my race*
> *A one-way ticket to Nowhere, got no town or any place.*

Queenslander Ceddy McGrady, who fought 135 television and club preliminary bouts (he lost 95 of them!) and recorded a Dire Straits-ish album called *Culture Country* in Tamworth in the late 80s, may have been the last of this breed (at least until Anthony Mundine and his recent, short-lived hip-hop career).

George Bracken was a better fighter than any of these men, if not necessarily a better singer. Born George Brackenbridge on Queensland's Palm Island settlement (or prison camp) in 1934, he first took the Australian lightweight title in 1955. Bracken was an articulate and outspoken Aborigine at a time in the 50s when Aborigines, if they were seen at all, were still not heard. He was one of the first successful black sportsmen to stand up for civil rights generally and for exploited black boxers in particular. "When I was a kid," he remembered, "I would sing at all the concerts there . . . hillbilly songs, Hank Williams songs, play the guitar. Every Aboriginal kid back then could play guitar or some instrument. And then I got pushed into the fight game with Jimmy Sharman, because I was

George Bracken fronts his band the Blue Jeans at the Dutch Inn, Geelong, late 1950s

interested in boxing. Jack Hassen was my foster-brother, you see." Hassen won the Australian lightweight championship in 1949, allowing him to indulge his passion for hillbilly music by collecting 78s.

"When I was 17, in Townsville," recalls Bracken, "I had a couple of fights there, beat an Air Force champion, so Sharman said, George, you might be able to make a bit of money, you ever thought about boxing? I thought, well, what have I got to lose? . . . I always had my guitar, of course, and us boys got together. Music was the thing to get away from real life. Meditate within yourself and enjoy yourself, you know. A respite from life itself."

Bracken left Sharman after only six months on the road and signed on with a trainer in Geelong, former featherweight champion Kid Young. He bought a house in Geelong, got a job in a rope factory and moved his family down from Innisfail in Queensland.

"I thought if I didn't make it in boxing, I'd give the music a go. So when I got to Geelong and started boxing in four-rounders and that, I kept my music going. I used to do quite a bit of work with Pastor Doug Nicholls in Melbourne then too, in the churches for the Aboriginal people. I'd take my guitar with me and sing some songs. A couple years after that I started my own band, the Blue Jeans. Got some boys together from around the place, used to go to different dances and that."

With a kid called Lionel Rose helping out in his corner, Bracken held his title for three years before losing it in 1958 and then winning it back again in 1959. In 1957, he suffered a

George Bracken in the studio for W&G Records, Melbourne, 1960

severe bashing at the hands of the Innisfail police. He protested publicly, but white Australia didn't want to know.

It was around the same time that Bracken's music got going in earnest. His new combo, the Blue Jeans, local white pickers, started a residency at a Geelong coffee shop called the Dutch Inn. "We did mostly rock'n'roll, country and western, hit songs of the day. We made a few bob."

In 1960 Ron Tudor, a manager at fledgling Melbourne independent label W&G Records, approached Bracken with the idea of cutting a version of teen idol Fabian's new song, 'Turn Me Loose'. The name of the local music game in those days was to get a cover version of an overseas hit out before the original was released here. Jazz guitarist Bruce Clarke, who'd previously worked with Georgia Lee, produced Bracken singing 'Turn Me Loose' plus, for the flip side, a rousing version of New Orleans R&B star Frankie Ford's hit 'Sea Cruise'.

For his second single, Bracken recorded two of his own compositions, 'Blue Jean Rock' and 'Why Don't You Write?' When it was released at the end of 1960, *Tempo* magazine commented: "Although George has never had a music lesson in his life, he has developed a fine rhythmic style that is so popular today."

Like its predecessor, however, 'Blue Jean Rock' failed to scale the charts, and eventually Bracken largely gave up music in favour of fighting. "It started to be a bit of a grind after a while because I would have to come back and train. So I thought, well, I'm getting more money out of the fight game, big purses, so I went with that."

But Bracken did know when to quit – he started to suffer from headaches and retired from the ring in 1962. After that, with the help of his friend Col Joye, Bracken launched an agency to represent Aboriginal performers, but apart from getting gigs for his sister Cheryl Bracken, a good singer in her own right, on *Bandstand* and at Sammy Lee's infamous nightclub, the Latin Quarter, it was an idea before its time.

"I must say the reputation that went before me helped, in that people didn't see the Aboriginal there, they saw the fighter. I was known as a fella that was in the paper, a celebrity . . . But I don't care who you are, anyone that hears music, it clicks something up there."

"I COME FROM A FIGHTING FAMILY," says Lionel Rose.

My tribe is the Gunditjmara and out of our tribe came four Commonwealth and one world champion. Out of one line of blood.

We defended our land right up to the early 20s, resisted the white man's presence, never copped no shit from anyone. Pretty fierce tribe. On Mum's side, the violence wasn't there. Hers was more or less a placid tribe; they wiped a lot of them out around Port Albert – 150, 200 in a tribe. Shot 'em all.

Lionel was born in 1948 at Jackson's Track, near Drouin, east of Melbourne. He was the oldest of 11 children. Jackson's Track was not a mission, it was a logger's camp owned by the

Tonkin brothers, and it attracted Aborigines from all over Victoria because it was a relatively equitable, happy place.

I wanted to be a boxer since I was about eight or nine. My Dad was a tent fighter. Being the first born and a boy too, as soon as I was high enough to hold my hands up, he started to teach me how to throw these punches. I'd sit around the campfire and listen to them talk about all the great fighters like Dave Sands and Frankie Flannery . . . That's what I wanted to be.

Music was part of my life even prior to boxing. Most of my family play instruments, and they all sing. My dad was a musician, and my mum, they used to do the harmonies together. Music's been a big part of my background. Especially indigenous people, they love country music: the Carter Family, Jimmie Rodgers, Hank Snow, Hank Williams. And Jimmy Little. I like all sorts, all types of music . . . I can't cop the opera, but I can everything else. I like rock'n'roll, I like jazz, I like Willie Nelson.

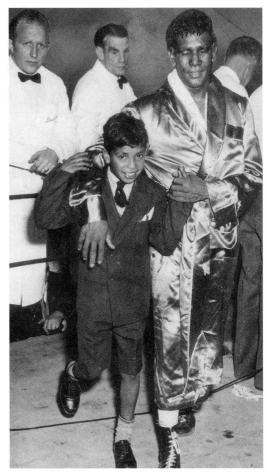

I was singing Slim Dusty stuff when I was eight years old. Slim Dusty's my roots of country music. He's the main man, top of the range. Through my career and the success that I've had, touch wood, I've met Slim Dusty, one of the greatest pleasures of my life. He's my idol, Slim Dusty.

Lionel's mother Gina and dad Roy used to perform in all the talent quests around the area. The family huddled around Grandma Adelaide's wireless to listen to the hillbilly shows on 3UL, Warragul.

Of course they were all mill workers and Saturday night was party night, get-together night, they would get together and have a sing-song. I'd be in bed in the hut, but I could hear them next door playing and I'd sit awake listening to them all night, 'cos they were good, they were really good.

Despite an impressive run of junior bouts, Lionel missed selection for the Australian team at the 1964 Tokyo Olympics. He moved to Melbourne and turned pro, being taken in by trainer/manager Jack Rennie and his

Master and apprentice: George Bracken and Lionel Rose

Lionel meets his idol Slim Dusty, 2TM-Slim Dusty Show, Tamworth, June, 1970

wife Shirley. Lionel was disciplined and determined. He fought 19 bouts and lost only two on his way to winning the Australian bantamweight title in 1966. Unlike earlier Aboriginal small men – Bindi Jack, Teddy Rainbow, Johnny Jarrett – Lionel was well-matched in his preliminary fights; he not only packed a punch and refused to go down, he was also very fast and very clever. He was actually lucky to get a shot at the world title – he was ranked only sixth when Fighting Harada offered him a mere $7,500 for what the champ thought was a soft challenge – but Lionel lasted the distance and narrowly won on points.

When he came home to Melbourne it was the biggest thing since the Beatles. "I didn't think so many people cared," Lionel muttered. He was crowned King of Moomba. He even had a song written about him, 'The Ballad of Lionel Rose', by Maori singer Rim D. Paul: "This is a simple story," it began, to the tune of '(The Man Who Shot) Liberty Valance', "Of one man's fight for glory/Fought for his race, for a place, underneath the sun/Equal and free, like you and me, fought till the battle had been won."

Through all this, under the wing of the Rennies, Lionel actually led a fairly insular life. "A big night out for me was a night at the pictures, going to see *Gone with the Wind* or *My Fair Lady*. It was boxing seven days a week. There was no time to go to pubs and so on. I never went to places where I was put in a position to be racially abused."

When Lionel won his second title defense, beating Castillo at the LA Forum in 1968 (the time he met Elvis), the Mexican's fans ran riot and set fire to the stadium. When he lost the title in August 1969, to 'Rockabye' Rueben Olivares at the same venue, it was only his third ever defeat, and his first by a knockout. By the time he lost his next fight, a challenge to Yoshiaki Numata for a lightweight title in May 1970, 'I Thank You' was still riding high in the charts. He got out of boxing straightaway and moved out of the Rennies' house.

Deprived of boxing's discipline, Lionel seems to have succumbed to the lures of pop stardom. Part of the problem was a variation on the theme that 80s Melbourne outlaw band the Dead Livers expressed in their song 'I'd Like to Have a Joint with Willie' (which was itself a variation on Slim Dusty's 'Duncan') – people loved Lionel, and everyone wanted to buy him a beer. Women loved him too. Ever the gentleman, Lionel has never been able to say no, or refuse a shout.

> I do have a little strife like that. I've been in pubs where I haven't spent a penny and walked out blind drunk, well . . . in a bad way. That happens quite a bit. You like to buy your own beers but people come out of the woodwork, you're sitting there and they come around the corner and say, Here's a pot, have one on me. Christ, half a dozen blokes buy you a pot each and you're halfway in trouble.

FOLLOWING HIS MUSIC'S STAR was a dangerous course for Lionel to take, because in show business the workplace environment itself is alcohol-soaked.

"We did a couple of tours," he remembers. "I did a tour with the Hawking Brothers. We did a six-day tour of Queensland, back in 1970. Myself, the Hawking Brothers, Kamahl and Johnny O'Keefe. Went from Brisbane right up to Townsville. It was a good buzz. A legend, Johnny O'Keefe . . . so's Kamahl. Packed houses every night. They loved O'Keefe. The master showman."

In 1971 Lionel joined Ashton's Circus; Laurie Allen was hired to direct a band behind him. Allen recalls, "I was a member of the Melbourne country music fraternity, I suppose you could say, and that included the Hawking Brothers, and of course Lionel was in thick with the Hawkings. Bobby & Laurie did a show in Adelaide once, and Lionel was on this show, so we met, and it just went on from there. We all used to sit around and pick and sing together."

Bobby & Laurie broke up in 1970. Laurie and Lionel's first gig was under the big top in Adelaide.

> I mean, Lionel had never done anything like that before either. It was an experience, let me tell you. We had a plane booked, so we all get out there to the airport – no Lionel. Time came to board the plane and still no Lionel, so we have to get on and leave without him. We're still not too worried though because there's a couple of days in Adelaide before we have to play. Anyway, we land in Adelaide, and there's all these people at the airport, obviously waiting for Lionel. We look out the porthole and a clown walks past, and then an elephant – the whole circus is there

★ *Black Knight* ★

Dempsey Knight was the first Aboriginal country singer to tour and record overseas – in Poland, of all places. It was the culmination, as the *Western Herald* put it in 1969, "of a meteoric rise to stardom." Knight was discovered in Bourke, in north-western New South Wales, in 1967, when a TV crew that was there to shoot a documentary on the drought came across him singing on the street in his "husky, haunting style." In 1968 he moved to Sydney under the guidance of manager/benefactor Mrs Dominique Millnick, who put him up and got him gigs in the clubs. "When he first went the general opinion was that he wouldn't last," said the *Western Herald*. "The change in environment has had a sobering effect on the young singer. Only once in the two years he has been in the city did he 'go walkabout'. He is now a respected member of the community in which he lives."

Millnick was talking the big talk, like a film based on Knight's life, but all that eventuated was a trip to Europe, where Millnick believed, according to *Dawn*, that "an Aboriginal singer would strike it rich."

Knight went to Poland, in spite of the fact that the Poles' taste in western music tends more towards Frank Zappa and Lou Reed, because Millnick was Polish. A short film of his tour there was shot, and he even recorded a single, 'Annabelle', for release through one of the state-owned record labels, but only a few copies of the disc seem to have survived, or at least made their way to Australia, and the film hasn't been seen since 1970, when it was screened in Bourke upon Knight's return to town.

In 1986, Knight got a part in a movie called *Frog Dreaming*, which was shot near Bourke. It was a blaxploitation film of sorts, made by Australia's King of the Bs, Brian Trenchard-Smith – a kiddie horror flick in which the monster is based on Aboriginal mythology. Improbably, Knight plays a country singer called Charlie Pride. Knight went on to score roles in a couple of other telemovies, 1991's *Rose Against the Odds* (a Lionel Rose biopic, in which, incongruously, no-one sings) and 2002's *Road from Coorain*. He still occasionally performs at community events. Poland, his whole shot at international stardom, now just seems like a distant dream.

●●●

to meet Lionel. It was like the Beatles arriving again, or Bobby & Laurie in their heyday. We got off the plane and all these photographers ran straight past us, looking for Lionel. No Lionel. So they just packed up the elephants and everyone went home disappointed. Lionel arrived quietly a couple of hours later.

The accommodation they had for us was double-beds in these caravans, with all these circus types – and they were all poofs! Well, Lionel wasn't going to have a bar of that, so we got new accommodation in this nice motel. Later on, I learnt Lionel paid for it himself.

Lionel runs away with the circus

We wanted to rehearse and they wouldn't let us; they said, whaddya want to rehearse for? We tested the PA, and it sounded worse than the loudspeakers at one of Lionel's fights.

Recorded at Channel 9 in Melbourne, *Jackson's Track* developed naturally out of the regard Lionel and Laurie developed for each other. "I don't even remember how it came about," says Laurie.

Maybe because the first one was so bad – it was just as if they'd pulled in this unsuspecting bloke and put him together with these musicians who, you know, weren't country players . . . And Lionel was happy enough with that, but I thought he deserved better, he could do better. Lionel just asked me, he said, Could you write a song about Jackson's Track? Could you write a bluegrass song? As it turned out, I wrote eight of the songs on it.

"If I only could, I'd turn the time back," Lionel sings on the title track, the album's opener, and from there he does just that, taking a journey back along the 'Gippsland Line', as another song puts it.

"I took him out there one day on the Jackson's Track," Lionel recalls. "We had a couple of bottles of Jim Beam and that, so we went down and I said this is where I used to live, corduroy road and that, so he wrote a song about it."

AUSTRALIAN COUNTRY MUSIC CHANGED with the onset of rock'n'roll. Parts of it, notably the bush ballad tradition, didn't change much, and it's surprising that a form so archaic and sexless still survives at all, let alone flourishes. But Australian country became broader in the 60s, when the bush ballad was supplemented by other forms; a younger generation of musicians – including many, like Laurie Allen, whose background was equal parts country and rock'n'roll – brought in more contemporary, often American, influences. Laurie Allen might have been an Australian Waylon Jennings, linking Buddy Holly to the outlaw movement. With hits like 1965's 'Crazy Country Hop', the 1966 number one 'Hitchhiker' and 1969's 'Carroll County Accident', Bobby & Laurie pioneered a uniquely Australian folk-country-rock sound that paralleled the work of Gram Parsons and Crosby, Stills, Nash & Young in America, and foreshadowed both the Dingoes and the Little River Band. It was almost xenophobic of purist Australian country to resist American influences as strongly as it did – especially when it all derives from Jimmie Rodgers anyway. *Jackson's Track* proved the potency of an open-minded approach, long before it was appreciated.

What is remarkable about the album, though, is that for all its American influences – even the inclusion of such American standards as 'Old Kentucky Home' and Johnny Cash's 'Folsom Prison Blues' – it paints a quintessentially Australian picture. Why would you not do 'Old Kentucky Home' when it was a song known and sung by so many Aboriginal people, after all? Why would you not pluck out a Merle Haggard prison song like 'Sing Me Back Home', when its resonances seem so uncannily appropriate?

Lionel and Laurie Allen become almost one on *Jackson's Track*, the singer and the songs fusing in nostalgic reverie. Scenes from Lionel's own memory are bought to life by Allen's pen and by the hottest band in the land, featuring Kenny Kitching on pedal steel. "Backings are kept very basic," said *Go-Set*. "Guitar dominant. Some fiddle. Some steel guitar. At times Laurie joins Lionel in close harmony . . . Lionel does sing quite well and Laurie has given him some entertaining songs and album [*sic*]."

No-one seems to have noticed the stories the album told. It was as pure a distillation of country music as could be— it was a landmark album and almost no-one, Lionel included, realised it.

"I think country music is really close to your heart," says Lionel, getting at one of the strengths of *Jackson's Track*. "It sings about the life, the life that every common man leads every day. The hard times, the good times and the bad."

After *Jackson's Track* flopped, Lionel was drawn back into boxing. "You see," says Laurie Allen:

There was a lot of people in the business who thought that Lionel really shouldn't be singing, but even some of *them* thought he wasn't that bad. I mean, Lionel's not what you'd call a true singer, but he's as good as Slim or any of them really.

Lionel was partly responsible for the state he was in, but not entirely. People put all these expectations on him. People let him go too, sometimes, because they had to, Lionel just had to be let loose. But nobody ever really seemed to put Lionel's interests first. It was the age-old thing, they just thought if you hung Lionel's name out the front, people would come. There's an adage in show business, you go where the people are, rather than try and pull the people. And they booked Lionel into some real toilets.

Stepping back into the ring, battling his drinking, his smoking and his weight, Lionel's slide continued unabated. Of the 16 bouts he fought after he lost his world title in 1969, which was only his third-ever loss, Lionel was defeated in eight, four of them by knockout.

In 1976 Lionel hung up the gloves for good. He was losing his centre. His wife, childhood sweetheart Jenny, divorced him. Lionel went into the studio one more time with Laurie Allen, at the behest of RCA Records, to record the single 'Had to Leave Her'.

"It was just a session," says Allen, "and if it showed any promise they might have gone on with something, but like everyone, they just thought anything with Lionel's name on it would be enough. Nothing came of it."

Lionel drifted deeper into the netherworld, getting into drugs. He might have made more than half a million out of boxing, all up, and he even made some wise investments, but by 1982 it was all well and truly gone. Within a couple more years Lionel hit rock bottom, sentenced to 60 days for driving while disqualified.

"They reckon I blew $600,000 on wine, women and song," Lionel once said. "I don't know if it was that much, but I do remember a lot of great women, a lot of so-so songs and in the later days, some pretty bad wine."

In 1987, at the age of 39, Lionel suffered a serious heart attack. By the time he was 46 he'd suffered two more.

IF LEGENDARY DELTA BLUESMAN ROBERT JOHNSON sold his soul to the devil down at the crossroads, as he put it, then it may be that at a quite different crossroads, Lionel Rose stole *his* soul back.

It was in Kempsey in 1987. Lionel was visiting the NSW coastal town in his capacity as a sports consultant for the Department of Aboriginal Affairs. Kempsey, of course, is the birthplace of two prominent Australians who have particular significance for Lionel, Dave Sands and Slim Dusty.

Lionel went down to the crossroads of Lionel Rose Street and Dave Sands Street:

They got a guitar from somewhere, and we gave them a bit of a concert for about half an hour. Then we went to a party in Lionel Rose Street. There's ten houses in Lionel Rose Street . . . and it took me a week to get out of the street! I had to stop in every house – this is fair dinkum – there was a guitar in nearly every house. It was great. I'd never experienced anything like that before. I felt like I wanted to get back to the motel, but they produced shaving gear and said, oh, you're sweet here. We'd sit down and talk a few yarns. They'd take me out and show me their fishing grounds. Bush tucker. Bush medicine. I learnt more in that week than in ten years of learning about my people.

By the early 90s, while taking his mother's advice to take things a bit easier, Lionel was back to making the odd appearance at Aboriginal functions and festivals. "I've still got to be careful," he said, "I'm just trying to stay alive."

He eased off on the grog and the smokes: "I never let it get in the way of a gig though. I don't do anything before the show, but afterward, yeah, I like to relax and have a few."

Lionel smiles a smile of guilty pleasure. He is such a sweet man that he can get away with almost anything.

Lionel was playing in Tasmania in 1992 when he bumped into the Howie Brothers, singing twins from Warragul who remembered playing football against him as kids. They encouraged him to take music a bit more seriously again.

"We all went back to the hotel and there was a kitchen area on the first floor set aside for the musicians," Graeme Howie recalled:

> We all took our instruments out, guitars, mandolins, the whole thing, and stayed up till three in the morning singing all these old songs: 'Blue Moon of Kentucky', all these old tear-jerking songs.
>
> People said to me when we were starting out, he'll never turn up, but that's not true. Lionel's turned up and been in good nick for 95 percent of it. And he loves it.

In 1993, the same time he got back together again with Jenny, Lionel went into a recording studio for the first time in 17 years and cut a track with the Howie Brothers called 'You Knock Me Out'. It led to a full album called *Getting Sentimental*.

"If I died tomorrow I wouldn't regret it," says Lionel.

> I couldn't regret the life I've led, it's been a beautiful life. I've had everything in life that I've struggled for, it all came true. There's a few things I wish hadn't come true, but still, that's life.
>
> I achieved the ultimate in my profession and that's a goal in itself. But then to come back and do something which has always been a hobby, my music, to have the experience of making a successful record and meeting people in that field, well, that's a bonus.

❧❧❧

Vic Simms on stage in the chapel at Parramatta Jail, July, 1973

PRISON SONGS

★ Vic Simms ★

*"I've sat down to dine with kings and queens and I've rolled
in the gutter with dogs, and I don't regret any of it."*
Vic Simms

othing to declare, Vic? the screws at the gate ask, and Vic Simms lets out a small
smile. "Nah, just got my wallet and a packet of smokes," he says. They wave him
through.

In a strange way, Vic Simms feels as comfortable behind bars as anywhere. He gets respect
in jail, that's why. He did the crime and he did the time, and now when he returns to jail it is
of his own volition, to sing for the boys. But that smile he gives is more than diffident – it's
nervous and fleeting, as if he always has one eye over his shoulder . . .

Jail is, of course, a constant threat to Aboriginal people. The statistics reveal the terrible
truth of institutionalised persecution: the tiny proportion of Australia's total populace who
are Aborigines, as opposed to their near majority in the jail population. For young Aboriginal
men, jail is now almost a rite of passage, as if it were a tragic update of Dreamtime initiations.
Black deaths in custody continue unabated.

As 70s South Australian singer-songwriter Cherie Watkins put it in song:

Prison's nothing special, to any Nyunga I know
Because the white man makes it prison most everywhere we go.

Blues and country, as musics of the underclass, have long had close associations with jails
and jail life. Leadbelly was 'discovered' on a Louisiana chain-gang, and prison songs – from
Jimmie Rodgers's 'In the Jailhouse Now' to Elvis's 'Jailhouse Rock' and beyond – have become
one of the great country sub-genres. American country music's lineage is such that when
Johnny Cash, who had already written such classics as 'Folsom Prison Blues', recorded his
Live at San Quentin album, among the captive audience that day was none other than Merle
Haggard, who would himself go on to pen such penitentiary classics as 'I'm a Lonesome
Fugitive' and 'Branded Man', not to mention 'Sing Me Back Home', which was later covered
by Lionel Rose as well as Gram Parsons.

Convict life was central to early Australian folk songs, and in country music the theme was pioneered by Tex Morton ('Fanny Bay Blues') and Buddy Williams ('Pentridge Jail'). Unsurprisingly, prison pervades Aboriginal writing, from its beginnings in Colin Johnson's 1965 novel *Wildcat Falling* to Warumpi Band's 'Jailanguru Pakarnu' and Archie Weller's classic short story 'Going Home', to the more recent 'Bird in a Concrete Cage', by Western Australian country artist Percy Hansen.

Vic Simms was only young when he went inside. It was the culmination of his fall from grace. He had been a child prodigy, a black kid from La Perouse who in 1958, at the age of 12, became a member of Col Joye's travelling troupe and the only other Aboriginal rock'n'roller besides Candy Williams on the fledgling Sydney scene. Simms cut two singles for Festival in 1961/62, when he was 15. By the time he was 18, his career might as well have been over.

Images spring to mind . . . of Frankie Lymon, whose 'Why Do Fools Fall in Love?' catapulted him to stardom in 1955 when he was just 13, but who was dead of a drug overdose by the time he was 26. Of Little Willie John, the teenage creator of 'Fever' and other classics, who died at 31 while serving a jail sentence. As it happens, both those deaths took place in 1968, the same year the 22-year-old Vic Simms was sent down for a long stretch. He had hit the piss and made some mistakes that led to jail.

By the time Vic was released in 1977, at the age of 30, he had already achieved something else extraordinary – and then seen that achievement undone. While he was at Bathurst Jail in the early 70s, not long before the riots that razed the place, he recorded the album *The Loner*, live at the jail, for RCA Records. It is one of the great forgotten treasures of Australian music.

The Loner tells not of prison life but of the black life in Australia that Simms knew before he went to prison. It was a first in so many ways, but most significantly it was a cogent and pointed statement of suffering and protest at a time when Aborigines were only just starting to assert themselves politically.

Vic will contend that in being allowed to pursue his music he was used by the Department of Corrective Services; he also implies that he suffered at the hands of other inmates because of that, or because that was perceived to be the case. It is certainly true that the Department of Corrective Services needed all the help it could get, in terms of public relations, at the time. After nearly two centuries of intractable brutality, its system was imploding at that very moment, so it was helpful for them to be able to pluck out a Vic Simms and say: Look, see what a shining example!

They sent Vic out on to the streets to play; they put him in suburban shopping centres, even the Opera House, as if he was some sort of freak. So yes, the Department did that – but when they were done with him, by which time their prisons were burning anyway, they threw Vic Simms back inside, back on the heap. By the time he got out a few years later, he had already been forgotten again. Perhaps partially as a result of that, Vic had another 'little alcoholic lapse', as he would put it. But before he hit rock bottom again, he succeeded in arresting his decline. He might still wrestle with the bottle to this day – he has the rheumy eyes of a drinker – but Vic has never again let it get on top of him.

As if it wasn't extraordinary enough that Vic's music career had a second act with *The Loner*, he came back for a third act in the 80s. He did some recording in Tamworth as part of the *Koori Classics* project, but he also started playing regular shows in prisons. And while his music has taken a considerable change in direction yet again, he's still playing prisons, still giving back to the boys inside.

"I've been going in there for more than ten years now," Vic sighs. "Some of the faces have been the same all that time."

Vic knows that there but for the grace of God . . .

WILLIAM VINCENT 'BUNNA' SIMMS was born in La Perouse in 1946, part of the clan that includes Rugby League legend Eric Simms. "The Simmses were there when Cook came into the bay," Vic says, "and they're still there today." Vic now lives in nearby Mascot in a council flat. He is married and has grown-up twin sons.

"I started in 1957," he says.

I went to a football social one night, we were regulars, my mum and dad and all of us went, and Col Joye was there. They were taking a break and they said, Does anybody want to sing a song? And so of course all my mates start nudging me because we used to sit around the campfire at La Perouse and just sing songs. They said, He can sing. So I got up, I sang 'Tutti Frutti'. Col said, Look, we're only starting out, but if anything comes up, you're with us! So the weeks went by and then he came around – I was living on the reserve – and he said, we've got a show coming up, the Jazzorama, at Manly, at the old picture theatre. O'Keefe was on it that night; it was sort of a mixture, because they had the Port Jackson Jazz Band too. Col said, this is our first big show and we'd like you to come along with us.

So I didn't look for it, it found me. I was lucky. The right place at the right time – and then I just worked.

Simms is a small man, jockey-like, who could almost be taken for Indian. In the late 1950s, he was a tiny, cute black kid who was just bursting with energy. It wasn't so much his potential perhaps as his immediate novelty appeal that the astute Col Joye and his brother Kevin Jacobsen could see. (Col Joye plays down their long-standing friendship and involvement with Aboriginal people. "We just used to help out if they needed new football jerseys, that sort of thing," he claims.)

Music was not something Vic ever hoped to make a career out of. Urban Aboriginal boys in the 50s couldn't afford dreams of any sort. The most Australia's capital cities wanted of its Aborigines was simply for them to stay out of sight.

I was lucky, Jimmy [Little] was lucky. In those days it was the movie star syndrome. They'd come into the milk bar and say to a pretty girl, we can make you a star. That doesn't happen anymore. I look around now and there are no child stars anymore.

When I was around there was a lot: Little Pattie, the Bee Gees, Billy Thorpe . . .

I just love to sing. I'm a mission boy. No-one wanted to live out there because of the blacks, there was just shacks, run-down . . . now you've got all the trendies moving in. I look back on my roots, it was tough, living through the Welfare Act, living in a rusty tin shack, under the thumb of the local police . . . remembering the curfews, if you walked outside your boundaries, you were likely to find yourself in an institution, or if you were an adult, you would go to jail. And this existed up until 1969, two years after Aboriginal people got the right to vote!

But, 11 years of age, I found that music saved my life. And without it I don't feel I could survive today, because I don't know anything else.

No-one in my family was ever really musically inclined. A couple of my sisters don't sing a bad song, but they never thought much of it. Radio was the thing, and it was in a country vein, Aboriginal people were pretty big on country music. Still are. But more so then back in the 50s and 60s, because that's what we'd grown up on.

Country was around long before rock'n'roll came. Elvis Presley, you know, after that, it took away the country concept of music in me. Up until then it was all Slim Whitman and all these type of guys, early Burl Ives, Gene Autry, Roy Rodgers and all of them, the Australian guys like Tex Morton and Tim McNamara, early Slim Dusty. But then, we had a milk bar down the road, and that was our social hang-out, and it was a big influence because we'd go down there and play the jukebox. And I got more enjoyment from Little Richard and Fats Domino and people like this, and that sort of influenced me to sing rock'n'roll.

After the Jazzorama show, Vic joined Judy Stone, Sandy Scott, the Allen Brothers and the DeKroo Brothers, among others, as a member of the Col Joye stable, effectively the 'Bandstand Family', the all-conquering clean-cut alternative to Johnny O'Keefe's less-well-scrubbed 'Six O'Clock Rockers'. Joye was the archetypal Aussie boy next door who beat even the Wild One to the punch in scoring Australia's first number one rock'n'roll record, 'Oh Yeah, Uh-Huh', in October 1957.

If O'Keefe was more inclined towards lascivious New Orleans R&B, Col Joye was the rockabilly kid, an erstwhile hillbilly singer who, like Elvis, Ricky Nelson, Digby Richards and countless other first-generation rock'n'rollers, eventually ended up musically back where he'd started, singing almost pure country.

Another gentle country-rocker, 'Bye Bye Baby', continued what would become a long string of hits for Col and the Joy Boys. The troupe was almost constantly on the road, exploiting the almost insatiable need of the newly identified Australian teenager for this equally newfangled thing called rock'n'roll.

I couldn't really pick an Australian black man for a role model because there wasn't really any around. I had to look to the Americans. Little Richard and Chuck Berry. You did 'Long Tall Sally', 'Tutti Frutti'. . . Jerry Lee, Bill Haley.

13-year-old Vicky Simms as part of Col Joye's troupe at Bill McColl's famous Manly Jazzorama gig, October, 1957

Everyone at that time was doing that. Col was the same, with a bit of country mixed in, Leroy Van Dyke, Don Gibson, 'Sea of Heartbreak'. Everyone sang 'Oh, Lonesome Me'.

We were playing the rock'n'roll dance circuit that there was in Sydney, the Bankstown Capitol, Bronte, Paddington Police Boys Club, these were the stamping grounds, and I was doing interstate, *In Melbourne Tonight*, which was all the rage then. I was doing hotels too, the Enfield Boulevard and the Swansea up in Newcastle, but I had to be out at a certain time, I had to be chaperoned, because I was a minor. Had to be out by nine o'clock.

But then as I got older, they said, well, you've either got to leave school or . . . it was difficult because I'd be in Dubbo or Walgett and they were concerned about truancy at school. If you missed a certain number of days, inexplicable absences, you'd be taken up before the courts, and I was up before the courts a couple of times for not being at school. And back then it was more or less looked upon as a criminal offence.

So because I wasn't at school because I was away musically, I was given an eighteen-month bond. So I had to exist with that as well. I'm sure if those laws hadn't been around then I could have gone a lot further as a youngster. I had this fear of being taken before the courts.

In those days you could leave school at 14 years and 10 months. So I spoke to Mum. I got a job in a factory to supplement my income.

AROUND THE SAME TIME, towards the end of 1961, Vic cut his first single, 'Yo-Yo Heart'. "As Col moved into Festival and started recording his things, they said, now it's your turn."

With backing by the Joy Boys, 'Yo-Yo Heart' was an attempt to cash in on a schoolyard craze as legitimate as any concurrent surfing record. It was unremarkable but it was a minor hit. As the *Teenager's Weekly* pop supplement inside *Women's Weekly* put it, "Vicky [as he was then billed, sometimes causing confusion about his gender] has a great sense of rhythm and when viewers get a close-up of those brown eyes – wow!"

A second single followed in 1962. 'I'm Counting Up My Love' was written by Brisbane boy Steve Kipner, son of emigre American entrepreneur Nat Kipner, who at 14 was even younger than Vic, and would go on to write the worldwide hit 'Toast and Marmalade for Tea' for his own band Tin-Tin, and 'Physical' for Olivia Newton-John. This was the way the record business worked in those days: much more like a studio system, in which singers were assigned songs and producers. It was the Beatles and Bob Dylan who ushered in the idea of singer-songwriters. At Festival, A&R Manager Ken Taylor decided who would do what, and how. Vic was relatively privileged in being able to choose the B-side himself, 'You Got Soul', an American R&B number that made for his best early recording.

'I'm Counting Up My Love' fared less well than the novelty 'Yo-Yo Heart', but although that meant Vic would not again record for Festival, he continued to tour as part of the Joy Boys package.

Vic had already attained everything that was hitherto out of reach, if not forbidden – and he wasn't even 15 yet! The stories of wild life on the road that Joy Boys' drummer John Bogie still tells are legendary. It was a world laced with sex and violence. And lots of grog. Money, freedom, glamour, Vic had it all. Still, he could not escape the reality of discrimination entirely, as he recalls:

One time we went to Moree with Judy Stone, Peter Allen, and it was a hot day so when we arrived in town we thought we'd go down to the pool for a swim. But I was asked to leave, because I was black. I'd never encountered that before. The others were all good enough to say, Well, if he's not good enough to swim here neither are we! And we all left.

I WANNA BOP
(Harlan-Morgan) (Joye) (2:25)

Festival   a New World of Sound

MX-9854
Made in Australia

FK-161

VICKY SIMMS
Vocal
With the Joy Boys

45 rpm

It was at the same Moree pool only a couple of years later that Charlie Perkins and his busload of civil rights activists, the Freedom Riders, tested such racism and exposed it to a national media audience. The winds of change were beginning to blow, but this experience left a lasting impression on Vic.

That was my first experience of racial prejudice outside of La Perouse, and it really hurt me because . . .I was 14, 15 at the time, and it really knocked the hell out of me, you know? I thought, I wonder if this is what it's like further down the line . . . And as I got older and I got more politically aware, I sort of had this chip on my shoulder: You know, are all whites like that?

In a way, Vic was out of his depth, with little control over his destiny. He was a ticking time bomb, resentful on the one hand of the inequity of his celebrity and his Aboriginality, and on the other hand resentful of Jimmy Little's greater success.

He was always up for a stir. As John Bogie says, Vic had "a wicked humour to match mine," and he was a willing accomplice in Bogie's legendary practical jokes that played on his colour. On one occasion, Bogie led Vic around the streets of Surfers Paradise on a leash like a dog, snarling at him, "Siddown, you black bastard!"

"Vicky would cower – what a performer! – and no response," says Bogie. "I mean, nobody even said boo to me. I learnt Australians did not give two shits about Aboriginals. So the fight goes on today."

Whoever or whatever did control Vic's destiny had no say in what happened next, though: the Beatles hit. Overnight, the goalposts of pop had moved radically. All of a sudden, all the greasy old first-generation rockers seemed completely passé, including Vic Simms. The Jacobsens dealt with this by going – along with their audience – into a new, previously untapped network of venues, the RSL and Leagues clubs. Jimmy Little took the same step. But not Vic Simms.

"All of a sudden there was a lot of competition around," Vic says ruefully.

It was a fast period of time, very fast . . .As they all went from strength to strength, I sort of dropped off. I've a tendency to go on drinking binges . . . I went through a period where I had a really bad time.

I started to drink a lot, and that sort of got the best of me. What money I had I blew on grog, and my mates. Things happened which I wouldn't like to go into.

"There can be no questions about jail," Colin Johnson wrote in *Wildcat Falling*. But as much as Vic has a right to his privacy, there are questions to be asked, if only to help explain *The Loner*. After all, you don't serve seven years, before being released on parole, without having committed a fairly grave offence.

Vic is clearly nervous. The small flat is empty of family. "I have a tendency to go out and catch up with old mates," he says, drawing on a cigarette. "I still like to sit around under

★ *From Little Things . . .* ★

In 1971 RCA Records released an epochal single called 'Gurindji Blues'. Sung by Galarrwuy Yunupingu and written by whitefella Ted Egan, it was the first land rights song and it's an Australian classic.

When stockman Vincent Lingiari led the Gurindji people off Wave Hill station in 1966 and squatted, on strike, at Wattie Creek, their campaign found a good degree of popular support. "I was employed by the Office of Aboriginal Affairs," Ted Egan remembered. "I was moved to write 'Gurindji Blues' on the night of 9 September, 1969, after Peter Nixon, Minister for the Interior, said in Parliament that if the Gurindji wanted land they should save up and buy it, just as any other good Australian would."

In a way, since 'Gurindji Blues' is hardly a blues, Egan was picking up on the old Aboriginal (jabbi-jabbi) gossip song tradition, which he then applied to a bush ballad foundation. He found a singer in Galarrwuy Yunupingu, a young man from Yirrkala who in the early 60s had featured on the EMI album *Land of the Morning Star* singing traditional Arnhem Land songs.

Egan: "My mate Jenny Isaacs at the Aboriginal Arts Board organised funds for Galarrwuy Yunupingu and Vincent Lingiari to come to Sydney, and Galarrwuy and I recorded the song."

Said RCA producer Ron Wills: "We booked a session, and somehow the press got wind of it. So we had all these newspapermen clamouring all over the place. I said, alright, that's enough, out! You can come back when we have a break for a cup of tea. There were three old Aboriginal elders who just stood in the corner the whole time, didn't move. But it was a good session, and it kicked off Ted Egan's career."

Says Yunupingu: "Vincent Lingiari and myself were seen as a messenger to be able to tell that there is a land rights struggle emerging out of Aboriginal people."

Pop journal *Go-Set* reviewed the single, describing it as "easily one of the most controversial songs put down inside or outside Australia . . . we'd like to feel that the majority of *Go-Set* readers are moved enough to take some kind of action." The record's impact was limited somewhat by radio's inevitable refusal to give it airplay, but it nevertheless filtered through.

Egan: "When the recorded version of the song was released, the secretary of Nixon's Department in Canberra rang Dr Nugget Coombs to demand that I be

Land Rights Record

A record has been made, under the RCA label, of two folk songs with an Aboriginal land rights theme.

On one side of the record, Vincent Lingiari, leader of the Gurindji people, speaks an introduction to a rhythmic song of protest called "The Gurindji Blues". Written by Ted Egan, it has guitar, didgeridoo and clapstick accompaniment.

On the reverse side, "The Tribal Land" is sung by young Aboriginal Galarrwuy Yunupingu of Yirrkala, to his own guitar accompaniment.

Galarrwuy Yunupingu, 23 years old, is a social worker at Yirrkala Mission and hopes to become a Methodist minister. He has lived at Yirrkala all his life except for three years at the Methodist Training College in Brisbane.

He says he wanted to make the record to "get the message across so that people would write to the Prime Minister and protest about Aboriginal land rights".

Galarrwuy Yunupingu of Yirrkala during the recording of "The Tribal Land" for RCA of Australia.

Recording for land rights. Galarrwuy Yunupingu meets Vincent Lingiari who spoke the introduction to the record, "The Gurindji Blues".

sacked from the public service. Dr Coombs replied that he rather liked the song, and felt it was a fairly succinct summary of what had transpired.

"Through Chicka Dixon we eventually sold thousands of copies of the recording, and that was one of the main means of financing the Aboriginal Tent Embassy."

Egan eventually recorded his own version of the song for his 1987 album *The Aboriginals*. Galarrwuy Yunupingu went on to work for the Northern Lands Council, leaving music to his younger brother Mandawuy, the leader of Yothu Yindi. The Gurindji got their land back in 1976. And the whole episode would inspire even more bush ballads in the future.

◗◗◗

a tree and have a drink with the boys. I think that's . . ." – now Vic grins like a naughty schoolboy almost – "well, it's been my undoing on a few occasions."

Something happens when I go out and see the boys. I can stay off it for years. But then I'll say, I'm going to go out and see the boys today. I see my mates quite often, but usually I'll just have a soft drink.

I got involved – I needed money – with a robbery that went dreadfully wrong, I'll go so far as to say that. I didn't have a leg to stand on. I had no money for a lawyer, because there was no Aboriginal Legal Service in those days. And so it was very much, plead guilty and throw yourself at the mercy of the court – but sometimes the courts weren't too merciful. But as I say, I've got no regrets. It made a better person of me. Gave me the will to say, well, it's not going to happen again. Which it hasn't. And through that, the achievement.

IT WAS A SUNDAY IN FEBRUARY 1974, during a screening of *Women in Love* in the chapel, when the petrol bomb was thrown that incited the riot that saw Bathurst Jail almost burn to the ground.

It was the last battle in a drawn-out war that took place at Bathurst, and it triggered a royal commission into the notorious NSW prison system. It was as if nothing had changed since NSW itself was founded as a penal colony – and no jail in the state was older or tougher than Bathurst.

The first disturbance at Bathurst, a sit-in, occurred in October 1970, ostensibly over the cancellation of the once-weekly sports session. Of course, this was just a catalyst for dissatisfaction with conditions in the prison as a whole.

"In common with all maximum-security jails built last century," the Nagle Royal Commission Report would subsequently state, "Bathurst has no glass in the windows. Prisoners, who spent about eighteen hours a day in their cells, frequently had their bedding wet by rain and sleet. There was no heating in the cells despite the extreme cold."

In the aftermath of that first sit-in of 1970, prisoners were openly and systematically beaten. The report went on, "Sewerage created health problems when lavatories regularly overflowed or cisterns jammed."

Yet out of this environment came not only *The Loner* but also Bob Merrett's play *The Cake Man*, one of the earliest Aboriginal excursions into 'legitimate' drama after Kevin Gilbert's *The Cherry Pickers* (which was also written in jail). Merrett was one of Vic's cellmates; he drafted his first

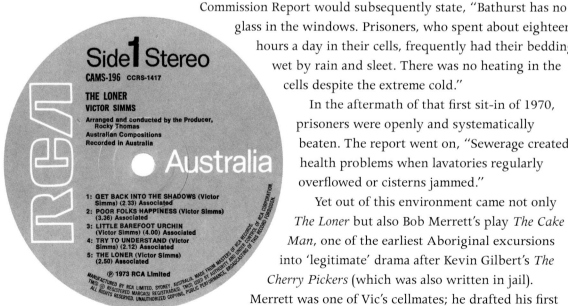

Side 1 Stereo

CAMS-196 CCRS-1417

THE LONER
VICTOR SIMMS
Arranged and conducted by the Producer,
Rocky Thomas
Australian Compositions
Recorded in Australia

● Australia

RCA

1: GET BACK INTO THE SHADOWS (Victor Simms) (2.33) Associated
2: POOR FOLKS HAPPINESS (Victor Simms) (3.36) Associated
3: LITTLE BAREFOOT URCHIN (Victor Simms) (4.00) Associated
4: TRY TO UNDERSTAND (Victor Simms) (2.12) Associated
5: THE LONER (Victor Simms) (2.50) Associated

℗ 1973 RCA Limited

MANUFACTURED BY RCA LIMITED, SYDNEY, AUSTRALIA. MADE FROM MASTERS OF RCA RECORDS. USED BY AUTHORITY AND UNDER CONTROL OF RCA CORPORATION. TM(S) ® REGISTERED MARCA(S) REGISTRADA(S). TM(S) USED BY AUTHORITY. BROADCASTING OF THIS RECORD FORBIDDEN. ALL RIGHTS RESERVED. UNAUTHORIZED COPYING, PUBLIC PERFORMANCE, play while Vic was nutting out the songs that would make up *The Loner*, which was recorded in a single session in the jail's old dining hall, one June afternoon in the winter of 1973.

"It had been a cold winter," the Royal Commission report read. "Prisoners in their cells remained open to the elements. Water often froze in the pipes, making the lavatories and washbasins unusable. Most prisoners went straight to bed after the evening meal [eaten at 4 pm] for the warmth that the regulation nine blankets issued gave them. It was too cold to read in bed, even to hold a book."

Just months later, in October, another sit-in took place, precipitating the final blow-up three months after that. The atmosphere was fetid and oppressive. Prisoners were denied buy-ups (of goods from the store, paid for with their own money), and they were extremely limited, 'for security reasons', as to what they could have in their cells. They weren't allowed to keep more than six letters. Vic had his subscription copies of *Identity*, the new glossy Aboriginal magazine, confiscated.

After the October sit-in, which ended peacefully, the prisoners were confined to their cells for a week. "Discipline had been tightened even more," the royal commission found. "Prisoners were not allowed to sit down in the yards despite the long periods they spent there . . . [they] were locked up or punished for trivial violations, such as having a shirt button undone."

All through summer the jail simmered. It was front-page news all round Australia when it finally blew its top in February. As 250 inmates ran riot, causing damage worth $6m, 12 were shot, two seriously. It was the ultimate indictment of a system long overdue for reform, and indeed, when the royal commission report was published in 1976, it called for a complete overhaul from the top down.

The commission specified six topics in its reform agenda, but though one of them was Aboriginal prisoners, barely two of the report's five hundred pages were dedicated to them. Little oral evidence was given to the commission by Aborigines, and only one of the 252 recommendations concerned Aboriginal prisoners. Aboriginal deaths in custody continued to rise, but this didn't become an issue for a few years yet.

"Yeah, it was tough," says Vic.

I mean you couldn't sit down, you had to be on your feet 24 hours a day. The winters were really unbearable, and you had no jackets or anything like this. You had to toe the line, or they'd toe the line for you. But in jail you can make it tough for yourself, go against the system and get into a lot more trouble. I just run my own race and people said hello, I'll say hello. You were never in there to win friends anyway, because there is no-one you can trust, so you just had to keep to yourself. And I found my outlet in sanity and companionship was the songs that I wrote, and night after night, when I got to learn to play the guitar, I'd sit there in my cell . . . I never experienced trouble in Bathurst, I just say, well, thankfully I got out of there – I went to the Opera House concerts just before the riots, so . . . I sort of sung my way out of trouble, so to speak. And in the end I sung my way out of jail.

VIC SIMMS TREASURES a tattered, leather-bound journal that has his proper name, 'William V. Simms', embossed on the cover. He worked in the Bathurst Jail bookbinding shop, so he was allowed to keep it for himself – and it was in this book he started writing what would become the songs on *The Loner*. Vic had never written before that, and the book became, as he says, his saviour, the thing that kept him sane through those long, hard and lonely days and nights inside.

Vic had never played guitar before either. But after he had a set of lyrics written and tunes worked out, he bought an acoustic guitar for a couple of packets of tobacco ("the currency was just tobacco, you could buy anything"), and in the back of his book you can still see the chord-fingering illustrations from which he taught himself to play.

> The ten tracks I recorded for RCA were all self-written, but were more politically inspired, and autobiographical. More up-tempo. I just wrote what I thought at the time, what was happening around me, politically, and I just put a tune to it. I didn't think it would go anywhere or anything would come of it, but it just happened it was heard by certain people and they said it should be recorded . . . But I never pursued songwriting after that. I'm prepared to go along with what's already been written.

That Vic wasn't subsequently encouraged to write more songs amounts to criminal negligence. *The Loner* is a masterpiece of straight talking. Set to rollicking country-rock grooves complete with a 'Ring of Fire'-like horn section, Vic's lyrics state, in very direct language, the things he saw around him, to paraphrase Slim Dusty. Vic turns the pages of his book with wonder and reverence, as if even he still finds it hard to believe.

> It sort of kept me mentally occupied during the bad old days. And, ahh, you had to have permission – there's the old jail number . . . It kept me sane, remembering all the repertoire I did, writing . . . then one day when guitars were allowed in I learnt to play guitar. I started off with just basic chords and basic lyrics, but through the combination on the album, with the brass and everything, it fitted in okay.
>
> How the album came about, I was playing in the yard one day and there was this social group coming through, and they said, oh, we like that. We've got people back in Sydney we can make contact with. The deal was done with RCA and the Department of Corrective Services that I would record.
>
> I wasn't writing, 'Down with the white man, give us back our land', I just wrote what I seen around me. If I had any dissent I kept it to myself. Oh, there was a strong message there, I wanted to do that but not heavy-handed, so to speak.
>
> I wrote all the words down, probably twelve months before I decided to put some music to them, some chords. I had the melodies but I didn't know where to put my fingers, so someone would tell me and I'd write it down.
>
> The lyrics are quite to the heart, because I wrote them from my own experience.

I wrote 'Poor Folks' Happiness' because I knew this girl who was the daughter of a well-known socialite, and she used to turn up at these dive pubs, you know, and I used to say to her, what are you doing here?

And being at Bathurst, I met a lot of Aboriginal people from the country who'd never seen a city. One was telling me how he went to Sydney to see the big smoke, and so I thought, I can see what he's about, maybe I can put some lyrics to it. He told me how he came to Sydney, so I wrote it as I saw him.

It was a party of visitors from the Robin Hood Foundation, a short-lived honorary organisation convened to 'develop Australian socio-cultural qualities and to invite world participation', who overheard Vic singing in the yard that day. Joy Alston, the foundation's head, organised a tape recorder for Vic, and took the resulting spool to RCA Records. Rocky Thomas, RCA's A&R manager, was sufficiently impressed to get in touch with the Department of Corrective Services about the idea of recording a live album behind bars. *Live at San Quentin* had just been a huge hit all round the world for CBS Records, and RCA in Sydney took that as a cue. The Department of Corrective Services, in turn, thought that allowing such an endeavor might do something to improve its tattered image.

Vic says : "They took me down to Sydney, we negotiated, then they took me back to Bathurst. Went back to Bathurst and they sent a mobile team up, some great musos too."

Thomas, who went on to produce *The Loner*, thought Vic's tape 'had something' the first time he heard it. "It was enormously difficult, the whole project," he recalls.

Part of the fun, I suppose, was just to see if we could do it. Because everybody told us we couldn't. I think it helped, though, as far as the jail was concerned, that we were a company of great prestige, not some fly-by-night operation.

When I first met Vic, he was just an ordinary guy like anyone else, although he is an inward sort of person. I knew he was an Aborigine before I heard the tape, but I didn't know any of the rest of his history, that he'd recorded for Festival. To me he was just a new talent.

I gave him manuscript papers, tapes, whatever he needed, and although he couldn't actually write [music], he had this form of notation I was able to decipher in order to rehearse the band.

Anyway, we all went up there, like a convoy, we had an OB van and the band in a bus.

Vic on stage in the chapel at Parramatta Jail, July 1973

With bluesman Black Allan Barker as part of the RCA team too, serving as Aboriginal liason, Vic and the band met and they had to get everything down first take. Remarkably, they succeeded. The horn parts were overdubbed later in the studio. "That was just me strumming on guitar and singing." says Vic. "We didn't have much time, we had two hours and we couldn't go over. It was one take and that's it. Put it down and onto the next track."

The album was released at the same time as B.B. King's *Live in Cook County Jail*, and it's fair to say King got all the reviews. Yet at a time in 1973 when the Americanised Brian Cadd, a local country-rock singer-songwriter, dominated the local charts, *The Loner* was at least on a par with such great and very Australian albums of that era as the Dingoes' self-titled debut, Matt Taylor's *Straight as a Die* and Slim Dusty's *Lights on the Hill*.

The best albums transport you to a completely other world. *The Loner* takes you inside black Australia. For whitefellas, it was perhaps a squeamish experience. RCA lifted 'Back Into the Shadows' as the single. It was a loaded choice: it had the hooks, but it was a straight rewrite of Big Bill Broonzy. Either way, in the wake of the controversy caused by 'Gurindji Blues', RCA did well just to get it out. However, 'Stranger in My Country' was – and still is – an anthem waiting to be adopted.

> After the release of the album – it wasn't given much publicity – the persistence of these charity groups, Corrective Services, saying, get it out as quickly as possible, we want the publicity. I did a few concerts, they were taking me out of the prison to do the Opera House . . . brought me down to Sydney to do one of the first shows at the Opera House, and around the malls, shopping centres, things like this . . .

The Opera House had just opened, yet even the *Sydney Morning Herald*'s special column covering the festivities makes no mention of the all-Aboriginal concert that took place on October 6, 1973. Perhaps this sort of 'popular music' as performed by Aborigines on the bill – Jimmy Little, Auriel Andrew and Heathermae Reading, in addition to Vic – was beneath the notice of the high culture snobs, who still seem to think that subsidised, imported and archaic European art forms are superior to all others. With a backing band called Blacksmith's Blues, Vic sang 'The Skye Boat Song', 'On Broadway', 'Honky-Tonk Women', 'My Girl' and 'Hey Jude', and only a couple of numbers from *The Loner*. Perhaps it was just too hot to touch.

"People expected a bit too much from me," says Vic now.

> I was getting nothing out of it. Corrective Services were getting the publicity and the pats on the back; I was getting praise from the highest quarters of Corrective Services which, again, might have caused the rest of the prison population to get pissed off. They thought I was making Corrective Services look good. It was really hard times. Then, after that, they felt they'd got their value, and it all dropped off.

Vic served out the remainder of his time at the minimum security Milton Island facility on the Hawkesbury River. *The Loner* was quickly deleted. Rocky Thomas was frustrated:

> I didn't think the record would be hard to sell; in fact, I thought the uniqueness of the whole thing would work in its favour. It wasn't until after the event that I realised otherwise. The thing was, we couldn't promote the album. We had problems then with the Robin Hood people. They'd had this vision of making a record and we did that, but as far as they were concerned that was the end of it. When, as you know, in the record business it's just the beginning. We wanted to go inside to do a shoot with Vic – we had interviews on tape – but they wouldn't let us. They were saying, it's an invasion of his privacy. They just didn't understand that we had to get out there and sell the record. So in the end I was disappointed with the sales we got for it. Because there was nothing wrong with the record.

When Vic eventually got out a few years later he went and saw RCA again. By then Rocky Thomas had left the company, but his successor, Barry Forrester, was keeping up the policy of recording quality local country. Lionel Rose had just released a single on the label. Vic recorded one too, a children's song – but it was never released.

The comedown was too much for Vic to bear. He hit the piss again.

VIC WAS IN A SERIOUS SPIRAL, but somewhere amid the madness and decay he saw a way out. He repaired to Nowra, Jimmy Little's home town on the NSW south coast, and got together with Bobby McLeod to dry out. McLeod's own experience ran virtually parallel to Vic's: he too was a singer now out of jail, trying to get off the grog – and like Vic he would get his music going again too.

By 1987 both men were in Tamworth, recording at Enrec Studios. Bobby was belatedly putting some of his great original folk-country songs down for the first time, while Vic was contributing to the *Koori Classics* series of albums alongside other black country acts like Roger Knox, Mac Silva and Mop and the Drop-Outs.

It was around the same time – and in the same company, with Bobby McLeod, Roger Knox and Mac Silva – that Vic first started playing prison shows. Although the quartet had many different permutations and combinations, it could almost be considered an Aboriginal equivalent of the Highwaymen, the 80s country supergroup formed by Johnny Cash, Willie Nelson, Waylon Jennings and Kris Kristofferson.

"Bobby McLeod, he's a great asset," says Vic.

He went through the drunken binges, and the police things and things like this too, but in the end we survived and we are on top of the world. And I've got, you know, myself to thank. I thought, well, I was really hitting it bad, so I just stopped one day. I said, I've got to do something, I've got this track record of being an entertainer and that's all I know, I'm not a pick and shovel person. So I went into a few talent quests to get some confidence back and I won a few. And I happened to be over at one of our local clubs one night and they were doing the Johnny O'Keefe Memorial Show, and they said, Well, look, we haven't seen you for quite some time. I said, Oh, well, you know, I've had problems and things like this. They said, Well, do you want to join our show? And I said, Yeah.

Most of my mates are dead, who I grew up with, through the grog, you know, cirrhosis of the liver and like this, and I thought, that's not for me, you know. This is just part and parcel of the oppressive state Aboriginal people are living under. The sadness . . . I've seen people die through oppression and, you know, I think we drink through the sadness and the reason to say, well, no-one's going to stop me now, you know.

Vic went to Tamworth because of Roger Knox, who he met via the prison shows. Long-time Aboriginal activist Chicka Dixon was the one who brought them all together, co-ordinating the shows. Roger Knox was the young buck of Koori country at the time, leading a charge in Tamworth aided by the Enrec studio and label. The *Koori Classics* series was conceived as a project to parallel the many official celebrations of Australia's bicentennial in 1988. One of the albums was, indeed, a collection called *Prison Songs*. Vic contributed versions of 'Branded Man', 'I Fought the Law', 'Muddy Water' and 'Riot in Cellblock Number 9'. He couldn't seem to escape the theme; he also cut a version of 'Hey Sheriff' for release as a single.

When Vic goes back inside to perform now, he's lucky if he gets petrol money. "You see them there, the radiance comes out of their faces," he says of the audiences.

They just bop along and you can see the lifting of their hearts, you know. All the tension's gone, because when you come in you can feel this tightness, in the atmosphere itself, it's really, really stiff, and you think – we look at each other and we say – we've got to relax these guys, you know. And the next minute we rope it up into some great 12-bar rock'n'roll-blues, and the next minute they're snapping along and then they sort of unwind. Next minute, they're up dancing around. And they'll come up to you and they'll shake your hand, say, good on you, brother, you know.

Maybe some of them have got chips on their shoulders, which you can't blame them for because, even though it's a lot easier today, jail is still jail. The loved ones are out here and they're in there, but we try to alleviate the sadness and the pain, through music, and they appreciate it. We try to deliver a message too, to say, we've been there, we did all that, you know, and there's a better life out there.

In 1990, not long after Mac Silva's untimely death, Vic, Roger and Bobby went to Canada at the behest of the First Nations people there, to play prisons and reservations. "I was really surprised because it's a mirror image to what we live out here," Vic said.

Vic recording The Loner, *Bathurst Jail, June 1973*

We sort of never really left home. The reserves, the missions are the same, the old cars were there, the dogs and, you know, the poor people who'd say, come in and have a feed. And the food was basically the same too, they'd have their damper, which they call bannock, alright, and they'd mix up curried mince and things like this. They've got this great togetherness like Aboriginal people have out here. Everywhere we went we did all the reservations, did the schools and we did the federal and state prisons right throughout Alberta down to Montana, up to the Alaskan border, everywhere we went people appreciated us. And it enlightened us too. But the greatest thrill we got was when we come back. Our personal chauffeur and confidante [in Canada] was a guy coming down through problems too. He said, I'm going in a movie next month, and he said, you'll probably get to see it out there – and everyone laughed because we've heard it all before. And you wouldn't want to know, when I went down to the city to watch *Dances with Wolves*, there's this guy up on screen, his name is Jimmy Hermann. And he's gone on to make *Geronimo* and things like this, so what goes around, comes around, this is my philosophy on life. Never take anything for granted; if it happens, it happens. And that's what it is all about.

By being involved in music we're delivering something to our people as well as going to the mainstream of the music scene in Australia, and this is really fine. If you do well, you do well, if you don't, you don't. This is the way it is in show business. But if you can deliver happiness out of sadness, that's what it's all about, and that's what I'm about.

Vic came back from Canada energised. He applied to the Australia Council for a grant to record an album, and in 1996 Bunyip Records released *From the Heart*. The CD is representative of the sets Vic presents in the clubs nowadays. He professes an affinity with pre-rock'n'roll crooners like Sinatra and Perry Como, and so now he covers them alongside Willie Nelson, Rod McKuen, Eric Burdon, and erstwhile stablemates the Bee Gees and Peter Allen. Compared to the sweep of vision of a record like *The Loner*, *From the Heart* marks a staggering shift: its mix of songs seems almost random, and the backing sounds as soulless as karaoke.

Vic still sings in clubs and at Aboriginal functions. His true heart he finds when he reunites with his brothers and they play the jails or for Aboriginal people. Then Vic sings the songs he really loves, that he's always sung – country and rock'n'roll, the songs he has the voice for – and Roger's band Euraba has the perfect sound, laid-back but sharp, and the audience relates directly to the songs and their singer. This is the real centre of Vic Simms's music.

It's not unusual for us to get called away to raise funds for funerals, for people who are hard done by to try and get enough money together to bury a relative or whatever. We've gone to great distances and we've travelled, you know, we've just said, we'll be there. We may be a little bit late but we'll be there. If we are a little bit late, we'll play a little bit late, but we'll definitely be there to help you raise your money.

And it's just been a way of life with us because we have that memory, you know, the dirt floors, the tin shacks and, you know, we might make a million dollars tomorrow, but it'll never change our attitudes, everything comes from the heart. When a blackfella does things, I think 90 percent of it comes from his heart, more so than his head. This is the way it is with Aboriginal people. They say, look, we need you. Okay, we'll be there. If we can get transport, we'll be there. And they say, we can't give you any money, but we can give you petrol money. We say, that's okay, we'll be there.

ɋɋɋ

Bobby McLeod (with guitar) sings on the steps of Parliament House, October 1973

GUNFIGHTER BALLADS

★ Bobby McLeod ★

I'm a lover not a fighter go the words of the old Kinks song. Bobby McLeod was a lover *and* a fighter, a violent man and a poet, a romantic figure who, during Australia's turbulent late 60s and early 70s, fought in the ring, on the streets and from the stage. Bobby became notorious in 1974 when, armed with a gun, he held hostages at the Department of Aboriginal Affairs, but it would be a travesty if he was remembered only for such volatile activism.

Possessing a voice and presence oozing danger and sexuality, and a battery of ballads uniquely didactic yet keenly sensual, Bobby McLeod could have been our first black superstar. He wrote his first song, 'Wayward Dreams', in 1973 while on day-release from prison after attending his father's funeral, and developed into a renegade singer-songwriter of extraordinary richness and power – yet he remains perhaps the single most undervalued talent in the history of Australian popular music.

As Bobby himself admits, sitting astride a tree stump down at Nowra on the NSW south coast, where he grew up and returned to live again, he was wild and he refused to be tamed. This was his both his strength and the reason for his undoing.

Born in 1947, a descendent of the Monaro tribe, Bobby served a total of six years behind bars; he fathered nine children with five women, and he never had anything approaching a hit record. But he got sober in 1983 and stayed that way, belatedly cutting his first album in 1988, and as an erstwhile Black Power pin-up, a sort of Che Guevara with Nat Cole's voice, Woody Guthrie's pen and Django Reinhardt's guitar, he enjoyed elder status.

He could take your breath away with a song or just his aura, the sparkle in his eye. Bobby McLeod was larger than life, an imposingly big man. He came of age in an era when one of the catchphrases was 'black is beautiful', and he epitomised the notion. 'Golden-Brown' is a name in Bobby's family, and it well describes his own colouring, which was highlighted by black doe eyes and – in later years – a long white mane of hair. He had a huge chest and huge hands (missing a finger on one) – you can see how he would have made a good boxer, or rugby league player, and he was both.

"He was a bit of a goer, Bobby McLeod," chuckles Lionel Rose, "but he was musically minded . . . a good singer. He was a guitarist too. But he'd sing these spiritual songs, he'd sing protest songs. Spiritual songs *and* protest songs. That was the first time I ever heard that."

Bobby McLeod's brilliance was to take protest songs into the realm of the sensual. His musical foundation always remained a sort of folk-country, in many ways inspired by Kris

Kristofferson. But in the way he created a body of work that is paradoxically luscious, that gives a sexual charge to political issues, he can perhaps be compared to Curtis Mayfield or Marvin Gaye, even Leonard Cohen.

At a time in the early 70s when the Australian music industry was rapidly maturing and Aboriginal people were becoming even more militant – a time when Australia in general was high on Whitlam-era optimism (these were the 60s we never had) – Bobby led a band in Melbourne called the Kooriers, who might be described as a sort of Aboriginal country take of the MC5, Detroit's self-styled 'White Panthers' of 60s rock.

The Kooriers burnt out, or were snuffed out, after a brief blaze of glory; they were a band that existed in a mist of alcohol and anger, not to mention dope smoke, and still only exist in a haze of failing memory and fleeting sightings. The sole surviving evidence of the band is a C60 cassette's worth of material, a demo of live and rough studio recordings. Its rediscovery confirms the Kooriers' enormous, albeit hitherto totally unappreciated, significance: Here are the ultimate gunfighter ballads. It all adds up to an irresistible myth.

The Kooriers formed when the young Bobby, fresh from his second prison term, bumped into legendary Murri pickers Dudley and Paul Meredith at the Aboriginal Tent Embassy on the lawns in front of Parliament House in Canberra. As evidenced by the unearthed demo, the trio boasted not only Bobby's great voice and emerging original songs, but also sublime three-part harmonies and a terrific interplay on guitars between the Meredith brothers, who bought some jazzier inflections ('old timey', in country terms) with them.

But the Kooriers were almost literally a band on the run, with Bobby some sort of enemy of the state as a result of the DAA hold-up. The band was hot, as they say in the music industry, but perhaps too hot. Their implosion after only a couple of years was as inevitable as the fact that almost no-one would pay it any mind.

Bobby eventually beat the gun charges, defending himself in court, but when Dudley and Paul took off for Darwin to take up a gig as a duo (which was how they had started out in Brisbane in the late 50s), and then Dudley died, the Kooriers died too. It is one of the great tragedies of Australian music that the Kooriers were not allowed to fulfil their destiny. Awesome as they already were, the band's full potential had not even begun to be tapped.

Bobby sank deeper into alcoholism and shiftlessness. It wasn't till he came out of a week-long coma in 1983 that he gave up the grog for good and got his music going again. The Kooriers' moment had passed, but at least Bobby eventually got some of those songs out on record, releasing two great albums for Larrikin, *Culture Up Front* and *Spirit Mother*.

On the back of his first album in 1988, Bobby appeared on ABC-TV's *7:30 Report*. Wearing a sharkskin suit and white shoes, his salt and pepper hair in a quiff so he looked like a young Charlie Rich (country music's 'Silver Fox' himself), Bobby sat on a stool on a bare sound-stage and, accompanying himself on acoustic guitar, sang the autobiographical 'The Resurrection':

Lyin' here down in the gutter, brother
Couldn't get no relief.

It was an extraordinary performance. Bobby slightly slurred the bittersweet melody, but still he seemed coiled, squinting into the camera in a way that emphasised his mystique, his cynicism and defiance, the tragedy and triumph of his words so great he framed them, as a final gesture, as a question, as if the only response at the end of it all is: Why?

"WELL, BOBBY MCLEOD IS A MAN I love dearly because he went through the mill," says Vic Simms.

> He went through the same thing I did. He was quite an activist and in the end
> his salvation, so to speak, was music. He had some hard times, round the streets,
> causing havoc, creating problems for people as well as himself, and knowing Bobby
> McLeod, you know, when we got together, he'd say, well, we're there brother, we're
> there. He was a role model for everyone on the south coast . . . Even the police,
> they'd say, hello Robert. And he came back with his music with a vengeance.

Robert Arthur John McLeod was born at the Crown Street hospital in Sydney in 1947, the oldest of six kids. His maternal grandfather was Robert Brown, Australia's first Aboriginal stipendiary magistrate. His father's father, like Jimmy Little's paternal grandfather, was a black tracker on the NSW south coast. His father, Arthur, was a labourer, a boxer and an alcoholic.

Living at Worragee, the Aboriginal settlement outside Nowra, Bobby grew up alongside Jimmy Little and his family. His mother was active in the Worragee-Wreck Bay chapter of the CWA (Country Women's Association) and the local Baptist church.

"All my family could sing," his mother says, "but I don't know about his father's mob!"

"My mum is a real good singer, but she's a Brown, you know," says Bobby.

> I grew up with Jimmy Little, so it was their influence that got me started, sitting
> down with his younger brothers and sisters, Freddie and Betty, and Colin. When I
> first started off I was in Baptist Youth Fellowship Choirs. And that was good for later
> on when I started singing and that . . . but the Littles, with guitar, they taught me
> the basics of that, and then Dudley and Paul took me a lot further.

As different as the two men are, when Jimmy Little left Worragee in the 50s to follow his dream – and found such great success – he provided the young Bobby McLeod with a very real role model. Additionally, Bobby said, "My grandfather was pretty independent and that influenced me a lot too."

After he'd completed his Intermediate at Nowra High, excelling at sport, in 1963 Bobby and his family, as perhaps a model Aboriginal family, were chosen to take a home in the new model suburb of Green Valley in Sydney's south-west. The McLeods were guinea pigs in that most wayward dream of all, assimilation. Green Valley was the post-war Australian dream – a house in the suburbs for everyone, even wogs and boongs – that turned into a nightmare.

The McLeod family (Bobby top left) as pictured in Dawn *magazine on the eve of moving to Green Valley, 1963*

The Housing Commission first bought 1500 acres of farmland near Liverpool in 1960. In 1961, construction of the £20m project began. By 1964 the estate contained 6,400 houses — but precious little else. And it was still growing. It was a human dumping ground in a clay desert, just waiting to erupt.

Today the sprawling Green Valley suburb is a settled and relatively pleasant, if poor, neighbourhood. But it had to go bad before it came good. Says Bobby, "To me, Green Valley was the sort of dregs of society, rounded up, to give them a new start. It was called the satellite city, we were just sort of locked in all these little boxes ..."

Bobby was 16 when he arrived at Green Valley in 1963, a bright kid. Within just a couple of years, he'd been sentenced to five years jail for assault and robbery, his first offence.

When the McLeods first got to the Valley, hopes ran high. 'Four Keys to Racial Integration' declared the *Sydney Morning Herald*, featuring the McLeods as one of four privileged Aboriginal families standing on the front verandah of a bold new social order, opening the door, as *Dawn* magazine put it, "to a new world for Aboriginal families anxious to attain full assimilation."

Work had been pre-arranged for Arthur, who told the *Sydney Morning Herald* the new house was a palace compared to Worragee. "We lived for six years in a six-roomed tin shack," he said. "We had no sanitary or cooking facilities and no electric light, and conditions were just shocking." *Dawn* reported: "Their new home in Charter Street, Sadlier, Green Valley, is a four bedroom asbestos-sheeted cottage, with coloured tile roof, sewerage, gas stove, gas bath heater and a gas copper."

Mr. C.A. Kelly, chief secretary of the Welfare Board, boasted: "The Aboriginal families who have taken up these homes have shown considerable courage in leaving their old familiar areas for the new, more impersonal surroundings of city life, with its greater pressures and problems . . . opportunities for them will improve if they are also willing to accept commensurate obligations."

Green Valley became the subject of great scrutiny as a sort of possible future for Australia. The image quickly soured. As early as 1966 a Sydney City Mission report decried "a lack of community life, a breakdown in family life . . . large numbers of deserted wives, needy children and bewildered people."

The *Sunday Telegraph*, unable to resist the headline 'How Green Was My Valley', began: "Broken homes, bad debts, teenage delinquency . . . catering for kids has meant almost totally ignoring the needs of adolescents and adults . . . The lack of entertainment for adolescents has led to skirmishes."

Bobby was just knocking around, doing his best to stay out of any skirmishes. Reverend D.H. Kemsley, pastor of the local Baptist church, to which the McLeods belonged, was proud of Aborigines' acceptance in Green Valley: "There is no discrimination at all," he said. "In a way it's amazing – but perhaps the troubles and trials of setting up a new life have been the common bond."

Bobby's mother was indeed a pillar of society, a religious woman, a JP and member of the school P&C. Bobby's father was an alcoholic on the road to an early grave, and as Bobby recalls, "I was into methylated spirits and everything . . . from the time I was 16. My dad used to drink too, so it wasn't a real issue about not stopping drinking, because we were both there together."

Bobby tried to join the navy in 1964, when he was 17, but the navy didn't want him. Bobby was a strapping lad, but there was a certain insouciance about him. Plus he was black, after all.

"That was the first time you went to Blacktown RSL and discovered you could sing," remembers his mother over the ironing. "I started singing rock," Bobby concurs, "but it never ever took off. Cause I was too young. I was only about 16 or 17, I used to do 'Be Bop a Lula'. But that's when I first met Dudley and that's when I started to change."

Next thing you know, I get into a fight there, because gangs started, I was 18 and I got five years' jail! You're getting around in a gang of blokes and next minute, you're fighting anybody, you know, it doesn't matter who. You had to sorta pick sides. I sorta helped a young white kid, I ended up getting charged with assault and robbery, and because we had no money for lawyers or anything, and there was no Legal Service in those days, I pleaded guilty.

We were involved with the church and all that, but they made an example of me. First offence and I got five years!

I think now I'm glad I had that experience. At the time I didn't think it was too crash hot, but where I was at with my drinking, if I hadn't done those two years when I did, I might not have even lived.

BOBBY WAS SENT TO BERRIMA, a minimum-security prison farm. When he got out on parole a couple of years later in 1968, aged 21, he was a very angry young man indeed.

While he was inside, Bobby kept his nose clean. He was quite capable of looking after himself, after all. He kept fit; he worked in the prison library, completed a couple of high school subjects, and learnt a trade (signwriting).

When he walked out of Berrima's gate in 1968, it was a different world altogether. Martin Luther King had just been shot in Memphis, the second great black leader lost in the 60s, after Malcolm X. Such was the power of music that the man called upon to forestall a potential America-wide ghetto uprising was James Brown, Soul Brother Number One – he appeared on national television to urge the rioting crowds to restrain themselves. It seemed like the whole world was in an uprising. In Vietnam the jungle war raged. In Paris students rioted. In San Francisco flower power, acid rock and the Black Panthers were all blossoming.

In Australia, the mobilisation of Aborigines had led to a landslide victory in the 1967 referendum that called for the belated acknowledgement of Aborigines as actual citizens in their own country. The increasing reach of television, just as it revealed the atrocities and futility of the escalating Vietnam war, had brought fourth-world Aboriginal living conditions into the lounge rooms of middle Australia. White Australia was shocked to learn the reality of life for its country's indigenous population.

But even if the referendum represented a resounding vote for the humanity of Aboriginal people, in practical terms little changed. Consequently, as the 60s became the 70s, increasingly frustrated but emboldened Aboriginal people started taking matters into their own hands.

The community of Yirrkala in Arnhem Land mounted a case against bauxite mining company Nabalco over its diggings on Gove Peninsula. The anti-war moratorium movement was growing (its twin demands were a total and unconditional withdrawal of Australian and other troops from Vietnam, and the immediate abolition of conscription), public protests were being stepped up, and there was increasing solidarity between students, the unions and Aborigines which raised the profile and pitch of such issues as racism, civil rights and land rights. This was the atmosphere Bobby McLeod walked into when he got out of prison and returned to Sydney.

Bobby was invited to trial for first grade rugby league club Canterbury-Bankstown, but he preferred to play for the Redfern All-Blacks. He preferred not to have to play football too seriously at all, actually – he was hardened and fit from jail as it was, and he needed plenty of space for carousing, drinking and chasing women, which were other things he really liked doing too.

"I used to sing around in the hotels and that, but I was too radical, I was drinkin' too much, fightin' too much, getting into too much trouble with the police. I wasn't settled down. See, I didn't stop drinkin' till I was 36."

Bobby's court appearances number over 70, he once estimated, and that doesn't include the rapes he eventually confessed to at a Sydney seminar, but for which he was never charged.

"I used to go into talent quests everywhere, the Sundowner, the Rex, all the big hotels, Blacktown RSL. I used to sing, ah, 'Born Free', lots of Kristofferson stuff." 'Born Free' became something of an ironic anthem for Bobby. Written by veteran English composer John Barry as the theme song for the African wildlife film of the same name, it not only won an Academy Award in 1966, it was adopted by jailbirds the world over.

Similarly, Kris Kristofferson had emerged while Bobby was inside, and he had an enormous impact on both country and rock. A new-wave (long-haired) singer-songwriter who turned Nashville upside down, Kristofferson wrote 'Me and Bobby McGee', which was a huge hit for Janis Joplin just before she died in 1970, and he struck a real chord with Aboriginal people too. Though it was a staple of Bobby's live repertoire, he would never record Kristofferson's hangover classic 'Sunday Morning Coming Down', although Harry Williams did. But Kristofferson's narrative balladry also presaged the type of songs Bobby himself would soon start writing.

At the same time, Bobby was inevitably drawn to the good fight. The times themselves were a hotbed.

"It was really hard not to do," he says. "We were a fighting family. Ambrose, one of my uncles on Mum's side, he was one of the radicals walkin' around. Everyone was in Melbourne and then they went over to that big thing in Western Australia with everybody protesting and that."

Returning from the sit-in at Noonkanbah in 1971, Ambrose Golden-Brown went back to his home in Canberra, the traditional high country belonging to the Monaro, and Bobby went to stay with him. "Ambrose," said Bobby, "was the one who took me to the tents in front of Parliament House. He said, You need to learn a bit about being a black man."

"WHEN I WAS INVOLVED WITH THE FOUNDATION for Aboriginal Affairs in the late 1960s," James Wilson-Miller wrote in his book *Koori*, "many activists spoke of our black brothers in America and imitated them with Afro-style hair. In those days everyone was black and few people were Aborigines, let alone Koories. But it was in the early 1970s that the black movement became a Koori movement."

Bobby McLeod himself came of age as a player in a very violent period in Australian political history, and this – as much as alcohol, holy-roller religion and sex – shaped his unique music.

Thanks to the new marvel of satellite television, even in Australia people saw African-American medallists Tommy Smith and John Carlos controversially give the Black Power salute at the 1968 Olympic Games in Mexico City. It was the expression of a mood that carried strong resonances for Aboriginal people in Australia.

Young Aborigines in the early 70s like Kevin Gilbert, Bruce McGuinness, Denis Walker and Gary Foley were well aware of the new generation of African-American activists, such as Eldridge Cleaver, Huey P. Newton and H. Rap Brown. The Australians similarly styled themselves as urban guerilla freedom fighters. But even alongside such notorious hotheads as Denis Walker and Gary Foley, Bobby McLeod was a real loose cannon.

In 1969, when Bruce McGuinness took over leadership of the long-standing Aborigines Advancement League in Melbourne, he invited Caribbean activist Roosevelt Brown to come and speak. The government promptly discontinued the league's funding. In Sydney at the

Bobby McLeod plots the downfall of the racist Australian government, Aboriginal Tent Embassy, Canberra, 1972

same time, Gary Foley and Paul Coe sought to overthrow the old Redfern establishment represented by the Foundation for Aboriginal Affairs.

In Brisbane, where Queensland premier Joh Bjelke-Petersen made life for blacks a special hell, Denis Walker, son of poet Oodgeroo Noonuccal (nee Kath Walker), headed up the new National Aboriginal Tribal Council. It sent four delegates to a Black Power congress in the USA.

The year 1970, marking the bicentennial of Cook's 'discovery' of Australia, presented a perfect opportunity for Aboriginal people to protest. At La Perouse, Botany Bay, where Cook first landed in Australia (and where Aborigines still lived on the old reserve), a public mourning was held. Media coverage guaranteed a reaction. At a wild demonstration in support of the Gurindji in Sydney, 70 people were arrested. Amid tabloid headlines, Bruce McGuinness warned, "It is going to come to violent racial conflict."

All around the country Aboriginal legal and medical services and theatres were springing up. Kevin Gilbert was writing *Because a White Man'll Never Do It*, a polemic firmly in the tradition of Black Power polemics like *Soul on Ice* and *Die, Nigger, Die*. Playwright Jack Davis took over the editorship of *Identity* magazine and relaunched it in the style of glossy Afro-American magazine *Ebony*.

The climate was hot and getting hotter. In 1971 the South African Springboks rugby union team toured Australia, inciting a wave of anti-apartheid protest that perhaps only pointed to a greater hypocrisy at home (at least apartheid was explicitly government policy in South Africa).

Then the courts threw out the Yirrkala case, ruling that Australia had been *terra nullius* until European settlers arrived, and that Aboriginal people therefore had no pre-existing title to land under Australian law. The Gurindji campaign continued in earnest, prompting the release of the single 'Gurindji Blues', but the Yirrkala loss was a fundamental blow. Assassination threats were made against Neville Bonner, the first Aboriginal senator, and against both the Queensland and federal directors of Aboriginal Affairs. But when conservative Prime Minister William McMahon announced his notorious land denial policy on Australia Day 1972, Aboriginal people hit a low ebb.

Consequently, on an unseasonably cold night a couple of days later, three blackfellas from NSW, Michael Anderson, Billy Craigie and Kevin Johnson, raised a beach umbrella on the lawns in front of Parliament House in Canberra that bore the cardboard sign, 'Aboriginal Embassy'. This was the organic birth of one of the great non-violent protests, and a protest and symbolic rallying point to rival the Eureka Stockade in Australian history.

THE INSTIGATOR OF THE TENT EMBASSY was Kevin Gilbert, although he was unable to be involved directly because he was on parole at the time. He later wrote: "I called together a number of young Aboriginal militants, Michael Anderson, Gary Williams, Tony Coorey, Billy Craigie and Gary Foley, and discussed with them the need for a permanent peaceful land rights demonstration outside Parliament House."

With $70 in cash and a car lent by Communist Party paper the *Tribune*, the first trio drove from Sydney to Canberra to take advantage of a loophole in the law that allowed Aborigines to camp on Crown land in federal territories.

The bush telegraph was already chattering, and black Australia quickly got on the road to this makeshift mecca. "It's impossible to adequately describe the ad hoc operation of the embassy and the emotions that we all shared," Roberta Sykes wrote in *Snake Dancing*. "By the time we arrived, the beach umbrella that had constituted the embassy for the first few hours had been replaced with a small tent. When large numbers of supporters began to roll into Canberra, local people supplied even more tents and, within a few days, we had the beginnings of a small tent city."

By March, under the surveillance of ASIO (Australia's CIA) and the federal police, eleven tents were pegged out on the lawns. The media was having a field day. At the same time, the Larrakia people of Darwin sent a petition to McMahon demanding a treaty. Chicka Dixon, then working on the waterfront in Sydney, was raising money selling copies of 'Gurindji Blues'.

By the end of April the first trio had gone and the cardboard sign was replaced by a painted wooden one that resembled those inside Parliament House. Bobby's uncle Ambrose Golden-Brown told journalist Noel Pratt: "We haven't made the government change its policy, but we've succeeded in embarrassing it, and we've made people think about the Aboriginal cause."

Geraldine Willesee reported, quite sympathetically, for *Woman's Day*, quoting 'a young Aboriginal': "I want equality, I want my rights and I'm going to get them. If I'm not given what is legally mine, the next time the white pigs pick up a gun, I'll pick up mine too. When he fires a shot, I'll fire back." Might this have been Bobby McLeod?

By May, Gary Foley had arrived, and Canberra was getting colder as winter approached. Sam Watson sent blankets from Sydney. Inside the tents, the National Black Caucus was planning protest marches all round the country in July to commemorate National Aborigines Day. But the embassy itself would not last that long.

It was first torn down by police on July 20. Minister for the Interior Ralph Hunt had gazetted a bill to make it possible, and the not-so-happy campers were arrested for trespassing. Ten days later, a couple of tents sprang up again. Again they were removed, this time apparently for good, despite the resistance of 1500 protesters singing 'We Shall Not Be Moved'. Bobby linked arms with Gary Foley, Roberta Sykes and Faith Bandler, among others, and resisted the temptation to lash out at the cops. Being dragged away, he still somehow managed to find a TV camera and pronounce right into it, "People of Australia – get fucked!"

But if the embassy battle was lost, the bigger war was looking better. By December 1972, McMahon was gone as Prime Minister, replaced in a landslide by the left-of-centre Labor Party's Gough Whitlam, who had actually visited the embassy and promised in his major election speech, "We will legislate to give Aborigines land rights – not just because their case is beyond argument, but because all of us as Australians are diminished while the Aborigines are denied their rightful place in the nation."

"When Labor came into power," Jack Davis editorialised in *Identity*, "politically minded Aborigines breathed the first genuine sigh of relief for over one hundred years."

DRINKING HEAVILY AND VERY VOLATILE, Bobby ended up back in jail again. But it was during this term in Cooma that he wrote 'Wayward Dreams', his first song, after attending his father's funeral in handcuffs in 1973.

It was about, then and now, how people . . . Dad died young, at 45, and they didn't understand. I was doing eight months jail at the time – see, I was angry because my father died, and I was in jail because of that. There was assault charges, larceny, all this sort of stuff, you know, like I started to write songs about what it was like to be an Aboriginal person. He died so young, and how people couldn't understand and I just wanted to understand . . .

At the same time I was in the tents in front of Parliament House, I was one of the young radicals at the time too. I got sick of talkin' to people so I had to write songs! This is how me songs started off, see.

What influenced me was, when I was in the tents, right, Paulie and Dudley Meredith, see, from Brisbane, was down, and I knew Dudley earlier, he used to sing about at some of the things in Sydney and that, and in clubs and stuff, with the Maori Troubadours, All-Stars. Excellent guitarist, excellent singer, used to be able to take people off, like Nat King Cole, that sort of thing. And his brother was asked to teach at the Conservatorium in Brisbane, couldn't read music but was an excellent

'We Shall Not Be Moved': Bobby on the right

guitarist, both of them were. They'd be playing augmented sixteenths and I'd be lost . . . but we were in the tents and they were the ones that influenced me into ballads, because I used to like rock'n'roll.

With Aboriginal people, see, there's always music, sitting around, you know, have a drink, around the campfire when you're drunk everyone's got a guitar, so it was just natural.

It just sort of come natural to me. I can sort of sit there, I could have the words and the music and everything, the whole lot, it just happens. I used to write a lot of poetry, when I was in jail. For instance, later, I wrote a song about my daughter, called 'Raquel'. That took me – I was thinking about her, I was trying to find her and I couldn't find her – and I thought, oh, old Aboriginal people, they used to be able to sing people sick or better or whatever, I was practising my ceremony and law at the time, I was sobered up, I had no alcohol, no cigarettes, nothing, so I thought, I'll write a song about her, see if I can do that. I was thinkin' about it, and this Mike Tyson fight come on TV, world title fight. And at the same time, this song hit me too, so I'm watching the fight, and it went six rounds, and from the time of starting the fight to the time it finished, I had the song written down. So I went and recorded it then, and as soon as I sung that song, a week later – and I've been trying to find my daughter all my life – she showed up, eh. Fair dinkum. Like, she didn't hear it, but if you follow those things . . .

WHEN THE GREAT REFORMER GOUGH WHITLAM first took office, prospects for Aboriginal people looked good. Whitlam appointed as Minister for Aboriginal Affairs Gordon Bryant, a long-time friend of black Australia. But when Bryant was sacked in September 1973, disenchantment set in among Aboriginal people.

Bobby was back out on the streets again by this time. After a demonstration over Bryant's sacking on the steps of Parliament House in October – at which Bobby was photographed, armed with a guitar, singing, and which Jack Davis said in *Identity* "could have been an ugly affair if it had not been for a few cool heads" – the Tent Embassy was erected once more. Bobby again moved in. It was at this time that he met Dudley and Paul Meredith, and the first inklings of the Kooriers emerged.

With the Queen due to open Parliament in February 1974, even Neville Bonner was warning that 'armed radical Aborigines' could spoil the party. Then, just days before the Queen's arrival, Charlie Perkins was sacked from the Department of Aboriginal Affairs for calling the conservative opposition 'racist'. Charlie Perkins was a lifeline for black Australia, and now that was lost. The mood turned even more sour.

It was an embarrassment, then, when a few hundred Aboriginal protesters greeted the Queen at Parliament House on February 28. More disturbing was the incident that took place simultaneously just around the corner. Bobby McLeod, armed with an unloaded pistol and aided and abetted by two followers, went into the Department of Aboriginal Affairs and held four public servants hostage for an hour, hysterically demanding Charlie Perkins's reinstatement. This might have been Australia's first act of modern 'terrorism'.

"We didn't think whether it was the right or wrong thing to do, you know, we just went and did it," Bobby shrugs. "We went down there and said, right, we're holding you hostage for the murder of black kids. The whole thing was about Charlie. I said, You stopped our only spokesman, and I could walk in here and shoot any one of you anytime. You don't care about our kids dying."

Bobby stormed into the DAA at about 3:15, the same time the Queen was speaking at Parliament House. He found the most senior bureaucrat in the building and barricaded his office. One of the hostages described the ordeal as "very confusing, very loud and very aggressive," and said he couldn't tell exactly what Bobby wanted. Bobby phoned the newspapers. Riot police sped over from Parliament House.

Bobby: "My cousin came down first, Burnum Burnum everyone calls him, but I said, no, you go and get Charlie."

At around 3:45, the same time that police armed with automatic shotguns, tear gas, riot shields and bullet-proof vests entered the building, Charlie Perkins arrived and calmed Bobby down, eventually persuading him to surrender.

Bobby was charged only with being in possession of an unlicensed firearm, to which he pleaded guilty (the four hostages had agreed before their release that they would not bring charges); he was fined $40 and put on a 12-month good behaviour bond. Bobby's lawyer argued, as the *Sydney Morning Herald* reported, that his "action was intended to be a charade of a violent act to demonstrate that this was something that could happen. There was no intention that violence should be carried out." Minister for Aboriginal Affairs Cavanagh astonished the house when he said Bobby would face no more serious charges. "But," he added, "the police want him to be medically examined."

Charlie Perkins wrote in his autobiography *A Bastard Like Me* shortly afterwards: "We totter now on the brink of a bloody new era in race relations in this country. People have condemned Bobby McLeod . . . Bobby, to me, is highly motivated with a genuine concern for his people. He is like a brother to me. His heart is good and he has soul . . . Some Aborigines feel they have nothing to lose but their lives. We want justice, whether the white man wants to give it to us or not. We will take it or deny him the opportunity to live with his conscience, or live at all."

$40 fine, bond over pistol in Govt office

CANBERRA, Friday.— A 26-year-old man who took a pistol to the Department of Aboriginal Affairs office in Canberra yesterday was fined $40 today and placed on a 12-month good behaviour bond.

Canberra Court of Petty Sessions was told by a police witness that the pistol carried by Robert Arthur John McLeod, an entertainer, of Scrivener Street, O'Connor, was not loaded.

McLeod's counsel, Mr T. Higgins, said his action was a political gesture.

McLeod pleaded guilty to a charge of having carried a .22 revolver between 7 am and 7 pm while not being the holder of a pistol licence.

Detective Sergeant Arthur Brown, of Canberra CID, said he went to the Department of Aboriginal Affairs, where he was handed a small .22 calibre pistol.

Sergeant Brown told Mr Higgins that the gun was not loaded, and that McLeod had been very co-operative

Later, Mr Higgins said McLeod's action was intended to be a charade of a violent act to demonstrate that this was something that could happen.

There was no intention that violence should be carried out.

The magistrate, Mr W. Nicholl, said that McLeod chose to use a pistol to further political motives and to draw attention to causes that McLeod believed to be valid and not receiving sufficient attention.

He had carried the pistol in a very public situation and in a sit ation where it w possible that some u happy consequence might have followed.

He said altho McLeod was aware the pistol was unlo other people ma have been.

Robert McLeod

Sydney Morning Herald, 2 March 1974

BOBBY HIGHTAILED IT TO MELBOURNE to escape the heat in Canberra, and to rendezvous with Dudley and Paul Meredith. Now, for Bobby, his music called the shots.

"I met Bobby many, many years ago when he was a boy," Paul Meredith recalls.

I hadn't seen him for ten years and then we run into him in Canberra, at the tents, after the Brisbane floods. Him and my brother wrote all these things and they wanted me to come down, and so we were sittin' there in the tents in front of Parliament House and we come up with the name the Kooriers.

We got this deal, this bloke, I can't remember his name now, he set us up to work for the Trades & Labor Council in Melbourne and so we done all the work sites, and they set us up to do that recording at the ABC studios there.

Bobby recalls: "We ended up on the same stage with AC/DC when they were first starting off! Chet Atkins rung us up from America. See, we were doing these union things, around Melbourne, the workshops, the Westgate Bridge after those blokes died. We did a show at the Dallas Brooks Hall with Jeannie Lewis. Chet Atkins rang us up, wanted us to go to America."

Dudley and Paul Meredith had already enjoyed successful music careers, together and separately, prior to forming the Kooriers. Hailing originally from Cherbourg in south-east Queensland, they "started off," as Paul put it, "at an early age, of course, on the ukulele and the old box guitar."

In the late 50s they broke onto the Brisbane pub circuit as a duo act called Peter & Paul. "It was rock'n'roll, it was that era, so my brother and I played the clubs, just a duo, two guitars."

"Paulie and Dudley, they were playin' but they weren't playin' at the Murri things," says Les Collins, another Cherbourg boy who played in black Brisbane bands. "The Aboriginal scene kept to itself, and we wanted to get out there," Paul explains.

"Paulie's a magical musician," says Collins, "and his brother Dudley was just a great entertainer, he could sing any type of music."

In the early 60s, while Dudley went off and joined the Maori Troubadours, Paul stayed in Brisbane and played with the Tommy Day Combo, which had a Friday afternoon Channel 7 TV show called *Swinging School*, before he too hit the road.

"A couple of times we had to pose as Maoris, you know? Because there was an influx of Maoris at the time, the Troubadours, Hi-Five, Hi-Liners, a big heap of Maori bands around at the time and I played in a heap of them too."

Maori bands were especially popular in the new luxury hotels springing up on the Gold Coast, and it was this connection that inducted Dudley and Paul into a funkier, jazzier – blacker! – sound, which was one of the influences that distinguished the Kooriers. At the same time, as Paul testifies, "We were more influenced by American country than the old hillbilly stuff here, you know. I'm not knocking Slim Dusty, I like Slim and I've played with him a few times and he's a nice guy, but [the American stuff] swings more, it grabs you more."

Like Malcolm and Angus Young of AC/DC, or bluegrass legends Charlie and Ira Louvin, Dudley and Paul were brothers who boasted a rare telepathy as pickers, and they took

Kooriers at Dallas Brooks Hall in Melbourne, July 1975, at a Chilean solidarity concert with Quilapayun and Jeannie Lewis

Australian country to a unique place somewhere between Hawaiian music and Western Swing. It's sometimes called 'old timey' music in America, with blues and rags reminiscent of the 'Hot Club of France' French gypsy jazz of Django Reinhardt and Stephane Grappelli. 'Hillbilly jazz' is another term for it.

"Dudley and Paulie were my kind of blokes," says Bobby. "They were my style, because they couldn't read music but they were excellent at what they did – and, you know, I trusted them. That's the way it is."

What Bobby brought to the band was a gospel or spiritual dimension. "I loved harmony," Bobby concurs, "the way the church songs went." Perhaps because his background was Baptist, the denomination out of which American gospel music grew, Bobby was able to update the gentle country-gospel of 'Royal Telephone', say, with a little bit of a soul.

"We sort of got together," says Paul, "the three of us, and that was it, we had the three-part harmony coming down. We got into protest songs, see, that Bobby and I and me brother wrote. There was a lot of feeling, for land rights …"

Says Lionel Rose: "I first met Bobby McLeod at the Builders Arms Hotel in Fitzroy. That was a sort of meeting place, and then he sang at the Collingwood Town Hall a couple of times, with the band. Well, they played there, they played a lot out at the Sir Douglas Nicholls Centre out in Westgarth, that was our meeting place there. You know, the boys come in and set their gear up and into it. It was a community thing. That was the first place where we could hold a concert, you know – unless you wanted to hire the Melbourne Town Hall, which we couldn't afford."

AS A MUSICAL GENRE, 'protest' is usually associated with 60s white folk acts like Pete Seeger and Bob Dylan. In African-American music, protest was usually more subtly stated, as in hits like Sam Cooke's 'A Change is Gonna Come' or the Impressions' 'People Get Ready', until the rise of Black Power encouraged a more confrontational attitude. Acts like the Last Poets and Gil Scott-Heron, and albums by activists like Stanley Crouch and Angela Davis and pimps like Iceberg Slim, prefigured hip-hop and rap – although social portrait soul records like Marvin Gaye's album *What's Goin' On*, or Curtis Mayfield's *Superfly*, probably drew more attention to the situation in the ghetto.

In Australia the Kooriers defied any and all conventions; they were a black country vocal and instrumental trio whose material, as Bobby himself once put it, "show[ed] the confusion and frustration of Aborigines and their cultural dilemma which came as a result of Westernisation," yet was expressed not aggressively, or obtusely, but like reggae, with something bordering on languor and a disarming directness.

The Kooriers' long-lost demo tape, produced for pioneering Melbourne indie record store/ label Archie & Jugheads, is a mixture of covers, from 'Sea of Heartbreak' to 'Snowbird' and 'Born Free', to guitar-instrumental rags (some with fellow Murri picker Darcy Cummins guesting on pedal steel), to classic early McLeod originals like 'Wayward Dreams' and 'Friendship Road', even the fabled 'Sick of Being Treated like a Low-Down Mangy Dog' (which was the first song ever danced to at the Black Theatre in Sydney, but has never been released in any form).

At a time when acts as diverse as Skyhooks and Richard Clapton were winning kudos for introducing vernacular language to Australian rock, the Kooriers could have been the ideal black counterpoint. But while Bobby and Paul Meredith will agree that the band was hot, that it was feted, and that it generated, as they say in the business, a vibe, they also acknowledge that in a way it was its own worst enemy. "I put it down to the fact," says Bobby, "that we were drinkin' too much."

Melbourne in the mid-70s was enjoying a real renaissance of both country and rock. Sydney was still the centre of the country music business; Tamworth was starting to assert itself, but perhaps only Nev Nicholls, with his truckin' songs, could challenge the old guard

supremacy of Slim Dusty and Reg Lindsay.
Overseas the West Coast country-rock of Gram
Parsons and the Eagles, and the Texas outlaw
movement led by Willie Nelson and Waylon
Jennings, had marked a shift in emphasis
away from Nashville. In Australia, that
shift was paralleled in Melbourne, which
spawned a kind of country underground,
from the bluegrassy Hawking Brothers
and Hayes Brothers to stoner western
swing merchants Moose Malone, from the
country blues of the Dingoes to the soft-
rock LA sound of the Little River Band and the 'ockerbilly'
of the Pelaco Brothers and the Relaxed Mechanics. This new wave of country-
rockers were no longer cow cockies come to town but dope-smoking city long-hairs whose
politics were radical rather than redneck, and in this environment the Kooriers should have
found their niche.

But success, as Bobby says, simply "wasn't an issue. We just loved to drink and sing, you
know. We knew how good we were. Like" – Bobby laughs – "we could sing as good as anyone
else around the place, if not better, you know."

"Oh yeah, we had the goods, we knew that," says Paul Meredith. "It was within our grasp
– but just out of reach."

"It wasn't an issue," says Bobby. "At the time, there's no way in the world I'd have had
white managers, because there was no trust there. All we wanted to do was prove a point to
ourselves and that's what we did. It wasn't how high or how far you could get, because we
weren't bought up with that sort of thing. When you're sitting around a campfire drinkin' a
flagon, you know, you don't consider yourself up there like a rock star."

Bobby has no idea how Chet Atkins, the godfather of the Nashville sound, producer of
everyone from Elvis to Dolly Parton, got into the band, but his interest was another lost
opportunity. "He rang me brother's place," Bobby remembered, "me brother was laying
around drunk at the time, and he thought he was calling from Queensland. My brother
thought he was joking."

When Dudley and Paul up and left Melbourne to take up a resident gig in their old duo
format at a tourist resort at Mount Dora, across the harbour from Darwin, Bobby was left
reeling. He got even more drunk and he stayed that way.

"I was never worried about tomorrow, having everything worked out to have a long
career," he said. "I just used to live from day to day."

"We played up there in Darwin for a long time," says Paul, "but then I came back here
[Brisbane] because I had a family, and then he [Dudley] passed away. I don't know what
happened, actually. He had a rheumatic heart, it was a heart attack."

★ *Get Outta Dodge!* ★

Eric Watson's liner notes for Col Hardy's belated 1972 debut EP *Protest; Protest!* begin: "How has an artist with so much ability, polish and professionalism managed to stay out of a recording studio for so long?" Because he was black perhaps?

Like Jimmy Little, Col Hardy is an interpretive singer, the owner of a rich country baritone who has released four albums since 1973 and is a winner of Tamworth's highest accolade, the Golden Guitar.

Hardy was born in Brewarrina in north-western New South Wales in 1942. Brewarrina, whose Aboriginal community is sometimes called 'Dodge City', can claim a strong tradition of country music – it was also home to the late Essie Coffey and her band Black Images. Col's first step in the right direction was to 'get outta Dodge'; Essie Coffey's, by contrast, was to stay put. She became an all-round Aboriginal legend – social worker, film-maker, activist, leader of Black Images and author of such country classics as 'She Moves with the Wind' and her signature song, 'Bush Queen'.

"I was working around the sheds, fencing," recalled Col later, sitting at home with his family at Kogarah in Sydney. "And there was this show that came through, Willie Fennell, and it had a talent quest, and I went into that."

Col ended up going on tour with Fennell, and from there to Sydney, where he arrived wide-eyed in 1962. He was taken in by a white patron – or rather matron – Myrtle Cox, who was a great activist for Aboriginal people. Mrs Cox got Col got a job at the Water Board, which he held until his retirement in 1999, and he started doing spots on the Sydney circuit: teenage cabarets, church socials, clubs. He was part of Jimmy Little's touring All-Coloured Revue, and when the Foundation for Aboriginal Affairs opened in Redfern in 1964, he became a regular at its events alongside Candy Williams and Jimmy himself.

It took a decade, however, before Col scored a recording deal, with Tamworth independent label Opal. Opal first released the EP *Protest; Protest!*, whose title track is a conservative American song protesting against protesting. On the eve of the 1973 release of his first full album *Black Gold*, Col won a Golden

All-Coloured Show's house band, the Opals, featuring Col Hardy (centre) and Jimmy's little brother Freddie (far right)

Guitar for most popular radio artist at the very first Tamworth awards. It would be 20 years before another Aborigine repeated the feat.

"His style is ultra-modern country," wrote Eric Watson. "His voice – firm, true and distinctive – carries that characteristic quality found in such fine artists as Jimmy Little, Lionel Rose, Kevin Bonny and Candy Williams – that formidable and growing list of dark people striding towards their rightful place in our country music heritage."

The NSW club circuit boomed in the 70s, and Col rode that wave all the way into the 80s. Steel guitarist Norm Bodkin wrote on 1978's *Col Hardy Country*: "As a musician working beside him onstage, whether at the Tamworth Town Hall, Canterbury Leagues Club or at a lonely northern mission station, I have felt his warmth and appeal, and saw the ecstatic eyes focused on this man as he performed their favorite songs."

Col no longer plays as much as he used to. The circuit has shrunk, and in any case he can't really compete with electro duos and DJs. But when he does get hold of a song, as he still can to this day, Col Hardy is a gentle giant of country-soul.

●●●

Failing to survive the mid-70s, the Kooriers echoed the changing times themselves. Many of the broader hopes of Aboriginal people evaporated too when Labor prime minister Gough Whitlam was controversially removed from office in November 1975.

"From then on," rues Bobby, "it was just a matter of, I'd sing here and there. But alcohol ruled my life at that time. After my dad died, I didn't care. Until I was 36, when I sobered up. I was drunk for the last nine of those years, every day."

Paul Meredith never gave up music completely, but it's tragically typical that it wasn't until 2000, over 30 years since he first played professionally, that he finally released a recording, a single track on a 4AAA compilation album.

IN THE LATE 70S Bobby went to Darwin to see his wife and kids and ended up staying a while. "I was trying to find out who I was, sort of thing. I was up there drinkin' around with all the lads from Elcho Island. I did a couple of shows with Soft Sands, I wasn't singin' with them, they just backed me up. But you know, like, I didn't really do a lot up in Darwin, I was just there."

Bobby was on a near-terminal spiral. At one point he threw himself out of a speeding car. He can barely account for a period as long as seven years. It was a criminal waste. He hit bottom in 1983. "I went into a coma for seven days, down in Bairnsdale, back down home. Some might call it the DTs. I nearly died."

Surviving that, Bobby was born again. He went back to live in his home town of Nowra after 20 years away, and got off the grog.

> Jimmy [Little] was a role model for me, the way he could go through life without alcohol, and Chicka Dixon was the next one, because he used to be into metho and all that, and he used to say to me, come on, you can get off this stuff.
>
> When that happened, I had to look at my life and see what I could do – so I started to get back into singing.

With a repertoire, as he puts it, ranging through "country and western, blues and ballads", Bobby recalls:

> I had to go and do a sort of a club thing, to do with health, one of the hotels in Sydney there, where Heathermae Reading was doin' a show, and it was the first time I'd ever sung sober. And it was good, and people liked it, so I thought . . . I haven't touched alcohol since.

In 1985 Bobby was invited to appear at the Pacific Arts Festival in Townsville. "Paul [Meredith] was up there," he remembers, "and I met some people from Hall's Creek and ended up going over there and meeting up with a man called Hittier Gordon, one of the lawkeepers over there, and I'm still doing work with him now. And that's when I started Donooch Dancers off."

Bobby McLeod on the ABC's 7:30 Report, *1988, after the release of his first album* Culture Up Front

Bobby took his four-year-old son Larry on the road around Australia in a sort of quest for spiritual direction. He found it in the traditional Aboriginal 'Spirit Mother'. He went back to Nowra and, rounding up his older sons, founded the Donooch Dance Group as a way for his boys to avoid drugs and alcohol, to have gainful employment and to approach a cultural and spiritual awakening.

In 1987, after Chicka Dixon had got him in to play prison shows with Roger Knox and Vic Simms, Bobby went to Tamworth for the first time to play the Koori Country Music Association's festival show. This opened the door for him to a belated recording career.

"As soon as I went up there I met the Enrec mob, and so I recorded with them and Buddy Knox, Mick Liber. It was real fun making that recording."

Culture Up Front, Bobby's debut album, was released by long-standing Australian folk label Larrikin Records in 1988. "That's probably one of the better records I've done," remembers Randall Wilson, drummer in the Enrec studio house band. "Because Bobby sings like Nat King Cole for a start, which is a wonderful thing to listen to and for a musician to back. He's got a good nature in the studio, lovely. He's got his other ways about him, but that's Bobby. He's a strong man. I liked the way he talked."

The album caught up on the backlog of great songs Bobby had never recorded, and added new ones like 'The Resurrection'. It is testament to the quality of these songs that even in 1987, a decade after most of them were written, they still had terrific freshness and relevance. As Sydney's *Daily Telegraph* described it, the album was "a challenging fusion of hypnotic rhythms and potent lyricism . . . It is a musical journey beginning with the anguish of oppression, leading through the path of rediscovery and finding renewed strength in one's own Aboriginality – and ending on a distinctly optimistic note: 'Friendship Road'."

At the same time that Larrikin released *Culture Up Front*, many years after Bobby had started singing, the label also put out *Pillars of Society*, the debut album by Kev Carmody, a folk-country singer-songwriter of the new generation, from Queensland. Carmody was building on foundations laid by Bobby McLeod – and would surpass Bobby in the broader marketplace. The same would subsequently be true of Archie Roach, who was well aware of Bobby's history in the Kooriers. Paul Meredith recalls: "Once I was on a gig up in Rockhampton . . . Archie was up there and he said he used to follow us, when he was a little street kid. He said he was greatly influenced by us, we sort of put him on the track."

It was a mark of the Australian music industry's increasing maturity that by the late 80s Kev Carmody and Archie Roach were both able to establish themselves relatively readily on the professional circuit. At the same time, Bobby was already unable to dedicate himself full-time to music because he had by now founded the Donooch Self-Healing Centre in Nowra.

In 1990 Bobby went to North America at the behest of native Indians to play prisons and reservations with Vic Simms and Roger Knox and Euraba. When he returned he cut his second album *Spirit Mother*.

Spirit Mother was recorded in Sydney with backing by the Flying Emus, one of the brighter lights of Australian country in the 80s. It was a more polished product but it lacked some of the sting of *Culture Up Front*. Bobby explains:

> What I found out after doing my first album, it was based on too much sorrow. It's the same thing with a lot of country and western, sorrow that people are talkin' about, it's more about sorrow than anything else. So then I started changing my ideas. With the CD I wrote, it wasn't . . . it was as if you sing about the sorrow of things, it sort of keeps people in that sadness. So what I did was I started to try and change it to find out what was good about being me and stuff.
>
> But see, what I did, after that, I put all my thing into my boys' dancing, and I stopped singing. I was seeing so much destruction through alcohol and that, I decided to try and get hold of my kids and help them get away from it. And I was running the drug and alcohol place for all the young kids down here then too.

Bobby applied the lessons he learnt in his music career, or rather anti-career.

> It's not till now that I realise, right, there should have been more effort put into it. That's why I'm really strict with my dancers now, you know. And I'm taking them

around the world, New York, Vietnam, we're off to Scotland and Cyprus . . . Slow down on the alcohol and drugs. Let them get an international perspective on who they are. That they're capable of being up there with all the big stars, which they have been. The people are seeing them because they're different, right, and because they do know their dancing and they do know their culture, the people see them as equal, they can do what we can't do, you know what I mean? These are kids who are really, really good at what they're doing. And so I got hold of that and I said, you cannot muck around.

It teaches them responsibility, which is something that I never really looked at when I was doing my stuff. Because I didn't have anyone pushin' me. Not only that, I wouldn't have listened anyhow because I was too much of an alcoholic. But because I don't drink now I push it with these kids: if you're doing this, make sure you're sober.

ꙭꙭꙭ

Harry and Wilga on the cover of the Country Outcasts' second album, Tamworth, 1981

STAND BY YOUR MAN

★ Harry and Wilga Williams ★
and the Country Outcasts

"If you can cry to a song, laugh to a song or dance to a song, it's going over."
Wilga Williams

They made a stunning couple, Harry and Wilga. Harry, with his electric shock of salt-and-pepper hair and mutton-chops, was the black silver bodgie, a wildfella – he was typecast as such, in fact, as a bit-part contract player for TV drama company Crawford Productions in the early 70s; Wilga was lean and handsome with deep dark eyes. They sit together on the cover of the second (and last) Country Outcasts album, under the dappled shade of the gums, a soft warm breeze caressing them. Wilga wears an equestrian red jacket (she had been a star sportswoman in her younger years), Harry a flash western shirt. If there's any strain in their smiles, it's because of the struggles they've gone through, and it's underpinned by drive, talent and grace.

Harry Williams, who died in 1991, was the godfather of Koori country. Wilga was the first lady. They worked and lived together for over 20 years, leading the charge for an independent, identifiably black Australian sound, not only setting an example with their own music but also providing encouragement through ventures like the National Aboriginal Country Music Festival, which they promoted into the early 80s.

"Well, I mean, he was the guiding light, Harry. And Wilga," says Lionel Rose. "Especially in Victoria, because they were the first Koori band that performed professional. And he was a good bloke, Harry was, we lost a good fella when we lost him."

Following Jimmy Little's second (mid-60s all-black) trio, the Country Outcasts were only the second Aboriginal band on record. Like most black bands until recently, their recorded legacy is slim, just two albums – but their achievement was immense. In creating the definitive Koori country sound as they did on tracks like 'Home-Made Didgeridoo', 'Streets of Fitzroy' or 'Blue Gums Calling Me Back Home', the Outcasts synthesised the south-eastern Aboriginal sensibility with more modern and often unashamedly American influences, infusing the bush ballad archetype with some welcome sensuality and swing. The tragedy is that so few of Harry's great original songs were recorded.

Despite the fact that the Country Outcasts' self-titled debut album was released by RCA Records in 1979 (the major label that had released Vic Simms's *The Loner* in 1973), the band was barely promoted by the Australian music business. Although it was a crying-in-your-beer masterpiece, the album came out with not a bang but with a whimper. The Outcasts' second album (also self-titled, rather confusingly) was recorded in Tamworth in 1981 and again was an unsung classic. But Harry's health was already beginning to falter, and the quality of the band as a live act (it was always a shifting aggregation anyway) was starting to decline.

Eventually the family moved back to Cowra, where Harry was born – and where he would die. Wilga still cries about it. "When Harry died, the heart went out of it and everything else," she says, wiping away a tear and then collecting herself.

> When he died, people were ringing, saying, we want a story. That annoys me. They wasn't interested when he was alive. Why do it now that he's gone? What benefit's it doing him?
>
> We always said, we'd like to go to the top – but not stay there. Just to go to the top, say you went there, say, I achieved that. Well, a lot we achieved going through, more or less opened the gateway for Aboriginal entertainers.
>
> Whether they were frightened of us . . . but look at the Aboriginal entertainers today – they're treated A1. They're getting recognition for something that we done 20 years ago. This is how hard it was for us.

BORN OF WIRADJURI BLOOD at the Eurambie Mission near Cowra, western NSW, in 1927, Harry Williams was preceded on the music scene by his brother Candy. His other three brothers were black stars too; Merv 'Boomanulla' Williams, for instance, had appeared at Doug Nicholls's Moomba show in Melbourne in 1951, and brought the house down with his version of 'Jackie-Jackie'.

Charlie Perkins knew all the Williams boys, as he recalled in his memoir *A Bastard Like Me*:

> Boomanulla was a real drunk and most people called him a no-hoper. He would come down to the Foundation and help me in numerous ways. He was brilliant in social efforts like running dances.
>
> Well, this was Booma. He did not smoke. But he drank. Harry did not drink. But he smoked. And Candy did neither. Yet they could all play musical instruments. They could sing, dance and entertain and play sports.

Wilga: "Harry was bought up with music. In their day, they entertained themselves. They had this one big night, he told me, in this house like a shed, all the walls opened up . . . Word got out, and all the whitefellas used to sit on the boundary and listen!"

Like Jimmy Little Snr, Harry's father 'Knocker' Williams was the leader of a travelling tent show that played around the Lachlan Valley in the 1930s. "Harry could play any sort of string instrument you'd like to stick in his hand," says Wilga. "Him and his uncles and his father. They used to make costumes out of old hessian bags."

Harry first learnt to play Tex Morton songs on guitar. After he left the mission school, vehemently rejecting Christianity, he became an itinerant fruitpicker. It was while he was doing this during the Second World War, according to Jazzer Smith's *Book of Australian Country Music*, that he found himself in Griffith, where "he was befriended by some Spanish folk who were excellent guitarists and who passed on some of their techniques."

After the war, Harry, now in his twenties, settled in Sydney. Booma and another brother, Sugar Ray Williams, both played rugby league for the Redfern All-Blacks, and Harry, who'd got a job in a factory, joined the team too. Football and music went hand in hand. Aboriginal boxer Keith Saunders recalls in his memoir *Learning the Ropes* how in the early 50s everyone would repair after games to Auntie Bunnie's place in Redfern "for a singsong and a dance":

> The entertainment was fantastic. The people that passed through Auntie Bunnie's place were celebrities, or on their way to becoming celebrities: Jimmy Little, singer, recording star; Alan Saunders, entertainer; Jack Hassen, lightweight champion of Australia; Harry Williams, actor, country and western singer; and Claude Williams, his brother.

Harry and Candy (as Claude was always known) would sing Ink Spots songs. Alan Saunders would yodel. Harry and Alan hit it off straight away and took to trading licks. From Taree via Newcastle, Saunders was a black urban cowboy renowned for his chops on guitar and vocals. Said his brother Keith: "He was once just beaten for first place on the *Amateur Hour* in Sydney by Reg Lindsay."

Harry was "more or less a drifter" at this time, Wilga says. He left Sydney, went on the wallaby again. He got married and settled in Shepparton, on the Murray. Shepparton was a centre of country music; Harry joined an Hawaiian club, where he learnt to play pedal steel.

When his marriage came apart, Harry moved on to Melbourne. During the 60s he was spotted regularly playing steel guitar, in a duet with Alice Thomas on piano, at the dances Eric Onus put on at Manchester Unity Hall in Collingwood. As part of a 1968 remembrance event organised on what was then called National Aborigines Day, he performed in Melbourne's City Square with Cummera man Herb Patten, gumleaf-player extraordinaire and author of the country classic 'Numerella Pines'.

Before the end of the 60s Harry would move on again and reunite with Alan Saunders in Newcastle. "Alan and Harry were like two peas in a pod," Keith Saunders wrote, "because [they] had the same intentions. Which were summed up in the typical query: 'Come on, brother, [do] you have the clues as to where we can find a party with women?'" Was it inevitable, then, that they would fall out over a woman?

WHEN THE COUNTRY OUTCASTS TOURED Papua Niugini in the mid-80s, Wilga remembers, "Word got around, go and see this big tall woman playing bass! They'd never seen anything like it before – and they were so short!"

★ Gubba Country ★

Tex Morton sings to some friends

If country music was at first a whitefella or gubba form co-opted by Aboriginal people, the relationship has definitely worked both ways since then. In his 1981 book *Walk a Country Mile*, Slim Dusty wrote that as a boy he loved bush music, but "one night I heard something different that made a lasting impression. An Aboriginal from the Bellbrook Mission pulled out a home-made acoustic guitar and sang 'The Drunkard's Child'. He made chords with a steel bar, moving it up and down the frets Hawaiian-style. It was a wistful sound I had never heard before, and I was entranced."

That Aboriginal slide guitarist was Clivie Kelly, and although he was never destined to enjoy a career quite like Slim's, there's no doubt that the line between black and white in Australian country sometimes becomes fuzzy. Family duo act the LeGarde Twins went to Nashville to further their career in the late 50s, and Aboriginality was a distinct part of their bushlands image, even though they were white.

Even before World War II, Tex Morton and Buddy Williams made pioneering tours of remote Aboriginal communities in the outback. Slim Dusty joined them in the 1960s. The experience naturally started to seep into the songs; Morton's 'Cream in Between' emerged at around the same time in the late 60s as Bob Randall's groundbreaking song on the same subject, 'Brown Skin Baby'. Slim was loved by black and white alike for songs like 'Trumby', as was Buddy Williams for 'Les Dingo', about actor Ernie Dingo's father.

Herb Laughton's story about Buddy Williams's confession at the end of his life – that he did indeed have Aboriginal blood – gets at a reality that was perhaps not so unusual. Much of Buddy's biography certainly fits with his claim: he grew up in an orphanage, to start with, and spent a lifetime looking for his mother. Country music researcher Andrew Smith has calculated that between 1939 (when Buddy cut his first session for EMI) and 1950, fully 13 percent of his songs dealt with the theme of parents and children, and the disconnection between them. Which at the very least would explain why so many Aborigines identified with them. Certainly, Buddy was very pale-skinned, but then so is Herb Laughton. Chad Morgan is another example:

Jimmy Little and Brian Young

in the recent documentary *I'm Not Dead Yet*, he admitted that he was raised by his grandmother, who was Aboriginal. "It was something I never hid," he said, "but then I didn't flaunt it around either."

Aboriginal pickers have enlivened many an otherwise white country band too. In Sydney in the 50s, enigmatic Hank Williams acolyte Ned Kelly led a band called the Western Five that boasted not one but two black guitarists, Trevor Roberts and Johnny Tonga. Rick and Thel Carey, like Slim, took to touring outback settlements in the 60s, and they've nurtured many fine musicians, both black and white, from Brian Young to Kevin Gunn and Jimmy Knox. Brian Young himself was a whitefella who would go on to enjoy special status among Aboriginal people. Sitting at the bar at the Oasis Hotel in Tamworth, Youngie draws up a list of all the Aboriginal artists he's given a gig to since he started touring nationally in 1977. It reads like a roll call, from Jimmy Little, Auriel Andrew, Col Hardy, Roger Knox and Troy Cassar-Daley to specialist guitarists Sammy Butcher, Kevin Gunn and Buddy Knox.

Perhaps the ultimate crossover music is Ted Egan's 1987 country-rock opera *The Aboriginals*. But then, as the author of both 'Gurindji Blues' and 'Arnhem Land Lullaby', Egan has given as much as he's taken.

Today, the songlines continue to intertwine, for example in the way that John Williamson and Warren H. Williams have become virtually inseparable touring partners since the success of their 1998 single together, 'Raining on the Rock'. An album of ebony-and-ivory duets is surely ahead of them.

●●●

At the 1980 Tamworth Aboriginal Country Music Festival

She was quoted in the paper: "Women and blacks can do it too." She laughs now almost in self-mockery:

> I can play anything! I started on the piano accordion. Then I learnt to play guitar from my father and mother and that, so it was naturally easy to switch to bass. It was Harry who taught me bass. We had to do a big show with Rolf Harris, and so I had 24 hours to learn bass because the bass player skipped.
>
> I was bought up with music too. Harry and I more or less done the same thing. In every Aboriginal person you'll find music of some sort . . .

Wilga Munro was born in Tamworth in 1940, and it's ironic that among the first strains of live country music heard in the town that became Australia's answer to Nashville, where Aboriginal artists have mostly been fringe-dwellers, were those made by Wilga Williams. Wilga was an exceptional young woman who could have done anything with her life.

'Wilga' means wild orange tree – Wilga was born under one. Her family is well known in the New England area. Today she lives on the NSW south coast. She is still imposing, a chain-smoking matriarch surrounded by a large, loving family.

"I wasn't bought up on the mission, but my mother and father were. We had a radio, and the old 78 records. Plus, there was a lot of church music, both sides."

When she first started singing publicly in the 60s, Wilga had just returned to Tamworth from serving in the air force, and she had already distinguished herself as a netball player. She got a job on the switchboard at the Tamworth exchange, and she continued to play both netball and the piano accordion.

Growing up in Tamworth was sort of hard for me, but it was not a racist sort of place, broad out, and we sort of pushed our way through with sport and everything else to sort of get noticed. A lot of the boys were in the fight game, boxing game . . . Then I sort of stuck to music, even though I'd played sport and everything. But to get involved in music there was very hard.

The official histories date Tamworth's inauguration as Australia's country music capital to 1964, when John Minson started his *Hoedown* show on 2TM and the Tamworth Country Music Club was founded by Geoff Brown, the man who opened up Joe Maguire's Hotel to live bands and launched the Capital Country Music Association, which is still the pre-eminent body in Tamworth today. Brown organised the CCMA's first annual Australia Day talent quest and jamboree in 1967, and it was when this event joined forces with 2TM and *Hoedown*, in 1972, that the festival in its current form, complete with the Golden Guitar awards, began.

"In Tamworth itself, when we first started," Wilga recalls, "there was only Geoff Brown, [then] there was me and a red-headed fella, young fella, can't remember his name. We were more or less the only ones in Tamworth then, [playing] this little coffee lounge. [People] used to go to the pictures and then after the pictures they'd all go to this coffee lounge."

The coffee lounge was called the Hayshed; it was located in the basement of Upjohn's Produce store. "That was where we first started with the country music. Got noted and John Minson asked me to go in a talent quest. I got third and I didn't think any more of it . . . I just used to get up and do a few songs at sporting events and picnics and everything else, and it was all country music."

Wilga got married and moved to Newcastle, but her marriage ran aground just like Harry's.

Harry was up there with one of his mates, Alan Saunders. They used to travel round, just the two of them, going into pubs and singing and earning a bit of money. The agent they had at the time said, You could do with a female in the band. So they had trials, me and three other women went along, and I got on, and then me and Harry sort of drifted together from there.

It was the beginning of the rest of their lives together.

CALLING THEMSELVES THE TJURINGAS (tjuringa means 'sacred object'), the band played the thriving Newcastle circuit through 1969, with Harry and Alan as dual frontmen, Wilga on bass and vocals and Alan's nephew Keith on drums. Their set contained no original material. Wilga recalls:

It was a big circuit. Some of the clubs that we done, we were like a local artist along with a big name artist, overseas artists as well as the locals. So that sort of made us open our eyes really to that, to the profession of it.

Harry used to play a lot of instrumental stuff, I think they were fascinated with the way that he played, and how we sort of all fitted with harmonies . . . Harry used

to play guitar. We mixed it up. Country, some old 50s rock stuff, instrumentals like 'Guitar Boogie'.

'Guitar Boogie', written and first recorded in 1945 by Arthur 'Guitar' Smith, was not only a set piece for Harry Williams – it became a standard of Aboriginal music that's still being played today.

This agent, she said, no way I'll let you fellas go to Sydney because I'll lose you. So then the band broke up and me and Harry, we done a duo. I was in the mini-dress!

It could also be that the Tjuringas broke up because Wilga's presence on the scene meant the end of Harry and Alan's male bonding.

Harry and Wilga didn't play for long as a duo. They went down to Melbourne one time, just to spend a weekend with Harry's sister, and ended up staying there for the entire decade of the 1970s, starting a family as well as a new band, the Country Outcasts.

At first the couple ran an artefacts shop in Fitzroy, selling Harry's velvet paintings and boomerangs. Their first break came when Harry was appointed musical director of the Nindethana Theatre. The Nindethana was a sort of Melbourne equivalent of Bettie Fisher's Black Theatre in Redfern. It was run by Joyce Johnson, a former member of radio show *The Hillbilly Club*; she greatly encouraged Harry and Wilga, and later became their manager.

Following in the footsteps of his brother Candy, who appeared in a couple of ABC-TV dramas in the early 60s, Harry signed on with Crawford Productions and got occasional parts in such shows as *Matlock Police* and *Division Four*. In *Cash & Co*, he was even hanged as a bushranger! "They said to him, Never cut your hair," Wilga laughs. Harry played a drunk on the trail of trouble in the landmark 1972 short drama film *Come Out Fighting*. "He got all the drunk parts," she says, "and he never ever had a drink in his life." But he lost two brothers and a son to the grog.

Harry always said, you know . . . he was offered jobs in big bands, he said, he'll do it for his people.

We went to see Lionel Rose, he was performing in a club one night, and Lionel said, "We've got another performer in the audience and he plays guitar pretty well, do you want to hear him?" And the crowd went, yeah, yeah. So Harry got up, Lionel played rhythm, and Harry said, "Do you know 'Guitar Boogie'? But you've gotta play fast." He could never play slow, he made all the mistakes in the world playing slow. So Lionel turned to the band and said, "And he means fast!" So bang, away he went, and the applause went up. This fella came up afterwards and said, "Are you in a band?" He said, "Come over my house on the weekend" – and that's how we ended up getting a band together.

The occasion was the Miss Aboriginal Victoria Quest. Lionel Rose remembers:

When he got up there he played, he just blew me out. His guitar, Wilga, all the country stuff, and then he sang a couple. Shows us how to do it. I took them back to my room, we stayed up and played all night. He drank tea and I drank beer. He was still singing in tune!

It was whitefella Ian 'Ocker' Mackay who'd approached Harry and Wilga about forming a band. And it was he, alongside Harry and Wilga and Harry's son from his first marriage, the late Bert Williams, on drums, who comprised the original line-up of the Country Outcasts.

"When we first started the band," remembers Wilga, "we went into all the country music festival competitions and everything else, so then the bookings started coming out of that."

They were declared the most promising new band at the Wandong Truck'n'Country Festival. At the Mooroopna Festival, Harry shared the songwriting award with Bernie O'Brien of Saltbush for one of his first original compositions, 'Home-Made Didgeridoo'.

This was the important next step Harry took, to start writing songs. Not even Candy got that far. Wilga remembers:

He wrote 'Home-Made Didgeridoo' at four in the morning. He woke me up and said, listen to this. So we went to Mooroopna and entered in the competition, and they announced the winner, Harry Williams, and all the blackfellas along the fence screamed out, Yeah!"

'Home-Made Didgeridoo' became the Outcasts' first single. They pressed it themselves, backed with a version of Ted Egan's 'Arnhem Land Lullaby' sung by Wilga. It was an Aboriginal turntable hit.

According to Harry, in one of his few surviving comments for the record:

I haven't been writing songs very long, but I think when you're writing songs, you write about things that relate to you. So I write about when I lived in Fitzroy one time, and the didgeridoo, my home-made didgeridoo. We lost our culture, as you know, down in the eastern states, and I don't think there ever was a didgeridoo in our tribal areas. People asked me to play the didgeridoo and I felt a bit ashamed about it so I turned around and made my own didgeridoo, and wrote a song about it.

"It was real home-town country music," says Lionel Rose. "Nowadays you play the up-tempo stuff. But they played the good stuff from the heart."

Then suddenly, Harry's son and Outcasts' drummer Bert Williams died. The family, the band, all of black Melbourne was dealt a devastating blow.

Harry went on to star in the premiere of his son's play, *Mission & Urban*, at the 1974 Adelaide Festival. And when Angelwood Records of Tamworth released the Outcasts' second single, 'Nullabor Prayer', in 1975, it was a fitting tribute, since the track was essentially an oration by Bert set to 'Just a Closer Walk'. But the future of the band itself was hanging in the balance.

THE GRANDVIEW HOTEL, FAIRFIELD – it's quite a mouthful, but something of a misnomer. Fairfield is a rather dull, flat suburb in Melbourne's semi-industrial north, and it's lacking in views that are anything like grand; virtually next door stands the women's prison. But the Grandview is a pub that should be ranked alongside Surf City or the Bondi Lifesaver, or the Crystal Ballroom or the now-demolished Cloudland in Brisbane, as one of the sacred sites of Australian music. Because it was at the Grandview, in the mid-1970s, that Harry and Wilga ran a weekly black night every Monday for a couple of years, and it became legendary, not only establishing the Country Outcasts as a band but also laying the foundations of a modern Aboriginal music tradition in Melbourne. A very young Archie Roach, for one, regularly sat in on these sessions.

At one point the Outcasts reconfigured with Joyce Johnson's son Ian on guitar and Henry Thorpe on drums, but this pair would leave to form black power-trio Hard Times. When the Outcasts were booked to play a groundbreaking Australia Council-sponsored tour of the Northern Territory in 1975, Harry, as Wilga put it, "called in the professionals" – Laurie Ingram and Candy on guitars, and Mac Silva on drums. They also invited Auriel Andrew along to add extra spice with her voice.

Organised by Ted Egan in Alice Springs, the tour had a strong impact both on music in the Centre – Australia's vast desert interior, where a lot of the Aboriginal population lives – and on the Outcasts themselves, and it marked the beginning of a long and fruitful relationship between the band and the Australia Council. Founded in the wake of early-1970s black activism and Whitlam-era reform, the Australia Council became an arbiter and sanctioner of culture whose commitment to Aboriginal arts was so fundamental that it always maintained the subsidiary Aboriginal Arts Board. It was Candy Williams, in Sydney, who first saw the opportunity the Board was offering; he roped Harry in to help and they seized that opportunity.

Aboriginal bands were always starting from behind the eight ball. They still are. Funding from bodies like the Australia Council helps them get around the obstacles that white bands never even have to face. Black bands, sadly, still need that bit of a leg up. With the assistance of sympatico white Australia Council officer Chris McGuigan, Harry and Candy quickly came to understand the system. They rightly convinced the Australia Council that country music was the contemporary popular voice of Aboriginal people, and, after the success of the 1975 Territory tour, they began plotting another major event.

 Not long after Harry and Wilga returned to Melbourne from Alice Springs they started their own country music radio show on community station 3CR, which was just getting started following the great opening up of the airwaves. "We wasn't getting enough airplay from the big stations," says Wilga, "so 3CR, we approached them for an Aboriginal program and they said, Yeah. We used to call it the *Country Music Shindig*. And that was playing a lot of the Aboriginal artists. But it wasn't just strictly for Aboriginals. We played the Hawking Bros, Chad Morgan – as long as it was country music. And I think a lot of people noticed that as well, because the feedback was coming in . . ."

By now Monday night at the Grandview was a veritable institution, and the Country Outcasts were themselves something of a juggernaut, as Wilga recalls:

All the young kids used to come out of the audience; we'd give them a chance to come up on stage. And then it gradually got that big they had to close the doors. Then when it changed hands, the new management said they didn't want . . . country music, so they squashed it.

Wilga still turns up her nose in distaste at the recollection of such a racist smokescreen. The Country Outcasts were at once outgrowing their origins and hitting the glass ceiling.

Country music was big, very big. The hotels down there – they never had clubs, although they had bowling clubs, RSL clubs – but the biggest lot of it was hotels. But the Aboriginal entertainer still didn't get a go. Because they say, oh, it's an Aboriginal band. One of the instances I'll point out, where it's raw and it's not right, one time in Gosford, this booking came through, we gave our quote, the manager rang, and he said could you send your records and bios, so we done that; well, as soon as he seen it was an Aboriginal band he squashed it.

What it is, with the Aboriginal entertainers, you can't stop a following. Everybody's got their following, like any big name. So with an Aboriginal band in you're going to have a lot of blacks in. Trouble.

Wilga explains: "We used to say, when we took bookings, you know that we are an Aboriginal band. We had to say it. You still got the looks and everything though. You only had to look at Harry, and they'd say" – she laughs fondly – "Look at this wildfella!"

Harry was a charismatic, driven man, strict but good-humoured.

Scenes from the festivals, left to right: Vi Chitty in Perth, 1978; Fairbridge and Ridgeway, Joan and Jim, Perth

To me, what we done was more or less open the public's eye to what the Aboriginal entertainer can do. A lot of these fellas, Roger Knox was one, when we first got together with him, yarnin', he said, how do you present yourself on stage? Because a lot of these fellas had no idea. And Harry said, be yourself. Always just be yourself, but be careful of the words that you talk. Because when you're an entertainer, you're performing to black, white, blue or brindle.

That's what he said to a lot of these young kids, you can't have that Black Power attitude while you're performing. What you do outside that performance is your own business, but you never bring it on stage.

The rules that he had: nobody goes on stage drunk. And there'd be no language. And most of all, he said, there'll be no militant attitude, Black Power.

It was a strange mixture of Elvis and James Brown.

"This was another point to prove: that we're not all down-in-the-gutter drunks and no-hopers. So we set that example too."

At bottom, Harry himself believed simply in the redemptive power of country music. He once said:

Because of Aboriginals' assimilation into the urban community, much of our culture – language, corroborees and way of life – has been lost. Country music I believe has taken its place. We can all play it, sing it, enjoy it, sing along with it. I think that's the reason country is so popular with Australia's Aborigines – because they so easily identify with it. It's true-to-life music. Down to earth. It's our heritage. Our music!

WHEN THE ARTS BOARD granted Harry and Candy a paltry $4,000 to stage a National Aboriginal Country Music Festival in Canberra in 1976, it barely covered phone bills and the Outcasts' air fares.

Held at the Narrabundah-cum-Boomanulla Oval, with the Outcasts as house band, the show boasted 63 performers on the bill and attracted a crowd of over 2,000. It was a great

Alan Saunders, Perth; the Country Outcasts on stage in Perth; Laurie Ingram in front of Wilga Williams, Canberra, 1976

gathering of the tribes, of songmen and pickers, so successful that the festival became a roving annual event that virtually defined an era as it made its way around the continent over the next several years, until its demise in the early 80s.

"We knew there was a lot of singers out there, guitarists, whatever, songwriters, everything," says Wilga, "and the festivals were a way of them coming out and showing what they've got."

Indeed, in the 1976 talent quest, Black Lace won the Bill Reid Trophy in the group section; the Leila Rankine Trophy for female soloist was won by Bonnie Quayle, followed by Carole Fraser and Val Power. The Dick Roughsey Trophy for songwriters was won by Mick Donovan, followed by their Bobnesses McLeod and Randall. The Kitty Dick Trophy for male soloist was won by Douglas Williams, followed by Merv Torres and Vince Quayle. This was the biggest singalong there had ever been. The vibe and everything, music included, was wonderful. It was important because at that time Aborigines didn't enjoy the sort of forums other Australians shared and took for granted, whether it was *Bandstand*, *Countdown* or the Grand Final.

The second festival was also held in Canberra, at the Yarralumla Woolshed, over Easter 1977. Candy and drummer Mac Silva were up on stage all day; they were the engine room; when Harry and Wilga and Laurie Ingram got up it was the Outcasts, and when the younger fellas from Redfern got up, led by Mac, it was Black Lace. Laurie Ingram led a set by his own band, the Bidgee Wanderers. The day was a great celebration. It was almost fashionable. "These days," reported *Australian Men's Vogue*:

> Harry plays steel guitar, rhythm guitar, country fiddle and piano with the Outcasts, while brother Candy plays guitar on the Sydney club circuit.
>
> When they get together, Candy likes to spice up Harry's more country and western (Nashville) style with some fancy guitar work on a few Chuck Berry classics, along with some original blues lyrics: "And I know sometime/I'll be called back to the Dreamtime/Where the white man's ways/Won't bother me no more".

The festival went on to play Perth in 1978 and Adelaide in 79. "Candy said, If there's any discrimination going on in that city, we'll find out," recalls Wilga. "So all we used to do is

contact the police, say there's going to be a big show, the Aboriginals will be coming, let 'em know why all the Aboriginals are coming together. So they were notified and we said, we don't want no hassles from you, we're just letting you know now. There was no problems, we had no problem with drink."

In 1979, in addition to playing the festival in Adelaide, the Country Outcasts toured Australia as part of the Chequerboard Country Roadshow with Reg Poole, an attempt to bridge the gulf between black and white audiences. They also toured overseas, Papua Niugini, for the first time, and they finally recorded their debut album.

The Arts Board gave the band a grant of $6,000 to spend in the studio. This was a pretty healthy budget by independent standards, although it wouldn't have even paid the catering bill for a contemporaneous Split Enz session. But it was money well spent, because the results are there on vinyl.

The Aboriginal Artists Agency in Sydney, with whom Candy was now also working, in tandem with the Arts Board, licensed the album for release to RCA Records. It didn't have much of a profile next to RCA's and Australia's biggest hit country album of the year, the Hawking Brothers' *One Day at a Time*, but it is a classic nonetheless. Opening with 'Streets of Fitzroy', the album contained only three other original songs, 'Tears on the Sidewalk', 'I Don't Want to be the One' and 'Just Waiting Here for You'. But even when they tackled chestnuts like 'Take Me to Your World', 'Pretty Paper' or 'Sunday Mornin' Comin' Down', the Country Outcasts retained their own distinctive flavour, an almost parched sound, given resonance by a beautifully lazy rhythm section plus Wilga's harmonies and some ringing slide guitar.

With their special fondness for the likes of Buck Owens and Merle Haggard, the Outcasts might have been trying to turn Melbourne into an antipodean Bakersfield! But the real beauty of the band, even though the album consisted largely of tearjerker ballads, was that it had a freshness and vitality very much related to its time and place.

John Stokes wrote of the band's appearance at the 1979 Adelaide Festival:

Harry Williams in striped sneakers and painter's cap, wife Wilga and the Country Outcasts continue a seemingly endless string of songs and jokes. Early settlers here found to their dismay that the Australians could mimic any sound they heard, from a dingo's howl to a Scottish brogue. Hearing the Outcasts imitate that American

nasal C&W twang, you can appreciate the settlers' alarm. But
Australia has its own country style and sound too, and the Outcasts
are real flash characters. But they still retain the same inexpressible,
unpretentious, uninhibited love of expression that circumvents
self-consciousness and leaves the senses – so neatly glad-wrapped
today by premeditated stage acts – stunned and humming with a
renewed sense of (Ab)originality.

The festival went on to Sydney in 1980 and Alice Springs in
1981, but as Candy's health started to deteriorate due to diabetes,
it lost momentum. Going to Townsville in 1982 was its last time
around. It had run its course anyway.

"We didn't do Brisbane, we done Townsville, because we
knew what Brisbane was like!" says Wilga.

Indeed, at the same time in 1982, Brisbane played host to a
Rock Against Racism gig to protest the Commonwealth Games
being held there, and it exploded into violence. It's noteworthy,
though, that the show's joint headliners, reggae-rockers No Fixed
Address and local Murri country legends Mop and the Drop-Outs,
signalled a new breadth in Aboriginal music. All of a sudden, black
bands were springing up all over the place. This was how far things
had come since the Outcasts started setting the pace just a few years
earlier.

WHEN CHARLIE PERKINS ORGANISED A HOUSE for Harry
and Wilga in Canberra they jumped at the chance. Melbourne, with
its cold and damp, was not good for Harry's health, which was already
deteriorating. They moved in 1981.

Everything seemed to be happening so fast. That same year, Wilga
enjoyed something of a homecoming to Tamworth, when the Outcasts
went to its annual festival. She and Harry were inducted into the
Hands of Fame by sticking their mitts in wet cement, and the band
recorded their second album. But at the same time things were starting
to tumble down. Back in Melbourne, Joyce Johnson died.

The Outcasts were like one of those dark stars, going supernova
before finally fading away. In 1982, they went on tour to Canada with
Top-End country-rock and gospel outfit Soft Sands, representing
Australia's Aborigines at indigenous pow-wows in Saskatchewan,
Peterborough and Curve Lake Reservation.

After they got back, in 1983, Candy died. Now an era was really coming to an end. The
Outcasts toured PNG again that year, plus the Solomon Islands and Vanuatu – and they would

ultimately visit PNG three more times – but generally after Candy's death they slowed down considerably.

Their second album is an appropriate epitaph. It came about when the owner of Hadley Records, Eric Scott, offered to record the band in his studio. With Scott as producer, sessions were organised with some of the hottest pickers in town, including pedal steel player Norm Bodkin.

Wilga remembers: "Both of us had the flu! Eric Scott said, Well, you've only got 24 hours to get better!"

One of the album's highlights is a version of the old cowboy song 'Home on the Prairie'; its other covers are two Hank Williams songs ('Kawliga' and 'Mind Your Own Business'), plus Buck Owens's 'I Don't Care', sung by Wilga (Harry had sung 'Crying Time' on the first album), and a version of the Leadbelly standard, 'Goodnight Irene'. But the record is particularly remarkable for its original songs: it offers at least two classics by Harry, 'The Ghost of the Jolly Old Swagman' and 'Blue Gums Calling Me Back Home', plus a version of 'Jackie-Jackie' that is almost definitive, and another great black Australian song called 'Heartaches COD', written by Mary Duroux. Duroux was an Aboriginal poet and songwriter from Kempsey whose 'Outcast Halfcaste' was reported to have been released as a single in the early 70s by Mick and Aileen Donovan, a duo from Eungai.

"What we wanted to do," Wilga says, "was record a lot of Harry's own material . . . but Eric Scott said no, it wouldn't go over. Australia's not ready for it, that's what they said."

And yet No Fixed Address had just appeared on *Countdown* with their militant catchcry 'We Have Survived'. Wilga still rues the opportunity that was lost: "Harry had a lot of songs, I've got a folder that thick . . ."

While the Outcasts continued a light schedule of touring – though only "until Harry got sick," as Wilga put it – they only recorded one more time, in 1984, at the behest of the Aboriginal Development Corporation. But that material – more of Harry's songs – has never seen the light of day. If there is any way it could be salvaged and released, like the Dougie Young CD, it should be.

When the Outcasts went to Tamworth for the festival in 1985 it was for the last time. It was as if their work was done. Already Roger Knox had taken 'Streets of Fitzroy' and remade it as his own 'Streets of Tamworth'. Wilga reflects:

Well, we had six kids and we done all the tours. The first year we didn't take them overseas. The next time we did. It was good, because what the kids seen they haven't got in books. Same as us – if we wasn't in the music field, we wouldn't have seen what we had. We met a lot of people, different tribes and all that, and the way we were treated was great.

Eventually Harry's deteriorating health caught up with him. "We were living in Swan Hill," remembers Wilga:

He just sort of walked up to the fence and grabbed it and said, Quick, quick! He was puffing and I thought, He's just carrying a little overweight, but the way he grabbed onto the gate, I thought, Nah, something's wrong with this fella. So I got him back down to the house and he was right the following day. Nothing again then for about . . . when we moved to Cowra. Back home, back to the mission – and that's where he started really deteriorating.

He said, I nearly passed out at the fence. He sort of never really picked up from there.

He had a pulled muscle of the heart, was what they told us. Fluid used to build up. But the way that he died was not satisfactory to any of us. Maybe it's the way he chose to go, but I'll always question it. He died in his sleep. He could have said he was sick that night. And I knew he wasn't well.

But even as sick as he was, he'd still get the guitar and play around.

When they lowered Harry into the ground, Wilga's will to sing was buried with him. She tried a couple of times, but it just wasn't the same.

Harry's final resting place in Cowra Cemetery isn't exactly in the shade of his beloved bluegums, but back in town a tree was planted in his memory.

It was the biggest funeral they've ever had in that town; they still talk about it today, black and white. At the same time they had a service in Victoria, and it was just as full.

They had the service on the mission, a real big tent they set up because the church, you wouldn't have fitted them all in a church, and then going to the cemetery from town, I sort of turned around and I was about the third or fourth car, and they were still leaving the mission. Now that's about eight kilometres, five to eight kilometres away, and the cars were still leaving the mission, you know. So that's – the police had to control the roads because there was that much traffic. It was marvellous. I never thought it would have such a big impact, but it did.

Wilga bites her lip and butts another cigarette. "We can all still feel the gap."

ଠଠଠ

Gus Williams with the Warrabri Country Bluegrass Band at the Warrabri Aboriginal Country Music Festival he organised, 1980

NAMATJIRA'S GRAMOPHONE

★ Gus Williams ★

If Herb Laughton was the spark that ignited country music in the Northern Territory, it was Gus Williams who kept the fire burning. Although not a songwriter, he was a singer, bandleader, organiser, motivator and advocate. His significance is so great, not just to country music but to all Territory Aborigines, that he was celebrated in song by no less a figure than Isaac Yamma.

"It's 1999 now," says Gus, "and I've done very well, got grandkids. I married in '58 and my children started singing when they were four, five, six. Up till now my son Warren Williams is doing really well. All my nephews, they're all musicians, Daryl Kantawara. I think the Williams family has done very well."

Gus himself has cut four albums, although he had to wait till the 90s, after he'd been gigging for twenty years, to start his recording career in earnest. Regardless of his own artistry though – and his albums reveal a sensitive, deeply-burnished singer, backed by a great band made up of his sons – it is Gus's selfless spirit that is responsible for perhaps his greatest achievement: he has applied music generally as a means of providing Aboriginal people with self-worth and meaning, as the *Centralian Advocate* once put it, "to give bored youngsters an outlet for their creativity and to deter them from turning to petrol sniffing, alcohol or drugs." In 1983 he won an Order of Australia medal for this work in the community.

"Gus is the co-ordinator who's kept it alive," says Bob Randall. "Gus used to bring guest artists here to put on the many special shows he organised, the festivals. It doesn't happen as much as it used to, it faded out in the 80s. But the Australia Council kept appointing people like Gus Williams because he did keep the music alive."

Gus will concede that he was something of an innovator – he literally electrified country music in the Centre – but his humility is unwavering. "When I talk about us laying the foundation," he says, "it's going from the remoteness of Central Australia into the city. Go back through history: Jimmy Little, Col Hardy, they were the starters for Aboriginal people round in the big cities, Auriel Andrew and the Country Outcasts, Harry and Wilga . . . Candy . . . yeah."

Gus's son Warren H. Williams is among the most prominent Aboriginal country artists in Australia today, right after Troy Cassar-Daley. After serving an apprenticeship in his father's bands, Warren recorded his first solo album, *Western Wind*, for CAAMA (Central Australian Aboriginal Media Association) in 1995, and has gone on to release a string of fine albums.

"Without Dad and Uncle Herbie, I wouldn't be doing this," says Warren in between announcing discs on his weekly CAAMA radio country music show. "He's a pioneer, him and Isaac and Herbie too, they're the first ones I ever seen play music . . . I reckon what he thought, with music you probably find a lot of peace in doing it, get away from trouble. What I found from music, it takes over when you're feeling bad, or feeling sad, takes you away and you get to some other space and time. Dad just – he loved it. It was always something in him. As soon as he'd get that guitar, well," Warren shakes his head fondly, "he's in a world of his own when he gets on a guitar."

KASPER GUS NTJALKA WILLIAMS WAS BORN at Larabuntja, just outside Alice Springs, in 1937. "My dad came from Hermannsburg," he says. "I grew up in Alice Springs because my dad was, like, looking for work. My mum came from another tribe around Tennant Creek. And then they both passed on in the 50s. So then about '52, I think, we were bought back here [to Hermannsburg], to my grandfather on my dad's side. And I grew up here."

Hermannsburg is the oldest and probably the best-known Aboriginal mission in all the Northern Territory, the place that produced painter Albert Namatjira, not to mention the famous Hermannsburg Choir. Established by Lutherans in 1877 (Germans still make up a large percentage of the tourists who visit the Centre), Hermannsburg was the only nineteenth-century mission to survive into the twentieth century. And while it was in some ways an oasis, a source of food and some sort of faith, it was also a death camp. Lawlessness and chaos were widespread during Australia's frontier period – not unlike the Wild West, in fact (another reason why it's not surprising that country music struck a chord) – Aboriginal people, entire tribes, were disappearing, dying or being massacred. Starvation, disease and alcohol claimed thousands of lives. Many people resorted to Christianity.

Namatjira, born in 1902 and destined to become not only the first great modern Aboriginal painter but also the first Aborigine universally acknowledged by white Australia, exemplifies the balancing act that was required in order to survive – up to a point, at least. Namatjira was an initiated Arrernte man but he was also a good Christian and an attentive student at the Hermannsburg school. In the 1930s, mission boss Pastor F.W. Albrecht went on holiday to Adelaide and noticed Aboriginal artefacts for sale in shops there. On his return to Hermannsburg he showed the people how to use hot fence wire to burn designs in boomerangs, as a means of generating employment and raising money for the mission. Just as he was a fine singer in the choir, Namatjira excelled at this too, and when a local policeman ordered a dozen items from him at five shillings a pop in 1932, Albert got to thinking. After a number of artists from the southern states (Violet Teague, Arthur Murch and Rex Battarbee) had visited Hermannsburg and variously given

Albert equipment (paint, brushes and paper) and lessons, Albert eagerly took to this new medium. In 1936 Battarbee included three of his watercolours in an exhibition in Adelaide; two years later Albert had his first one-man show in Melbourne – and he was an overnight sensation.

Namatjira's success was a blessing and a curse, both for himself and for Hermannsburg. His wealth bought useful material goods – artist's equipment, a gramophone, a refrigerator and a truck – to the mission, but it also brought grog.

Gus Williams was a teenager when he arrived at Hermannsburg in the early 50s. The gospel music prevalent there gave him a good grounding.

"That's how Dad started," says Warren Williams, "he was in the choir. And then – you could probably say he was a rebel – he sort of broke away and moved on to singing country music. He was the first one to do that."

"I was also at that age already working as an adult, doing things as an adult," recalled Gus.

And of course there was a lot of singing, you know, choirs in the church. A few of my great uncles were all evangelists and they all sang, and I grew up and at 17, 18, 19, I sang in the choir, the men's choir and I was lead singer.

That's when I heard the 78 records through a gramophone . . . It was really the artists that bought gramophones, that had a little bit of money from their painting and all that, and they brought in country records. It was mainly country music. I just managed to sneak over and listen to gramophones. My great cousin, Albert Namatjira, I think he was the first person, the first one to bring gramophones into the community.

And that's when I first heard it [country music] and picked up a guitar and started strumming.

We weren't allowed to sing any other songs outside the church songs. The only songs we were allowed to do in front of the white missionaries were hymns like 'Jesus Loves Me'. Wasn't most popular for us to hear or practise or sing another song outside the church circle – oh, we would have a got a flogging nearly. Which I did in the 50s, the white missionaries forced my Aboriginal church council at that time, telling them that I was singing songs outside of the church.

"There was a lot of talk," says Warren, "people at the mission saying it was evil. Like people didn't understand rock'n'roll. People didn't understand Aboriginal people singing other sorts of music." In 1959 Albert Namatjira died after serving a six-month sentence for supplying alcohol to people at Hermannsburg. It was illegal to supply alcohol to Aborigines; Albert had acquired an exemption certificate (a 'dog tag' that made him an honorary white) so he was allowed alcohol himself. Even though it was the black drinkers and not their suppliers (white publicans) who were usually punished for the crime, Albert was caught in the crossfire. He was, inevitably, too young to die, but jail killed his spirit.

Gus Williams has never let alcohol pass his lips.

BY THE 1960s, HERMANNSBURG WAS a relatively affluent community, a self-contained village only a few hours' drive from Alice with its own modern school and hospital, an airstrip and a shortwave radio link.

Given this closer contact with the outside world and the social revolution that was going on (the 'Swinging 60s'), the Lutherans had to soften their attitude to secular music. The Hermannsburg Choir, after dedicating the community's new Bethlehem Church in 1966, went on tour in 1967 to celebrate their ninetieth anniversary. The show, as captured on a memorial album recorded at Adelaide Town Hall, was a modern production boasting elaborate staging and lighting, and incorporating, as the liner notes described, "hymns, extended chorales, negro spirituals and campfire singsongs." The latter was country material performed by former boy soprano Gus Williams, complete with clap sticks accompanying his acoustic guitar. The album's liner notes went on:

> Although it is musicologically unfortunate that indigenous music has been discarded for many decades, the aboriginal adoption of European music has so amplified their musical ability and appreciation that the extended Bach chorales are admirably mastered, and are their greatest delight. This musical assimilation has bought into their homes guitars and record players, and into their new church a two-manual full-foot pedalboard electronic organ valued at $2,500.

This flood of new input only encouraged the swing away from sacred music. Gus was branching out to play to the tourist trade, which was growing rapidly with the increase in air travel. A souvenir 10-inch album called *Campfire Concert*, put out by the Sundowner Safari Tour Company, provided Gus with his second appearance on vinyl.

The album was recorded around the campfire in Palm Valley. "They used to have tents set up a few miles down the Finke River," says Gus, "and we used to go down to sing to tourists round the campfire. We mixed the songs up, country and sort of gospel songs in our language, western Arrernte dialect."

The album has echoes of the Aboriginal vaudeville shows that toured the south decades earlier. Opening with two Arrernte-language hymns sung by the girls' choir, the remaining three tracks on Side One are country tunes led by Gus with "his group of Aboriginal guitarists," as Alan Edenborough's liner notes put it. "Gus has no formal musical schooling, but has trained himself by listening to records and much practice. He is the unofficial leader of a group of guitarists at the Mission who specialise in country and western numbers."

Gus opens the set with his signature song, a lilting tune matched to Arrernte words, whose title translates as 'God Be With You Until We Meet Again'. The next song, 'I'm Moving Out', boasts "a strange blending of English words and that peculiar rhythm which seems common to all Aborigines."

After closing Side One with a version of 'My Son Calls Another Man Daddy', Side Two opens with a version, of all things, of 'Cotton Fields'! Then, after Gus leads the children's choir again on 'Showers of Blessing', the spotlight is given over, according to Edenborough, to 'Tiger':

> . . . apparently the oldest man at Hermannsburg – one of the few men on the mission who can remember life in the true tribal environment and I hope that may have a genuine Aboriginal chant or song. He rather stuns us when he begins an Arunta version of 'Silent Night'. By now the campfire is little more than ashes. Supper has been served; boiling hot cups of strong billy tea are passed around, and everyone is preparing to turn in for the night.
>
> Suddenly there is silence as Edwin calls to his people to sing what they call the Benediction Hymn. The stillness settles on the Aborigines and tourists as they gather round the fading fire. Overhead the magnificent stars form a dome and everyone feels the presence of this ancient land.
>
> As the last notes die away there is silence. The majesty of the night overwhelms all and it is a long time before anyone speaks.

Then Edenborough asks Gus if he can reprise his first song at half its original tempo:

> He tells me he isn't sure but after five minutes of strumming and humming with his group, he announces that they are willing to make a try.
>
> I record this version with the group crouched around the dying campfire. It seems to me to symbolise the Centre and its inhabitants; a lyrical, easy-going piece

of music, played with the enthusiasm of a people who love their country and their way of life.

"We got no money," says Gus, "it was really just for the enjoyment of singing, I think."

"THERE WERE FRIENDS THAT USED TO play guitar in Alice Springs," Gus remembers. "Herb Laughton, I used to watch him do it. Herb, we're still very close friends after so long, you know. But mainly, because a lot of the music I play is just by ear, I'd pick it up anywhere."

Gus had stepped up his activities by the mid-70s – he had almost enough gear to mount a fully-fledged rock concert (Gibson guitars, Marshall stacks and a PA!), and his sons were now old enough to play behind him. He was fast becoming the media spokesman for Hermannsburg. Gus coaxed Herb Laughton out of retirement and the pair joined forces to play shows – especially in remote communities, where the hunger for music was growing.

"I set up for myself in Alice," recalled Ted Egan, who arrived in the Centre around 1974, "and I was the only thing that even resembled entertainment for years. There were no bands or nothing. Gus was really the only one, he used to do his stuff, but that was at Hermannsburg, and he used to go round the bush ..."

"I was about six years old when I first started playing," laughs Warren Williams now. "Playing bass, and then guitar."

Gus and Herb got a gig going at the youth club in Alice Springs, a regular country music show with a talent quest.

"It was for the betterment of kids to grow up to be musicians," said Gus, "which some of them are doing very well now. It wasn't only our . . . We guided them, we got them on the cracked notes singing."

"Gus Williams and Herbie Laughton always organised the country music shows," remembers Frank Yamma, who started playing with *his* father Isaac around the same time, in the late 70s. "We won a trophy one time for Best Band. Everyone would come in and see the show, it was great, the place was always packed out. Everybody was just challenging each other through music."

Gus: "It was a bit slow to take off, they had to get confidence, you know. The confidence was missing. I built up confidence to teach other people too. It wasn't easy. And so then I travelled round and I taught quite a few different tribes to be musicians."

Gus trained up his own boys to form the Territory's first electric country band, the Warrabri

Country Bluegrass Band, named after the settlement where Gus had become community council president.

After taking the Warrabri Country Bluegrass Band to the third annual National Aboriginal Country Music Festival in Perth in 1978 – and finishing second in the talent quest's group section – Gus organised the first Northern Territory Aboriginal Country Music Festival in Alice Springs.

After that the festival moved to Warrabri (now renamed Ali-Curung), where it thrived for a few years. Its peak was probably 1981, when it attracted 1,200 spectators and showcased a dozen top bands, including Soft Sands, from as far north as Elcho Island. The talent quest ran in six categories – Group, Male Solo, Female Solo, Junior, Songwriter and Country-Gospel, and was open, as the entry form put it, "to any amateur or semi-professional artist of Aboriginal descent." Adjudicator Barry Thornton, legendary former Slim Dusty guitarist, was flown in courtesy of TAA. "Competing artists," the entry form went on, "will be required to perform country & western style music only."

"What Dad and Uncle Herbie went through," says Warren, "it was so hard for them in those days. Like, they didn't have the opportunity to record. If they did have the opportunity to record in those days, I reckon they would have done pretty good. Because they did a lot of good stuff, like, people wrote a lot of good stuff in those days. But they weren't given a helping hand to play it."

The following year, 1982, Gus premiered his 'new' band, Country Ebony. Country Ebony was merely a further refinement of the band Gus had always had with his sons, but it was the vehicle, with Daryl Kantawara on bass, that would take him and Warren into the realm of recording.

Yet even when CAAMA came along in the 80s, with its radio station 8KIN and the record label Imparja, it offered no support to Gus either. Perhaps it was because he was perceived to be of sufficiently independent means (in other words, he had money); perhaps it was because he didn't write his own material, didn't do 'Aboriginal songs'. Certainly, CAAMA was most interested in the new black rock bands, like Warumpi and Coloured Stone. Either way, while even Herb Laughton was recorded for the first time ever by CAAMA, Gus was left to fend for himself.

Ironically, Gus was awarded the Order of Australia in 1983 – and yet he couldn't get a record deal in his own home town! At the same time, his son Warren, as documented in Herbie Laughton's song 'Your Careless Ways', was drinking and running off the rails. Balancing his commitment to family and community with his music, Gus just made it on to record before the decade was out, releasing his first cassette album, *Storm in My Heart*, whose title track is a Herb Laughton song, on his own Ntjalka Records label.

"My style is still in the way of traditional old country," says Gus.

There are changes by young country music singers . . . I still like our style, but that's sort of phasing out slowly. But there's still a few around that's the old traditional way of playing: how to pick a guitar by thumbing, not just by plectrum like most of the fellas play today. They play the whole lot, whereas old country you just pick what strings need to be heard. There's a style in that, really.

When we started off we just sang with one guitar, then we started in our own small way getting electrical guitars and all that. The foundation is there for us now. Music followers are waiting to hear good music which can be provided by indigenous musicians.

"What Dad and Uncle Herbie did," says Warren, "without them realising it, they opened the gates for us."

"COUNTRY MUSIC IN ALICE is pretty slow now," says Gus:

Because, even a lot of Aboriginal communities, they'd rather go for rock and country-rock. Because they think in Alice Springs country music is only second grade, because lots of the top bands in Darwin and around the communities, they like to play rock'n'roll. If we have a country music festival, even if we have one side by side, country music and a rock concert, the rock band will draw more crowd than the country. We tried a few out here but we just continue doing it because of love of music.

In the 90s Gus prepared the way for his son Warren to carry on the family name. In 1991, riding on the back of their album *I'm Not Trying to Forget*, Country Ebony went to the Tamworth festival for the first time, starting a tradition that's been kept alive every year right up to the present.

"That was like a dream, I think, going one day to Tamworth," says Gus.

It's like playing in Nashville to us. Now people ring up around December asking us to go.

We travelled on our own holiday pay. And if we had tapes we'd survive on that. From there we never looked back, it just got better and better. There were a lot of obstacles in Tamworth for us. The message we were receiving from our cousins was that Tamworth wasn't for Aboriginals, it was just for them. But we never got aggressive or nasty, we just came back home, packed our swag again next year and went back again.

I remember a few times we were on stage, even my son Warren, we could see the audience after they'd had a few drinks, singing out, get the blacks off stage! We sort of felt down, you know, but after . . . comes next January, and we're packing our swags to go back again.

But for my son Warren, playing at the awards, that's gone further again. We've achieved in music, and it's really good to see our Australian cousins have really accepted us as musicians like them.

Gus and Country Ebony play Peel St, Tamworth, 1993

In 1992 Ntjalka released Gus's third album, *Straight from the Heart*, followed the next year by his gospel album, *My Kind of Heaven*, and the first stand-alone Country Ebony album, an instrumental collection called *Southern Cross*. At the same time, Country Ebony backed Shorty Ranger on his album *My Kinda Country Music*.

In 1994 Gus released his penultimate album with Country Ebony, *Through the Years*. Nine of its 14 songs were written by Slim Dusty. "I never was a songwriter," says Gus. "But I've always sung other Australian fellows, Australian songs."

In 1995 Warren Williams released *his* first solo album, of all original material, *Western Wind*. Gus has not returned to the studio since then; Warren stepped up to share the spotlight in front of Country Ebony, and went on to release *Country Friends and Me* in 1998.

"Probably when they first seen us, a lot of the white people [in Tamworth] didn't know how to take us," says Warren, "because here was this mob of people from the bush . . . But it was funny, as soon as they seen us play, it was a different thing altogether: Wow! you know – and we were playing music just like any other people. So from then on, for the last, whatever, ten years, it's been pretty good."

If Warren Williams grew up in public as a musician in the Centre, in the 90s he went to finishing school, breaking through at Tamworth and, inevitably, touring with Brian Young, as replacement for Troy Cassar-Daley in Youngie's band.

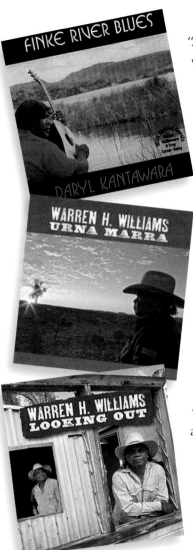

"I mean, well, it took me a long time to write a song," he says. "And then just – when I did – like, you know, it was hard to stop writing songs!"

Western Wind was an extremely accomplished debut. "There's two kinds of country," says Warren, "there's the real hardcore country – and country. Lee Kernaghan and all them, they're sort of country. But old Slim and whatever, Brian Young, they're hardcore country."

Warren is very much his father's son: his apprenticeship gave him a real head start, and now he picks up where Gus left off. His songs, scenes from black and white life in the Centre, are raw, unaffected and direct, and in the country-rock groove of *Western Wind*, they come across with an urgency that Warren has in common with Frank Yamma. Much of the album, in fact, sees Warren confessing the sins of his drinking, purging it perhaps. What it most often sounds like, remarkably, is a cross between Dobie 'Drift Away' Gray and Dire Straits.

"That's what I like about country music, because they make it so clear, I mean, listening to old Slim sing a song about – if you listen to the song 'Namatjira' or something like that – you know what he's all about, who he's singing about. That's the best thing about country music." The stories.

'Raining on the Rock', songwriter John Williamson's tribute to Albert Namatjira, has made Warren into something of a national folk hero, a practical symbol of reconciliation. When Warren first heard the song he felt it could have been written about him. That's why he asked Williamson to sing a duet with him on it. When the pair debuted before a crowd of 6,000 at Tamworth's Golden Guitar Awards in 1998, the sense of elation was palpable. "People sometimes label country music fans as being a bit redneck," Williamson told the *Sydney Morning Herald*. "But the two of us got a standing ovation. If any of my supporters don't like it, well, I don't want them."

"That song has changed my life," says Warren. "I go to big cities with that song and everyone knows it. But here at home it's more laid-back," Warren laughs, "because they knew who I was before." Looking out of the 8KIN studio's fishbowl window at Alice's dusty main drag, he smiles wryly. "They always know who I am." In other words, he can't get away with shit at home: it's the tall poppy syndrome the way it should be, cutting down pretension.

Warren refuses to forget his roots. He could probably up and chase rainbows all over Australia, desperately trying to become a country-rock star, but he remains firmly based in Alice, solid ground, where he continues to fly the flag for country music almost single-handedly. "There was one time things just got out of hand for a while, sort of rolled along too quick," says Warren alluding to his drinking days, "so I had to get back into the groove, and it just sort of slowed down."

To listen to 8KIN today is to hear R&B, hip-hop, reggae, blues, rock and pop in addition to contemporary Aboriginal music, which tends to blend all the above. Country hardly gets a look-in anymore.

"I don't think CAAMA ever got into country music," says Gus without a trace of bitterness.

They more got into rock. Not country-rock but really rock. It's only just recently that they play a few country [songs] and all that; they agreed to play country music on Thursday night with Warren Williams and also on Sunday night with Clarrie Satour. I think CAAMA mainly looked at Aboriginal songs, you know. We gave them a CD and all that but hardly heard it on air.

At least now Warren plays country occasionally on 8KIN. And if he has to, when he's asked, he'll play some of his own stuff.

"What I realised was," says Warren, "people don't really know what our country's all about, you know. Not only the white but black Australia too. Our country's so big, like the city mob don't know what we do out here. So the best way to tell it is probably through music. And I've found it easy doing that. Because I live out here and it's right in front of me."

Warren Williams is doing his old man proud.

"He'd never admit it, but he's very – he's, you know . . . Probably my generation sort of just carry on my dad's name. But if the other generation, I mean my kids' generation – if they want to do it I will help them, but I would not force them. I would let them do whatever they want to do."

☙☙☙

TRUCK-STOP SWEETHEART

★ Auriel Andrew ★

Auriel Andrew is just a tiny little thing, but she has a huge heart. She is a ball of nervous energy and, almost as importantly in terms of her projection as an artist, she has these enchanting brown eyes.

In the early 70s, when Auriel burst onto the Australian country scene as a regular on Reg Lindsay's weekly national TV show, she was one of few successful Aboriginal women in show business and a sex symbol to boot. She was drop-dead gorgeous, as the pin-up pictures prove.

Born in Darwin in 1947 but growing up around Alice Springs (her mother was Arrernte), Auriel left the Centre shortly after she turned 21 in order to pursue a professional career as a singer. Living in Adelaide, appearing regularly on TV, recording her debut album *Just for You* and gigging constantly, Auriel achieved an awful lot very quickly. She was young and she loved it – the attention, the challenge, the freedom.

The pitch of Auriel's career may have dropped since she moved east in 1974, but in a way she has become even more valuable. She has taken greater charge of her material and become the foremost interpreter of Aboriginal standards like Bob Randall's 'Brown Skin Baby' and those of other songwriters such as Herb Laughton, Harry Williams and Ted Egan.

Today, Auriel's eyes are somewhat obscured behind thick glasses. She sits in the sunroom of her home in Newcastle, NSW, chain-smoking cigarettes from a roll-up machine and joking about her advancing years and the toll they have taken on her sex appeal. She is an inveterate ham. Her humour has made her popular among children of all colours and ages. She still works in a hospital on weekday mornings.

"My husband growls at me: You never tell people about yourself," she says. "And I think it's sorta not important. But it is."

She crinkles her nose, apparently bemused, and amused, by the concept.

AURIEL'S FATHER, MERV ANDREW, was a white Australian of Cornish extraction. "Dad used to do drilling for water," Auriel remembers, "all round the Territory." Auriel's family left Darwin for Alice Springs when she was still just a baby.

It is a beautiful name, Auriel. It derives from the Latin word for golden, but the name itself just seems to sing. Auriel herself mentions an American bird, the oriole, that is red, black and gold, just like the Land Rights flag.

Alice Springs – see, our tribe is the Arrernte tribe, so Alice Springs is sort of like home. Dad's work was mainly out on the station, mining, so we were out bush most of the time. And of course Dad would never leave us in town. Because Mum was Aboriginal and he was white, he wouldn't leave us in town for the simple reason that welfare would come and take us away. Every time he had to go bush and work, he'd make sure that he took Mum and my sister Lorraine and myself, so even if it was for a couple of days, we'd go bush with him, because otherwise once he left the camp, you know, where we lived on the banks of the river, the welfare or the police would come and take the children. Especially with our colouring, we weren't black, we weren't white, we were what they used to call half-caste then. The point was a lot of kids were taken away and they weren't put into schools, they were put into homes and made to work . . . Our education – Dad would teach us. We'd sit down and do some spelling or some sums.

Then her parents broke up, and her mother met Jim Simmonds, who became 'Dad Simmo':

When Mum and Dad broke up, Dad took all the kids, but we were too little to go into St Mary's, that's the kids home . . . Lorraine was four and I was three. Faye, Clive and Rhonda went in there, so Lorraine and I were with different relations of Dad's.

My first memory of singing was when our cousin, Gladys Cartwright, and her husband took us to Mount Isa. This is before Dad gave us back to Mum. I can remember they had this old wireless, big thing, and we built this cubby-house and got inside the wireless, and Lorraine would say, Oh, I think I'll turn the wireless on now, and she'd pretend, click, and I'd start singing: "Down at the station, early in the morning . . ."

They'd stand me on the table and I'd sing 'Blackboard of My Heart'. They'd give me two bob: sing it again. And as long as they kept giving me money, I'd keep singing!

Then finally Dad gave us back to Mum. And that's when we moved over to Queensland, travelled in a little panel van all the way from Alice Springs to Mount Isa. And lived around there, Mount Isa, Cloncurry. Dad Simmo used to be a fencer, did a lot of work around that area, and in the lime quarries. Copper mines. He worked on the stations, fixed trucks, he was a jack of all trades.

Mum used to play the harmonica, or the mouth-organ we used to call it. Dad Simmo could play it, and he'd play the button-accordion. Of course we didn't have TV then. Every now and then they'd play and we'd play musical chairs, or statues.

And the old gramophone, we had Jimmy Shand, I wish we could find some of his old records. We loved him, because Dad used to play a lot of his stuff too. And another one that we listened to a lot was Winifred Atwell, 'Black and White Rag' and all that, we loved her.

Atwell was a Trinidad-born English honky-tonk pianist whose recording of 'Black and White Rag' was a huge hit in the mid-50s, and who became perhaps the most significant role model for Aboriginal women in music. She toured Australia many times, eventually settling in Sydney, and inspired not just Aboriginal pianists like Dora Hunter, Noel Wilson and Frankie Franklin but also singers like Auriel.

And of course we listened to Slim Dusty and different singers. He'd come through once a year, so if Dad had a job we'd try and save up so we could go. I remember he used to come through with a big tent, put the chairs out. Old Buddy Williams used to come through, then Reg Lindsay.

They'd pack the halls too, because we didn't have TV, and I can remember one time, we was in the old town hall and this young girl was singing and I could see myself up there. I never dreamed that I would become a singer. You think, oh yeah, I wish I could do that, but never thought it would come about.

We were out in the bush until I was 16, so I was only in town every now and then. Dad would get a job and we'd live on the banks of the old Leichhardt River. Even when the Beatles hit, I didn't get involved as much as all the other kids, because I'd only hear a bit now and then. If Dad was down in the mines I'd switch on the wireless before he got back.

When she was 14, in the early 60s, Auriel got a guitar for Christmas.

We'd just sit around the campfire with the guitar with three strings, four if you were lucky. Mum and Dad would have a party, we'd all do a couple of songs each. Someone would play the piano.

I went into a couple of talent quests in Mount Isa. Won one. I was that nervous. I was only about six stone, and I was wearing black slacks, a frilly white top and black vest. Mum used to call me Catwoman. I can't remember what I sung.

I never thought I'd be a singer. Because there was not much then for Aboriginal kids. As far as spelling goes, writing, I taught myself. The teacher in school, in my class, I was the only Aboriginal kid there, and the only time he really took any notice of me was when there was head lice inspection. It was really difficult because I couldn't read. I taught myself, and now I'm a real crossword fanatic.

On 23 January, 1967, Auriel had her first child, Sarina, in Mount Isa. She was 19. Not long after that, her mother died. The late 60s were a time of great change for Auriel, as indeed they were for the whole world.

By the time she turned 21 in October 1968, Auriel would be back in Alice Springs. By then she'd also made her first paid performance – "in Coober Pedy, at the Italian Club . . . it was just a tin shed. I still get nervous and I've performed that many times, so you can imagine what I was like then . . . I suppose the first thing you think is you're not good enough. I don't have a good voice. By gee, the confidence I've got now I wish I had then."

Auriel bundled up the infant Sarina and returned to Alice Springs to live with her natural father again. By this time, Merv was married again – to Rosaline, an African-European piano teacher.

> When Sarina was little and I still lived there, Friday and Saturday night was going-
> out night. The only bands you'd go and dance to at the pub on a Saturday night.
> There was no Aboriginal songs sung then. I remember 'Brown Skin Baby' that Uncle
> Bob Randall wrote, but that wasn't till I was in Adelaide. But in those days if you
> got up and said, this is a song about the children being taken away, people would
> say, oh, what a lot of rubbish, that never happened.
>
> They had pubs there, and they'd have a band and you'd meet everyone and party
> on and then go back to someone's place and sing. We'd sit around the campfire.
> Because in those days you didn't have clubs to go to after the hotels closed, so we'd
> go out along the road a bit and make a big campfire, all the young people, and we'd
> have a couple of guitars and we'd sit around.

By the time she was 22, Auriel was in Adelaide with a professional singing career beckoning. She had been caught on tape, so the legend goes, by an opal miner who saw her performing at Bill Amiott's Sound Lounge in Mount Isa. The self-appointed talent scout sent the tape to John Crossing in Adelaide, who arranged Auriel's television audition and went on to become her producer. Auriel left Sarina behind in Alice with her grandparents.

MOVING TO PORT LINCOLN NEAR ADELAIDE, Auriel's first television appearance was on SAS 10's *New Faces* in 1969. Within 18 months she had become a regular on TV, released her first record, an EP, and toured South Australia with Chad Morgan.

Starring on *New Faces* opened the door for Auriel.

> I went to Channel 7. The big boss there, he said to come in and sing a song, so I
> went along and I'm shaking that much. I think I know five chords on the guitar,
> and back then I knew three. So I was strumming away and singing, and he was just
> picking his fingernails, he wouldn't look at me, and I thought, oh, I've stuffed up.
> When I finished he didn't smile or anything, he just said, Come on the show next
> week! I nearly fell over.
>
> At that time it was called *The Roger Cartwell Show*, and then, not long after that,
> Johnny Mac took over. *The Johnny Mac Show*. I then went over to Channel 9 – there
> was such rivalry then – to *The Reg Lindsay Show*.

In the early 70s there might also have been an unacknowledged battle going on for the title of Australian country music capital. It wasn't until 1973, after all, that Tamworth produced its first festival proper. By that time, the Sydney scene had lost much of its former glory, while Melbourne and Adelaide each had a fair claim to pre-eminence. Melbourne was home to a new wave of Australian country that even extended to Aboriginal acts like Lionel Rose, the Kooriers and the Country Outcasts, and it had the independent record companies, like Astor and Fable. But Adelaide had the media – the TV programs that kept Auriel so busy and which reached a massive national audience.

Under the radical government of South Australian Premier Don Dunstan, Adelaide in the early 70s was creating its own cultural renaissance. Since its founding by free settlers, Adelaide had maintained a long tradition of liberalism and artiness. In the 1890s one of its most popular theatrical attractions was the glee club from Point McLeay, the nearby big Aboriginal mission.

Seventy years later, the city produced seminal 1960s bands the Masters Apprentices, the Twilights and the Zoot. In the early 70s, when the Tamworth Country Music Festival had just been launched and the Adelaide Festival was well established as the nation's premier annual arts event, Adelaide's cultural underbelly was still thriving, spawning Cold Chisel, the Angels, Redgum and Robyn Archer as well as sustaining an entire country music circuit.

"It was really big in Adelaide, really big," says Auriel. "You know, there was the two TV shows, and oh, nearly every hotel had a country music band, Thursday, Friday, Saturday nights."

Adelaide's liberal tradition assured at least the appearance of greater tolerance towards Aborigines. People from satellite centres like Point McLeay, Point Pearce and Murray Bridge all gravitated to the city, as did people from the central desert and Darwin. John Bingapore, Stan Karpany and Les Sumner were country pickers from Point McLeay, for example, who played the Adelaide circuit, leading bands like Country Freedom and Black Pearl. "Uncle Bob Randall, I met him in Adelaide," Auriel remembers. "We used to all meet in this old building and sit around and sing. That was our only experience of singing in front of people, unless you were on stage."

Most importantly, the King of Country right then was Reg Lindsay, thanks to his TV show. It was the one time this could be said of Reg; he only fleetingly stole the crown from his brother-in-law, Slim Dusty. Reg was familiar with both Adelaide people and Aborigines, having worked the stations of South Australia before he became a star in Sydney in the early 50s. He succeeded because when the travelling country roadshows were squeezed out of business in the 60s, a victim of television as much as anything, he made a successful transition to the enemy camp. And television has proven to give an instant boost to any music career.

The Reg Lindsay Show, seen all over the country, was Australian television's equivalent of the Grand Ole Opry. For Auriel to become a regular on the show was a guaranteed meal ticket. But it was more than that: it was as like joining a family, one built around Reg in the same way Johnny O'Keefe had once cultivated his own exclusive stable or Col Joye headed 'the *Bandstand* family'.

Auriel's only misgiving was that it meant being separated from her daughter.

Being on my own . . . and I had Sarina then, she was only a little baby, so I had to, you know, leave her with my daddy and my stepmother while I was trying to get somewhere, and that was difficult. I've been on tour with Brian Young, four times, around Australia and the first time I went was one month and, oh, it was the longest month. I'd get all the photos out and sit there and cry nearly every night.

In 1970 Auriel released her first EP on the Adelaide indie label Nationwide Records, produced by John Crossing and featuring the immortal 'Truck Driving Woman'. It helped that Crossing was also the musical director of *The Reg Lindsay Show*. "I was the one that added colour to the show," Auriel deadpans.

There was really only Jimmy Little and myself. I remember once Jimmy came over to Adelaide and did the show, and that was the first time I'd spoken to Jimmy. I remembered him for all those old songs, and we were so proud of him.

I just . . . got going on TV . . . when I used to go and do shows, I'd look at the house as we drove away and I used to think, the next time I see the house it's going to be all over. That's how nervous I used to get. But I'd remember, just walk in like you own the place. And so I did. I don't know, I used to think I wasn't ambitious enough. But when you think about it, I am a bit cheeky . . .

IN 1971 AURIEL WENT TO TAMWORTH for the first time, to headline at the precursor to the festival itself, the fifth annual Australia Day Country Music Jamboree.

The visit coincided with Nationwide's release of her debut album *Just for You*. Michael Hudson reviewed it in Adelaide's *Sunday Mail*: "The Darwin girl shows the talent that has made her one of the stars of the *National Country Music Hour*. Backed by the Viscounts and a sextet led by pianist John Crossing she swings her way through 'My Big Iron Skillet', switches pace for Buck Owens's slow and beautiful 'Together Again' – and maintains the variety throughout the album."

"Mainly, it was American country," says Auriel. "Because even then a lot of people didn't do Australian songs. The American stuff was good, but now I chuck in 'Blue Gums Calling Me Home', Australian songs, a lot of Uncle Herbie's stuff I do, Uncle Bob."

Just for You reflected the assertive persona Auriel had developed. Just as Auriel opens the album hiding behind the kitchen door waiting for her man, against whom she's going to wield 'My Big Iron Skillet', women in country music have long been quite the opposite of shrinking violets. In fact, from the Carter Family to Australia's McKean Sisters, women have often been at the very forefront of country music, as its pioneers and innovators. In America in the 50s and 60s it was singer-songwriters like Kitty Wells, Patsy Cline, Loretta Lynn, Dolly Parton and Tammy Wynette who first injected feminist social realism into popular culture.

In the context of the gingham and hay bales of *The Reg Lindsay Show*, it was clear that even though Auriel was – gasp! – *dark*, she was a good girl at heart. (If only they'd known she was a

'single mother' who'd deserted her daughter to chase the bright lights of show business!)

"Usually, you picked your own songs," she remembers. "You'd say, why don't we do so-and-so, and they'd say, Righty-o. They didn't tell you what to do, which was good."

Still, it was probably the lack of great original songs that let *Just for You* down. That and the somewhat stiff backing: the version of the Hank Williams standard 'I Can't Help It' is probably its swingingest track, while a trio of Wanda Jackson-like rockabilly tracks, 'Get While the Getting's Good', 'Tippy-Toeing' and 'Ride, Ride, Ride', could do with being much looser. The album nonetheless propelled Auriel into a dizzying whirl.

My very first little record was a little EP. I couldn't believe it, I'm playing a record and Auriel Andrew was singing, I'm listening to my voice. I used to work in the Riverside Hotel in Alice Springs, back in 1968, and of course Johnny Farnham was big then and his record was on the jukebox and I used to think, oh, if only I could have, you know, a record of mine on the jukebox. And when this little one came out they put it on the jukebox in the Riverside, so I was quite proud. And everyone used to play it: Oh, that's our cousin, that's our sister girl. And then of course the big LP came out, *Just For You*, and it's a lovely thing too, all the family in Alice Springs, they'd play it at a party and they'd be all dancing and then they'd all think of me and then they'd all start crying: our little sister girl, look she's a singer now – so it was lovely.

It was funny though, because sometimes people would come up and say, but you're not that dark. You could pass for someone who's just got a good tan. I'd say,

Auriel on stage in Adelaide with her part-time backing band

Yes, isn't it a pity, if only I was blacker! It's been pretty good, a few things happened along the way, but if I had the attitude, Oh gee, I'm not on this show or not on that show or not doing this because I'm Aboriginal, then I might as well have gone home and forgotten all about singing. You've got to have a positive attitude.

In any case, Auriel's schedule didn't allow much pause for reflection in 1971, once the album was out. In September she returned to Alice Springs, where she played a triumphant homecoming at the Memorial Club. In October she jetted to Perth for the Aboriginal Football Festival.

In December, the *Adelaide Advertiser* was able to declare, 'Big time beckons dusky Auriel'. "The little Chocolate Princess," it read, "has her fingers crossed about getting into the big time." Auriel now had a manager, who was talking of interest from Nashville.

Of course, it all fell apart. First, *The Reg Lindsay Show* was cancelled. Losing that security was Auriel's first stumble. Being blinded by Nashville's light was her second.

In March 1972, *TV Times* reported that Auriel's new manager, Ronda Parkin, an "Adelaide housewife and mother of three, herself a performer and writer of songs," proclaimed "I want [Auriel] to be the biggest thing in country and western in Australia, and I want her to get to Nashville and appear at the Grand Ole Opry. And I want it to happen this year."

Auriel told *Women's World* in August, "I want to show people we're not always going walkabout. We CAN stick to things. It's not often you find an Aboriginal who can't sing. We're like the Welsh – a singing people. I want to shout it to the world." Under the headline 'She's the Evonne Goolagong of Song', she told the *Advertiser*, "Aborigines have beautiful, natural singing voices. They've got something similar to the US negro – the rhythm or something like that – but Aborigines are just naturally shy. They won't make the first move."

It soon became apparent, however, that Ronda Parkin's ambitions amounted to little more than 'the dreams of the everyday housewife', to quote country prophet Glen Campbell. When Nashville's interest amounted to nothing, Auriel found herself out in the cold. She got pregnant again, and fell ill with diabetes. Her *life* was threatened, not just her career.

A LITTLE LATER, WHEN JIMMY LITTLE asked if Auriel would come to Sydney to appear with him, Vic Simms and Heathermae Reading at the special all-Aboriginal show to celebrate the opening of the Opera House in October 1973, Auriel knew she had to make the most of the opportunity. Her son Reuben would soon be born.

> I was over here for a couple of weeks. I did one show at the Opera House – it was like standing out on the plains on the stage there, it was so big, I looked back and saw the band and said, can you hear me? When they handed me the cheque, I looked at it and thought, I think they've made a mistake, this is too much. They said, no, that's right. So I said, Righty-o – and I moved straight over!

Auriel established a foothold in Sydney on Bill Kelly's country show at the Cabra-Vale RSL. She toured NSW with Jimmy Little, and in 1975 she returned to Alice Springs as part of the groundbreaking tour captured in the Film Australia documentary *Country Outcasts*, with Harry and Wilga Williams and Ted Egan.

> When I went back in 1975, Sarina was nine and Reuben was a little baby, ten months old. We went and did a tour of the Territory, even some of the settlements outside of Alice Springs, and that was the greatest experience because Harry and Wilga had never seen my country before, you know, and they just couldn't get over it. It was wonderful because I had a little baby that my family hadn't seen.
>
> I think it got a lot of young kids thinking, Gee, if Auntie Auriel is up there singing, we can do the same. We did the show at one of the parks there and it was just packed out, there was Aboriginal people everywhere, so I think they come along and thought, if they can do it, so can we. And this is what I'd like a lot of young kids to think today. You know, if someone says you can't do it, say to yourself, just watch me . . .

★ Across the Borderline ★

The colour line is much less distinctly drawn within music itself than it is in its audiences or its analysis. How country was Chuck Berry, after all (a lot); and who were those funky white dudes playing behind Aretha Franklin?

But as much as Aboriginal people have made an idol of Charley Pride (who is merely the biggest star in a long line of African-American country singers), there is arguably more kinship between black Australian music and Native American or Mexican-American music than there is with African-American music. Freddy Fender is the towering icon of Tex-Mex music, and it's uncanny the way black Australian bands have echoed his border barrio sound. It's just as uncanny how the development of Native American music and Aboriginal music seem to run parallel to one another. "It's the mirror image of us," says Roger Knox, who has toured Canadian reservations and jails. "Everything about it – the culture, the dances, the stories . . ."

Although many important American musicians are known or believed to have some Native American ancestry, including Elvis, Hank Williams, and Bo Diddley – and in the case of Chuck Berry, for example, this was proudly acknowledged – the first clearly Native American musical star, following a number of wrestlers, was 50s rock'n'roller Marvin Rainwater. The strongest Native American tradition in modern music lies somewhere between folk and country. From Buffy Sainte-Marie to Pete La Farge (whose 'Ballad of Ira Hayes' was made famous by Johnny Cash), from Jimmie Dale Gilmour to present-day singer-songwriters like Sharon Burch,

(Left) Charley Pride, African-American country star, could almost call Australia his second home he tours here so often; (right) Markeeta Little Wolf

Joanne Shenandoah and Bill Miller, Native American music has been ghettoised just like its Australian counterpart.

Australia even had a Navajo country singer of its own. Markeeta Little Wolf was the daughter of wrestler Big Chief Little Wolf, who was a big star in Australia in the 50s. Markeeta started singing professionally in Sydney at age 12, and in 1975, when she was still just 17, she released the album *Sunbird* through Festival, which showcased her powerful, gritty country-rock sound on great songs like 'Never Been a Horse that Couldn't Be Rode' ("never was a cowboy that couldn't be throwed"). When her father's health began to deteriorate, however, Markeeta Little Wolf accompanied him back to the USA in 1980. She tried to keep up her music career back in America, but found "they didn't know what to do with me." She retired from the stage to sell real estate.

"When I got to Nashville," Bill Miller has related, "publishers would say, Man, there's too much sad Indian stuff in your songs. It makes us white people feel guilty." It's a refrain that sounds eerily familiar.

❧❧❧

I think they nearly had to knock me out to put me back on the plane again. I sort of didn't want to leave Alice, but I had to continue my career.

In the late 70s Auriel worked the clubs in NSW, often as a double act with Col Hardy. In 1978 and again in 1980 she toured the outback with Brian Young. All the while, she was a stalwart of the National Aboriginal Country Music Festival, and most every January she also made the pilgrimage to Tamworth.

I used to go to Tamworth a lot. Every year. That was a great thing, because you'd see everyone you hadn't seen. You go along and go to a pub and they'd say, hey, get up and do a song. Then you'd go on to the next venue. But now it's just sort of . . . You've got big business coming in now, so you can't just walk into a hotel and have a drink and get up.

Youngie, I've been on tour with him four times altogether now, around Australia. That's an experience, because sometimes you'd sleep in the schoolrooms.

I did some bass. It was funny because Brian asked me. He always calls me Big Mama. He said, You coming on tour, Big Mama? Err, how much you paying? I said,

Auriel on stage with the Country Outcasts at the 1978 Victorian Aboriginal Country Music Festival

I said, Look, if I play bass, will you pay me such and such? He said, I'll think about it. He came back straight away and said, okay. I put the phone down and said to my husband, What am I going to do now, I can't play bass! I sat down to learn. But Youngie's stuff was good, because it was the old country stuff . . .

I've been singing for many years now and you never stop learning. Performing in different places, like with Youngie, you might be in a big, flash club one night and then singing under the gum trees the next, because he was flying around then.

In 1981, after a support spot on an Australian tour by Maori country singer Eddie Lowe, himself fresh from supporting Charley Pride, Auriel went to Tamworth to cut her second album, *Chocolate Princess*, for Ross Murphy's independent Opal Records label. Auriel remembers, "Ross said, would you be interested? So I said, Righty-o then. All American stuff. Quite a good sound."

The album was produced by Murphy and recorded with the cream of Tamworth session men, including pedal steel players Pee Wee Clark and the late Norm Bodkin, and guitarist Lindsay Butler. Kevin Knapp, compere of the annual awards, wrote the liner notes:

The first time I ever saw Auriel was on the Tamworth Town Hall stage, early 70s, for one of the 2TM Supershows. This particular one was headlined by Jimmy Little and I recall how enthusiastic Jim was about this emerging singer at the time . . . But then I lost track of AA.

Now she's back on record with a new vitality, back to TV with voluminous exuberance and back on stage, as Jazzer Smith puts it, beautiful, bouncy and bright! If I was a songwriter I think I would insist Auriel work the product.

The clarity and meaning given to words and the sell given the song is something an Andrew performance never lacks – a tribute to the Tamworth musicianship that showcases the vocal work is very much in order too. Tasteful licks and superb if short guitar soloing, passive but poignant piano, complements perfectly the rich vocal artistry. Whether it's a lullaby (Ted Egan's 'Arnhem Land'), a torch song ('Something to Forget You By') or a waltz ('Loveliest Night of the Year' – in a premiere country setting, surely?), here's a set as varied as you would want, but every title presented with a joy in the voice that's uniquely Auriel.

As producer of the album, Ross Murphy was quite satisfied with it; but in his role as head of the record company he was disappointed it didn't sell. "I always felt she was a good little singer," he says, "good entertainer, a combination of both. But who knows in this industry why one thing does well and another doesn't?" Murphy laughs and shakes his head. "Some of my best products have been absolute bombs."

Maybe it was the material. It might also have been the cover – and the title didn't help either. But the rub was in the grooves: Auriel might have been any one of dozens of experienced Australian country singers struggling to keep up with the changes the 80s seemed to be ringing in.

IN LATE 1982 AURIEL MOVED from Sydney to Newcastle, where Sarina was going to school. She continued to work as she always had – in 1983, she went on tour with Jimmy Little – but over the next few years she would finally, and most satisfyingly, channel an expression of her Aboriginality through her music.

In 1985, with CAAMA up and running in Alice Springs, Auriel returned home to release the cassette album *Mbitjana*, a collection of great black Australian country songs, and it established her as the elder stateswoman of Aboriginal music.

> The 1980s, it definitely changed for us, in a good way. Because we can sing songs like 'Brown Skin Baby' and explain the story, and you'll see people sitting there crying and saying, We never knew that happened to Aboriginal children, that they were taken away from their parents and family, even little tiny baby ones. So these songs that we are singing about our feelings, songs about Aboriginal peoples' feelings with the earth: she's our mother, she looks after us, she provides food and water and everything and we've got to look after her otherwise if she gets ill, what happens to us? We're her babies. We've got to look after her. So now songs are coming out, people are singing songs about their tribe, their grandparents, all that sort of thing and it's all being promoted, so that's good.

Mbitjana proffered a clutch of songs by Herb Laughton ('Ghan to the Alice', 'Alice Springs Waltz', 'Arunta Man's Dream', 'Old Bungalow Days' and 'Old MacDonnell Ranges') next to others by Ted Egan, Rod McCormack and Jimmy Little. But its real discovery was a song called 'Easy Going', written by Jim Ridgeway and Joan Fairbridge, the team behind 'Ticket to Nowhere'. 'Easy Going' is a great song that, as country songs love doing, turns on a double meaning in its catchphrase title: You may be an easygoing person, but it's never easy going when you have to leave your loved one . . .

Rather than playing the clubs, Auriel, was now more inclined to play, say, the Tin Sheds in Sydney, a legendary venue connected to the University of Sydney at which Radio Redfern ran regular gigs. Many people, both black and white, first heard songs like 'Brown Skin Baby' or 'Arnhem Land Lullaby' when Auriel sang them. It was Auriel who turned Bob Randall's lament into the anthem it is today; she's the one who turned people on to the true stories of Aboriginal people in song.

Then Auriel took on what she considers the two greatest challenges of her life: she got married, in 1988, and she started singing for kids.

"I was asked to sing at a school, and I thought it would be easy. But I've never been so nervous in my life. They're the toughest audience. They don't care – if you're not interesting, they'll just start talking or plaiting each other's hair, whatever . . ."

As well as guest-starring in TV soap *A Country Practice*, Auriel, like fellow country singer Colin Buchanan, has appeared on *Playschool*, and in 1995 she recorded the cassette *Let's Get Together* for the NSW Department of Education.

My greatest satisfaction is, I love singing on stage. I still get nervous but I love it. You get out there and you get going, your adrenaline is going, and also, I teach Aboriginal culture in the schools, from little weeny ones up to school teachers, right up through high school, I tell children about our culture. Singing the little Aboriginal songs and, you know, I feel like I'm giving back instead of taking, so every time I finish a show and children come up and talk and put their little arms around me and cuddle you, and so many times you have little non-Aboriginal kids coming up and saying . . . [Auriel goes into coy baby-talk] *I wish I was an Aboriginal*. Well, that makes you feel great. So that's the satisfaction.

Singing on stage and performing to children, and adults too, it's really – it makes me, it gives me a good feeling. A very good feeling.

ꙩꙩꙩ

Bob Randall at Stanwell Park on the NSW south coast, 1999

CRYING TIME

★ Bob Randall ★

G*ot to laugh to keep from crying*: it's a common adage in African-American culture. It describes equally well the Aboriginal sense of humour – the blackest humour imaginable, way beyond the gallows, in hell already.

Bob Randall has a way of telling a story, a horror story from his own life, and laughing about it – but laughing in an odd way. It has the effect of drawing his listeners in closer.

Even in his seventies, Bob still has a (brown skin) baby face, only now it is framed by an electric shock of frizzy grey hair and beard, with a cowboy hat jammed on top. A smile frequently bursts forth from this dishevelment, his brown eyes light up, pierce the atmosphere.

Bob is a rotund little fellow, almost leprechaun-like. He pulls his pants up high around his waist and wears them tucked into his cowboy boots. His somewhat dreamy demeanour belies an iron will and his hard-won talent as a communicator. For 40 years Bob has been singing, telling stories, preaching, talking, orating . . . singing his songs. He is the author of 'Brown Skin Baby', no less, the first great song of the stolen generation. He may be a diminutive figure but he casts a large shadow.

Bob is a stolen child himself, and the central theme of his work is reconciling the lives of all the world's cheated innocents and lost souls. When he finds dark comedy in the nightmare that's been a large part of his own life, there's a pattern to the stories he tells: at first he is quizzical, then bemused (he shakes his head), and then finally, it seems, relieved. He lets out a sigh and settles again into repose, crossing his hands over his tummy, staring out into the distance. And then slowly Bob's brow lifts again and his whole face lights up, as if he has finally arrived at a conclusion of child-like wonder, not at the beauty of a thing but at the reality, and the acceptance, the Christian sense of forgiveness as the only path to reconciliation and redemption.

When Bob Randall actually *preaches* – which is something he still does, in effect, any time he takes the floor – he is more grave. There's still a lightness to his delivery that keeps people hooked, but he skips the knock-out punchlines. Because he saves the stuff that *really* hurts for his songs. Sooner or later, whether he's at a lectern or in a pulpit, on a soapbox or a stage – or just sitting around at a barbeque – he will check that his guitar's in tune and start singing. And it's when Bob Randall starts singing that he cries. He straps on his old Maton acoustic with the red, black and gold Jesus fish sticker on it, and his songs are his tears.

"It was one of the means by which I was able to keep myself together after the experience of losing my family when we was on the reservation, on a place called Croker Island, or Minjilang, on the Arnhem Land reservation," he explains. "Those of us who could play and sing, we found a way of release. Some of us handled it different ways. My way of handling it was to sing the story as I refer to it, because I still do sing my songs in my workshops. People say they've never heard history told like that. It's been so successful in putting the message across about what's been happening to us."

Where he's living, south of Sydney on the coast near Wollongong, is familiar territory to Bob; it's where he spent the war years, along with all the other stolen children transported from the Northern Territory to the safe haven of Bombaderry Mission; he returned here in the 80s to teach at the university. Overlooking the ocean, he was working on his autobiography while still travelling and teaching – singing and healing. There are still flashes of the lost child, but they are infrequent now and pass quickly; Bob dismisses them and focuses on a more immediate task.

> I just know that today, you know, whatever bad experience we had, we've got to release it. Don't hold it within, share it out. That's what happened to me in our family; healing was terrific for myself and for a lot of my people because it gave them a chance of release too. And the release was enormous, you know, the relief of really letting it out with tears and anger, frustration – all that was released, you know. It's magic, it came at the right time.

IF BOB RANDALL HAD NEVER WRITTEN another song after 'Brown Skin Baby', his place in music history would still be assured. Archie Roach's 'Took the Children Away' won a Human Rights and Equal Opportunity award when it was released in 1990, a number of years before the Stolen Generation report was finally tabled in federal Parliament; but it was 'Brown Skin Baby' that first opened people's eyes, 20 years earlier.

'Brown Skin Baby' was the first song Bob Randall wrote, around 1964. Country music, with its long tradition of both sentimental mother songs and lost-child-in-the-wilderness songs, presented Bob with the ideal vehicle for his story. Legend has it that the first time he sang 'Brown Skin Baby' in public, people openly wept – and it still makes people cry.

The song has become an Australian standard almost by stealth, taking on a life of its own despite a lack of interest from the music industry; today it is sung by school choirs, opera singers, folk singers. Even though the ABC first recorded Bob singing it in 1970, it wasn't until 1978 that it was released on record, when he cut it as a track for the Aboriginal Artists Agency compilation album *The First Australians*.

The song remains so potent, such an archetypal folk-country classic, because it grew so organically out of a truth and because – for that reason – it so powerfully captured that truth; but also because its intentions were never compromised or sullied – it was only ever used as pure expression, as a salve and a protest, and not for any commercial purposes.

Bob and the song – and the truth – shot to prominence in 1970, when ABC-TV produced a documentary called *My Brown Skin Baby, They Take 'Im Away*. Introducing Bob as a "lay preacher, folk singer, a leader among his people, the half-caste Aborigines of northern Australia," the film showed him searching for his family. It was explained that because of his mixed parentage he'd been taken from his Aboriginal mother when he was a child and put in an institution. This was a shocking revelation at the time, before white people 'in the south' either accepted or were aware that such a practice had ever taken place – might

Singin' in the kitchen: Bob as he appeared at his Darwin home in the ABC-TV documentary Brown Skin Baby, *1970*

still have been taking place! – whether it was explicitly government policy or not.

"Everything in that song really happened," Bob testified in the film. "A policeman came and got me and some others I know. They split them into three church denominations."

People in the south were aghast to learn that the policy of assimilation had sunk to such ugly depths. 'Brown Skin Baby' was a flower in the dustbin of history: the song and the documentary may well have marked the beginning of the end of assimilationism.

The ABC went on to produce a follow-up film, *Mixed-Up Man*. "Who am I?" Bob asks in the title song, tapping into a universal theme, "What am I? What will happen before I die?" The film shows Bob finding his mother – but only in her grave. His mission, then, was only half-complete. Bob had found his place: he discovered that he is one of the traditional owners of Uluru (Ayers Rock), the massive rock formation in central Australia (he and his family sang at the ceremony in 1985 when it was formally handed back to them). Yet the lines that had been broken, he knew, could never properly be joined up again. Perhaps this accounts for his higher calling, and his subsequent wanderlust: Bob's personal search became his greater mission, and he redoubled his dedication to helping all the world's lost children, all the scatterlings like himself.

Bob has gone on to sing the stories of his people all round the world, creating a unique body of work that includes other such classics as 'Let Me Loose', 'My Pony Hookey', 'Red Sun, Black Moon', 'It's Time, My People', 'I'm Still Waiting' and 'Ringer's Girl'. Yet he still doesn't regard his music as anything more than a means by which to pursue his higher calling. He will go so far as to deny ownership of his single greatest hit: he believes 'Brown Skin Baby' was given to him by his long-lost mother, and that it belongs not to him but to everyone who wants to share it, which is why he never accepts royalties for it.

I never set myself up to become famous for singing my songs. That was never one of my goals. I got surprised when I realised money could be made from it. That was the first time, the ABC . . . A thousand dollars was paid my way. Money? For singing?

★ Country-Rock ★ against Racism

Rock and racism are avowed enemies; the series of Rock Against Racism concerts in Australia in the early 80s are a testament to that fact.

When the Twilights became the first Australian rock group to use a didgeridoo on record, on their 1968 *Once upon a Twilight* album, it was largely as part of their attempt to emulate *Sergeant Pepper's*. Australian rock matured immensely in the 70s, however, and in the 80s Aboriginal themes became pervasive.

The 'Aboriginal question' first entered the charts in 1976, when Ross Wilson, former leader of the very successful Daddy Cool, released the country-reggae style single 'Livin' in the Land of Oz': "And I'm livin' here because," its lyric went on, "two hundred years ago . . ." Folk-blues singer Margaret Roadknight later cut a version of the song complete with a didj part. Also released in 1976 was LA-based expatriate Australian Ray Rivamonte's *Birth of the Sun*, a remarkable country-rock concept album about his homeland. Rivamonte was a folk singer who went to America and apparently became a roadie for Delanie and Bonnie. He must have had some good connections, at least, because *Birth of the Sun* is a major-label production, complete with some of the hottest session pickers in town. With a loping sound not unlike Waylon Jennings, the album is a song-cycle in which Rivamonte paints a fond picture of his long lost past on the edge of Aboriginal Australia.

In the 80s, as multiculturalism became a buzzword, artists interested in what it means to be Australian could not avoid Aboriginality. Midnight Oil did it with a highly polished, dynamic form of pub rock. Paul Kelly did it with the acoustic singer-songwriter values of folk-country-rock, as did Shane Howard's band Goanna. Today Paul Kelly is virtually our songwriter laureate, and he's done much to build bridges – but then he's Black Irish, after all! In 1988, a number of years before he would

co-write Yothu Yindi's 'Treaty', Kelly's song 'Bicentennial' was the perfect riposte to any would-be anthem John Farnham might have trumpeted: "I have got no mind for dancing," he sang quietly, "on someone else's grave." Paul has subsequently written such songs as 'Maralinga', 'Pigeon' and 'Special Treatment'; produced Archie Roach; co-written 'From Little Things, Big Things Grow' and 'This Land Is Mine' with Kev Carmody; covered Joe Geia; been covered by Jimmy Little; collaborated with Danny Marr and Troy Cassar-Daley; and been remixed by Christine Anu. This is the criss-crossing of modern songlines that so enriches Australian music.

●●●

You've got to be joking. I love singing, no-one has to pay me to sing! And so that helped me with sending my kids to school. But that didn't come till later.

What my people call the 'kanyini' part of life, our love and responsibility of spiritual connectedness, has been stolen, we've been robbed of it, and we need to regain that . . . Which is my responsibility, just with love, you know.

I'm Pitjantjatjara, you know. Where I was born was a cattle station in the Northern Territory, south of Alice Springs, called Tempe Downs, in 1934. I'm from the Bindara nation. And from Tempe Downs I went to Angus Downs and from Angus Downs . . . A constable, Bill McKinnon, came in the policy period when they used to take children away from families whose father was white or of non-Aboriginal descent, and so from there to Alice, then from Alice Springs to Croker Island.

I found my wife's people first. Her place was at Ti Tree. The old people said, they killed a big mob of our people at Coniston. Now Coniston was just a few miles from Ti Tree, to the west, and they said you might be from there, because there was a Randall Stafford there. So my in-laws took me out to Coniston and the people who remembered the massacre told me the story, that's why I wrote that song, 'Red Sun, Black Moon'.

'Red Sun, Black Moon' is the first in a trilogy of Bob's songs that cover the Killing Times, the Stolen Generation and Reconciliation. The second, of course, is 'Brown Skin Baby', and the third is a song in the true cowboy tradition, 'The Trail Leads On'.

We went to the west, we went to the east, and then I found some family members who thought they knew who I was, that I belonged to the Liddle family. Because quite often they give you another name. And then once I knew Liddle, I found my older brother and he said, yeah, I remember when they took you away.

Bob's father, Bill Liddle, the owner of Angus Downs station, had children by four Aboriginal women. Bob has only faint memories of life at Angus Downs before he was taken, first to the Bungalow in Alice Springs, where Herb Laughton was raised.

"He was taken away on a camel, fella by the name McKinnon took him there," his sister Jean told the ABC in 1970. "The creek was there and we was on the other side, everybody cryin' and you know how they carry on, mothers and grandmothers . . ."

"Bill McKinnon knew about all of us anyway," says Bob, "because he used to visit now and again."

And so while my father, old Bill Liddle, was away, he came and took me with some other people he'd arrested for offences like spearing cattle, you know. I was taken away with some of my aunties into Alice Springs on one of his patrols. That happened about 1939, when the war just started.

It's a very traumatic thing to happen to any kid at that age, you know. That's how that song came about, 'Brown Skin Baby', that deep psychological effect it had on me, you know, such a shock that you are just numb for years and you are just doing the best you can to survive under whatever condition rises, you learn to develop skills to adjust to what's happening in the present. I think that's what kept me going, then when I was able to tell the story, I started singing.

Growing up after the Second World War on Croker Island, a Methodist mission, was alien country to Bob – it was Top End saltwater country, and he was from the desert. He remembers:

We used to play country music, we really liked the old American singers, we had 78s, the church people from the south would donate these 78s to our mission. So when I started, my influence was from the American greats in olden times, and then Herbie Laughton coming out with his guitar.

I still sing a lot of Hank Williams, it fits into the blue that's in us. The longing, the great country songs have that same longing.

We used to hear some of the TI pearlers with their guitars, but they had a different strum, they had a little vamping kind of beat, a different beat . . . when I grew up I realised it was of the ocean, the rhythm of the seas. Then Herbie turned up with very strong country, with his guitar, and he entertained us, and for the time he stayed he shared his talents and abilities with us kids. After he left, one of the older boys said, We should make a guitar, I can remember the shape. So they'd outline the shape of the guitar on brown paper.

They had this tea-chest, which was a musical instrument in itself when it was empty, it became the bass with a broom handle and a string – boom, boom, boom! Off a tea-chest, the boys cut out the guitar shape, two sides, one tea-chest would make one guitar. They stole the glue from the carpentry shop. The handle was made from the kapok tree, because it's a good wood to work with, soft. The frets were cut from the wire wrappings around boxes on the ships. The winder was made similar to the ukulele, a peg through a hole. A special wood, milk wood, because you could spit on it if it was getting too dry and loose, and it would swell and be tight again. The strings were taken from an aeroplane that had crashed during the war, an American plane. Some of us would get really flash and make a scratchplate out of turtle-shell.

On this home-made guitar everybody could play, at the reservation. The community had access to these guitars, and one person who knew something would teach the next person. Those of us who had good memories, we'd learn the songs off the 78s and teach the others, and in concerts we'd play them.

The songs we could relate to because they were story songs about sad experiences, quite often: you'd lost your horse, you'd lost your dog, you lost your girl, you lost your wife. It was similar to us. We could relate to that, because we'd lost everything. Because we had so much loss, country music gave us something we could gain. A lot of us were stockmen, see, and I remember a song I loved at the beginning, 'Old Shep', we could relate to that. That's one of the things the church taught us, you could be a stockman. We were all stockmen, we were all carpenters, we were all boat builders and mechanics, farmers, by the time you left the reservation really, you could look after anybody. I started ordering stuff through the R.M. Williams catalogue when I was 12 years of age, and they were worth a lot of money, those silk shirts and cowboy hats! But that's what you were, you was a cowboy, a ringer as we called 'em here, and of course, guitar was part of that. Sitting on a horse was part of that, having a dog was part of that, having a relationship, begin and end, was part of that.

Then some of us started to create our own songs, good fun songs that was about people everybody knew, and things that was happening, like the Christmas races, I wrote a song about that because my horse won it. Singing helped me cope, express what was in my heart, what was in my mind.

When Bob finished school at 16 in 1950, he got his first job on Croker Island, as a buffalo-shooter. But even though he was soon to marry, he still felt his life was not his own on the mission:

You used to think, there'll be a time when I'm going to walk out of this place and be free, because you're imprisoned in an institution . . . You cannot do anything you want to do when you want to do it, you are living under a system and controlled every moment of your life until you are 18 or 20.

Bob left Croker when he was in his early twenties, in the late 1950s. "I was banished because I criticised the white superintendent for nearly burning the mission. See, he lit a fire and it nearly burnt a couple of the schools down. I said, who was that stupid idiot who lit that fire? Should have had more sense, you know, to make a firebreak first. Not realising it was him who did it, and he didn't like what I said so he had me sacked" – Bob laughs – "from the job I was doing. I was a carpenter at that stage, and he me ordered off the island. That's the kind of power they had."

DARWIN IN THE 1950s, when Bob and his wife settled there, was a frontier town whose music scene was at best impromptu; nearly all the music was home made. This much it had in common with Aboriginal music in Australia's other major cities at the time, but in other ways it was very different. In the same way a port city like Liverpool could produce the Beatles as a synthesis of all the influences arriving there by ship, Australia's entire northern coastline, from Broome in the west to Queensland's Deep North, with Darwin in between, was a melting pot that threw together Aboriginal, whitefella, Islander and even some Asian influences.

Ted Egan wrote of the period in *Sitdown Up North*:

"The songs we could relate to because they were story songs about bad experiences, quite often: you'd lost your horse, you'd lost your dog, you lost your girl, you lost your wife. It was similar to us. We could relate to that, because we'd lost everything."

We would get a case and go to the wharf, or to the grandstand of the Darwin Oval. There were quite a few good musicians in Darwin, particularly among the people of Filipino-Aboriginal extraction, and invariably somebody produced a guitar. I came to learn all the old Darwin songs, most of which had their origins in the pearling industry of pre-war times. 'O Mariana' derives from, I think, the Trobriand Islands, but nobody really knows: the work songs of the pearling luggers came from anywhere in the world, and each person singing felt free to add his or her words.

Various people at singalongs in Darwin had their party pieces. I sang some of the great American favourites of the day, songs like 'Mule Train', 'Ghost Riders in the Sky', 'High Noon' and 'Cool Water'. Jaffa Ah Mat was always asked to sing his own composition, 'Old TI'. Babe Damaso's special favourite was 'Mañana' and if pressed, or pissed, or both, Babe would also demonstrate the Charleston. Cyril Ah Mat used to make up hilarious songs in pidgin English. Rusty Perez, Dolph Cubillo and Peter Cardona would lead us all in 'Goodbye to You, My Nona Mani'.

"In Darwin, everybody plays the guitar," says Bob. "You get together and the guitar comes out and you're singing. Everybody likes what you're doing so you get invited to more parties! The Mills Sisters started up at the same time I was there. I can't remember anyone who didn't play a musical instrument."

After working at the hospital and getting a diploma in educating the handicapped, Bob got a job for a while in the early 60s with one of the Territory's air services, until he returned to work at the hospital.

In those days, we were travelling round the Top End in the old DC3. Mail delivery, supply delivery and passenger carrying, and I was one of the workers on that plane. Now that song, 'Brown Skin Baby', come from when I was sitting in an aeroplane flying over Arnhem Land and . . . it was an amazing experience, how that song come to me, I refer to it as my mother's spirit came and sat beside me, you know, and she said, I got a song for you, my son, and that's when I knew who it was, you know.

It was one of many songs that I wrote in the 60s, and then performed around Darwin. You see, I used to work with a Police Boys' Club with all our kids and sitting around campfires, we'd just pass the guitar around. We were the first group, my own people and the Police Boys' Club, you see, working in that social structure. We used to look after our kids, you know, we had a pony club and we would often go out to Adelaide River Gymkhana and Katherine Gymkhana and the Darwin shows, and we'd always have a couple of guitars and then we'd sing a few songs.

When I started to think about our social status in this country and I saw the injustice and felt that – not that I didn't know it existed, I always did, but I used to get so angry about it, so I started to sing songs about that as well.

I used to play at all the folk clubs, I was the number one member of our Darwin folk club because we developed that and I was part of that, a group of us, other Australians, white Australians, we were good mates, and we did all the folk clubs. Wherever I went in the southern states, Adelaide, Melbourne, Sydney, I'd go to find out the folk clubs to sing. Groups like the Friendship Society, other organisations, the Quakers, used to fly me down to the southern states and I'd present my stuff. There was a period in the 60s when folk clubs were everywhere, everyone had a folk club.

My band I had in the 60s in Darwin had the didj and the clap sticks with the steel guitar. And a tea-chest bass! We had no amps. No amps to vamp it all up, that's all recent stuff, like the Warumpi Band, Yothu Yindi. I had three didgeridoos, because of the three chords I use which is D, C and G. And then the other thing I had was the steel guitar, the little one, the little square one because I learnt that from the TI guys, because they love that steel guitar. It fitted in with the waves, fitted in beautifully. You know, that was my little band and we only played where we were asked to and not for money, just for fun.

★ *Seven Sisters* ★

Darwin's Mills Sisters live in Tamworth, early 90s

Confusingly, there are two sets of Mills Sisters in black Australian music. Both were active during the same period, the 80s and 90s; one was from Darwin, the other from the Torres Strait. Both were made up of actual sisters, although only the Darwin quartet used their real names, and they shared similar influences – from string bands to country music to Island songs, gospel and hula jazz, carried here along the sea lanes of the pearling trade.

Darwin's June, Allyson, Barbara and Violet Mills were the four daughters of Larrakia poets and musicians Kathleen and David Mills; their great uncle was Darwin string band legend Val McGuinness. "Mum and Dad were always singing and writing songs," Allyson, or Ali, told *Vibe*. "Dad would set up a theatre stage in the loungeroom and he'd dress up in lots of crazy costumes." Their first gig proper was for the Northern Country Music Association in 1980. They sang country and gospel songs in sweet harmonies, and put their mother's poetry to music. They trod a big stage for the first time in 1982 supporting the Bushwackers and Bullamakanka. In 1987, they released their debut (cassette) album, *Arafura Pearls*, whose title track is their signature song: a country-gospel ode to inter-marriage, written by their mother, that's become a Top End anthem.

The three Mills Sisters from Thursday Island – twins Ina Titasey and Cessa Nakata, plus Rita Fell-Tyrell – first started singing publicly at the Grand Hotel on Thursday Island in the late 70s. Rita, the youngest, was the motivator. She started out wanting to be a country and western singer and got her sisters in on her gig at the Grand, along with Seaman Dan, who'd learnt guitar off none other than Val McGuinness (when they were both working at the Silver Plains cattle station on Cape York). In the book *Verandah Music*, Dan describes the melting-pot of influences they all felt: "In Torres Strait we've got Island blues, Island country, Island hula, Island jazz,

Island folk. It's all just good music to us, done Island style."

Crossing over to the mainland in the late 80s, Ina, Cessa and Rita quickly became darlings of the then-emerging world music/festival circuit, where they were dubbed the 'hula nans'. In 1993, they released their debut CD *Frangipani Land*, which contained traditional songs along with more contemporary standards like Jaffa Ah Mat's 'Old TI' and Seaman Dan's 'TI Blues'. After a second album in 1996, *Those Beautiful TI Girls*, the group broke up and Rita went solo. She released two terrific albums, *Blue Mountain*

TI's Mills Sisters at Cairns indigenous radio station 4BBM (Bumma Bippera Media), 2001, from left, Rita, DJ Marcus Smith, Cessa and Ina

(1998) and *Mata Nice* (2001), which had an almost saltwater country-rock sound, and toured the US with her band the Descendents before finally succumbing to Alzheimer's. She died in 2004, and Ina and Cessa laid the Mills Sisters to rest.

Darwin's Mills Sisters, after two volumes of *Sing Along With the Mills Sisters* in 1995, also disbanded in the late 90s. They got back together in 2002, though, and staged the Darwin Festival show *String Bands and Shake Hands*, a tribute to their uncle Val McGuinness and his music. June Mills went on to release a solo album *I'll Be the One*, in 2005; Ali's self-titled solo debut followed. "Basically this album is a thank you to my elders," Ali told *Vibe*, "for what they gave me, what they taught me in terms of song and music, laughter, joy, culture, identity and heritage. It's all in my songs. Through my songs I can say so much about my culture and our political issues. And what a wonderful way to get messages out, through storytelling and dance. We've been doing that for thousands of years, so why stop now?"

◖◖◖

Bob can't remember what the band was called. It might have been Minjaling, after Croker Island's indigenous name. But then, the existence of Robert Brown's Mystics, supposedly *the* Aboriginal band in Darwin in the 60s, cannot be verified either. Uncle Bob Randall's band, which in common with the Mills Sisters sometimes also included ukulele, epitomised the saltwater country sound.

[At first] we did ones that I could remember, Hank Williams, Jimmie Rogers. But then I started bringing in the stuff I composed myself, and they became popular, people would request them. People said, that's a good song, is it true? I'd say, yeah, that's my story. You see? They didn't know.

I was also working for my church as a counsellor for my people, because more of us was coming into Darwin from the reservations, you see, and a lot of us was getting into some sticky situations in relationships. On Croker Island you just learned to trust everybody, and a lot of our girls were absolutely gorgeous and they attracted men that I think were more users and abusers, and they had these relationships which led into terrible conflict situations, you know. And then the 60s, the late 60s, the right to drink came in, you know, which made things worse. Some relationships were very good and very successful; there were others which mixed up with the grog became very traumatic not only to our women but to the children. So I was working as a counsellor, and it was during that period I wrote a lot of the heavy emotional songs about relationships. Because when I write songs it helps me release the anger and frustration I'm feeling when I work with my people.

You know, when I had that experience of writing that song in the aeroplane flying over Arnhem Land . . . I brought it back and said, I've got a new song I want to sing. There was a lot of people at my house in Stuart Park, Darwin, and I sing and most of the adult people there walked out crying. See, it was powerful from the first day I was writing it. I was crying and writing it, it was a very strong healing song for those of us who have that experience. It really is a powerful healing song.

It isn't my song, it belongs to my people, because we've shared, it's our experience, and that's why I would never, ever receive money from anyone who performed it. The money was directed back into promoting other young composers and singers. I always wanted it to be like that because it's our story, our Aboriginal people's story of this nation.

Man, all these hidden secrets the governments were doing to our people, was made wide open through these songs.

"I WORKED AT THE DARWIN HOSPITAL," continues Bob, "you had leave and they'd pay you four weeks leave money and I saved up until I got enough to get an old car and then with that car I'd load my children up and go down south as far as I could with the money I had. And I had three, four different trips down there before I started to find my people."

In the early 70s, after Bob had traced himself back to his mother's grave at Areyonga, he

moved to Adelaide, where he was "doing these courses in sociology, you know, to become a social worker, a counsellor, and then I started to work at the Community College."

Founded in 1973, the Aboriginal Community College in Adelaide became an important focus for Aboriginal people throughout South Australia and the Northern Territory; among many other things, it encouraged such future musical talents as Buck McKenzie and Coloured Stone's Buna Lawrie.

By the time Bob was photographed singing in Adelaide at the Scots Church in 1973 – and as Bob asserts, "that's where I really started, when I went from Darwin to Adelaide" – he had abandoned the straightlaced shirt and tie of the first ABC documentary, had a groovy droopy moustache and was growing his hair out. It was a transformation like Willie Nelson's, from the modest backroom songsmith to born-again outlaw superstar. Bob was teaching at the Community College and was on the editorial board of *Identity*, regularly writing articles for the magazine; he was also writing songs and performing them regularly.

Aboriginal people in Adelaide in the mid-70s could congregate in relative safety at the Carrington Hotel. Music was encouraged at the Port Adelaide Friendship Club, and concerts staged at the Scots Church, where Leila Rankine and Val Power, graduates of the Salvation Army Band, held court. The younger generation was comprised of country singers like Bob and Gawler welfare worker Cherie Watkins, who wrote the much-quoted 'Prison's Nothing Special'. Alf Gollan and his country band Aces Wild sometimes put in an appearance too.

"In Adelaide I would sing at functions," remembers Bob. "I went and participated in the raising of awareness of our situation in Sydney."

The infamous 1971 Springbok tour of Australia unified and mobilised like-thinking blacks and whites. "I met up at that game in Sydney with Paul Coe, Billy Craigie, Billy Williams, and

I started then singing some of my songs as an opening to the addresses they gave. My cousin Charlie Perkins used to use me a lot when I was in Sydney. A place in the Cross, I'd go to the Wayside Chapel to do presentations, and I'd talk, as well, about the plight of Aboriginal people."

In 1976 Bob appeared at the first National Aboriginal Country Music Festival in Canberra. 'Brown Skin Baby', incredibly, only came third in the competition for the songwriting award, behind songs by Bobby McLeod and winner Mick Donovan. Not long after that, Bob left the Community College and Adelaide and went back to live in Alice Springs, for the first time since he'd left the Bungalow as a small child. He got a job as a director at the Central Australian Legal Service. He also kept singing, of course, leading to the release, finally, of his first (cassette) album, through CAAMA, in 1983.

In Alice, Gus Williams and Herb Laughton set the agenda. Isaac Yamma, like Bob, was still a relative newcomer at the time.

"With Gus and Herbie," says Bob, "we'd band together for presentations everywhere and anywhere. When I went back there, they were very much running competitions in communities and other places. I had my own little group called the Red Sands; we used to take out a lot of the prizes, because we were good!"

At the fourth annual Northern Territory Aboriginal Country Music Festival, held at Ali-Curung in 1981, Bob cleaned up, winning both the songwriting and country-gospel awards. It was extraordinary that over a decade after 'Brown Skin Baby' had first been recorded by the ABC, it still qualified for the competition as a 'non-contracted composition'.

Ballads by Bob Randall is a small token, barely a dozen tracks from a man who has written as many as 30 songs. It nevertheless reveals the considerable scope of Bob's artistry. One of its two traditional Arnhem Land children's songs, 'Nga Mounour', is one of its best tracks, a rollicking chant. Original songs like 'I'm Still Waiting', 'Ringer's Girl' and 'Why Are You Ashamed of Me?' see Bob convincingly singing from the point of view, perhaps, of one of those gorgeous girls from Croker Island who is left by her man, or, worse, used and abused by him.

By the time CAAMA released the cassette in 1983, however, Bob had already moved back to Darwin to work for the North Australian Aboriginal Legal Service. Before he left Darwin again to go and work at the Canberra College of Advanced Education, he served as a sort of outboard songwriter for white band True Country, with whom his sons also danced. But he never again gave music as much attention as he did in his years in Alice in the early 80s, when Alice was jumping.

From those recordings, that's where it stopped. I didn't follow through, I didn't develop a band, I suppose I could have but I preferred to work face to face in a classroom. But whenever the opportunity presents itself I sing the story.

I was in America in 1998 and, honestly, I was singing everywhere I went. The story was being listened to too. I think if I was just a politician, angry and shouting and all that, people would have just walked away.

Without a doubt, like I still perform here, wherever I go, and the story's still too new, even though it happened so long ago. A lot of the songs, a lot of people haven't heard about them because Australia is always presented as a country that was always perfect.

Bob laughs again. "These things were well hidden, you know, what I sing about. I exposed it all with the songs, isn't it amazing?" His eyes light up. "What a powerful tool, eh?"

"I'm still in the business," Bob continues, looking out at the beach from his hillside verandah. "I don't compose as much as I used to, I just seem to be overloaded with work, but I never stop writing songs. It's part of my living."

In the 1990s, Bob worked variously for the Department of Aboriginal Affairs, the University of Wollongong, the Australian National University and the Aboriginal Development Corporation; he has moved around between Canberra, Darwin and Alice Springs, as well as frequently travelling internationally. Lately he's been going to America as a guest of a group called the Healing Touch.

"I don't carry my guitar when I go overseas," he says, "but a guitar certainly springs up pretty quickly!"

For many artists their greatest hit can become a millstone around their neck as easily as it can make their reputation. Bob Randall has had to learn to live with 'Brown Skin Baby'. When he's asked to sing it, as he is always is, he'll plead, I've written other songs too, you know! But he's too gracious not to oblige, and he always puts in a controlled, heartfelt performance.

With its lilting 'Yow-a-yow-wee' chorus, tremulousness is the song's primary quality, as it is in most of Bob's music; 'Brown Skin Baby' walks a fine line between tears and total breakdown. In the middle years when Bob played it, it was as if the song was so powerful it had a mind of its own and got caught up on itself, tripped over the edge. Today Bob has taken back more control over the song, reined it in, so that now he finds more room in it for mystery and tension.

And Bob has a whole set of songs just as good, if not better.

"I still have difficulty doing it for money," he says shaking his head.

People say to me, you should charge, you should get paid for what you do, and I say, nah. It's a gift I've got from God and I'm meant to share it. And I'm only too glad to share it. It's not to make money.

I never, ever chose to follow my music career as a career itself. I've always put it on the side as a social thing that I enjoy doing. I sing for the benefit of the good feeling I have within myself, and the effect it has on others who are listening.

❧❧❧

COUNTRYMAN

★ Isaac Yamma ★

Even though he was preceded by Herb Laughton, Gus Williams and Bob Randall, Isaac Yamma is often referred to as the father, or godfather, of Central Desert music. Perhaps that's because he was a full-blood tribal man, Pitjantjatjara. Or because he bridged the gap between country and rock; or because he sold himself relentlessly but was uncompromising, singing only in (traditional) language; or because he was a magic man; or because he inspired a whole generation of musicians, not least his son Frank Yamma, the present-day Central Australian bad boy of country-blues guitar heroics (and himself a potential international superstar).

Isaac Yamma died in January 1990. He was only 50 years old. It is still criminally common for Aboriginal men to die that young of vaguely described heart complaints. Or was he sung? Such is the power of music in traditional Aboriginal society that songs could be used to kill – or, on the other hand, heal. Was Isaac Yamma perhaps sung into his grave? Certainly the restrictions on deadly spirits that usually stay in place for maybe seven years after a person's death – it is customary in traditional Aboriginal society that the deceased are not invoked by name, or image, or in any other way during this time – remained in place for much longer in Isaac's case, such was the extraordinary respect, or fear, or awe, commanded by this fella. What powerful songlines coursed through his veins?

"Poor Isaac, my old mate died," said Herb Laughton. "It's a cruel thing in Aboriginal law – now that he's dead they've stopped playin' his music. Isaac came back here and he said, Oh mate, when I'm dead and gone I wish they'd still play my songs. I said, if I'm still alive, I'll be playing your tapes all the time. He said, If you die before me, I'll still play your songs. They should be playing his songs."

"Sometimes it's hard," mumbles Frank, the family spokesman. "When people pass away they pass away, you can't bring them back to life."

Isaac Yamma's output was limited to two CAAMA cassettes and a live performance captured on the CAAMA video *Sing Loud, Play Strong*, a film of the first black rock festival in Darwin in 1988. But during the 80s, when he had his own show on CAAMA radio station 8KIN (which he used to promote himself as much as anything), and regularly busked the Todd Mall in typically ostentatious fashion, a can of beer hidden inside an empty flavoured-milk carton, Isaac Yamma was the man on whom musical tradition in the desert turned.

"He was probably the first that whitefellas recognised," says Ted Egan, "because he was such a gregarious little bloke. He wasn't . . . He had no reservations about white people, he'd come up to you and say, I'm Isaac Yamma!"

Since mourning restrictions are slowly being lifted, pictures of Isaac are beginning to emerge, even if they're sometimes hazy, like photos of a ghost, and a couple of previously unreleased tracks have trickled out on recent CAAMA compilation CDs. Frank Yamma pointed to a rare profile of his father, written by Paul Toohey for the short-lived *Independent*, as an accurate representation of him. It began:

> Even though he was never really known outside his home in Alice Springs, true stardom cannot be measured by album sales. Isaac Yamma proved this to whoever saw him. You knew he was a star because he told you he was. He dressed like a star and insisted that he be treated as one. And that's all a person ever needs to become a star. The fact that he played like one was a bonus.

Training up his boys – Hector, Frank, Peter and Paul, plus cousin Russell Yamma on drums – Isaac formed the Pitjantjatjara Country Band and developed a unique sound based on his own songs, which were written almost exclusively in the Pitjantjatjara tongue. A true black country beat from the desert, it was characterised by rollicking, twanging guitars and Isaac's towering personality. Isaac sang like no-one before or since, a laughing, crying kookaburra; it was almost like improvised talkin' blues. Isaac had a whole repertoire of whoops, yells and hollers to rival Bob Wills's immortal 'ashh-haa' trademark. He pushed together the old and the new – as if the Sex Pistols had been a Tex-Mex border band – and ignited in the 'settlement bands' that followed, from Warumpi to Yothu Yindi, a spirit not unlike the DIY ethic of the international punk movement that was happening at the same time.

These settlement bands took on more rock, reggae and other influences, but it was Isaac who provided the base. And the base for him was American country: Jim Reeves and the Hanks – Snow and Williams.

"He just picked up on the country feel early in the piece," says Bill Davis, a whitefella who lived for a long time among Pitjantjatjara and worked closely with Isaac as a sound engineer at CAAMA. Davis recalled:

> And you know, that way of talking across the top of something is something that's in Pitjantjatjara culture. Isaac would basically write a song with only a chorus and take off in a verbal description while he plunked away underneath, an extrapolation of what it was he was on about, and then he'd return to the chorus, which is like a traditional form as well . . .
>
> He picked up on what being flash was. He had a beautiful set of teeth. He never got the front ones knocked out, like most initiated men do up there. I'm not sure why that was. But he was definitely an excitement machine. He had real style and pizazz, and a laugh . . . that rang out. He was charismatic, a sort of luminary. He definitely was the one that got people going.

"Lot of people out there never heard no other Aboriginal country singer till him," says his son Frank. "He just performed. Any instrument we could pick up and play, we just try and make it sound better."

ISAAC YAMMA STARTED SINGING and playing publicly as a member of the Areyonga Desert Tigers some time around the late 60s, when he was nearly 30. He was born in 1940 by a waterhole near Docker River, in the Petermann Range near the Western Australian border. As the very first CAAMA press release and sales brochure, a photocopied ten-page booklet, read: "Isaac was born in the bush before his parents had seen white men. When he was around six years old, he went to Docker River, and after that he lived at Areyonga."

Graziers and then miners pushed Aboriginal people off their traditional lands in the Northern Territory. The tribal ways faded as people were drawn to the missions and towns for hand-outs, and the white man built outstations to keep them tethered.

Herb Laughton recalls:

When I was workin' on the roads here in Alice, I had two guitars, and Isaac Yamma was a little fella, and we had a cook on the road there, Lennie Warburton, he said, Oh, there's a young fella out there by the name of Isaac Yamma, he's mad on Jim Reeves, so I said, Well, here's an old guitar, you take it out to him. After a few weeks Isaac come into town and I showed him a few chords and that, and when he got goin' good I said, No, you go in town now, I said, you sing along, walk along the street . . . He went and done it! Singin' every day up and down, he said, it's good to have people like it. I said, Now, come back, you've got to try and make some songs in your own language, so your people understand. He said, I can't write songs. I just said for fun, Look, you know 'Three Blind Mice'? Well, you make words for that.

And so he was alright then. That was before he got married, and he had two sons then. One of his sons died, he was a guitarist, he was good, he used to chuck the guitar behind his back, and Frankie Yamma, well, him and Isaac used to come around and have a singalong, and Frank got good then and I said, you don't want to just learn country, you want to do all kinds of music. And he got going, he's a great guitarist now.

Says Frank of his father: "He showed me a real old photo of him at Areyonga, west of Alice Springs, standing with a guitar, long before I was born. He started playing a string, you know, just on a cardboard box. Then he started to pick up six-string guitar from listening to old American songs."

Isaac's father was a cameleer, and so Isaac spent much of his childhood travelling around with him; later, in the 60s, he travelled around himself as a stockman. As that very first CAAMA press release put it: "Isaac has played guitar and sang his songs in most of the territories, towns and settlements and plenty of dry creek beds in between as well."

According to Paul Toohey's account:

Somewhere along the line, somewhere in his mind, Isaac needed the clothes to match his vast ego and uncommonly out-there nature. He shopped at Don Thomas Stockman Outfitters in Alice, where he bought R.M. Williams Santa Fe boots, Long Horn jeans and mainly violent red New Breed satin shirts. When the money – and the shirt – was in town, he'd buy superior Texan-made H-C, paying up to $150 for them.

In many minds, the shirts remain long after the songs. Isaac was to some locals and passers-through a comical figure, a garish blackfella busker who had overcome the Anungu way of averting his eyes from white people and looking down in shame.

Frank: "He go round the communities and play, they used to have the Areyonga Desert Tigers back in the late 60s, early 70s, and he played with them, and they used to give a concert in the caves there. They put lights in the cave and people come to see them. I performed there when I was a kid too."

Isaac, however, didn't want to content himself with popular covers – he wanted to write his own songs, about his own experience, and he wanted to play those songs as he saw fit. He almost certainly wasn't the first contemporary Aboriginal musician to write songs in (traditional) language – both Bob Randall and Elcho Island band Soft Sands boasted the odd original song in language, and on CAAMA's 1983 compilation *Rebel Voices*, Wally Morris sings a country song in language about Alice Springs – but Isaac assumed possession of the idea. He shaped his boys into his own band even before they were in their teens, and by the start of the 80s, as Frank says, "We was a family band, solid family band."

Australia's celebrated 'rock brain of the universe', Glen A. Baker, has argued that it was the very isolation of Australian music that encouraged its mutant originality; certainly there is a lot of that in Isaac Yamma and the Pitjantjatjara Country Band, just as there is in the Loved Ones or the Missing Links.

Bill Davis remembers meeting Isaac:

We made a little performance that we recorded on a basic Superscope, at Jay Creek, in '82, and it's a pretty original version of Bobby Randall's song 'Brown Skin Baby'. Frank was about 12 or 13 then, this little prodigy playing lead guitar in the background. There was another kid there, Hector, but he got killed, you see. He was incredible, I mean, he was a better guitar-player than Frank. But he got killed in a hit and run accident.

If you listen to that recording, you'll hear a bunch of drunken people singing along in the background. And that's what it was, a drinking session and a singalong.

It was still . . . Back then, there hadn't been much music that was written in language, not written and recorded anyway – and then you can't broadcast anything if it's not recorded, so you've got to get to the point of recording. Which is easier said than done, of course.

WHEN BILL DAVIS FIRST ARRIVED among the Pitjantjatjara people in the late 60s, after finishing teacher training in Adelaide, he brought a piano with him. "The first time anybody out there had a piano," he laughed.

> I had nowhere to put it because all there was, was a caravan. It's only in the last 40 years things have gone from living in the bush to living in a house. So I dug this hole, much to the bemusement of everybody, and built this structure to house the piano. I'd sit there and play and everybody would sing, about 20 people in the hole and 40 outside . . .
>
> The big thing was hymns. It was such a traditional life, probably the main thing was religious music. There was harmony, and the idea that hymns were written in their own language was strong.

In contrast to the Hermannsburg Choir, whose Lutheran overseers largely forbade traditional practice, the Pitjantjatjara Ernabella Choir was a trail-blazing outfit, the first to sing hymns in language. (The innovative Pitjantjatjara gospel tradition flourished well into the 80s, most prominently through country-fusion artist Trevor Adamson). In the late 70s, Bill Davis was commissioned by the local council to write a choral land rights song in language; 'How Can You Buy My Grandfather' became something of an anthem. Davis also wrote a humorous tune, 'The Motor Car Song' which was another hit.

> There was a tradition of singalong. It tended to be country. Because there was this relationship that had developed with pastoralism, and that image of dress and stuff. But there was a tradition of contemporary songs in language too.
>
> When I was down in the bush there, I played with bush musicians, and we just jammed along on that basis, that funny talking-blues level that Isaac Yamma used . . . This is like whatever you could lay your hands on that made a sound. Whenever somebody had a guitar, it was mercilessly used and abused till it would eventually crumble, so no guitar anymore until another one showed up – and the same thing happened to that one!

Davis worked as administrator for the Pitjantjatjara land freeholding bodies in northern South Australia until the historic Land Rights Act was implemented in 1981, at which point he left that job and joined the fledgling CAAMA.

Founded in Alice Springs in 1980 as a radio broadcaster, CAAMA also set up a record label (and ultimately a TV station too), giving Aboriginal people in the Centre a modern media voice and encouraging an explosion of music that perhaps marked the beginning of the end of the black country tradition.

CAAMA station 8KIN was Australia's first black broadcaster – 'Aboriginal Radio in Aboriginal Country' was its slogan – and it paved the way for Aboriginal radio generally. Radio was the 80s' great connecting force, and today it is a fully fledged industry: the National Indigenous Radio Service's primary network numbers dozens of stations all round

★ *King Bands* ★

From left to right: Coloured Stone, No Fixed Address, Warumpi Band

Aboriginal music was transformed in the 1980s by three groups – No Fixed Address, Warumpi Band and Coloured Stone – who ushered in a new era of black rock and helped put an end to country's dominance. Aboriginal music exploded in their wake, giving rise to a wave of 'settlement bands' that led all the way to Yothu Yindi.

By the mid-80s almost every community in the outback had a band. A decade before, almost none of them did. Soft Sands, formed on East Arnhem Land's Elcho Island in 1971, might be the original settlement band; they used electric instruments and boldly blended country, gospel and traditional language material. But it wasn't until relatively recently – the Softies still exist – that they were heard outside their own community.

When No Fixed Address appeared on ABC-TV's *Countdown* in 1982 performing 'We Have Survived', an anthem was born and a precedent set. Warumpi Band and Coloured Stone followed in quick succession, all three bands blending country, rock and reggae to different degrees. NFA emerged from Adelaide's Centre for Aboriginal Studies in Music (CASM), which also fostered acts like Queenslander Joe Geia (who served time in NFA, too), Us Mob, Kuckles (from Broome) and Coloured Stone, whose leader Buna Lawrie, like NFA's Bart Willoughby, hailed from Ceduna, on the Great Australian Bight, where he cut his teeth covering Creedence Clearwater Revival songs. Blackfellas love Creedence.

The Warumpi Band formed at the Aboriginal outstation of Papunya, west of Alice Springs, where the acrylic dot painting movement originated in the early 70s. In late 1983, CAAMA joined forces with Sydney indie label Hot Records to release their debut single 'Jailanguru Pukarnu', a rockabilly song in traditional language that set the Australian music underground on its ear. In mid-1984, CAAMA formed its own

label, Imparja, and released a debut 45 by Coloured Stone, 'Black Boy' – it too was a seminal record. But it was Warumpi who penetrated deepest; they were also the band with the strongest country strains. Their song 'Fitzroy Crossing', which is a pure country lament, was a live favorite from the start, and 'Mulga and Spinifex Plain' was soaring country-rock worthy of the Eagles. Even 'My Island Home', before Christine Anu turned it into saltwater soul, felt like dusty landlocked country music. "The curious thing," the Melbourne *Age* said of the band, "is that what they often recall is the Tex-Mex sound, a connection the Warumpis themselves certainly haven't made and one that would intrigue musicologists."

When the Sing Loud, Play Strong black rock festival was held in Darwin in 1989, its bill, numbering no less than 26 acts from all over the Top End and central desert, reflected mostly the eclecticism that was coming to typify music in the oncoming global era. New Arnhem Land outfit Yothu Yindi had only just released its debut album *Homeland Movement*, on Mushroom Records. Initially a pub band in search of pop smarts, Yothu Yindi became the international spearhead of Aboriginal music when their recording of 'Treaty' was remixed by Melbourne DJ crew Filthy Lucre.

In the 1990s, by which time there were even Aboriginal nu metal bands starting to emerge (NoKTuRNL, for example), hardcore country was kept alive in the Territory by the Tableland Drifters, the Wild Brumbies, Daryl Kantawara, the Benning Brothers, and most prominently, Warren H. Williams. When Frank Yamma went electric, he started to sound more like Sonic Youth than Steve Earle. The country-rock-reggae hybrid that became the new standard form can now, strangely, sometimes sound as much like African highlife or township jive as Tex-Mex music. Which would be equally fascinating to musicologists.

●●●

the country, with maybe 200 more sub-outlets. John Macumba, the father of CAAMA, said in Canberra in 1980: "My people are being bombarded with western broadcasting. At the moment there are no Aboriginal people who have control over what goes on about them, or what does not go on about them . . . All that we are doing is developing our own style."

"CAAMA came along and offered the possibility of the point of expression, you know," said Bill Davis. "There was a realisation that these things could be done. Straight away CAAMA got stuck into doing recordings. It was very basic, on old Revox machines, straight on, done with the bloke sitting there in a chair. From the most scrappy resources, recorded and dubbed off onto cassettes."

CAAMA's first release was the *Desert Songs* compilation cassette in 1982. Cassettes, rather than records, were the prevailing form in the desert, given their easy portability. After the release of *Desert Songs 2* in 1983 (which again featured Isaac Yamma, Herb Laughton, and the Wingelina Choir), the Imparja label was established, and in 1984 six cassettes were released under that imprint which encapsulated the past, present and future of Aboriginal music. Along with another sampler, *Rebel Voices*, the cassettes comprised belated debuts by Herb Laughton and Bob Randall, and very timely debuts by Isaac Yamma, Warumpi Band and Coloured Stone. CAAMA went on to release tapes by bands like Ilkari Maru, Aroona and Soft Sands, defining the new direction of Aboriginal music as an equal-parts postmodern mix of country, rock, reggae, gospel and traditional influences.

"All this was rather astounding," said Davis.

People were excited and confounded and astounded and awe-struck. Suddenly, it was really clever, that this music was being converted into their language, or vice versa. And people would laugh, when they heard whatever it was in a song. People would stand stock still and listen . . . it was amazing participation. 'Jailanguru' [Warumpi's first single] is a sort of a joke too, about identifying who around the place was just out of jail . . . I remember driving around with kids in a school bus and they were singing it and pointing at people as we passed them on the footpath.

The way that bush mob listen to recordings of stuff in their own language is completely different to . . . well, no it's not: I mean, if there was a song on the radio about your family, how would you react?

THE RISE AND RISE OF ISAAC YAMMA and CAAMA go hand in hand. Isaac was more than just one of CAAMA's DJs, he was its first drawcard. He was in fact following in a venerable tradition, that of the self-promoting country singer-cum-DJ (or vice-versa), which included Waylon Jennings, Freddy Fender, and even John Laws. According to Paul Toohey:

Isaac would often make quick recordings of his own songs of an afternoon and plug them shamelessly on his Pitjantjatjara show the next morning. At the time, most of CAAMA's announcers were tribal people who read the news in language, talked between songs in language and played songs by local artists on mind-numbingly high rotation. A new cassette recording by some Central Desert artist came out of the studios once a month. Even if the songs were poorly rendered and recorded, no-one really cared. The Aboriginal community radio station was operating as both recording studio and live radio, in the manner of America's early rock'n'roll-belt stations.

Isaac lived at House No 1 at the Little Sisters camp, on the south side of the Gap in Alice Springs. Little Sisters is a sweet name for a town camp that is home to some of Alice Springs' ugliest violence. At the time Little Sisters was side by side with the CAAMA/8KIN studio. Anyone working there grew familiar with the routine. It started at eight or nine or ten p.m., with shouts and screams coming from Little Sisters. The studio, respected by all as a sanctuary, would be encircled by howls and running steps and dull thuds. Soon someone would be banging at the door. A limp body with chronic head wounds – usually a woman – would be left on CAAMA's steps. The attackers would disappear back into the night, and a radio worker would be left to deal with the near-corpse. Police and ambulance drivers got to know CAAMA staff by their first names.

Out of this mess walked Isaac Yamma, unbloodied and smiling, with his shirts pristine. Although quick-tempered and not opposed to using violence himself, Isaac was respected and feared, and usually drank in a way that at least resembled moderation. No matter how bad the night before had been, Isaac was always in the studio at five a.m. for his show. Often, he would sleep in the studio . . . With his contrived talk-show host patter and the fraudulent 'Ho ho ho' which punctuated his own and his guests' talk, whether it was funny or not, Isaac used radio and live music like no-one before him.

Frank remembers:

I hang out with the old man sometimes too, to know what he's on about in his life, and he works for his living, you know. I went to CAAMA with him, we camp there,

Jam in Alice, mid-1980s: (left) Auriel Andrew's husband Barry, Herb Laughton, Auriel; (right) Herb Laughton, Gus Williams, their eyes on Isaac Yamma, out of frame.

a caravan out the back, go inside at five o'clock in the morning, or sometimes he sleep in the studio, or sleep in the hallway. He'd get up at four o'clock to start the show . . . He'd play it all live to air.

ISAAC'S FIRST WIFE DIED when their four sons were still young, in the early 70s. He would also outlive a second wife, as well as his son Hector. Paul Toohey reported, "Isaac regularly belted his second wife, Isobel, and the boys copped it too. One day Isobel returned from hospital and received a particularly vicious public hiding. He made two of his sons watch. Three months later Isobel was dead."

Frank Yamma was born in 1968. He started playing guitar when he was five. By the age of six he could sing and play Hank Williams's 'Hey, Good Lookin'' and 'Cold, Cold Heart'. He debuted with the Pitjantjatjara Band when he was just a teenager, in the early 80s, and stepped up after his brother Hector was killed.

After playing at Western Australia's famous Seaman's Inquiry into land rights at Warburton in 1984, Frank first stepped outside his father's band in 1985, when he joined white country legend Brian Young's touring show, taking the guitarist slot left vacant by Sammy Butcher, who was by then on the road with Warumpi.

The Pitjantjatjara Country Band came back together to record a second cassette in 1987. It doubled up on a number of songs from the first album, but it was more concise.

It wasn't just the rawness and originality of Isaac Yamma's vision that made him compelling, it was his magnetism, his self-belief. Paul Toohey again:

> Isaac's success came from the fact that he could not alienate a crowd. His piercing tenor with its built-in laugh and cry modes caught everyone a little off-guard. Unlike a lot of Top End Aboriginal songwriters, who use hopeless platitudes to prop up their songs ("Modern technology killing Dreamtime survival"), Isaac's use of his own language meant he didn't steer into the realm of bullshit. Songs were stories, not complaints; he didn't miss his woman, he missed his country.

Like all great country music, Isaac's songs were at once old and new, borrowed and blue. Going a step beyond updating traditional gossip songs, Isaac translated ancient songlines into contemporary narratives. Curiously, there was something of a saltwater influence evident in his sound, right down to the occasional use of ukulele. 'Docker River Song' is based on the Fijian tune 'Isa Lei'. His signature song 'Pitjantjatjara Boy', a piece of self-aggrandisement worthy of the best gangsta rap, is set to the tune of 'Old TI'. And the refrain from Bob Randall's saltwater country classic 'Brown Skin Baby' kept cropping up in various forms.

Bill Davis: "The remark that gets made in music is repeated . . . There's a verse and chorus, so it gets repeated like a good joke and understood."

Frank recalls:

> He had papers full of songs. He'd write it down, he'd see it happening in real life, so . . . that's how life goes, so he'd write things like that, some in English, the

rest in language. It was really important to him. Performing on stage, or anywhere he like, he liked singing his traditional songs. Language stuff tells a story, what's the story about? That's stories happening in real life – so then I see things I didn't realise . . .

Yet while singing in language was a breakthrough that inspired Aborigines throughout the Territory, it limited Isaac's scope, too. Singing in Pitjantjatjara meant he was understood by a very small number of people. So while Bob Randall agrees that what Isaac did then "encouraged our people not to hesitate to sing positively in their own language to the modern musical instruments," he still also argues, "The message I give to the younger ones who are coming up now – if you sing in language, remember to put in a verse of interpretation, otherwise your market is limited, because if people don't understand what it's about, it won't sell."

Herb Laughton: "Before he died, we went down to Adelaide to record for the ABC, people wanted to air our songs for request. The manager of the studio, he put us in this hotel and he said he'd pick us up, so we were standing at the railing, Isaac had a big beard, and the traffic lights came on and there's this lot of kids in a station wagon staring at us, so I said, Have you heard Slim Dusty singing 'Trumby'? Well," Herbie laughs, "they jumped out of the car to get autographs!"

Such stories of Isaac – his power and his ego – are legion. Like the time he went to the Port Fairy Folk Festival in Victoria with Frank, Bill Davis and Ted Egan, and even though he still refused to sing in English, everyone there seemed to implicitly understand him anyway. An unmistakable wordless message was conveyed by his sheer front, after all. And then, so the story goes, when he got back to Alice, Isaac insisted on being driven on a lap of honour of the town, waving out of the bus as if it was a conquering king's homecoming – which in a way it was, even though the roads were empty of well-wishers.

Isaac injected some much-needed show into the business of country music in the Centre. Another of the tall stories surrounding him concerns the Sing Loud, Play Strong festival in Darwin in 1988, at which he apparently quieted the literally warring tribes with, again, the sheer force of his presence.

This first Darwin festival, at the same time, perhaps signalled a changing of the guard. For it was at this festival that Frank Yamma first premiered some of his solo material. After Hector was killed, the weight of expectation was transferred to Frank.

As a bandleader, Isaac was as stern as James Brown. The least indiscretion, on or off stage, invited savage reprisal. Isaac would stride on stage and stick out his left hand, and a guitar would materialise in it. One of the boys would hold his harmonica for him because he refused to wear a neck-brace. In turn, the abilities of the boys, certainly Frank, soon far outstripped their father's. Isaac always remained a three-chord wonder. But like country music at its core, he never needed any more; leave the fancy finger-pickin' to the Chets and Franks . . .

Towards the very end of the 80s it seemed perhaps as if Isaac knew he was going to die. He returned to Docker River, to reconnect with his birthplace. Yet it was still a shock when he died. Like too many Aboriginal men at too young an age, he just seemed to fade away. The official explanation – that he suffered a viral infection of the heart – is a standard euphemism for when white doctors don't understand black death. No-one will now talk about it, either way.

Paul Toohey: "After [his] death, Frank's brothers Peter and Paul got drunk and stayed drunk. Hector was already gone."

All Isaac's treasured shirts, everything, was burnt, including the photo he carried in his top pocket, of when he was a young guitarist at Areyonga. Frank was stabbed in the leg, tribal way, as part of the mourning ritual.

On the last day of January 1990, the *Centralian Advocate* ran a short obituary under the headline, 'Popular musician mourned by Alice people':

One of Central Australia's best-known Aboriginal musicians has died. Central Australian Aboriginal Media Association managing director Freda Glynn paid tribute to 'Kumantji', which in accordance with traditional Aboriginal custom is the name given to an Aboriginal person who has passed away.

Ms Glynn said that Central Australia would be a poorer place with the passing away of Kumantji. Ms Glynn paid respect to Kumantji saying he was instrumental in founding the now-healthy Aboriginal music industry. "Kumantji was a true folk musician playing and singing whenever he had the opportunity to both black and white audiences throughout Australia. His songs and spirit will live on in the hearts and minds of our people."

Isaac Yamma's spirit may live on, but it's only now that his songs are finally returning.

Frank Yamma, despite having subsequently buried his two other brothers Peter and Paul, has at least realised some of the heavy expectations imposed upon him. After the 1988 Darwin festival he formed the Ulpanyali Band, while at the same time moonlighting in the Secret Admirers, a sort of Aboriginal supergroup that toured the Territory in 1990. The Ulpanyali Band broke up in 1992, thus freeing Frank to pursue a true solo career. In 1997 he finally released his first album under his own name, *Solid Eagle*. Appropriately enough, it followed Warren Williams's debut album *Western Wind* and the Warumpi Band's 1996 comeback album *Too Much Humbug*, confirming the return of CAAMA as a record label after something of a lull following Isaac's death.

Frank's music is a strange brew: his stock in trade is driving blues-rock anthems that are as catchy as Scrap Metal. There is, then, an aspect of stadium rock, of the 'power ballad' about it – which would put Frank on a par with, say, Jimmy Barnes – but he also has more than enough country-blues roots to put his music in the same bag as, say, late Texan axe-hero Stevie Ray Vaughan. Frank is indeed an extraordinary guitarist, an unorthodox but brilliant one. It's as if he's worked out all the hard rock cliches for himself – but then there are different turns he takes, and there is a wide-open tone, characteristic of the desert, that stamps the whole as unique.

It is ironic that it could have been Aboriginal acts like Frank – and even the Warumpi Band, from the evidence of *Too Much Humbug* – who kept alive the great, and hitherto very much white, pub-circuit tradition of Oz rock, long after the lineage extended by bands like Cold Chisel, Midnight Oil and the Angels seemed all but exhausted.

"He heard my material," says Frank, referring to his father, "he knew what I was doing and he liked it. I only had about six or seven songs when he passed away. But I'll keep on continuing."

His second CD, *Playing with Fire* (recorded for CAAMA in Alice Springs with additional musicians such as bassist Jim Hilburn – of the aforementioned Angels – and European keyboardist Zeus B. Held), won the 1999 Deadly award for Album of the Year, so it seems all that's stopping Frank from attaining more widespread success is his own reluctance.

That much of his father's groundbreaking catalogue remains out of print is a cultural loss that should be rectified. Says Frank:

> If he was still alive, he'd say, play country music, so he could be lookin' down at the young ones and he'd say, Cool, no worries . . . all his nephews playin' country music, now his grand-daughter singin', that's three generations.
>
> He'd be sittin' down with a smile, proud.

Popular musician mourned by Alice people

One of Central Australia's best known Aboriginal musicians has died.

Central Australian Aboriginal Media Association managing director Freda Glynn paid tribute to "Kumantji", which in accordance with traditional Aboriginal custom, is the name give to an Aboriginal person who has passed a

Out of r
origin

●●●

THE MAN WHO WOULD BE KING

★ Roger Knox ★

Roger Knox, I think you're great,
That's what the people say.

Manny West, 'The Koori Lad', 1987

Buried deep down the back of Roger Knox's wardrobe in his cream-brick-veneer suburban home in Tamworth is a pair of cowboy boots the singer treasures above all his modest possessions. He cannot wear them. They are sacred. They are a memento of his journey to the centre of a flaming hell of death and back.

They are the boots Roger was wearing when he went down in not one but two planes on the same day, while touring with Brian Young in 1981. When he was almost burnt to death. They are charred black, flesh and leather fused, but still quite identifiably cowboy boots. The Cuban heels are stumps, and one boot was cut open so it could be removed from the wearer's foot. Roger's foot.

It was the 26th of July. "Our aircraft struck engine trouble near Oodnadatta and was forced down," says Brian Young. "Two rescue planes were sent out, and one of those ultimately crashed on take-off, killing our drummer and seriously injuring other members of the party. The remainder of the tour was cancelled, but we continued our air charters until 1984."

Kiwi drummer Ken Ramsay died on impact. Roger was dragged from the blazing wreckage by Maori country-gospel singer Stephen Bunz.

Roger was then in his early thirties, just starting to get ahead in country music. Yet while they were a major setback, the crashes, the near-death experience and his subsequent and on-going recovery, ultimately gave Roger a new and special sort of drive. As if he had been chosen. Roger connected with the spirits, and in a mix of Dreamtime and Old Testament imagery he claimed – and was granted – deliverance. "I crossed that valley twice," he said. "I was six months in hospital and two years in bed. And the pain . . . I wouldn't wish burns on anyone. I'm still going through pain. It's hard, it's hard." Roger squeezes out the words.

The wreckage of the plane crash near Oodnadatta that killed drummer Ken Ramsay (right) and seriously burnt Roger Knox, July 1981

Even though his injuries meant he could no longer play guitar, within a couple of years Roger had released his debut album with the Euraba Band, the classic *Give It a Go*, and for the guts of the 80s he would reign supreme as the King of Koori Country, an adopted Tamworth denizen who became something of a thorn in the side of Australia's self-proclaimed country music capital.

Roger had never played bass until he joined Brian Young's band. Sure, he played guitar – he was a good guitarist – and he'd always sung, from when he was just a little fella back on the mission at Toomelah, near Moree on the Queensland border. But he had to teach himself to play bass to go out with Youngie, and as shy as Roger was, it was an opportunity he couldn't let pass.

Brian Young was practically the last country star to make the outback rounds (although he remained earthbound after the mid-80s). At the time, Roger had to be able to sing *and* play bass for the same reason Auriel Andrew did when she went out with Youngie a year earlier – there was only room on the plane for one more person.

"He seen me in a couple of shows in Tamworth," Roger says. "I didn't have any expectations even then towards the music business. What persuaded me to go with him was that at the time I was down really bad with bronchial asthma." (Roger still wheezes, so it's quite a wonder how he manages to sing).

He said I should get some help, so that's why I took off with him.

I came home and then I went out again. I said, let's get serious – and that's when I had the plane crash, see, and I can't play guitar no more. And it's still holdin' me back now. Because I have trouble with me legs swelling up if I stand too long, ache, and me back and hands, I need more surgery on me hands. It's still very hard even today for travelling, all the burns.

DYING IN AN AIR CRASH IS, of course, a long music tradition, from Glenn Miller to Stevie Ray Vaughan. To paraphrase Waylon Jennings, it's just one of the hazards of life in a hillbilly band, rather than one of the pleasures. Plane crashes have claimed country stars like Patsy Cline, Jim Reeves and Ricky Nelson. And Waylon Jennings only lived as long as he did – and always felt some guilt about it – because he gave up his seat on the plane that went down with Buddy Holly, Richie Valens and the Big Bopper on board.

"I did three months touring with Brian," says Roger.

Up through the Top End, the Territory, through North Queensland, up through Bamaga, the islands and the west, the Kimberleys, right up – a lot of outback communities, you know, mining towns. And I really enjoyed that . . . just seeing these places and performing to these people who really liked music. Out in the desert, they know what they want!

So then we came home, and we were heading out for another four months or so. We went to Walgett and then to Bourke and then we were heading out to Oodnadatta. We cross Lake Eyre, we develop engine trouble. I was co-pilot at the time, I was sitting next to the pilot and he said, we're in trouble, we have to land. I think there was eight people behind me and I opened the door and I said, hey, we're going to crash [*laughs*]. Caused a big panic. So we got down, you know, we actually got down on a sort of a little bush track, it was pretty rough but we got out of it. It was about 10:30 that morning. We were there all day waiting to be rescued.

I think it was about one or two o'clock, a plane came over, spotted us. It was about 5:30, just before sundown, there was four of us left and we had to finish putting the equipment into this rescue plane to get to Oodnadatta to do the show that night – we were concerned about doing this show, see. And by the time we got all packed and ready to go, it was just after dark. We took off and what seemed to me like ages we were in the air, total darkness. I remember speaking to Ken Ramsay who was behind me – I was sitting next to the pilot – I remember saying to Ken, how do we know whether we are flying upside-down or if it's level or what, like that, and I turned around and when I turned around I seen the ground, because there was a light on the front of the plane and it must have hit the ground, I seen the ground coming up at me at a great speed, and that's all I remember waking up, waking up in the plane, fire, my foot was trapped, I couldn't get out. There was myself, the pilot, Ken Ramsay and Stephen Bunz.

I don't know what happened. All of a sudden I shot out, but I was well alight. Stephen Bunz seen me, he caught me and put me on the ground and put the flames out. That's how I burnt me hands – trying to put me clothes out like that. And I remember saying, Ken's in there, we have to get him out, you know, there was huge orange flames leaping up into the sky – and that's pretty much all I remember until waking up in Oodnadatta, you know, then getting on a plane and going to Adelaide, waking up some three or four days after that in hospital.

ROGER CAME BACK FROM THE DEAD because, he says, "I believe I have a strong spirit in me, a Dreamtime spirit, some force is there stronger than we are."

From the moment Roger stepped back into the ring, unsteady on his scorched, spindly legs, his hands still bandaged, everything just seemed to fall into place, even if he was still not overly confident or ambitious. The myths that grew matched the theory, as they do: "You know, surviving two plane crashes in the one day," Vic Simms shakes his head, "being declared dead and having the sheet over his head and all of a sudden a tear rolls out of his eyes, and they say, He's alive! He's alive! And he's brought back this wonderful music."

Recovering at Toomelah, the elder women sang to him, Roger recalls, and rubbed the balm of the 'eura' bush on his body, anointing him.

I walked away from there and I was supposed to go back to the doctor, have more operations. I never go back to see any doctor. I felt I was good, you know, I was getting back into music and from there I got my band and we started to perform, and we called ourselves Euraba.

There was now a fire burning deep within Roger, driving him beyond his previous frame of reference. He had the aura. Overnight he became the heir apparent, and once Harry and Wilga Williams pulled out of the Tamworth festival, well, it was as if they were handing it over to Roger, abdicating in his favour. And indeed, all of a sudden everyone seemed to defer to Roger as the new leader of the pack.

Although Roger wasn't himself a songwriter, and Euraba hadn't yet paid any real dues, they were the hottest act in all of Australian country from the moment *Give It a Go* was released in January 1984. Roger was messianic, his sound seemed to completely naturally to him – a soft, warm, unaffected, unadorned true Koori country sound.

Says Troy Cassar-Daley: "Roger Knox was a big influence on my life because we first saw him when we were relatively young. His son Buddy was playing guitar, he had his other boys in the band as well, and I think he sort of made it a bit more contemporary and accessible, because he was almost like this black Elvis we had, you know! He was slick, he sang deadly, and just had so much charisma, you couldn't help like him."

Says Roger: "We called ourselves Euraba, it was my auntie who give me that name, because Euraba was the first Aboriginal settlement in that north-west area, where my father was born. The name was associated with the eura bush too, associated with healing. So that's why we call it healing music – music is a form of medicine. It soothes your mind, soothes your soul."

In order to ease his own pain, Roger had to give to others. And his gift is song.

ROGER KNOX WAS BORN IN 1948 at Toomelah, one of nine children. His father was a cotton-pickin' drunk, his mother a stolen child, his grandmother a church worker. For Aboriginal people, some missions were relatively commodious, others were 'mongrels'. Toomelah was a mongrel. The settlement was the subject of an official inquiry as recently as 1987, following racial tension that erupted when 19 Toomelah people were arrested in nearby Goondiwindi after a mass brawl with local whites. It was revealed as massively overcrowded, with 80 percent unemployment; it provided no garbage collection, was supplied with water for only half an hour a day, and there was sewage collecting in open ponds.

"Growing up in Toomelah, wow . . . we were sort of segregated from everybody," Roger remembers.

White people weren't allowed to come in and we weren't allowed to go out . . .

See, my mother was a stolen child, she was taken away from her mother, from a little camp in Moree. All these things affect us in a lot of different ways . . . My father was an alcoholic. In those days, early mission days, alcoholism was just startin'. I seen that, and it didn't do me any good. I was around my grandmother a lot and she also helped alcoholics, because she was living in Bogabilla, which is just nine miles from Toomelah, and if those old fellas were caught in town after dark . . . ! So she would put 'em up in the shed. I still have a fear of the police today. But I seen what I can do too, if I can help people. Well, that's been my downfall, I've helped too many people and I don't help myself! But I believe there will come a time . . .

The only music I knew growing up on the mission was gospel music, Slim Dusty and gospel. See, because my grandmother, she was a missionary and, you know, everything was centred around gospel music, and we looked forward to that, you know, because we could sit around singing, singing gospel songs. Then came people like Slim Dusty, I know all of his songs. I learned them not from the radio but from other people singing them.

There was all me cousins and uncles and people who play guitar and who'd sing, you know, and I'd sit around listening to them. And they were brilliant musicians.

★ Tamworth Outlaws ★

In November 1981, just a few months after Roger Knox's plane crash, hot young Tamworth pickers Glenn Green and Eric Newton were killed in a car accident on the way home from a gig. Newton, the son of Slim 'Redback on the Toilet Seat' Newton, had been planning to open his own recording studio.

His brother Steve carried on the dream, however, and in March 1983, Enrec opened its doors, beginning a period in which it became synonymous with Koori country. "We never intended to do *just* Aboriginal stuff," remembers Ed Matzenik, a picker, producer and publicist who teamed up with Newton, "but it was the Aboriginal stuff that started selling."

"Koories just didn't feel comfortable doing business with white people in a lot of places. Once a few had recorded at Enrec it became the place to come to – and they came from everywhere!"

Other Tamworth studios-cum-labels like Hydra and Big Wheel dabbled in Aboriginal acts (Bill Wellington, Kevin Gunn, Moonie Atkinson), but Enrec was the one with legs. With Roger Knox and Euraba as its flagship attraction, Enrec's catalogue eventually numbered more than a hundred releases, including the seminal *Koori Classics* series of cassettes, featuring such acts as Mop and the Drop-Outs, Sarina Andrew, Moonie Atkinson, Manny West, Sharon Mann, Bill Wellington, Tracey Lee Gray, Johnny Huckle, Vic Simms, Mac Silva and others.

Ed Matzenik mastering the first Koori Classic *tape*

'Moonie' Atkinson, who disappeared the day he finished his album at Enrec and never even returned to pick up a copy

In 1987 Bobby McLeod went into the studio with house guitarist Mick Liber and drummer Randall Wilson. Enrec released the single 'Friendship Road' but, as Ed Matzenik said, "We'd do things like . . . We'd do singles, so we'd get airplay, but then we wouldn't have enough money to do an album, so we had nothing to sell." McLeod's long-overdue debut *Culture Up Front* eventually came out on Warren Fahey's Larrikin label.

Sharon Mann was the odd one out in Enrec's firmament. She wasn't a local – she was from Rockhampton in north Queensland, an Islander woman unusually untouched by saltwater rhythms, and she produced two solo albums around the turn into the 90s, *Reach Out* and *My Home in Joskeleigh*. But when her songwriting partner, politician and morals crusader Keith Wright, got caught up in a sex scandal, her career seemed to decline along with his.

By the early 90s, with the bottom dropping out of their country product, Enrec's saving grace was didgeridooist Mark Atkins. Finally, that wasn't enough either, and the label went into retirement. Its last release, Charlie Wilson's *Fighting Back*, trickled out in 1995. Steve Newton kept the studio alive, however, and forged a long partnership with modern bush balladeer John Williamson, and also went on to produce Warren H. Williams. A good selection of tracks from Enrec's *Koori Classics* series are now available as downloads online.

◗◗◗

I remember sitting around listening to the old fellas play the accordion, in the old days, foot-stompin', hand-clappin' stuff. I grew up with that.

One of me cousins, Charlie Duncan, taught me to play the guitar. I also give my grandmother credit for teaching me about gospel music and singing. That's why I did a gospel album. Well, it's the best thing I did vocal-wise. I'm not a Christian, you know, but I have a belief in divine power, fulfilment of divine prophecy . . . I credit her for givin' me the courage and strength to know where I'm going rather than fall down and then look for a way out.

When Roger was 15, in the early 60s, he left Toomelah to go to Tamworth.

I only moved here because of work, that's the only reason. One of my relations was working here on a tobacco farm at a place called Moore Creek. And he'd asked me to come down and work with him.

In my teenage years I wanted to be either a footballer or a fighter. I didn't have any ambitions or dreams to be a musician. I just sang me songs because people asked me to sing.

The first time I'd seen a live band . . . of a weekend we'd go out to Joe McGuire's Pub, see people like Geoff Brown. That was the first band that I seen perform and it just freaked me out. And they encouraged me to get up and sing.

In the 60s, before Tamworth christened itself the country music capital, when John Minson was only just establishing his *Hoedown* show on 2TM, Geoff Brown was the local artist who opened the town up to live country music. Today, Joe McGuire's Pub is a sacred site in Tamworth, although these days bands only play there during the festival.

"They used to come in on Friday and Saturday nights," Geoff Brown remembers. "They were playing guitars, and he used to get up and sing."

"It was an all-white audience," remembers

Roger not long after starting performing again, 1983. Note bandaged hand. Troy Cassar-Daley: "He was almost like this black Elvis we had, you know! He was slick, he sang deadly, and just had so much charisma, you couldn't help but like him."

Roger. "The band was all-white. Just going to town was something . . . I don't know how I did it, I just got up there and sang an old song. Then everybody started jumping up and clapping. I was shocked. I was really scared, but then when I saw this happen, I thought, Wow, I must be doing it right."

"He was just himself," said Brown, "he had a great voice, and charisma, Jimmy Little-like charisma. People loved him."

Roger: "You know what inspired me? People like Harry Williams. I seen him perform, and a fella like Col Hardy — it was 1971 I saw Col Hardy perform in Tamworth — I seen 'em perform before an all-white audience and I saw what they could do to an all-white audience, and I thought, Wow, that's fantastic, I can do that too. It took those black men for me to see."

In 1979 Roger entered the festival's Starmaker Quest. He finished in the Top 20. He entered again in 1980 and finished in the Top 10.

"I still didn't have any, you know, great desire to do this, but I liked doing it. So each time I did it I felt good. It's just that . . . people like Brian Young, he came and spotted me and I went out on the road with him."

The road, in fact, that led to the plane crash that purged Roger of a certain diffidence — fear, even — and instilled in him an absolute, if as yet unstated, sense of purpose.

"Music, like here in our communities," he says, "it's all about inspiration."

It's all about, you know, lifting each other up to reach these heights, to go from there, to continue on. And that's all it's about. If we can give each other a lift up, I mean, we can depend on other people to lift us up . . . [that's the] way it happens, from way back up until now. It happened to me. I was inspired and if I can inspire someone, they could do it and maybe as time goes on, it will be easier for these people, you know, being an Aboriginal person.

That's what we don't have, see, leaders who aren't in love with publicity and money. Leaders who are prepared to suffer and to bleed. Leaders who are prepared to die.

ROGER SPENT THREE MONTHS IN HOSPITAL in Adelaide after the accident, before being transferred to Tamworth Base Hospital. He left there early in 1982 in a wheelchair, and spent the rest of the year prostrate at Toomelah.

I had nightmares — I saw the fire. I was on heavy drugs for the pain. I was going crazy . . . then one night [a vision of] Ken appeared in front of me, looking really good, and he just looked down at me and left . . . after that I settled down.

I went back to Toomelah and my old great auntie was there . . . As a child growing up, no matter what sort of illness we had, or burns or cuts, she would fix us up. And when I went back, she rubbed this oil, goanna oil, on me. And I went from the wheelchair to crutches. She would give me something to chew on, she didn't tell me what it was. At this time I was on painkillers, and so what I did, I just quit all that, I went cold turkey, and I don't know what she was giving me but I seemed to get over the pain. The pain was still there but I could deal with it better, because she was humming or chanting while she was rubbing, you know, rubbing this stuff on me. Then she boiled this stuff, it was called the eura bush, it would be a real browny, purply tan; the water, you know, smelt like eucalyptus, and what she did was she poured it in an old bath and I would sit in it and soak in it. While she was rubbing, she was singing, like chanting, and I think that healed part of my mind, you know. I threw away the walking stick and, you know, got back on my feet again. I started to walk.

I did heal but during that 18-month period I also lost my mother, my father and 21-year-old sister. What helped me keep going was music. I realised I was in search of a particular feel to my music. I wanted to sing songs that linked awe and wonder with something more spiritual, like Woody Guthrie's lyrics and feelings mixed with the manner of the Dreamtime.

THIS WAS THE EPIPHANY that Roger experienced: he had to find his own sound, a true Koori country sound, and in order to do that he needed his own band. He knew he had to inject some of his own blood into his music.

The first step was teaching his son Buddy to play guitar. Today Buddy Knox is one of the tastiest guitar pickers in all Australia, a fella who looks something like a young Muddy Waters and who, as well as serving as his father's right-hand man, has toured with Warumpi Band and freelanced on other sessions.

"I used to play with other bands," says Roger, "but I felt better and I felt I could do more with my own band."

I was going through a lot of pain but I was still singing, and then I introduced my son, Buddy, to the band – like, to music – to play the guitar. And then I got another son Gene, Gene was only about 12 or 13, and that's how I introduced my family to music. And right up until today we still do it, you know, Buddy plays lead, I have John and Ruben, Ruben plays bass, John plays rhythm, and Gene plays the drums. So, you know, it's a family thing.

To me, it seems to work because we are family and, like, the family situation was a part of our culture. When we are together we know what time we are doing, know how we do it. And not necessarily with too many words.

At first, before Roger's other boys were old enough, Euraba coalesced around Buddy, guitarist Harold Brown (a veteran Aboriginal picker who taught Buddy more than a few tricks) and the three Graham brothers, Steven, George and Robert. Soon enough, the Graham boys would be replaced by Michael Knox, on bass, and whitefella drummer Randall Wilson, who produced *Give It a Go*.

Give It a Go began to coalesce when Roger first started walking again in 1983. He went

Roger and Euraba around the release of the first album: (top) Buddy Knox, the three Graham brothers; (below) Harold Brown, Roger Knox.

to see Steve Newton and Ed Matzenik, who had just opened Enrec Studios. Matzenik was a refugee from 60s rock'n'roll – an original member, in fact, of seminal Sydney surf instrumental outfit the Atlantics, of 'Bombora' fame. Steve Newton currently plays bass with and produces country legend John Williamson.

"Originally when Enrec got going it was in my house," remembers Randall Wilson. "I was out the front one day just working in the garden and this Aboriginal bloke came up and said, I need to talk to the guys from this new studio. I said, go inside."

Roger: "It just happened that, you know, we started recording that album, it was in Randall Wilson's old house in Darling Street, we did the whole recording on a four-track machine. That's how I first got into recording, not because I wanted to, you know, make millions and sell millions but because I was inspired by people, I felt I could inspire people too, Aboriginal people, and build it like this."

"He just came up one day and said, you know, he wanted to make an album," says Ed Matzenik.

"He had most of the songs already. He had a few songs with Koori content, but he didn't know whether he should do them; he said, they won't like it, they won't play it on 2TM. We said, Oh, do them! If they hate you, that's great, otherwise you'll just be one in the crowd anyway, so we encouraged that side of it . . . And then when it was finished we put it out ourselves."

Give It a Go was recorded over a couple of months with additional musicians including Newton and Mick Liber on guitars (Liber was another refugee from 60s rock'n'roll, who had played alongside Rod Stewart in Python Lee Jackson), hired hand Lawrie Minson (son of John) on dobro and harmonica, and Pixie Jenkins on fiddle. The inaugural album on the Enrec label, *Give It a Go* came out just in time for the 1984 Tamworth festival. It was an instant classic. Roger appeared at McGuire's and broke the house record.

Coming in on the back of Johnny Marshall's didgeridoo, *Give It a Go* opened with 'Blackman's Stories', a terrific opener written by Queensland whitefella country artist Buddy Weston. After recasting Harry Williams's 'Streets of Old Fitzroy' as 'Streets of Tamworth' (while still giving credit where it was due, to Harry), Side One closed out with definitive versions of Jimmy Little's 'Black Tracker' and 'Koorie Rose', one of the great black country love songs, also written by a whitefella, Merv Lowry. In the early 70s, Lowry had been the guitarist in Les and Joy Keats's band the Country Styles, who occasionally backed up Lionel Rose on live gigs, and 'Koorie Rose' originally came out as the B side of his 1979 solo single on Bullet Records, 'Truckies'.

Side Two opens with another song by Harry Williams, 'Blue Gums Calling Me Back Home', followed by another Jimmy Little song, 'Australia Down Under'. The centrepiece of the side is a version of Dennis Conlon's 'controversial' 'Our Reserves'. The album even gives vitality and passion to chestnuts like 'If You Love Me (Let Me Know)', Larry Gatlin's 'Help Me' (so widely adopted as to be virtually an Aboriginal standard) and 'Bridge over Troubled Water' – all nods to gospel roots.

Give It a Go struck a chord among Aboriginal people everywhere, and it also registered with a hip young urban audience which was tuning in to what *Rolling Stone* described as 'a watershed year' for black Australian music. "Some country singers are just milk bar cowboys," Bob Hudson said in the *National Times*; "Roger Knox is the real thing."

The Euraba revue went on a tour of eastern Australia, toting guest stars Ken Copeland, complete with quiff and shades, and songstress Sarina Andrew, daughter of Auriel. "Roger

Knox is an amiable mountain of a man with huge, strong hands that testify to a life of work," said a story for the *Age* in Melbourne. "Yet his singing voice is light and sweet, and on *Give It a Go* he renders sensitively songs that deal with peculiarly Aboriginal feelings. 'I believe music is a good way of making people understand one another', the singer says. 'If I'm black and I walk on stage, when we start the music we're all the same, and we can communicate'."

In January 1985, on the eve of the Golden Guitars in Tamworth, the *Moree Champion* claimed Roger Knox and John Williamson as its joint favourite sons and crowed, 'Moree artists thrill':

> Both black and white Moree entertainers are this week dominating the annual country and western festival in Tamworth. In the tradition of Woody Guthrie and Robeson, Roger Knox is a spokesman for his people in a gentle but firm manner, yet at the same time offers a universal appeal, with an impressive sincerity and simplicity.

Williamson was nominated in a number of categories at the 1985 Tammies, Roger in two – Best New Talent and Australian Heritage. Williamson scored one little trophy, his first, the APRA Song of the Year for 'Queen in the Sport of Kings'. Roger was beaten out for New Talent by Vic Lanyon, and for the heritage award by Reg Poole. Neither Lanyon nor Poole could ever really hold a candle to Roger Knox.

Roger wasn't perturbed. "We done all right to get into there with that old recording we did . . . you put it up against some million dollar recording people, so I reckon we did all right." Certainly, everyone involved in the album will still boast it was "the best thing anyone ever did with a quarter-inch four-track!"

"You see, people get you and tend to tokenise you," says Roger, "and I don't like that. When white people talk about integration, they mean tokenism. Tokenism benefits only a few. I could do it but I would feel not right in me. It would be just for myself and not encouraging or supporting others."

IN THE MID-80s, Roger and Euraba were as hot as anything in Australian country. The big record companies were still desperately seeking new Slim Dustys, and John Williamson came closer to what they wanted than James Blundell. Tamworth was becoming increasingly powerful and, inevitably, more conservative. It was only a handful of acts – like the Three Chord Wonders, the Flying Emus, and Roger and Euraba – who brightened up the annual pilgrimage to Tamworth.

Following up *Give It a Go*, in 1985 Roger released *The Gospel Album*, fulfilling a lifelong goal. Shortly after that Enrec released what would become the first in a series of *Koori Classics* cassettes that very much grew out of the court that now surrounded Roger.

As Randall Wilson put it, Roger was "the godfather and the ambassador." Everyone, whitefellas included, said Roger could have been a star, should have been a star. But it was the likes of Williamson, Blundell and Graeme Connors who would define the slick, nostalgic direction that Tamworth took.

★ Big Mac ★

When Mac Silva died in 1989, Redfern lost its musical linchpin. His passing, closely followed by the deaths of Isaac Yamma (in early 1990), Dougie Young and Harry Williams (both in 1991), signalled that an era was drawing to a close.

When Malcolm Silva first arrived in Sydney in the mid-60s, he took over the direction of the loose house band at the Foundation for Aboriginal Affairs from Candy Williams, christening it the Silver Linings (as in 'Every cloud has a . . .'). By the early 70s the band was known as Black Lace, referring not only to the chains once clamped around Aboriginal men's necks but also to the sprawling social network from which the band drew its ever-shifting membership. With Mac on drums and vocals (when he wasn't moonlighting with the Country Outcasts, or when Bettie Fisher or Syvanna Doolan weren't guest-singing), Black Lace's sound was country-rock with a Latin tinge, like Creedence crossed with Santana. It was a joyous, liberating sound, and into the 80s Black Lace were stalwarts of both the National Country Music Festival and Rock Against Racism.

Mac enjoyed one last hurrah in 1988, releasing his first recordings. He went to Tamworth to contribute a definitive version of 'Malabar Mansion', the great song about Long Bay Jail, to volume 4 of the *Koori Classics* cassette compilation series, *The Aboriginal Prison Song Collection*. Written by whitefella Dave Duncan and first cut by Gordon Parsons, 'Malabar Mansion' has long been claimed as one of their own by Aboriginal people. Also in 1988, Maya Records released Black Lace's only single, 'Deaths in Custody', written by poet Frank Doolan. The record's unsigned sleeve notes could be read as Mac's epitaph: "The future must be linked to the past by the living bonds of experience. The voice of the suffering past must not go unheeded. We must seek to share our knowledge or else we will build up barriers and illusions – the great illusion of separateness. All life is one, and he who wishes to save his own soul shall lose it."

●●●

The Gospel Album might not have been the shrewdest move commercially – like bluegrass, gospel is hard to sell even in the country market – but at a time when Roger's promise seemed unlimited, he felt it was appropriate to acknowledge an important part of his past before moving on.

"My biggest dream before anything was to do a gospel album for my grandmother," says Roger, "because it was her who inspired me to go for direction, you know, and not to fall off or to be, you know, get tricked. I wanted to pay her back somehow."

Roger doesn't wrestle with Christianity; rather, he uses of it what he needs. "I heard just recently about Dr Martin Luther King [saying], God gave us minds for thinking and bodies for working – he would be defeating his own purpose who committed to achieving through prayer what may come through hard work and intelligence."

With its set of old standards such as 'Put Your Hand in the Hand', *The Gospel Album* bears comparison to Elvis's inspirational recordings. Was this, then, singing for release from bondage? "Well, I think the soul goes back," says Roger. "Like, I grew up with it, see. You couldn't sing a song you don't feel good with, you wouldn't attempt it. To me, gospel also talked about . . . the struggles . . . If you don't feel right, you know, look to God and he will make you feel right."

The idea for Enrec's *Koori Classics* arose after Roger covered 'Our Reserves' on *Give It a Go*. It started out as some sort of cultural exchange between Tamworth and Brisbane. Dennis Conlon's Mop and the Drop-Outs came down with Angus Rabbit Jnr to go into the studio, and together with Roger, Sarina, Euraba and two other Tamworth-based black pickers, Manny West and Moonie Atkinson, they made up the cast of the album, which was a curious collection of 50s rock'n'roll, Murri country and weird covers like 'I Just Called to Say I Love You'.

In May 1985 Roger and whole Enrec crew returned the favour and went to Brisbane for a big show with Mop and the Drop-Outs and Charlie Bobongi, Cashmere, Barbara Little and Margaret Drahms. Mop and the Drop-Outs returned to Tamworth on numerous occasions. "When they first came down, Mop and the Drop-Outs were quite a big band in Brisbane," says Randall Wilson, "and they actually taught us a lot more about what's going on, the more topical things – they're the ones who bought down 'Malabar Mansion', some of those things, 'Tonight I'll Get Out of this Place'. . ."

"When the first *Koori Classics* came out," remembers Ed Matzenik, "we had an album launch, and it was booked for one of the pubs, and then they mysteriously cancelled it. You get so many mysterious cancellations . . . all the time. Any band gets cancellations, [but] Koori bands get ten or twenty times as many. Like, we broke the bar record at McGuire's, but they wouldn't put the show on the following year. Now, why wouldn't you put a show on that breaks your bar record?"

As Euraba became blacker – not only in its line-up, but its sound and its audience – it was met with racist resistance from fearful publicans.

Ed Matzenik: "You book a gig with a Koori band. You run around trying to rustle up the gear, then you run around trying to rustle up the musicians. Everything's difficult. Then, if

the publican doesn't mysteriously cancel, everyone's late, and everything breaks down. It's all a nightmare – and what's the performance like? Absolute magic!"

Euraba developed a natural feel and sound that was at once classic and unique.

"Obviously the didgeridoo is the first cliche," says Matzenik, trying to define the Koori sound. "Lots of spongy rhythm guitars . . . that's one thing. Another thing is, they can all tune drumkits. You can go into tin sheds out back of Alice Springs and if there's a drumkit in there covered in dust, you can hit it and it sounds good. And all the lead singers should sound like Elvis!"

Roger points out some of the double standards they were met with:

Like 'Our Reserves' . . . Some people say that's controversial, if they want to play it on radio. And yet, you know, you have fellas like Peter Garrett who can sing songs like 'Beds Are Burning' which is pretty much the same thing, but that's acceptable.

Like John Williamson, he talks about pioneer days, and you know, pioneer days to me, they weren't good days as far as we're concerned!

You get stopped at certain doors. You do. And you say, why? Aren't I good enough to do this? Of course I'm good enough. Just as good as anyone. I'm equal to anyone. The only thing I'm above is drugs and alcohol. I operate on total reality.

THE CHANGING OF THE GUARD can be pinpointed almost exactly. It was 1986, when two separate Aboriginal events were organised at the annual festival, one by Harry and Wilga Williams, the other by the newly convened Tamworth Koori Kountry Music Association.

The year before, in 1985, Col Hardy had put on a show at Tamworth's Regent Cinema featuring himself, Roger, Auriel Andrew and Euraba. In 1986, Harry and Wilga put on a talent quest at the town hall, but its impact paled in comparison to the week of events that had been planned by the TKKMA. Harry Williams would never again appear in Tamworth.

The TKKMA was a short-lived body but it had a strong motivating impact on Roger Knox particularly. With Sydney Aboriginal activist, author and one-time Silver Linings member James Wilson-Miller as president and Heather Perryman as secretary, the TKKMA, making use of a $4,000 grant, staged a carnival and evening concert/beauty pageant at the Tamworth Country Centre on the first Saturday of the 1986 festival, and on the second Saturday a showcase gig at St Andrew's Hall starring Roger and Euraba, Mop and the Drop-Outs, Manny

West, Sarina Andrew, James Miller and whitefella Keith Blinman. As the TKKMA's eventual report to the Australia Council noted, the show was "equal to any big-name event."

The TKKMA had the field to itself the following year, 1987, when they organised an Aboriginal talent quest and concert over two nights at the town hall. Roger and the band headlined the showcase Sunday night gig with Bobby McLeod, Sarina, Alice Springs country-gospeller Trevor Adamson, Western Australian 'piano man' Frankie Franklin, Jimmy Knox (Roger's cousin, who led Rick and Thel's band, the all-Aboriginal Country Shades), Keith Blinman, Vicki Slater and Johnny Marshall.

Enrec mounted its own showcase at the Locomotive Hotel, featuring talent both black and white. The big crossover, as they say in country music circles, was Roger. "In those days," as Heather Perryman says, "he was something pretty special."

It was not just that Roger was a black star rising; it was also that Euraba were musicians' musicians. The high regard they were held in can be gauged by the reception they got in 1987 at the Steel Jam, a regular festival feature celebrating the pedal steel guitar. *Capital Country News* reported on Euraba's performance with Harold Brown:

> Harold set up on a stage littered with thousands of dollars' worth of expensive 'knitting machines'. He had the most beat-up looking lap steel and he had a medicine bottle for a slide. But he wrought as pleasing a tone from his instrument as anyone else and showed that there is no substitute for playing from the heart. He won the respect of the musicians, and the crowd in general showed their feelings with a standing ovation.

Buoyed by the apparent groundswell of interest in Aboriginal artists, Enrec applied to the Bicentennial Authority for a grant to record more releases in the *Koori Classics* series. They were knocked back at first, but Ed Matzenik, a clever media manipulator, brewed up a storm in the Tamworth papers. 'Bicentennial snub!' they shouted. Having enlisted the support of Tamworth's own bicentennial committee (although conspicuously not the Capital Country Music Association or any other part of the festival establishment), Enrec were eventually awarded $20,000 by the NSW Bicentennial Authority's Aboriginal and Torres Strait Islander Program. Enrec stretched that money out to make six full albums, featuring no less than twenty Aboriginal acts.

Dennis 'Mop' Conlon of the Drop-Outs (top) and James Wilson-Miller, writer and president of the short-lived Tamworth Koori Kountry Music Association.

★ *Murri Country* ★

The Deep North may be the spiritual home of indigenous jazz, blues and soul, but in the rest of the sunshine state the country is drier and the music is country. In Brisbane today, radio station 4AAA is perhaps unique in the world with a format that's country and black at the same time.

Murri country developed into a distinctive strain as a result of the oppressive atmosphere in Queensland – the political climate as well as the tropical heat. Even white Brisbane bands like the Saints and the Go-Betweens were forced underground, and eventually into exile. There was black country in the north too (on Palm Island especially), but it was the disproportionately high number of singers and pickers from Cherbourg, the biggest and oldest Aboriginal reserve in the state, who led the Murri country charge. Cherbourg, just 200 km northwest of Brisbane, had previously produced Harold Blair; it was also home to Angus Rabbit, the Meredith brothers Dudley and Paul (who went on to form the Kooriers), Les Collins, Micky and Dennis 'Mop' Conlon, and Angus Rabbit Jnr.

Steel guitarist Darcy Cummins, from Cunnamulla in western Queensland, moved to Brisbane where he led the Ravens in the 60s. When the Ravens broke up, he formed the Opals (not to be confused with Sydney's earlier Opals starring Col Hardy and Freddie Little); the Brisbane Opals played the 'Open Door' dances Cummins organised for OPAL, the One People of Australia League. When they broke up, it was Mop and Micky Conlon's Magpies who took over the top perch in town. The Magpies started out doing covers like 'Wasted Days, Wasted Nights'. When they hired halls in the late 1970s and put on dances, they shared bills with punk bands like Razar – and Bjelke-Petersen's task force didn't know who to bust first! Mop then started to turn out disarming original songs like 'Don't Give In' and 'Brisbane Blacks'. After appearing at the famous Rock Against Racism gig to protest the Brisbane Commonwealth Games in 1982 and releasing a single on local indie label Sunset Records the same year, the renamed Mop and the Drop-Outs were the definitive Murri country travelling sideshow; they also became a mainstay of Enrec's late-80s *Koori Classics* family in Tamworth. "We just wanted to get up and put our statement in our music," said Mop. "Not putting anybody down. Just the way it was."

●●●

With typical bluster, Matzenik told the *Northern Daily Leader*: "The biggest thing the grant will do is enable us to sell Koori music as a movement rather than as individual albums . . . Koori music will now become a style. We can go to America and say, do you want to become the first company to release Koori music, rather than just say, Do you want to release this album?"

It was indeed a grand vision, but one that would clash with reality and, like Brian Young's plane with Roger in the co-pilot's seat, come crashing to the ground.

IN 1988 THE TKKMA again staged a show at the Tamworth festival that was headlined by Roger, but this time it was boycotted by some local Aborigines as a protest against the bicentennial celebrations. It was an inauspicious start to the year.

Enrec's subsequent release of four more *Koori Classics* cassettes diffused rather than concentrated Roger and Euraba's momentum. Roger may have been guided by spirits, but by the turn of the decade the Euraba juggernaut was faltering.

"It's difficult selling anything in Tamworth if you don't go through the established channels," says Randall Wilson. "If you don't take that path, you're pushing uphill at the best of times, it doesn't matter if you're black or white. They think dollars and cents [in Tamworth], and if it's got anything to do with actual music, they're confused. It doesn't fit into their agenda."

"The other thing is," says Ed Matzenik, "a lot of these things were financed by the Aboriginal Arts Board. But they would never . . . you know, there's an old adage in the record business, you've got to cut it when it's hot. And it would take them years to make their mind up. It would just be some dopey academic, sitting there reading a letter that's full of buzzwords like 'community' and all those . . . if it sounds politically correct, they'll give them the money – ten years after they're too burnt out to use it!"

If Roger was supposed to be the spearhead for a movement that might sweep the world, he seemed more intent on playing to neglected Aboriginal audiences. In April 1988, Roger and Euraba kicked off their first tour of the Northern Territory with a triumphant gig at the Alice Springs swimming pool, a Rock Against Grog outing with settlement band Ilkari Maru. After that they stepped up their commitment to playing prisons, banding together with Vic Simms, Mac Silva and Bobby McLeod (who had just recorded his debut album at Enrec).

For three years running, from 1985 to 1987, Roger celebrated his birthday in a jail. In 1989, after a proposed tour of Ireland fell through, he and Euraba played 24 shows with the assistance of the Office of Aboriginal Affairs, 22 in prisons and two at juvenile detention centres.

After Mac Silva died in 1989, Roger formed an even stronger bond with Vic and Bobby, and even though, unlike them, he had always been a non-drinker and had never served time, he too became a role model for Aboriginal inmates. In 1990 all three men, along with Euraba, would go to North America, not to mount a Koori country invasion so much as to tour neglected Canadian jails and remote Indian reservations.

"Well, I believe we're less than 3 percent of the population outside, but inside we're 50 to

60 percent," says Roger. "But I don't believe black people are criminals, they are victims of crime. In there because they did something under the influence, or against their own kind. I feel a lot of those people, once they get in there, they think that nobody cares about them, and I give them a feeling of, you know, being worth something."

THE APPALLING STATISTICS OF ABORIGINAL deaths in custody were symptomatic of a cycle of oppression, alcoholism and incarceration that blighted the lives of young black Australian men.

The issue first came to the attention of a broader Australian public in 1982, when, to widespread horror, Malcolm Smith died at Long Bay after driving one of his paintbrushes into his eye. The media followed the funeral parade. Later that year, 19-year-old Ricci Vincenti, on remand at Canning Vale Prison while awaiting trial for allegedly stealing groceries, was killed by a warder's bullet when he tried to escape. In 1983, John Pat died from head injuries sustained inside the Roebourne (Western Australia) lock-up; four police and an aide were charged but acquitted.

The death of 25-year-old Robbie Walker at Fremantle in 1984 was a national tragedy. Walker was a poet and musician who had won a Channel 10 talent quest and published a collection of his prison writings, *Up, Not Down, Mate!* On Tuesday, 28 August 1984, at about 4 a.m., he was taken from his cell at Fremantle Jail and savagely beaten in the yard for all to hear. By 5:15 he was pronounced dead. Kevin Gilbert, who had himself survived the prison system, wrote: "Isolated, subject to fear and hatred made even more intolerable by the claustrophobic walls of the prison cell, Robert Walker cut his wrists and began playing

Roger's cousin Jimmy Knox, leader of the Country Shades

his guitar. He didn't intend to die . . . his personality unerringly dictated that he protest his treatment, and he forced someone to take notice." The coroner eventually found the cause of death to be misadventure, and the case was closed.

When an Australian Institute of Criminology report was published claiming that 19 Aborigines had died in prison between 1980 and 1985, it was regarded as a gross underestimate. Aboriginal people, and many white Australians too, were outraged.

In July 1987 teenager Edward West hanged himself inside a cell at Cherbourg. Barely a month later, Lloyd Boney killed himself the same way in a Brewarrina prison cell, inciting a virtual riot on the streets. Five days after that, the federal government finally appointed a Royal Commission. Yet for all its eventual findings, black deaths in custody continued and continue to this day.

Roger, Vic and Bobby had no choice, then, but to try and help their brothers behind bars. "I mean, I go into the prisons here," says Roger, "and it's places like that where you have to work with the audience, get them going, do something for them. I've been doing it for years and I continue to do it today because they ring me up, and I never refuse."

He continues:

Nobody told us about alcohol. All they told me, my ancestors were myalls, uncivilised, cannibals, now they say. And that would tend to make me say, well, I'm not part of that then. So then I started to hate myself – and self-hate is the biggest problem in our community. Because if you turn against yourself, you're going to turn against everyone else too. I seen the destruction, the family breakdowns, I seen all this that alcohol causes. It just keeps us down, keeps us contained and confined.

"It's a bit scary, just being in there with a lot of desperate men," says Randall Wilson. "There's a lot of energy there you've got to convert into positive energy very quickly, because if you don't, they can turn on you."

Roger: "We get down singing and talking, and it just lifts their spirits, you know, makes them feel good."

Wilson: "It's incredibly hard to walk out on those men when you're done. Their faces are different when we leave from when we arrive. The moment Roger starts singing he gives them a bit of hope. He'll tell them too, it's your own bloody fault you're in here, nine times out of ten. He makes their time a bit shorter, and they talk to him when they're out. So there's a fairly good rapport. The ones who are crook, he really tells 'em, look, you're here because you deserve to be here. But a lot of the young kids in there, there's all sorts of people in there who should never be in there. And so he says to those ones, there's a lot of people know you're innocent, don't get down because of it."

"I don't even have a criminal record," says Roger.

But I still couldn't trust a policeman. And I know what the situation's like in jail. You can get a pat on the back, told, You a good blackfella, you not like those blackfellas over there, see, and then you'll start thinkin', No, I'm not like them. But fuck it, we are all the same – just some of us don't do drugs and alcohol.

IN 1990, AFTER A SCORCHING lone stand at the Tudor Hotel in Tamworth during festival time, Roger and Euraba went to America. It was a high they've struggled to replicate.

Appearing at the Tudor, the watering hole of Tamworth's young turks and outlaws, Euraba played the hottest set heard all week. "Euraba are not just the leading Koori band," exclaimed local critic Mort Fist, "they are simply one of the best bands in Australia. Extraordinary!"

The band was seen by visiting Native Canadian Chester Cunningham, and he invited them to tour prisons, juvenile detention centres and reserves there in April/May 1990.

"I was three weeks in Nashville and I was homesick so bad," says Roger, "but once we got to Canada with the Indian people it was just like home."

You get off the plane in Edmonton, Alberta, and they'll tell you, don't go to 96th Street – and so you immediately go straight there!

I did a song written by a fella over there [Daniel Beatty] called 'Warrior in Chains'. What it is, it talks about a similar situation we have here, deaths in custody. I visited reservations and they were just like our missions. I suppose controlled by the same people, white people. Country music went over real well over there. Like, you get some rock bands, you know, but the majority of people like country music. I was just so amazed, our culture was a mirror image.

Back in Tamworth for the 1991 festival, Euraba played a triumphant homecoming. "Euraba keeps setting the standard," the festival program said, and after playing a number of their own headline shows, the band went back into the studio to start work on a third album proper. But that album never emerged, and by the middle of the year Euraba could no longer get a gig in their own hometown.

After the TKKMA dissolved acrimoniously, Roger was left without white go-betweens, or champions, in Tamworth, and he had the door slammed in his face. Enrec scraped together a greatest-hits compilation CD called *Warrior in Chains*, after one of the few new tracks it contained, but when Enrec went bust and were virtually run out of town, the door was locked. Euraba lost momentum at that point and struggled to regain it.

But then, Enrec too was often frustrated by its flagship charges. Commercial success, as Ed Matzenik knows, is by no means music's only yardstick – but still there is a nagging element of unfulfilled potential about Roger. Says Randall Wilson:

Roger sells himself way too short, to be quite honest. I went on the road with him a lot . . . and he'd never even get them to include something to eat and somewhere to sleep. Other people take their rider very seriously. Roger would just say, we'll go with what you've got . . . When I go out now I say, Look, you blokes can sleep in the van, but I'll sleep in a motel, thanks very much.

"I tried to get the Aboriginal Arts Board to put a publicist on their Canadian tour," Ed Matzenik snorts.

One of their freeloaders, who was going on the trip with them, came up to Tamworth and said, Well, we're not going to fund whitefellas, for a start. So I said, Well, I dunno who's going to fly the plane! Roger came back from that tour with one box brownie photo of himself outside a motel opposite Elvis's house, which he pulled out of his back pocket and showed me! That's how much publicity they got off that tour of America! I thought, that's it, I can't promote these guys out of my dole cheque any more.

The *Northern Daily Leader* lamented, "Tamworth Aboriginal band Euraba is being forced to play on a street corner because it can't find an official venue. Band members claim they had already been kicked out of one city pub . . . They allege they have been told they 'attract the wrong kind of crowd'." And this is a band that had just returned from a tour of North America!

Says Roger:

When I started getting my own band I guess more Aboriginal people would congregate, see, and I think a lot of these people who control these venues couldn't accept that. I had a fella came in once, he's a whitefella and he went into some of these clubs and asked for a gig, and what they told him was that I attract the wrong type of people. And see, I interpret that as, I attract too many Aboriginal people.

Probably also because I started singing songs about my struggle too, Aboriginal songs, they couldn't accept that either. Like I mentioned earlier, I can sing 'Our Reserves' and, you know, they look at it different to what if some white man would sing songs similar to that. I don't understand it.

At the same time, as Roger himself knows, that's no reason not to continue singing those songs – which he does to this day, on a purely community level.

They're songs with good words, good meanings and that's what I pick up on, you know, a song that will say something. Like 'Warrior in Chains', which deals with deaths in custody, a real issue which has been happening and is still happening today. And these are stories that need to be told, you know.

That's what I look for in songs, something that says something, something people can understand. Something, you know, that is positive, something that's good because, you know, music, you can communicate better with music.

"I still live in Tamworth, country music capital. Still can't get a job here." Roger laughs, surveying the landscape surrounding him, lush green rolling hills on which he broke his back picking tobacco. He doesn't even have his handprints on the Walk of Fame – and everybody in Tamworth has their handprints on the Walk of Fame! "They give you the same old story, same old bullshit, that I attract the wrong type of people . . ."

But Roger isn't bitter. He has endured too much, been too close to the real edge, to know that personal ambition is irrelevant in the face of the good fight.

It wasn't till 2004 that he followed up his first album with a second containing (nearly) all-new material. Credited to Roger Knox solo rather than Roger and Euraba, but with backing from the usual Tamworth crew including Buddy on guitar and Gene and Randall Wilson on drums, *Goin' On, Still Strong* reprised a couple of his classic tracks, like 'Streets of Tamworth', 'Koorie Rose' and 'Malabar Mansion', but more importantly it brought together a clutch of versions of great original Aboriginal songs, some of which, like Mop Conlon's 'Mother's Eyes', were making their belated debut on disc. Others were Johnny Huckle's 'I Am', Bobby

McLeod's 'Friendship Road', Jimmy Little's 'Brighter Day', and a pair of Queensland songs, 'Murri Man' and 'Murri's Plea'. But the album had a minimal impact. Roger cut back on gigging as Buddy became ever busier with his own solo career as a born-again bluesman.

Perhaps the great thing about Roger is that even though he could see himself as a musical martyr, he refuses to. He is still singing when asked, and still trying to lift people up.

"Country music, I think it's threatened but it will not be eliminated," he says, "because, you know, you have to go back . . . you know, you can change it, rearrange it, modernise it, but you still have to come back where your heart is, you know."

❧❧❧

KIMBERLEY PICKIN'

★ Kevin Gunn and the North-Western ★ 'Desert-Surf' Sound

Kevin Gunn's been on the grog for a few days now. It's not uncommon for Gunnie to go on a bender. He may be a legend, but in country music circles, hard drinking only adds to a legend. And what else is there to do when you're back in home at Halls Creek (pop. 1,182) between engagements? Forty years and an entire continent on from Dougie Young, Kevin Gunn sings:

Drinking with my friends down by the creek,
Looks like I'll be drunk for a whole damn week.

Kevin Gunn is one of the last bad-ass guitarslingers. Sammy Butcher could have been Australia's first black axe hero, but family and community commitments meant he had to leave Warumpi Band. Buddy Knox, Euraba's original lead guitarist, Roger's son and Sammy's replacement in Warumpi, might be an even better musician than Gunnie, and now that Buddy's got the blues, having gone solo and swapped the country sound for a stinging, funky style of blues and rhythm, he might yet be the black man to rival the recent crop of rustic white Australian bluesmen. But it was Kevin Gunn who showed them all the way.

Born in 1956, Kevin Gunn is the most enduring and romantic figure (and there's plenty of competition) to have emerged from the Kimberley, an area in northern Western Australia where a long and extremely rich black musical tradition still thrives. In fact, the Kimberley may be one of the last strongholds of Aboriginal country music.

Divided by the Leopold Ranges, the Kimberley is comprised of distinct areas of coastal, river and desert country. In all but coastal towns like Broome and Port Hedland, where different influences have arrived by sea, the dominant tradition is country music, and in particular, space-age country-surf guitar music!

Western Australia is a very big place with a very small population. Broome is tiny, yet it almost overshadows Perth as the state's indigenous music capital; it's a cultural melting pot that was originally a pearling port and is now a tourist boom-town. There's hardcore country in Broome, for sure – artists like Geoffrey Fletcher and Francis Cox (one of a long line of Coxes) – but the place is best known as home to a whole generation of musicians, like

★ Seven Brothers ★

What's the top-selling souvenir among the tourists who flock to the beautiful, remote north Western Australian port town of Broome these days? It's not pearls, even though Broome is a centre of the pearlfishing industry. Nor is it DVDs or CDs of *Bran Nue Dae*, the 1990 hit musical by local Jimmy Chi that was made into a movie in 2010. No, it's *Saltwater Country*, the 1997 debut album by the Pigram Brothers.

The title *Saltwater Country* is apt both as a description of the band and of the land, the ground and the sound: the album is awash with all the breezy, lilting strains of Island music, set atop a rollicking country-rock base.

Stephen Pigram served an apprenticeship in Jimmy Chi's band Kuckles, as well as Johnny Albert's Scrap Metal, before finally corralling his six siblings (Alan, David, Colin, Gavin, Phillip and Peter) to form the Pigram Brothers in the mid-90s, with the stated objective of making music that was "as close to the spirit of place and being that one could possibly get."

That closeness was defined on *Saltwater Country* by the chemistry between the brothers on their shifting array of barely electrified string-band instruments, and their sunny, airy harmony singing – all of which was put in the service of terrific, nostalgic songs like 'Barefoot Kid', 'Saltwater Cowboy' and 'Going Back Home'.

But if *Saltwater Country* remains a highwater mark because its songs had been honed for as much as twenty years ('Going Back Home' first appeared as part of *Bran Nue Dae*), the Piggies have continued to put out consistently good CDs. They delivered their second album proper, *Jiir*, in 2001, produced by Australian country-rock legend Kerryn Tolhurst, formerly of the Dingoes. *Jiir* entrenched the pattern: it's like swamp rock crossed with calypso, a real Australian Cajun style – Islander, Indonesian, whitefella, Aboriginal; it has a power-ballad yet intimate quality; it's smooth yet earthy and down-home.

And if the Pigrams have generally seemed reluctant to leave their idyllic hometown, that's all part of their laidback charm. "We still try to go out fishing every week as a family and keep it a fairly natural kind of thing," Steve told Perth's *X-Press* magazine. "Some of the positive things [here in Broome] are that you get to play to a lot of people from all over the world as they come here, so if you are a musician you can position yourself to perform locally in your hometown and have a different audience every week."

●●●

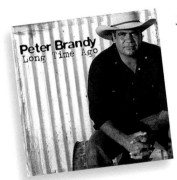

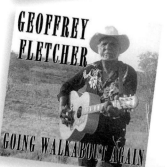

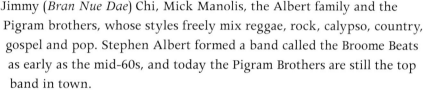

Jimmy (*Bran Nue Dae*) Chi, Mick Manolis, the Albert family and the Pigram brothers, whose styles freely mix reggae, rock, calypso, country, gospel and pop. Stephen Albert formed a band called the Broome Beats as early as the mid-60s, and today the Pigram Brothers are still the top band in town.

Saltwater influences peter out in the landlocked Kimberley, though. In dusty cattle country, Kevin Gunn is the archetypal local guitar hero, the leader of a pack that includes such long-standing stars as the Benning Brothers, Rodney Rivers, Frankie Shoveller, Peter Brandy, and Danny Marr and his country-rock band Fitzroy Xpress, from Fitzroy Crossing.

After the Benning Brothers, who formed as early as 1963, shifted base to Tenant Creek north of Alice Springs, Kevin Gunn's only serious local rival was Ernie Bridge, the 'singing politician' who also hails from Halls Creek and is the father of the modern bush ballad hit, 'Helicopter Ringer'. But with four albums to his credit since 1980, Gunnie has long sustained a national profile despite between-tours drinking binges. Looking like a bandito with his trademark Zapata moustache and lazy eyes, he irresistibly updates the Kimberley outlaw tradition that dates back over a hundred years to Tjandamurra.

The Kimberley guitar sound as practised by Kevin Gunn is a clean, chiming sound, free of distortion and with a delightful lightness of touch and whammy-bar restraint, more Chet Atkins or Barry Thornton than Dick Dale or Jimi Hendrix. People have long remarked on how strange it is that in the western desert, where water has to be finessed out of the landscape, wild surf instrumentals like 'Wipe Out', 'Pipeline' and 'Bombora' are the sort of standards Aboriginal musicians cut their teeth on. Maybe it just says something about the universality of the garage band style.

Certainly, though, it seems appropriate to the unspoiled rugged beauty of the Kimberley, with the sharpness of its clear blue skies and jagged outcrops of rock. It picks up on some of the history of the area, too, in the way 'Apache' by the Shadows also does.

Opened up late in the course of the all-engulfing frontier, the original inhabitants of the Kimberley, some 30 tribes, put up fierce resistance to white settlement. Tjandamurra was less a bushranger than a freedom fighter, and he is still celebrated in songs like Paul Kelly's 'Pigeon'. Because the area was virtually annexed by the cattle industry, the presence of the church was minimal, and the bloody violence continued until well into the twentieth century. The Coniston Massacre of 1928 was so horrific, though, that it prompted even some whitefellas to attempt to ensure such things never happened again. Yet the Kimberley remained a perilous place to be Aboriginal, with a particularly appalling record regarding alcoholism, imprisonment and deaths in custody.

Kevin Gunn knows he's done well just to have avoided a life punctuated by jail, or ended prematurely by alcoholism. But he might also wonder why he hasn't been rediscovered the way Dick Dale was after *Pulp Fiction*. Gunnie's been back in Halls Creek since the late 1990s, since his mother died. "I've been back up home for a while, trying to get away from the rat-race for a little while," he laughs.

Gunnie grew up on old-time Australian country, and those roots still inform much of what he does, just as the Kimberley's historical zest and spirit of defiance also seem present in his sound. It all adds up to a vibrant sort of ride-the-wind Western soundtrack that's restlessly in search of a film, or at least the way home. Gunnie still has dreams, like playing the Grand Ole Opry in Nashville the way Ernie Bridge did, but he shrugs, "I'll try and get there one day, but for now I'm not really worried about it."

"It's pretty hectic to write new songs and to play, get organised and produce it," he explains. "People think it's easy, but it's your mind that's doing all the work. It's not a physical work, it's a mental work. It tires you out."

Kevin Gunn is already revelling in semi-retirement, the glow of eldership. And just like the old leather cowboy hat that has became another of his trademarks, he wears it quite comfortably.

"Country music up here is very, very popular," he says.

It's starting to pick up more now from when I started, because when they have the country music festival up here, a lot of people enter it and they're the talents that are finally coming out of their shells. And when people say, where'd you get your country influence from, people mostly say – not all the time – Kevin Gunn, because we saw him first up there. And this is from different artists like Archie Roach and Troy [Cassar-Daley] too. Well, Troy's just lately on the scene.

When he was 11 years old, Troy used to watch me up in Ipswich, playing with Rick and Thel. And he said to me, one day I'm going to be just like you. And now, he's won three or four Golden Guitars!

"I was really attracted to Gunnie," concurs Troy. "I thought he was a great fella. He played good guitar, he was everything we wanted to be when we were young."

ACCORDING TO HIS OFFICIAL BIOGRAPHY, Kevin Gunn was born not under a bad sign but under a coolabah tree, at Go-Go Station near Fitzroy Crossing on 1 July 1956.

My mum and dad was travelling round a lot. My mum's a full-blood Aboriginal and my dad's an Irishman. We ended up in Halls Creek, Dad was doing a lot of bush work, like fencing and droving. And we used to have the old radio on and I used to listen to the Sunday country music from Perth. We had an old guitar there in the

Kevin Gunn (left) with Rick and Thel (centre) and Frank McHale on bass, early 80s

stock camp and I started playing that. I hadn't been much educated myself. I left school early in grade five and started working with Dad, and then I was playing a lot in the bush.

When I was growing up we mainly listed to, like, Tex Morton, you know, the old early stuff, Slim Dusty, Buddy Williams. And some of the American ones like Jim Reeves and Hank Williams. The only Aboriginal one I could focus on really was Jimmy Little. He was very popular but we only heard him now and then because we only had the radio.

At Saunders Creek Station in the late 60s, Kevin jammed with Jimmy and Charlie Wilson and old Uncle Jimmy Smiler.

I started playing a lot in the bush but the welfare got me back in school because I was too young, I was around 13. And so I started playing town [Halls Creek] a lot then. I played bass guitar with a band in town here and I was only about 14. I don't know if you know Ernie Bridge? Well, Ernie's brother Peter was in the band. They were older than me. I was the only young fella allowed in the pub because I was in the band!

The band was called Peter Polo and the Moon Men, but Gunnie stayed only long enough to learn some more chops before he moved on to the Zodiacs, and then Big Feets, and then finally formed his own band the Mysteries. The Mysteries played the Kimberley in the mid-70s – dances, rodeos, weddings, parties, anything – before Gunnie broke the band up to play drums with another outfit called the Fantastic Four.

★ 'The Singing Politician' ★

Country music and party politics might not seem to have much in common (even though Neville Bonner, the first Aborigine to become a member of Australia's federal parliament, listed 'country and western' as one of his hobbies alongside 'boomerang throwing'), but for Ernie Bridge they became quite comfortable bedfellows.

Born in Halls Creek in 1936, to a part-Aboriginal mother and a father whose family was among the Kimberley's first white settlers, Ernie Bridge was Western Australia's first Aboriginal state MP. He also happens to be a bush balladeer with five albums to his credit, and has even appeared at the Grand Ole Opry in Nashville.

Prior to recording his debut album, *Kimberley Favourites,* in 1979, Bridge had never set foot on stage or in a studio. In 1980, when he was elected state Labor Party member for the Kimberley, he went on his first tour of Western Australia and released his second album, *Helicopter Ringer*, which featured the great Rodney Rivers on guitar.

Politics took precedence over music after Labor won government in 1983 and Ernie was appointed to help set up the Seaman Inquiry into land rights, and then in 1986 was made Minister for Aboriginal Affairs. Since his musical comeback in 1990 with *The Great Australian Dream*, Ernie has inducted his son, guitarist Noel, into his act. "Ernie has a thing about singing only Australian songs," says his bio, "which he feels and hopes can be related to Australian people – in a wonderful land he is proud to possess."

◖◖◖

I was getting better and better I suppose, then Rick and Thel's travelling show used to come through a lot, and they asked me a few times to get up and play. This was back in '76, '77, '78. I was with the community service at the time, doing an office job and playing music on weekends, and then they invited me to go on tour with them, back in 1979, around Australia, so I accepted. And I was with Rick and Thel for five years, playing the guitar all over Australia for ten months a year for five years.

Rick and Thel Carey were the first couple of white Australian country. After meeting in suburban Sydney in the late 40s, they signed to EMI in 1954 and quickly joined the likes of Slim Dusty and Reg Lindsay at the top of the Australian country music tree. Album titles like *Mr and Mrs Country* and *Lovin' and Fightin'* give a good indication of the nature of their act.

In 1960 Rick and Thel roped in Athol McCoy, Brian Young and Gordon Parsons to mount their own first touring show. In 1967 they went to Western Australia for the first time, starting a love affair with the state that would eventually see them move there. The course of Rick and Thel's career was perhaps a metaphor for Australian country generally. With the drift off the land and the rise of rock music, country was superseded as a popular voice, and to survive it was forced to the perimeters. In 1974, Rick and Thel pioneered the sort of touring by charter plane that their protege Brian Young would later make famous, flying around between remote missions, stations and settlements. This was the beginning of their close relationship with Aboriginal people. In 1979, they were dropped by EMI after 25 years, and after a brief tenure with Tamworth's Hadley label, they formed their own label, Matilda Records (later RTC).

Kevin Gunn was called in to join the show in 1979, when guitarist Paul Lester dropped out in Cairns. Gunnie was the first Aboriginal musician Rick and Thel employed, but he wouldn't be the last. In fact, he ushered in a mixed-race approach that became characteristic of latter-day Rick and Thel line-ups.

During his time with Rick and Thel, Kevin Gunn released two albums on Matilda under his own name, *Travellin' Man* and *Country Variety*. After appearing on the live album *On*

Kimberley pickers (left to right): Francis Cox, Doug Brown and Frank McHale, who all played with Rick and Thel in the 80s

Tour! The Rick and Thel Show, Gunnie recorded his debut, *Travellin' Man,* at Hydra Studios in Tamworth in 1980, with a cast of super-session musicians and even the elusive Moonie Atkinson on backing vocals. "I'd like to dedicate this album to my mum and dad and all my fans and relations," Gunnie wrote in the liner notes. "As a boy I had always dreamed of recording an album of my own."

Exactly half of the album's twelve tracks were Kevin Gunn originals, including the turntable hit 'Heartache Blues'; the other six were classic covers like Roger Miller's 'Hitchhiker', Stan Coster's 'Halls Creek Rodeo' and Slim Dusty's 'Camooweal'. Even Floyd Cramer's Nashville piano instrumental, 'Last Date', was transposed to guitar.

"I started writing back in '78, '79, my older songs," says Gunnie. "The first one was 'Heartache Blues'. In 1980 I was voted on the radio in Perth the most requested country music singer for that year."

Gunnie played alongside bassist and Halls Creek countryman Frankie McHale, the second Aborigine to join Rick and Thel, for a few years until they both left in 1983. Rick and Thel went on to assemble an all-black backing band called the Country Shades, numbering, most commonly, Jimmy and Trevor Knox, cousins of Roger's, plus Doug Brown and Francis Cox, the latter a prodigiously talented multi-instrumentalist/vocalist from Broome who eventually produced his own solo recordings.

"After five years I called it quits," Gunnie recalls. "It was getting too much, it was pretty hectic doing one-night shows in one-horse towns and clubs and so on. That nearly wore me out, so I had a couple of years off for while at home here and played in a local band for a while."

Gunnie returned to the professional fray in 1985, when he joined up with Brian Young.

Jimmy Little, he was on tour with us. We flew in an aeroplane around Australia. I believe Brian's in the *Guinness Book of Records* for having the longest flying tour in the world. Some of the big names in America, they fly for two or three weeks on tour. We did it for about four months. Then I left Brian and went up and worked at the Argyle diamond mine for six months in '87. But I didn't like it, 'cos it was time-consuming up there and I couldn't play much music. So I left the job and I went back to Halls Creek.

In 1988 Gunnie was invited to tour America with Perth's Aboriginal dance theatre Middar.

I was over there for four weeks playing California. I was doing mainly a lot of bush ballad stuff. I was doing my own songs as well.

> After that I came back home and then went back on tour with Brian Young for a while in the early 90s. Then I came back home here and had a rest for a while and then went to Perth. Played Perth a lot, and Geraldton. And then I thought I'd come home for a while because my mother passed away.

Gunnie released his fourth and still most recent album, *Kimberley Roadtrain*, on Big Wheel Records in 1991. One side of the LP is instrumental, the other vocal. The album opens with the title track, an original Gunn instrumental, and leads through songs like Herb Alpert's 'Mexico' (transposed from trumpet to guitar), until the side closes with the grandaddy of 'em all, 'Guitar Boogie'. Side Two includes a telling version of Fats Domino's 'Hello Josephine', plus Gunnie's own 'Down by Banjo Bore', 'About Buddy Williams' and 'Drinking Again'. Drinking songs, it is perhaps superfluous to add, are another speciality of Gunnie's. 'Down by Banjo Bore', in particular, is terrific, not only for its inevitable banjo part but for lyrics that gets at something real essential:

> Down at Banjo Bore you'll find me sittin'
> With a friend who plays the country-style guitar
> We'll sing some Charley Pride and share a bottle
> When the doors are closed at the Kimberley Hotel Bar . . .
> There are many of my people who are sufferin'
> Like me beneath the trees at Banjo Bore.

"I can write songs and it gives me a chance to express those feelings," says Gunnie, "and people can relate to that and all those stories I sing about, because they been through the same, similar experience. That's why they love all the country stuff. Well, I reckon it's because it's sort of down to earth. There's a message in each song, you know, it's about country and it's about family and all the problems they have, and it's good music and they can relate to it. Good simple music."

Late in 1998, back at Halls Creek, Gunnie was asked by Goolarri Radio in Broome to write a new signature song about the Kimberley:

> I recorded this new song called 'Anywhere In The Kimberley Is Home Sweet Home To Me', and it's very popular now. I've been out in the community teaching young Aboriginal kids to play music. That's basically it really. Givin' back a bit to the community what they done for me.

But as much as Kevin Gunn likes to give himself plenty of breathing space, as much as he might even occasionally like a few drinks, he will eventually get back to touring. Because after nearly a quarter of a century on and off the road, you can't just kick it like that.

The fastest Gunn in the north-west will ride again, and when he does he will shoot down any gringo who dares doubt he is the baddest man in all the Kimberley badlands.

❡❡❡

Kev Carmody

NEW CORRIDOS

★ Kev Carmody, Archie Roach ★ and Ruby Hunter

In 1988, when a 42-year-old Queensland blackfella and former drover by the name of Kev Carmody released his debut album, *Pillars of Society*, it was hailed by *Rolling Stone* as "the best album ever released by an Aborigine, and arguably the best protest album ever made in Australia." Vic Simms's *The Loner* and Black Allan Barker's *Fire Burnin'* had not so much been forgotten as never noticed in the first place. Similarly, when Archie Roach's debut single 'Took the Children Away' was released two years later, in 1990, it was hailed as if 'Brown Skin Baby' didn't even exist. This is not in any way to downplay the achievements of what would become a whole new wave of Aboriginal corridos, rather to illustrate how broader white Australia was by now not just finally ready for Aboriginal music, but hungry for it, however ignorant it might be about that music's rich past.

The 1990s saw Yothu Yindi become the first Aboriginal band to break through onto the world stage as part of the greater surge of indigenous music that made an impact in Australia, along with the rise of dancefloor diva Christine Anu. At the same time, along came this new wave of reflective, necessarily politicised folk-country music: singer-songwriters like Kev and Archie and also Ruby Hunter, and the vocal group Tiddas. It was at once the consummation of a long tradition and the anointing of a new generation of Aboriginal musicians.

Australia's new black corridos found themselves part of the growth industry that was roots and world music in the 90s; this was a result not just of the digitisation of music and its concomitant globalisation and fragmentation into niche markets, but also of the rise of multi-culturalism in general. The wheel of fashion in popular music has continued to turn and recent times have seen a real revival of roots and acoustic genres like country, folk and blues. Australia today is awash with young, feral bluesmen, folkie fair maidens and bearded banjo players. Aboriginal singer-songwriters were ready and able to stride right onto this newly welcoming stage.

And with a sound full of echoes and tears – sometimes tears of joy – Kev, Archie, Ruby and Tiddas produced an overlapping body of work (a score of albums between them) that not only offered both consolation and inspiration for Aboriginal people, but was also keenly felt, far more than before, by white audiences. Albums like *Pillars of Society*, *Charcoal Lane* and *In My Kitchen* were quickly acknowledged as Australian classics, songs like 'Took the Children Away',

'Down City Streets' and 'From Little Things, Big Things Grow' as among our new standards.

How country was the music of these new corridos? Well, Carmody's 'Little Things' won a Golden Guitar at Tamworth, so it had to be pretty country. And in fact the country influence is fundamental, while at the same time it also drew on all the other usual stuff: gospel, folk, rock, pop, blues, soul, traditional music. For white Australia, it wasn't that much of a stretch: it was folk-country-rock with acoustic guitars and vocal harmonies, after all, singer-songwriters with confessional narrative stories. However harrowing those stories may be. Eventually, Archie and Ruby made it to Tamworth too…

But what really propelled this music was the way it so powerfully put into practice the idea that the personal is political, and its willingness to buck stereotypes. Almost as soon as *Pillars of Society* had been acclaimed as the greatest protest record ever made in Australia, Kev Carmody was rejecting the tag, damning it as patronising and inhibiting. This was a long way from Col Hardy. But even as Kev and his compadres moved further and further from the classic sound of Koori country, it was always part of their power that no matter how far they went, their roots provided a solid underpinning to everything they did.

It's perhaps a mark of the extent to which Aboriginal life in Australia is widely viewed as desperate and dissolute that when Ruby Hunter called her second album *Feeling Good*, this reclamation of pleasure (or happiness, or comfort, or just safety) seemed a more defiant gesture – certainly a more unorthodox one than, say, fiery rhetoric. Clearly, these were no longer just the sorrow songs, and that's a point these new corridos were all keen to make: if you only sing about sorry business, to paraphrase Bobby McLeod, it keeps people locked in that destructive cycle: a 'circle of negativity', as Kev Carmody has called it. There is a whole other side to the Aboriginal experience, and it's as important to celebrate that good side as it is to expose and rail against the bad. Again, the proof was in the pudding, or rather the grooves. Kev Carmody could be angry, corruscatingly so, but while the title and lyrics of an early classic like 'Thou Shalt Not Steal' may read like a sermon, the music was typically rich and sensual, in a way that brought everything together. And that's without even taking into account songs like 'I've Been Moved'. Archie Roach even called one of his later albums *Sensual Being*. In a way this represented a rebirth of the whole image of black Australia.

"I've often been called a protest singer, as a lot of other people have," says Kev.

Kev Carmody points the finger: shooting his first video, for 'Thou Shalt Not Steal'

> To me it's derogatory, too narrow. It ghettoises the music for a start: Oh, it's protest, it's negative. Whereas if you really listen to a lot of my stuff, there's lots of positivity in it.
>
> My grandfather was born in the bush, and he'd say, you are surrounded

by sound, boy. The brolga crying, the sound of the kangaroo, the dingo or the crocodile.

He said, you have to learn to listen to the wind. What he was saying was, use your imagination, widen it out, be aware of things around you. You learn to listen in another way. That's the key to my music. Just opening up to that sensory perception of sound.

KEV, ARCHIE, RUBY – THEY WERE ALL stolen children. And they had more than that in common. Although Kev was a bit older and from Queensland, while Archie and Ruby were a decade younger and from the south-east, they all fell almost accidently into a music career relatively late in life. Kev only began writing songs in earnest when he was 33, after he'd enrolled in university; he could still barely read and write, and music offered him a way to *sing* his dissertations, as oral history. Archie only started to take the idea of music seriously after his Uncle Banjo Clarke told him he was sick of hearing him sing all them American songs all the time: *Why don't you sing your own story?*

Their reaction to Australia's hollow Bicentennial of 1988 was something else the three of them shared. Both Kev's *Pillars of Society* and Archie and Ruby's first cassette together, 1989's *Koorie*, were designed as deliberate ripostes to the Bicentennial. (Discographers usually credit *Koorie* to Ruby alone, but regardless of the name on the marquee, Archie and Ruby have always been a double act.)

As well as embodying a transition from genocide to rebirth, Kev, Archie and Ruby also embody the transition from country to city (and from analog to digital, from vinyl and cassette to CD). Country music remained purer – or more traditional – in country areas. But as more Aboriginal people moved to urban centres, the style of their songs and the stories they told changed too. In a way, it wasn't such a big leap for Kev to go from bush poetry to suburban-ghetto raps, or for Archie to update the claypan dance into 'Charcoal Lane', which memorialises a Melbourne back alley where he and his homeless friends would gather to drink and pass the time – and hand a guitar around. You'd get there, as one of Ruby's songs has it, 'Down City Streets'.

Another important common element was folk-rock star Paul Kelly and the guitarist in his bands the Coloured Girls and the Messengers, the late Steve Connolly. Kelly and Connolly both became honorary members of Melbourne's Koori community as they wove their way through its music. It was Connolly who first saw Archie performing 'Took the Children Away', on the ABC TV show *Blackout* in 1989, and got him in to play a support spot with the band one night. At which gig Kelly, along with the entire crowd, was blown away by this gawky young blackfella with a dodgy mullet, coke-bottle glasses and these incredible songs. This led to Kelly and Connolly convincing their record company Mushroom to sign Archie to its roots music subsidiary label Aurora, and the pair co-producing his first album, *Charcoal Lane*.

Around this same time, in 1990, Kelly and Connolly were also working with Kev Carmody, producing his second album, *Eulogy (for a Black Person)*. Kev and Paul went on a camping trip together in Kev's country, and they co-wrote a little song called 'From Little Things, Big Things Grow'. The song itself would enact its title, growing from a throwaway B-side to encapsulate a burgeoning public sentiment in Australia: that the struggle for Aboriginal rights – land rights and other rights – is one worth fighting, by everyone. It's still something of a wonder that a more-or-less throwback bush ballad like this could become an anthem in contemporary Australia – but perhaps this merely shows the depth and power of such genuine songlines.

Today's online arbiters might describe 'Little Things' as a rock protest song, but in fact it couldn't *be* a more conventional bush ballad, with its almost nursery rhyme-like simplicity, its strummy couple of chords, singalong circular melody and central narrative drive. In that sense, it was no stretch for Tamworth to give it a gong in the Heritage category at its annual awards ceremony in 1994. The breakthrough was in the nature of its narrative. In a field full of gum trees and all the rest of the usual rural nostalgia, this was a song about blackfellas standing up and actually winning some ground back off the whitefellas.

By the mid-1990s Aboriginal music was hitting some kind of peak. Kev was already regarded as something of an elder statesman, with *Bloodlines*, his third album (and the one that contained 'Little Things'), a towering achievement. Archie had followed up *Charcoal Lane* with a second album, *Jamu Dreaming*, and had toured overseas with Ruby, who was just releasing her first album, *Thoughts Within*. Tiddas, whose vocal harmonies were a defining feature of Kev's sound, had signed a major label deal in their own right and delivered their own debut album, *Sing About Life*. Never before had a gaggle of Aboriginal artists like this occupied such a prominent place in Australia's musical landscape, and they opened the gates through which so much more could flow. When they toured the world together in 1995, it was just the icing on the cake.

"Mainstream media are trying to find out what to do with it because it's got such a power," Kev told the ABC.

> We talk about things that are so truthful, and so close to us as people, so it's a bit hard for the mainstream. But once they can categorise it, and utilize it some way . . . because the Top 40 only exists to sell a consumer con, sell motor cars, or drinks, or shoes, or a house, so the music in there can't be knocking the system. Whereas every black performer I've ever heard, I don't care who they are, they've always made a social statement about something, and it's very hard for that type of music to be utilized. But it's breaking through, we're breaking through, like black music in the US – that took 40 years, you know.

KEV CARMODY WAS BORN IN CAIRNS in 1946 to an Irish-Australian father and Aboriginal mother. It's one of the reasons, he's often said in interviews, that he does what he does – one of the reasons he's done so many interviews! He's such a great talker, storyteller, singer, polemicist and poet, because he is rooted in two of the world's great oral traditions, the Irish and the Aboriginal.

"His songs have about them the quality of a blessing, the odd sense of forgiveness, and the promise of hope," acclaimed Tasmanian novelist Richard Flanagan has written. "They reflect a life that embraces the profound historical change undergone by Aboriginal people over the last half century. Tex Morton and Henry Lawson, Dylan Thomas and Hank Williams, Joh Bjelke-Petersen, Jesus Christ and Vincent Lingiari. I can't bring them together. Kev Carmody can."

Trying to explain his skill set, Kev told Noel Mengle: "I'm from an oral tradition, taught to think in word images. When you are telling a story, you have to have an image to stick in the person's head, so they remember it."

In 1950, when Kev was four, he moved with his family from Cairns to the rich farming and grazing district of the Darling Downs, in Queensland's southeast. He grew up in a three-room shack on a station near Goranba, west of Dalby. These early years he remembers extremely fondly. His parents were drovers and he himself rode a horse from a young age. This, plus his Aboriginality (his mother was well versed in the ways of the bush), inculcated in him a love of the land so great it became part of his spirituality, and has fuelled some of his finest songs, like 'I've Been Moved'.

Richard Flanagan again: "In his songs it is possible to see a small Aboriginal boy in his swag waking in the middle of the night, the stories and songs of the campfire still swirling around his mind with dreams and flames, the wind a caress on his face he will never forget, the night sky a brilliant blanket, and that small boy being overwhelmed with a sense of belonging so powerful that he spends the rest of his life seeking to recapture it, explain it, convey it, become it."

Kev has told the story many times of the family getting an old dry-cell radio and the wonder of it, of the music that came out of it, that for him rivalled nature itself. He fell in thrall to both kinds of music, country and classical, Hank Williams and Chopin. He didn't go to school but he was getting a deep education as it was.

At the age of ten, though, in 1955, Kev and his younger brother Laurie were forcibly removed from their parents and put in a Catholic boarding school in Toowoomba. Kev hated it, has called it little better than an orphanage, and whether he jumped or was pushed, left before long and became a drover.

"Through the 50s we used to have packhorses," he told Andrew Stafford, "and they couldn't carry a guitar, but there was still music around the campfire every night, you know, mouth organ. But when we got a truck we could actually carry a guitar, and my uncle knew a few chords. That's why country music was so important to blackfellas, because you only needed two or three chords, and you could put your own words to it."

One story has Kev finding a songbook at the dump. He was hearing other things blowing in the wind too, like Dylan, and Leadbelly, and Woody Guthrie. He liked both Dylans actually, Bob and Thomas. He can still recite parts of *Under Milk Wood*. Profoundly motivated by the 1966 Gurindji strike, which would of course eventually become the subject of 'From Little Things, Big Things Grow', Kev started writing little verses of his own. He played representative rugby. He has recalled how in 1968 he first drafted the words that would become 'I've Been Moved' around a campfire, just as in the scene Richard Flanagan imagined so well.

"You can sit around any campfire from here to Cairns, from here to Wyndham," Kev told *Rolling Stone*, "and there'll be a Murri or a Koori with a guitar, who'll have a song. With white culture, someone will write something, then once the book goes on the shelf then that's it, it's finished, it stopped dead when that bloke did his last word on it. Whereas with oral cultures it's updated, it's dynamic, all the time it's evolving, and you've got to have people around to transmit it. It brings people together."

Motor transport may have brought guitars but it also brought the beginning of the end of droving, at least for Kev, and in the early 70s he took his first wife Helen and young family to live in Toowoomba. He got a job in a welding shed, and very seriously set to teaching himself to play guitar. He decided he wanted to study music theory, but despite his by now formidable technique on his instrument, he could not – because he had no formal qualifications. Instead, he was steered into enrolling at the Darling Downs Institute of Technology (now University of South Queensland) in Toowoomba, to study history, music and geography. Even though he was effectively illiterate. Thus it was that in 1978 he started taking his guitar into tutorials.

It is a perfect illustration of Kev's innate understanding of the power of word pictures, the way he's so often conjured up the image of his younger self going off to classes, riding his old motorcycle in his filthy work overalls, his guitar slung over his back and long beard billowing behind him in the slipstream.

He played his first semi-pro gigs at a little folk club in Toowoomba. He graduated, and contemplated stepping up to do a PhD, but at a family meeting it was decided that for the greater good of all Aboriginal people, he shouldn't confine his increasingly impressive songs to the halls of academe, but instead pursue what he's called 'this music caper'. He went to nearby Brisbane to hawk himself around. But under the iron fist of hillbilly dictator Joh Bjelke-Petersen, there weren't any gigs in Brisbane even for white bands, let alone black ones.

Mop and the Drop-Outs, for example, were constantly harassed by the police.

But there was community radio, 4ZZZ, and through the station's *Murri Hour* program, Kev recorded his first couple of songs. These tracks, including 'Thou Shalt Not Steal', started a groundswell of appreciation on Aboriginal radio all round the country, and with the 1988 Bicentennial approaching, Kev's mother lent him the money to make an album in an attempt to put the case against it.

The result, of course, was *Pillars of Society*, recorded in Sydney in just two days at Megaphon studios, and released towards the end of the year by a start-up label called Rutabagas. The album was a tribute, as its liner notes said, to "all humanity that has, does and will suffer and struggle for civil rights and human dignity as well as freedom from oppression – you are the fulcrum for what limited inspiration this album manifests." With tracks like 'Thou Shalt Not Steal', 'Black Deaths in Custody', 'Jack Deelin' (the single) and 'White Bourgeois Woman', delivered in a pure, acoustic folk-country-blues mode, *Pillars of Society* was an immediate turntable hit. But for all the praise *Rolling Stone*, among others, heaped on the album, it wasn't without qualification. To be really great like Dylan, the suggestion went, Kev would have to break out of the protest singer straightjacket, transcend sloganeering and divisive polemics; 'didactic' was a term that cropped up in more than one critique. "For every great line," said *Stone*, "there are lots that smack of undergraduate protest and political clichés rather than deeply felt rage."

"It's not entertainment," Kev spat back. "If I wanted to entertain I'd go and put out something like the latest pop group."

Andrew Stafford commented: "Where Midnight Oil's 'Beds are Burning' spoke of 'we', and Archie Roach limited his accounts of personal tragedy mainly to 'I', it is perhaps unsurprising that Carmody's accusatory 'you' would prove too difficult for white audiences to swallow."

But Kev was building a momentum that would become irresistible; the songs would simply outlast any critical carping or audience resistance.

IF KEV WAS THE FIREBRAND, the Old Testament charismatic, Archie Roach was a perfect complement, the shuffling, shy one. Both were counterpointed by Ruby Hunter, the flamboyant one with her trademark feathers and plumes and cheeky/cherubic demeanour. Together, Archie and Ruby – well, it's almost impossible to imagine one without the other. They were more than soulmates in life and music, they were part of – the heart of – an organism much larger than just the two of them. Archie was born in 1956, although he still seems confused about exactly where – he's variously given his birthplace as Mooroopna, near Shepparton on the Murray River, or Portland, near the Framlingham mission on Victoria's west coast. But then, confusion understandably runs all through Archie's childhood and adolescence.

Ruby was born a year earlier, in 1955, in the Coorong, at the South Australian mouth of the same Murray River. Music was in her blood – she's from the Hunter clan that has also included singer Isaac and pianist Dora. She was taken from her family at the age of eight, in 1963, and put in Adelaide's Seaforth Children's Home.

Archie was taken from his family at an even younger age and put in the Liam Booth Orphanage in Melbourne, along with his sisters Gladdie and Diana. From there, he went through a couple of abusive foster homes before finding some love and acceptance with a family called Cox. It was with the Coxes that he really fell for music. His foster sister played organ in church but it was her guitar he loved, the gospel songs, and Hank Williams songs.

Archie's world was turned upside down again, though, when another of his sisters, Myrtle, turned up to tell him their mother was dead. Archie went off the rails, and ran away. He was around 14 or 15, and all he took with him – again proving the power of word pictures, apocryphal or otherwise – was a guitar.

He led a vagabond existence, riding the rails. 'Itinerant farm labourer' might be the most polite description of what he did back then. "I just drifted around," he said. "A lot of people didn't know where to go, couldn't find their way home, didn't know where home was. So more often than not you ended up on the street, just drinking . . ."

One time when Archie was around 17, he had been fruit-picking in Mildura and then headed down to Adelaide. This was when he met Ruby.

"Archie and me, we were both pretty wild," Ruby remembered. "I didn't know he was trying to find his people like I was."

Ruby had been on the streets herself for a few years, after running away from Adelaide's Vaughan House for wayward girls when she was 15. Like Archie, like too many street people, just "drinkin' and fightin'," as she put it in 'Down City Streets'. She and Archie struck up an immediate rapport. Shuttling between Adelaide and Melbourne, Archie was dealt another blow when he found out his father and sister Gladdie had died too. Ruby would never see her parents again either.

"She met a boy," Archie sang in 'From Paradise', which like all his love songs, as he attests, is about Ruby:

Who kind of knew,
Some of the things,
She was going through.
But he was confused,
So he ran away,
But she found him again,
And here she is today.

After watching black bands like the Kooriers and the Country Outcasts, Archie got up at the 1978 Aboriginal Country Music Festival in Melbourne, and won a gong. "It was a part of life, playing music," he said. "No matter sort of like where you were or what you were doing, if there was a guitar handy you'd always . . . pull it out and strum it around and sing some songs."

Still drinking heavily and basically homeless, Archie and Ruby started having kids, their sons Amos and Eban. By 1981, Ruby had had enough. She went into rehab. Archie followed.

When they got out, Archie fell off the wagon. "You know, I went as low as I wanted to go. I hit rock bottom and I'm very lucky that I'm alive."

In 1983, after being hospitalised in Adelaide, Archie went into rehab again. "This time it was different," he said. "There was this lad there and he had a guitar – all my guitars were hocked or broken or whatever – and so I just picked that up again and started strumming around. I started going along to things, someone asked me if I wanted to come along and sing some songs at this coffee shop, and so I started playing there, and people started to come. All I was doing was singing country songs. But it was good."

Approaching the Big 3-0, Archie was getting his life back together. Reunited with his family – on Ruby's terms, which included keeping up his membership of Alcoholics Anonymous – Archie started working as a drug and alcohol counsellor. Ruby was working as a 'cottage mother' to no less than twelve kids. It was around this time that Archie had the epiphany that would alter the course of his life, via his uncle Banjo Clarke, who was one of the Framlingham elders to whom he went for guidance.

> He came up to me one time and said, you know, you write songs, why don't you write a song about your own experience, your life on the streets and what happened to you.

A very young Archie Roach wins a gong at the 1978 Victorian Aboriginal Country Music Festival

Thus was born 'Took the Children Away'. It wasn't the first song Archie had written, but it was the one that set him on the path. For a long time, as Archie has often said, he didn't understand what had happened to him, or why, but when old Uncle Banjo helped him understand, it all went into 'Children'.

Archie and Ruby have variously described two country bands they led, Altogether and Koori Kinaction, before they recorded the cassette *Koorie* in 1988, as a response to the Bicentennial. *Koorie* marked the recorded debut of 'Took the Children Away', and the song immediately cut through. Archie was invited to sing on new ABC-TV Aboriginal program *Blackout*, and was spotted by Steve Connolly.

"It was pretty accidental, yeah, as far as becoming professional, making a living from it," Archie said.

> I was working in the hostel for homeless people, and that's when Paul and Steve got in touch with me. It was weird. I mean, I had not thought of making . . . anything, I was just writing songs – a lot of the songs that ended up on *Charcoal Lane* – and singing them, at various venues around the place, pubs, small acoustic venues, on public radio, 3CR, and I was quite happy just doing that. But as soon as they said, would you like to do a record? I said, Wow, this'd be good.

With his regular guitarist Dave Arden in tow, Archie recorded *Charcoal Lane* under the tutelage of Kelly and Connolly, who were both very impressed by Archie's set of songs – they were so well-formed, they both testified, that all they had to do was stay out of the way and let him sing. They all bonded over a mutual love of George Jones. "Archie's got a double punch," said Kelly, "because he's not only a great songwriter, he's a great singer, a soul singer. He could put out an album of covers and it would be great."

When the album came out, with 'Took the Children Away' as its first single, and Ruby's song 'Down City Streets' one of its highlights, it seemed to be still more warmly received than *Pillars of Society*. Even decidedly mainstream media came out in support. "Archie Roach is a reluctant star and spokesman," said *New Woman*, of all magazines, "but there's no such shyness about his music. Like him, it is modest and unassuming, but not lacking in presence or power. *Charcoal Lane* is an unrelentingly sad record, but one that demands to be listened to."

One reason for *Charcoal Lane*'s greater penetration may be that it was on a major label, which *Pillars of Society* wasn't. Another may be that, unlike Kev, Archie preferred to avoid polemical lyrics.

I do. That's the way I am. When I was a bit angrier and a bit drunker I would have written some pretty awful stuff. I can tell people to jump up and down and hit them over the head with messages, slogans and stuff like that – but people are already doing that. Plus, as a songwriter, you know, I wanna develop and write about . . . although, I will, if I see something that happens, an injustice . . . but it's basically just how I feel, my own feelings towards things.

There were certain things I couldn't talk about, deal with in my life, so I started to write about it, sing about it, and it was, you know, such a release. I'm glad I discovered that – putting down your feelings in songs – otherwise I'd probably be committed somewhere by now. Or dead.

After appearing at Womadelaide in January 1992, Archie and Ruby went overseas, toured the US. *Charcoal Lane* had been released there and was meeting just as positive a response as it had at home. "One of the most distinctive singer-songwriters to emerge in recent memory," read a typical review. "His sadly beautiful songs and haunting voice illuminate the pain and misery of Aboriginal life."

Paul Kelly said: "I've seen Archie get more confident on stage, just as a result of the fact, he knows now . . . When I first heard his songs, he wasn't sure if he was connecting with the world at large. But now he's realised people are listening, and when you know that, you gain power, and confidence."

In 1993, Archie released his second album, *Jamu Dreaming*, produced by David Bridie. Sophomore recordings are often difficult and disappointing. A debut might have drawn on a lifetime's worth of material and development, and the follow-up is sometimes pushed through too quickly. But *Jamu Dreaming* suffered no such shortcomings. Songs like 'From Paradise', 'Tell Me Why', the title-track, and the single 'Walking into Doors', a Nick Cave-like piano ballad about domestic violence, were as strong as anything on *Charcoal Lane*.

Archie and Ruby toured overseas again in 1993, and the following year Ruby released her first CD, *Thoughts Within*. "It was in '88 that I actually first sang one of me songs that I wrote on the guitar," she said.

Two years of learning how to play, Archie taught me. He just showed us a couple of chords, they were the chords to 'Hang Down Your Head, Tom Dooley'. Just doing a little bit by bit every week, I'd go back to Archie and I'd say, have you got any more? So . . . I learnt to play the guitar, I just kept on asking questions because I started getting interested because I liked the sound, thinking, oh gee what are you doing? I want to do what you do.

★ *Harmony Rising* ★

Singing 'BVs' – studiospeak for backing vocals – is one of the few roles in the music business that black women have traditionally not just filled, but dominated and defined. And that's how Melbourne trio Tiddas got started.

Lou Bennett, Amy Saunders and Sally Dastey first sang together, doing BVs, for Amy Saunders's brother Richard Frankland's band Djaambi, in Melbourne in the late 80s. Saunders was an Aboriginal lass, from Portland, on Victoria's west coast; Bennett was a Koori too, Yorta Yorta from Echuca, north of Melbourne on the Murray River; Dastey was a white girl from the suburbs. Together, they were instantly – and seamlessly – greater than the sum of their parts. "The first time we sang together," said Dastey, "we just looked at each other – we knew we had something special."

Ruby Hunter named the group and gave them their first gig proper as part of Hot Jam Cooking, a show she organised at the Town Hall Hotel in Richmond in 1991. "We thought we'd do just one song," said Lou Bennett, "so we wrote a song, it was really daggy, but then we did some more of my material, that I just had in a notebook, and from there it just snowballed."

Unlike Olive & Eva or the Sapphires before them, Tiddas were able to carve out a career of sorts – at least, as much of a semi-professional career as most jobbing musicians in Australia can reasonably expect. On the eve of the so-called grunge era, when music was being changed by so many other influences – artists like k.d. lang, Tracy Chapman and the Indigo Girls, for example, were shaking up perceptions of black/folk/country/female music – Tiddas were so hot they almost incited a record company bidding war. After their first EP, 1992's *In My Kitchen*, was released by tiny Sydney indie BlackHeart Music and kept selling out re-pressings, the group signed a recording deal direct with major label PolyGram. Their debut album, *Sing About Life*, was released in 1993.

With an acoustic folk-country-ballad base and lovely three-part harmonies, the group were, as one critic put it, "so refreshing as to be breathtaking – a potent, beguiling blend – singing and songs that are as sharp as they are sweet. Yet while there is not unsurprisingly a quite sombre lilt to much of the Tiddas sound, it is the trio's effervescence, the sheer exuberance with which they attack the task at hand, that regularly causes scenes of rabid bliss at pub gigs."

Tiddas released a total of four albums during the 1990s. Perhaps they will be most fondly remembered for so beautifully bringing modern traditional songs like 'Inanay' and 'No Goon No Pah' into the contemporary realm, although original songs of their own like 'Anthem' and 'Spirit of the Winter Tree' also resonate still. The group toured the country and the world, won awards, and – not least of all! – became the BV chicks of choice for a whole generation of Melbourne musicians. They were the most consistent defining aspect of Kev Carmody's shifting sound, and lent their uplift to his otherwise minimal version of 'From Little Things, Big Things Grow.'

"There's a message behind the music," said Sally Dastey, "but we don't like it to be put into little boxes, like it's political, feminist, Koori or whatever. To us, it's just what we talk about and see around us, everyday life."

With the 1999 release of a live album, *Show Us Ya Tiddas*, whose title points to attitudes that continued to frustrate the group, Tiddas played an extensive farewell tour before breaking up in 2000. "It's been great," said Dastey, "but it's also taken a lot of hard work, to push ourselves, and not take the shit that some people put up, whether you're black or white, male or female. It was against all the odds."

●●●

Unsurprisingly, the recording of Ruby's *Thoughts Within* was a family affair. Archie played guitar and sang, while Dave Arden contributed some especially tasty picking and slide guitar, and Tiddas sang backing vocals.

Is it any wonder that Ruby and Archie, these two stolen children, defined themselves according to the family they'd (re)made themselves? Archie often speaks of how children are the redeemers, how it is they who teach the adults (not vice versa), completing a circle of love that keeps all those within it protected.

"Yeah," said Ruby, "family is very important to us. Family and music – that's what's held us together." She giggled in her typically infectious fashion: "Kind of like the Partridge Family, but black!"

AFTER CUTTING HIS FIRST ALBUM in a mere two days, Kev Carmody took six months to record the follow-up, *Eulogy (for a Black Person)*. The label that had put out *Pillars* had gone bust, so once again Kev borrowed money – more money this time – to record off his own bat. Kev was ambitious, artistically and commercially.

"That first album was acoustic because we didn't have enough money for anything else," he told Noel Mengle. "But as I went on, I was always exploring sound."

Eulogy was a satisfying progression from the first album. In retrospect it can be seen as transitional. With Steve Connolly now in the producer's chair, Kev returned to Megaphon studios in Sydney and called sessions whenever he could. Some tracks were recorded with bassist Paul Burton, who'd served as musical director on the first album, and others with Paul Kelly's band the Coloured Girls, in which Connolly, of course, was the guitarist. Other musicians were brought in for overdubs when the album was mixed in Melbourne: former Triffid Graham Lee on pedal steel, Cleis Pearce on violin, former Bushwacker Dobe Newton, and Bart Willoughby on didgeridoo.

Released at the end of 1990 on a lease deal through Festival, *Eulogy* lacked some of the punch of *Pillars*, but it proffered a clutch of what would quickly become new Kev Carmody classics: 'Cannot Buy My Soul', 'I've Been Moved', 'Elly', 'Droving Woman' and 'River of Tears'.

'Droving Woman', nominally about Kev's mother, was bush balladry on an epic scale, 21 verses spanning a good ten minutes. 'River of Tears' was an example of how Kev was perhaps taking some of the criticisms of *Pillars* to heart. Unlike, say, 'Black Deaths in Custody', which had a generalised perspective, 'River of Tears' homed in on a particular case, the police shooting of a Marrickville brother by the name David Gundy ("they gunned him down"), and it gained in power as a result. Another thing that gave the song wings was Kev's falsetto vocal. Isaac Yamma had made a trademark of his kookaburra laugh; Kev's pain and anguish here was all the more convincing when delivered with a howl like a wounded dingo.

'Elly' showed even more maturity. A poignant medium-tempo ballad about a girl gone wrong, its greater strength was that it could be about any girl, black, white or otherwise. Kev Carmody's politics may have started with race, but they clearly didn't end there. At its base, he saw the world's problems as spiritual, the result of a disconnection from the environment itself. Beneath his brown skin, he was deep green.

Kev complained about not getting mainstream radio play, but the fact is that no acts in Australia get commercial airplay unless they're safe and bland. Mainstream radio in Australia is a mire of mediocrity. On the other hand, Australia has some of the best public radio in the world. If it wasn't for stations like 3CR, 2SER, 4ZZZ and 4AAA, plus ABC radio programs like *Music Deli*, Aboriginal artists – really, any artists outside the lowest-common-denominator mainstream – would face an even more difficult struggle.

Eulogy may have been a refinement of its predecessor *Pillars of Society*, but it hardly prepared the way for its successor, *Bloodlines*. Kev's third album shot off in completely new directions, and still stands as his finest work. According to *Rolling Stone*:

> *Bloodlines* is an adventurous album that is quite clearly trying to reach out and touch more people. It's not as cohesive as *Pillars of Society*, but that's because it's refused to accept such a narrow precept, and even while it is quite fragmented, there are more likeable kinks and crevices. Much of it, in fact, is barely half-baked. But elsewhere it rises to sublime heights. Any Carmody fans crying Judas as Dylan's did in 1965 will only be missing out.

Rolling Stone's equivocation was totally misplaced on this occasion. *Bloodlines* was a triumph. Most of it is at least three-quarters baked, and if it is sprawling, it nevertheless pulls through by dint of its sheer urgency.

Bloodlines was very much a result of changes in Kev's life. After his first two albums, Kev wasn't drawn to play the pop star. Instead, he went even deeper into the underbelly of society. In 1991/92 he spent time working with disadvantaged youth, black and white alike, in Logan City, south of Brisbane. Logan is a housing commission ghetto – flat, hot, dry and dusty – stuck between Brisbane and the Gold Coast. Kev was profoundly affected by what he experienced there, and *Bloodlines* grew out of that experience, offering a provocative counterpoint to the other major musical export that bleak Logan City spawned at that time, world-beating synth-pop duo Savage Garden.

The first indicator of Kev's new direction came in early 1993, an EP called *Street Beat*, whose title alone suggested a drift away from the back country roads. *Street Beat* contained four tracks that all revolved around Logan, three of which – 'Living South of the Freeway', 'Darkside' and 'Rider in the Rain' – would later be included on *Bloodlines*.

Kev had effectively decamped to Sydney by now. He was living in a house in Marrickville, and had joined forces with a dreadlocked whitefella called Andrew O'Phee, who'd taken up his management. O'Phee also played mandolin, and would share co-production duties on *Bloodlines* with Kev. *Street Beat* was the first fruit of recording sessions back at Megaphon, and was a stunning mini-concept album in its own right. Only the acoustic 'Rider in the Rain' might have come from the earlier Kev Carmody, with its galloping headless-horseman sense of doom and O'Phee's clattering mandolin. 'South of the Freeway' was essentially strident pub rock, or an Australian equivalent to Steve Earle's 'Copperhead Road', complete with stinging guitar solo by Leroy Cummins (grandson of Darcy). But it was 'Darkside' that really turned heads, a sort of chamber-music rap set not to hip-hop beats but bittersweet layers of twelve-string guitar and trilling piano: it was bush poetry come to town, or at least the suburbs.

When the album itself came out a little later in 1993, its opening track, and first single, was a song called 'Freedom'. Co-written by Kev and Bart Willoughby to commemorate Nelson Mandela's visit to Australia, the track was South African township jive more than reggae, appropriately enough, and it was a supremely auspicious beginning. Part of its uplift came from the vocals supplied by the girls from Tiddas; indeed they would add sweetness to Kev's fire throughout the album.

Bloodlines' second track, 'Asbestosis', could be the post-punk blues of Nick Cave's first band, the Birthday Party (and obviously, again, an issue not restricted to blackfellas), and this is a perhaps curious influence that, fused also with a certain dub style, infects a number of the album's other tracks, like 'Bloodlines' itself (a sort of barbeque rap), 'BDP' and 'Sorry Business'.

Apart from 'Messenger', another chamber rap that is similar in theme to 'I've Been Moved' (awe in the face of mother nature), most of the rest of the album returns to more familiar territory. 'On the Wire' is a junkie's lament, and though the junkie in question is clearly black, he may just as well have been white, so universal and identifiable is his plight. The album closes with 'From Little Things, Big Things Grow', and if it seems somewhat tacked-on, like an afterthought, in this context, that's because it was. After Kev and Paul Kelly wrote the song in 1990, it was Kelly who first recorded it, in 1991, for his album *Comedy*.

In his wonderful book *How to Make Gravy*, Paul recalls them writing the song around the campfire. It started with a Bruce Springsteen couplet ("From small things, mamma/Big things one day come") that Paul thought they could improve on. That's how songwriters often work, borrowing and bending. "With Kev doodling a few chords on the mandolin," Paul wrote, "me playing a capoed guitar and the ghosts of Hattie Carroll and Woody Guthrie's 'Deportees' hovering overhead, we conjured most of the song in a couple of hours under the bright, bright stars."

The very minimal version of the song that closes *Bloodlines*, a mere three-hander that has Kev and Kelly trading verses in between fluttering choruses from Tiddas, was actually originally recorded for a short film about Kev and Paul called *Blood Brothers*, and was added to the album after it had first appeared as the B side to the single 'Freedom'. It turned out to be the ultimate sleeper, a little thing that grew to a very big thing indeed.

When 'Little Things' won the Heritage Song of the Year at Tamworth in 1994, making Kev the first blackfella to collect a Golden Guitar since Col Hardy twenty years earlier in 1973, the award was not without controversy. At an event dominated by new hat act Lee Kernaghan – while Black Allan Barker was on the street outside, busking to next to no-one – *Australian Country Music* magazine reported that many were surprised that Kev and Paul, "both fringe country performers, snatched the award." *Capital Country News*, Tamworth's journal of record, admitted that people were 'astonished'. The Tamworth brains trust should perhaps be commended for taking a decision they must have known would cause consternation, but that doesn't make the reaction any less deplorable. Neither Kev nor Paul were in attendance, and so, as *Capital Country News* reported, Jimmy Little, who was at the ceremony to be inducted into the Hall of Fame, "accepted the award on their behalf, and took it all in his stride."

Today, 'Little Things' nestles alongside 'A Pub with No Beer', 'I'm the Sheik of Scrubby Creek' and 'Raining on the Rock' as one of the classics of Australian country. "It's a creaky song with a Sunday school melody that makes me cringe sometimes," wrote Paul, "but it just keeps on going, like an old buggy bumping down the road."

SO WHAT DID KEV DO as soon as he was reluctantly accepted into the pantheon? He seemed almost perversely determined to negate his hard-won gains; certainly he's never returned to the dais at Tamworth, where Paul Kelly has by now won a total of five Golden Guitars. Kev may not have gone quite as far as Native Canadian singer-songwriter Buffy Sainte-Marie, who ended up experimenting with electronic music, but he was certainly pushing the envelope. He hooked up with Steve Kilbey, the mercurial, drug-addled leader of cosmic rock band the Church, to produce his next album.

Preceded by the single 'The Young Dancer is Dead' – which Kev's own publicity release described as being "about deaths in custody [albeit again a specific case, that of Daniel Yock], but . . . no thin-lipped protest song" – *Images and Illusions* opened with a track called 'Some Strange, Strange People', which threw down the gauntlet with its synthesised textures. Was this Kev's equivalent to Neil Young's *Trans*? But the remainder of the album didn't carry on the hiss and grind of the first track. 'The Young Dancer is Dead' was another instant classic in the mould of 'Rider in the Rain'; 'Images of London' hit at the heart of the Empire, and the neo-rockabilly 'Needles in the Nursery' was close to the bone, given that its producer was an old junkie and young father. But otherwise the material, which included more than a couple of incidental instrumentals, seemed to lack some of the power of the songs on *Bloodlines*.

It did not quell the momentum, though. Kev joined Archie and Ruby and Tiddas on a 1995 world tour that started at Canada's Music West Convention in Vancouver and ended in Europe, at a 'Corroboree' season of concerts in London. The rest of the world had never seen anything like it: Kev, the leader of the pack, the stern patriarch, looking not unlike Karl Marx now with his new long white frizzy beard, blasting out songs like rounds from a Gatling gun; Archie, the wayward son, the dreamy one with faraway eyes and songs like pleas; Ruby, the earth mother-cum-Gumnut baby with her throaty voice; and Tiddas, the younger sisters with their sweet harmonies that held everything together.

As British folk-protest singer Billy Bragg put it at the time: "For us in England, the voice of Aboriginal Australia has come either through the white editorial system, the media, or in the traditional Dreamtime form. But there hasn't been anything about contemporary Aboriginal issues. So Kevin, writing about the subjects he writes about from the angle he writes them, is quite refreshing." To say the least.

AFTER THIS HIGH POINT, Kev withdrew from the scene. He was now almost 50, and feeling the strain both physically and mentally. He was fed up with the mendacity of the music business and plagued by a bad back and arthritis, acquired over too many years of too-hard manual work. With his second wife Beryl, he repaired to his bush block on the Queensland side of the Tweed River, just south of Stanthorpe, and revelled in the company of his children and grandchildren, and the surroundings of his garden.

Archie and Ruby and Tiddas pressed on, although Tiddas, who played the pub circuit most diligently, would be ground down by it, and disbanded before the decade was out. Archie released a third album, *Looking for Butterboy*, in 1997, which yielded the single 'Hold on Tight', and then he and Ruby embarked on a tour of Queensland jails and Cape York. After that, they started to take advantage of some of the new possibilities that were opening up. In 2000, they made a film called *Land of Little Kings*, about the stolen generations, and then Archie collaborated with Sydney's Bangarra Dance Theatre on a production called *Skin*. It was an enormous leap to have made, over the course of just a couple of decades, and symptomatic of a profound shift in Australian life. As Archie himself has said: "Thirty years ago we were marching for justice down the city streets, but now we're telling our stories in the concert halls." The opportunities that weren't available to a Roger Knox or Bobby McLeod, let alone a Dougie Young, were now flowing freely. Lou Bennett of Tiddas traded her razor cut and harem pants for the top hat and tails of the legitimate musical stage.

Ruby also released her second album in 2000, and if there had been any critical reservations about *Thoughts Within*, they were quickly dispelled by *Feeling Good*. Produced by Mick Thomas, former leader of Weddings, Parties, Anything (a band that itself changed Australian folk-rock in the 80s), *Feeling Good* was a crisper, more groove-oriented outing.

In 2001, the feature film *One Night the Moon* was released, starring, among others, Paul Kelly and Ruby, and with music by Kelly and Kev Carmody. The soundtrack yielded at least two more classic songs: 'Moonstruck' and, in another nod to Woody Guthrie, 'This Land is Mine'. Archie went into feature films too, providing the music for *The Tracker* in 2002, the same year he released his fourth album, *Sensual Being*.

The wave was building again and about to break, for a real last hurrah. In 2003, Kev made a comeback with his first album in eight years, *Mirrors*. By now, with the albatross of the 'protest singer' tag a thing of the past, the internet was about to give Kev his revenge anyway: "Bob Dylan wishes he was Kev Carmody," one wit posted online.

In 2005, *Cannot Buy My Soul* and *Ruby* put a capper on everything. *Ruby* was a collaboration between Archie and Ruby and composer Paul Grabowski and his Australian Art Orchestra. It was a sort of jazz-folk opera, like a reprise of that first cassette Archie and Ruby

made in 1988 but on a grander scale, stringing their greatest hits together in a single, coherent song-cycle for the theatrical stage. "It's easy with Archie and Ruby," Grabowski told the *Age*, "because the roots of the music they like and the roots of the music I like are very similar. Whether it be gospel, country or blues, all that stuff has played a role in the evolution of jazz, so there's plenty of crossover points."

Apart from an ill-advised Vegas-like treatment of 'Took the Children Away', and a tendency on Archie's part to overdo the vibrato, the album was really quite magnificent, with Grabowski's 22-piece ensemble (not unlike Charlie Haden's Liberation Music Orchestra at times) recasting material of relatively modest means into gloriously widescreen chiaroscuro. *Sydney Morning Herald* jazz critic John Shand called it "the finest, most moving work the AAO has undertaken."

"You'll hear about my birthing," said Ruby, "to playing games with my sister, little stories that were told to me about the river, other songs about the taking, and meeting Archie, our life on the street . . . There is sadness, but there's happiness too. It's enlightening. It's not to leave people with heavy hearts. There's too much heaviness and deep thoughts now."

Cannot Buy My Soul was a Kev tribute show/film/album that soared far above the banality this genre usually entails. With white as well as black acts covering Kev's greatest songs – and driven, of course, by Paul Kelly – it actually added another dimension to Kev's already enormous legacy. That artists as different as Troy Cassar-Daley, Missy Higgins, Archie Roach, the Pigram Brothers, the Herd, the Last Kinection, Steve Kilbey, Tex Perkins, and the Drones could remain true to themselves and true to the songs is a testament first and foremost to the quality of the songs. The Last Kinection, an indigenous hip-hop crew from north Queensland featuring Naomi Wenitong, mixed up 'The Young Dancer is Dead' for a new young generation, while Archie Roach reduced the title track 'Cannot Buy My Soul' to an essential statement of pride.

Richard Flanagan was asked to provide liner notes for the album, and he wrote:

I met Kev Carmody on the eve of a major concert in Melbourne by Australia's leading indigenous musicians showcasing the best of black music over the last thirty years. The concert was in part inspired, lost, elegiac, driven, mad, overwhelming. At the concert's end 2,000 people rose and gave ovation after ovation. Huge waves of emotion buffeted the hall. There was goodwill there upon which a different country could be built.

And at that moment I realised it was never about the past. Why is it we are so frightened of who we are? Could it be that what black Australia offers is not guilt about our history, but the invitation to a future as diverse, as large as the songs played that night in that hall – as remarkable as the songs by Kev Carmody.

Cannot Buy My Soul was a hit, and as Paul Kelly noted, when the project was completed, Kev quipped, "Now I can lay my guitar down for a while."

Richard Flanagan again: "Representative of a people and culture that has been excluded and denied, Kev Carmody's world is open to all and everything. Everybody is included, each thing connects, and we are all related to each other and all of us to the wind and the stars, the dust and the scrub."

As Kev told the *Courier Mail*: "I always say, no matter what, we're the one biological race, homo sapiens. We come from a heap of different countries and cultures. If we were all the same we would be a boring society. Okay, we might have been kicked around a bit, but every bugger has. You have to have the optimism that comes from looking at the positive things."

Such incredible grace and equanimity is a big part of what gives Kev's music its greatness. It's a sentiment echoed by Archie Roach as well.

"If it hadn't been for what happened to me," Archie said, "I probably wouldn't have been a musician. We are the sum total of our lives, of what's happened to us. A lot of things are sad, but I would never ask to be different. Terrible things happen because of misunderstandings, but I know I would be a poorer person if I had not been through these things."

ꙭꙭꙭ

Proud Young Man: 20-year-old Troy Cassar-Daley records his debut single at Enrec, Tamworth, 1990

OPEN ROAD

★ Troy Cassar-Daley ★

Troy Cassar-Daley is feeding his two-year-old son Clay. A Brisbane thunderstorm is about to roll in, obscuring the spectacular view of the city Troy usually enjoys from his leafy back verandah. Clay enjoys his food and Troy enjoys his son. The storm could be light years away instead of just across the river.

Troy Cassar-Daley is one of the hardest-working men in Australian show business. He is also the nicest guy in the business. Everyone agrees on that.

It used to be that in country music, stars could get away with almost anything: beating up their wives, being a drunk and a vandal, not turning up for shows – and that was just George Jones! But even George Jones couldn't get away with getting above his audience. The country star who considers himself superior to his audience will soon lose it.

"One of the things Troy does that's so right, aside from the music, is the kind of person he is," says Gina Mendello, the American who signed Troy to Sony Music in Sydney.

And in country, that makes a huge difference. A lot of times in pop acts, bad attitude is popular. Well, in country, good attitude is popular. You've got to really reach out to people, befriend them, show that you're not up yourself. The kind of guy Troy is, he makes everyone feel like they're his best friend.

Troy has been called the Johnny Farnham of Aboriginal country. It is meant as an insult. John Farnham may be some people's idea of Australia's perfect pop star, but to others his songs are bombastic and his nice guy persona seems forced, a bit like his too-golden hue. Troy, too, is almost too good to be true. Maybe if he's still wearing exactly that same crooked smile in 20 years time it might look like cracking. But right now, with his happy young family the ideal accompaniment, Troy has all the genuine enthusiasm of a neophyte. He's warm, open, down to earth, he's got a good sense of humour, he's charming and he's a lot of girls' idea of hunky. And, let's not forget, he's got a fair degree of talent.

From the moment he won the 1990 Tamworth Starmaker Quest at age 20, Troy's career traced an upward curve that couldn't be smoother.

Music today is more than ever a sprawling big business, a voracious machine that chews up an endless stream of wannabes. It is perhaps a measure not only of the changing state of the Australian music industry, but also the changing status of Aborigines, that Troy seemingly effortlessly scored a deal with Sony (formerly CBS), the biggest multinational label in the country and the world, and so was thrust straight into major contention, the big paddock. Yet even though Troy certainly hasn't achieved the massive crossover success of an antipodean Garth Brooks, or a male Shania Twain, he's still standing with his career and his credibility all intact. Survival itself is often achievement enough.

Right now, balancing his son on his knee as he chats, oblivious to the downpour taking place outside, Troy is eager to please and equally convincing. He could be an Australian Everyman: the guy who can balance a career and personal life; a good family man but not one who can't still be one of the boys; a guy who balances his background between black and white, city and country; a guy who, with his music, is balancing an instinct for core quality and self-expression with the commercial imperatives of survival.

"I'm a big believer in what Slim Dusty has done," Troy said.

If you don't get to the people, they don't buy the records and they never hear of you. I said to Slim at his fiftieth anniversary celebration, if there was anything I wanted in my life it was to end up like him, playing the music you love, having the woman that's loved you all through your life, and still enjoying what you're doing.

Once country gets into your heart, it's very hard to shake. And I think that's what's kept me going for so long. I've never wanted to be a crossover artist. Crossover, you know, my manager and I, Doug Trevor, nicknamed it the 'c' word because, I don't know, the harder a country artist tries to cross over, the more unattractive they look to me. A lot of people try to push you that way in your career path, but I've just always been proud of playing country music, I suppose. Compared to a lot of the use-by-date stuff that is around these days, it's a genre I think is going to be around for a long, long time.

BY THE 1990s, LEE KERNAGHAN was the dominant figure in Australian country music. At the same time, the presence of Aboriginal artists in Australian pop had become sufficiently widespread that it was almost taken for granted. During the 90s Troy Cassar-Daley became another accepted black face on the Australian pop scene, alongside an impressive gallery that included Mandawuy Yunupingu, Christine Anu, a reborn Jimmy Little and all the new black corridos.

There is, however, still a degree of ghettoisation to Aboriginal music. Almost as soon as world music got that name in the mid-80s, Aboriginal music seemed to get absorbed into it. The didgeridoo is Australia's world music instrument, no doubt about that, and its present-day masters like Alan Dargin, Mark Atkins, Adrian Ross and Richard Walley are among Aboriginal music's most successful exports. After white didgeridoo-synthesizer duo Gondwanaland Project introduced the sound to experimental rock audiences in the 80s, Bangarra Dance Theatre Musical Director David Page has made much of a postmodern fusion. In the late 90s, for its full fifteen-minute allotment, the didgeridoo was a cliche of the jungle/drum'n'bass remix; now, it's used freely by new age snake-oil salesmen as some sort of sound therapy instrument! The protests coming from Aboriginal people, asking for respect for their traditional culture, seem to be falling on deaf ears in a world where appropriation and sampling are the building blocks of the era's most exciting new music.

Since the broader category of world music also seemed to absorb what was left of the folk tradition, it makes sense that artists like Archie Roach, Kev Carmody, Tiddas, TI's Mills Sisters, even Maroochy, became staples on the festival circuit from Woodford to Port Fairy. But while world music happily takes in pumped-up settlement bands like Yothu Yindi or Sunrize, both basically rock acts with exotic choreography, it seems to have no interest in the grass-roots black country music of Kevin Gunn, or Roger Knox, or Troy Cassar-Daley. There is clearly some sort of inequity at work here. Is country music still looked down upon by white liberal audiences, even when it gets the guilt vote for being made by Aboriginals? Is it too close a reminder of the bad old days (as the blues are for present-day African Americans)? Or is it that country as a genre is simply too successful – too popular, too effective – to be allowed into world music's comfort zone?

Or is it that Koori country somehow offends elitist notions of purity? If so, that's pretty ironic, given that to most Aboriginal people country music is still their *traditional* music.

Indeed, country-based music is still the favorite type of music of a great many Australians. Country trails only rock and pop in its share of the contemporary music market. Classical, jazz, world music – these all have a small audience share. Hip-hop and urban dance music a bigger share. And when it comes to crossover, country-pop is still the biggest crossover market there is.

Back in the 90s, however, country music – as defined by Tamworth – never really threatened to cross over. Nor did it ever surprise anyone. Perhaps the only serious threat to Lee Kernaghan's supremacy ever came from Troy. James Blundell was too uptight by half. And Keith Urban, virtually as soon as he got out of the blocks in Australia in the early 90s, skipped town for Nashville. Back home, both Lee Kernaghan and Troy, like Urban, have blended a radio-friendly fusion of rock and country, a balance of American and Australian influences, contemporary and traditional. It is in part a reaction against the syrupy Nashville sound, in part also a need to progress beyond the almost xenophobic obsession Tamworth has with preserving the purity of the outmoded Australian bush ballad.

In the 80s, country music in America and Australia was revitalised by a new wave of artists who all at once got back to roots but also shared some of the iconoclastic spirit of punk: this was the start of what is now known as alternative country, a sort of update of the 70s outlaw movement of Waylon 'n' Willie or, in Australian terms, Digby Richards or Laurie Allen. In Australia, rock acts as diverse as Mental As Anything, Paul Kelly, Tex Perkins, Cold Chisel and Dave Graney all sought to reconnect with their roots, which as much as anything means vintage American country. This was a new kind of crossover that in the 90s attracted the likes of Kernaghan and Troy, who were country artists with a traditional background yet unafraid of new and unorthodox influences like – gasp! – rock, and – even more shocking! – American country!

Tamworth is still Australia's undisputed capital of country music, but these days the hippie haven of Byron Bay, a little further north on the New South Wales coast, hosts its own annual festival of 'blues and roots' music that provides a provocative contrast to all the old histrionics of the Golden Guitar awards. To a large extent its audience is one that's grown out of teen angst and bubblegum and dug so deeply into music that it has inevitably reached the roots of blues and country; equally, many attendees are young urban cultists who revel in rejecting the mainstream bland-out. There are quite a lot of bikers. Few in the audience have much affinity with traditional Australian country like, say, Slim Dusty, and almost none will base their aesthetic decisions on political criteria, as so many world music aficionados do.

Not a lot of Australian artists could play both Byron Bay and Tamworth. Paul Kelly is one. Blues guitarists like Dave Hole or Matt Walker will probably never get to Tamworth. But Troy Cassar-Daley has long been a favorite at both events.

Troy is a local hero to both audiences, in fact. He grew up, after all, in Grafton, smack in the middle of NSW's lush northern rivers district, and he served his musical apprenticeship on the area's thriving pub circuit, which takes in both Tamworth and Byron Bay. To this day he will describe his roots as equal parts rock and country, equally Australian and American, with just a bit of blues thrown in for good measure. So if it's still possible to hear traces of the Eagles in Troy alongside Slim Dusty, or Merle Haggard, what makes him unique is his Aboriginality.

Troy grew up on seminal Aboriginal artists like Harry and Wilga Williams and Roger Knox, and his songs still carry their echoes as well. Nor has Troy shied away from hard Aboriginal issues; the title track of his 1995 debut album, *Beyond the Dancing,* was about black deaths in custody.

Even his brief foray to Nashville to record his second album, *True Believer,* which can only be considered a nominal success, didn't knock any of the self-determination out of Troy. It's just that now he's got a family in Brisbane to manage as well as his career. It's a new aspect of life that only feeds the smart artist.

Given that Troy has a foot in either camp, if Tamworth does eventually die out (if nothing else, its audience is getting older . . .), then Troy will be able to transfer all his weight to the other foot. Which suggests a promising possible future for Australian country more generally. If it keys in to broader trends than just rural nostalgia – widespread underclass disenfranchisement, for example – it might even catch up with the rest of the world. In that sense, Troy is Australian country's great not-so-white hope.

"Back when I was a kid," Troy remembers, "my mother was working on the railway. She could only afford one LP a fortnight, so we'd buy the groceries and everything, and we'd go round to this little record shop and buy a country album, whether it was *Slim Dusty Live at Wagga Wagga,* or Merle Haggard or a George Jones . . ."

It is a really universal music, country, to be able to affect a little Aboriginal kid growing up in Grafton the same way it affects, say, a kid growing up in Nashville,

Tennessee. The fact that there is a story to this music and it takes a lot of pride in the lyric, I think that's the thing that really gets you in the first place.

Aboriginal families love country music and I think the main reason is because of its honesty. It tells about real things. It tells about getting up in the morning and feeling down, perhaps. It doesn't necessarily have to be from Australia. It can be an American song and you can think, Gee, I can relate to that. That's what attracted me to the music when I was a kid, its lyrics, its honesty, and I think that's what really still holds me there.

BORN IN 1970 TO A MALTESE FATHER and Aboriginal mother, Troy Cassar-Daley was already treading the boards before he was a teenager. Growing up part-Aboriginal and with an absent father, Troy, in classic country fashion, gives great credit to his mother Irene.

"I mean, I never had a family that said, no, you can't do that, you've got to go and get a proper job. I was going to be a shearers' cook or a chef or something, at least I knew I could travel with that. So I went and did a home economics course at the Grafton TAFE. But I was never good at cooking and whenever we had to do something outside cooking, I'd always do music. And so my life just evolved into this musician's life of wanting to travel, and the band started taking over from the restaurant I was working in."

Troy first went to Tamworth in the early 80s. He was keen on motorbikes but he was also keen on music, and he busked – conspicuously and precociously – on Peel Street.

When I got out there, it was my guitar teacher who really encouraged me to sing. I only wanted to be a guitar player, because we always wanted to be like Lindsay Butler or, you know, Barry Thornton. But by the time I got to Tamworth she really pushed me to get up there. She organised a little busking spot for me. She always encouraged me to sing at our little concerts we had once a year – we'd go to the old folks' home, we'd go to the local jail, just to practise what we had been learning all year.

By the time he was 16, in 1986, Troy was fronting his own band, Little Eagle, that toured the northern NSW circuit and provided a staple local support act for headliners from Mental As Anything or the Angels to Charley Pride. "When we first started playing, we wanted to play Creedence, the Eagles, Dobie Gray, Charley Pride, that sort of stuff."

The next step was obviously to start writing original material. Troy's favorite subject at school had always been English, and his mother was a bush poet. Troy was inspired by the veritable renaissance in Aboriginal music he was hearing.

That was a big point for us when we realised indigenous people were making music. I mean, there was Roger Knox, we'd go and see Roger when he come through town, we'd go and see Col Hardy, Harry and Wilga Williams, when they came through town, Jimmy Little of course.

Those early Aboriginal country singers, they are role models. I think that as little kids running around listening to 'Streets of Old Fitzroy', 'Streets of Tamworth', to

★ *Little Big Man* ★

Jimmy is inducted into Tamworth's Roll of Renown by 'Mr Hoedown', John Minson, 1994

After spending time in the 1980s working as a teacher at the Aboriginal Eora Centre in Sydney, Jimmy Little eventually made a triumphant comeback to music. During a period when so many of his younger compatriots – Harry Williams, Dougie Young, Mac Silva and, in the Centre, Isaac Yamma – all died, Jimmy was being born again, reinventing himself.

In 1989, after making his acclaimed theatrical debut in *Black Cockatoos* and starring in artist Tracey Moffatt's film *Night Cries*, Jimmy was named Aboriginal of the Year for his community work. In 1991, he appeared in the Australian scenes in Wim Wenders's cosmic road movie *Until the End of the World* – but was regrettably not included on the hit soundtrack. In 1992, he moved back into live performing with the Tamworth on Parade roadshow, then spent most of '93 touring with the Kings of Country roadshow. At the 1994 Golden Guitars he was inducted into Tamworth's Roll of Renown; that same year he played a role in the Aboriginal opera *Black River*. In 1995 he finally released a new album, *Yorta Yorta Man*, on the independent Monitor label – his first recording since 1981. It was worth the wait for the title track alone. Jimmy might have written barely a dozen songs in his entire career, but 'Yorta Yorta Man' is his swan song – and a beautiful black swan at that.

Subsequently, Jimmy was taken back in by Festival, and the album *Messenger* was released in 1999. The rest, as summer gave way to a new century, is history: the album was a huge hit and Jimmy's place in Australia's cultural landscape was confirmed. He was inducted into the ARIA Hall of Fame. His wife Marj called *Messenger* 'way out', with its unplugged, minimalistic readings of recent Australian pop classics, from the Go-Betweens' 'Cattle & Cane' to the Reels' 'Quasimodo's Dream' to Paul Kelly's 'Randwick Bells'. Jimmy wasn't content, even in his sixties, to ride off into the sunset. Even though he'd already produced possibly the most elegant third act in Australian music history, and was already suffering health problems, he continued to push into new territory. First he released a follow-up to *Messenger* called *Resonate*, in 2001. In 2003, he returned to a harder country sound on the album *Down the Road*, singing duets with Troy Cassar-Daley and Melinda Schneider, as well as his grandson James Henry. In 2004, he was awarded the Order of Australia. That same year, he had a kidney transplant and subsequently reunited with *Messenger*'s producer Brendan Gallagher to record *Life's What You Make It*. It was his thirty-fourth album and it would be his last.

◖◖◖

me that gave us a little glimmer of hope, that because they were out there doing it, we thought, well, maybe it's not impossible for us to do it as well.

But then when we heard this stuff coming out of the desert, we'd never heard before: people singing lingo, people singing about taking a brown-skinned baby away. We were just really motivated by that as kids, and I thought, well, obviously there is a place out there for me, I've just got to find it.

In 1989 Troy entered the Starmaker Quest in Tamworth, and finished in the Top 10. Little Eagle was fast becoming a thing of the past, just like Troy's day job.

"It was a real turning point for me because I realised it was a chance to play your own material. I'd never been game to do that, and it taught me a lot about having the pride to just do your own thing."

The following year Troy won the Quest. This was the real beginning of his professional career. Part of the prize was a session at Enrec Studios; Troy recorded his debut single there, 'Proud Young Man'. After that, in a rite of passage for Aboriginal country artists, he went out on tour with Brian Young. He was following in the footsteps of black giants:

There is always going to be stumbling blocks due to being Aboriginal, whether you are a fair Aboriginal or a really dark Aboriginal. The only word of knowledge my grandmother gave me is that when you see a job, big or small, do it right or not at all. And I said, well, I don't mind that, I'm not afraid of a bit of hard work. Mum always had a pretty good work ethic as well, so it was really good to apply that to your own career and say, well, okay, I'm going to give it 150 percent because I have to, and I can.

Winning Starmaker in 1990 was a big step. I mean, I couldn't win an argument when I was a kid, but to win that made me realise people were listening because I was playing my own compositions. I suppose it was just a bit of a boost to your self-esteem, that I wasn't just some kid, I suppose, but you probably could do something special for yourself and your mob if you really got up and had a good go. And Mum was never discouraging.

On tour with Brian Young was a big, big motivational thing in life. The biggest lesson I think I learned from that was that I got to know myself and that's one thing I've really had to do, because I was a bit of a big fish in a small pond at the time. Until you get out there in the real world and play for people who don't care who Troy Cassar-Daley is, that's when you start learning about, well, maybe you should be a bit more humble. Maybe you should take a bit more time to talk to people and not think you are so deadly. And also, Brian had this really, really good way of being a professional musician, and he taught us all those qualities that an old-fashioned showman should have. He'd walk on, he'd treat the people with lots of respect, he's very humble, he's proud of his show and I think I still carry a lot of those characteristics with me now.

After his time with Youngie, Troy again didn't try to make the overambitious leap that can destroy young talent prematurely. It was as if he was actively trying to pay his dues. He replaced James Blundell in part-time country-rock supergroup the Blue Heeler Band, and he spent 1992 and '93 on the road.

> Tamworth was the first place I moved, and then I went up to Maryborough, to be with the Blue Heeler Band, then I came to Mullumbimby where I wrote *Beyond the Dancing*. And then from there on I just started progressing into the bigger towns, and it was pretty daunting. I mean, I can't say that I really like cities.

Playing for two years with the Blue Heeler Band, Troy honed both his performing and songwriting skills. At the end of 1993, he had enough good original material to go shopping for a publishing deal. Again, things fell straight into place. Tamworth powerbroker Doug Trevor (also the manager of James Blundell and Gina Jeffries) took on Troy's management. Warner-Chappell signed his publishing. One of the big generators of Australian catalogue, Warner-Chappell put Troy in the studio with veteran rock producer John Sayers, and they recorded, on spec, a full debut album. It was this tape that finally convinced Sony, too, to take Troy on.

Late in 1994 Sony released the EP *Dream Out Loud*. Straight away Troy was nominated for the Best Male Vocal Golden Guitar. He didn't win it, but using the Tamworth festival to launch the album *Beyond the Dancing* at the same time, he had fired an auspicious opening salvo, and before the year was out he would win the 1995 ARIA (Australian Record Industry Association) Award for Best Country Release – for his *debut* album! Now Troy was perhaps even surpassing his wildest dreams.

"HE'D ALREADY RECORDED THE ALBUM, with the help of Warner-Chappell," says Sony's Gina Mendello, "so basically it was very easy for us to commit to a tape-lease deal, with an option to do another album after that. So I worked with Troy from the beginning, getting him out there, and we worked all the way through to the release of *True Believer*."

Within a few months of winning the ARIA, Australia's equivalent of a Grammy, Troy collected his first Golden Guitar, the 1996 award for Best Male Vocalist, presented by Slim Dusty. Then he went out on the road supporting Merle Haggard's Australian tour. Having already supported the Highwaymen in 1995, Troy was entering a galaxy of superstars he once could only have dreamed of inhabiting (as other Aboriginal artists as recent as Roger Knox could never have allowed themselves to dream . . .).

"The intentions on my first album were to be as honest as I could," says Troy.

> I thought, people do know what real life is all about so we should write about that, and real life for me at the time I wrote *Beyond the Dancing* was sad. I was a bit of a loner and the album was quite dark. I mean, the title song was about black deaths in custody, you know, it was an issue that had happened, you know, close to me in a couple of instances, and I thought, Well, gee, I should write about this.

"I could never see the Maltese side of Troy coming into play that much," laughs Gina Mendello. "However, the indigenous part of him is the country. It's an awareness of the land that's deeper than most Australians'. So there's that part of it, and he can sing for the people, what it's like to grow up in a small town . . . He's done that, and he's done it in a close-knit circle of family and friends just like any country boy, and yet he's been well educated, he's very intelligent, and so he's got it all."

Now, almost overnight, Troy's sights were reset on Nashville. But he was still cautious. "If we can keep it as country as we can," he said in a press release, aware that while Nashville is the mecca of country music, it also has a habit of ironing out the too-country kinks in pursuit of the glittering crossover dollar. And that wasn't something Troy ever wanted to do. But still, he was ambitious. "If we want to make an impact internationally," he said, "we have to make international music as Australian people."

PERCEPTIONS OF AUSTRALIAN COUNTRY IN AMERICA, despite any boosterism to the contrary, are minimal and fuzzy. Sure, the Le Garde Twins and the Hawking Brothers, Ernie Bridge and even Troy have played the Grand Ole Opry, but as Gina Mendello, who is now working back in Nashville, puts it, "I used to come here and it was like, 'Really, country music in Australia?' Now they know it exists, people in the industry, but you couldn't ask the average American country music fan if he's heard of Australian country music . . ."

Troy Cassar-Daley in 1996 was simply the latest in a long line of Australians who have made the pilgrimage to Nashville and had a minimal impact. Troy's mistake, though, was not so much going to Nashville, as not staying there – in coming home. That's what Keith Urban got right; when he left Australia, he left for good. But then, perhaps Troy realised that making it in America, with all the sacrifices that entails, wasn't necessarily the be-all and end-all; there were more important things in life, like having a life.

"Nashville isn't New York or LA," says Gina Mendello. "This is the south and [people's attitude is], Well, what else is there besides Nashville? Besides America? So when someone's all the way in Australia, they might as well be on Mars. When Troy played at the Bluebird Cafe [a legendary Nashville venue], people were astounded. Everybody was like, where's this guy been? Well, he's been in Australia, that's where . . ."

Troy went to Nashville to appear at the annual Fan Fair, and he stayed on to record most of his second album *True Believer* with producer/songwriter Steve Dorff.

What I learned from the experience over there was daunting. It happened a bit quick, I sort of went in one end and came out the other with this album, you know.

I think that the thing that I've really learned is that a lot of my influences come from the States. Those influences have been there since day one.

The songs [for the album] came from all directions. I'd gone through lots of ups and downs after the first album came out. I'd been living in Sydney and getting pretty deep and dark for a while. Then the trip to Nashville bought out a lot of positive things in me because I'd been wanting to get there for so long and I got

so inspired over there that I got this really bad case of insomnia and I never stopped writing.

The result was that Troy emerged with an album that was 'world-class', as the odious Australian usage goes, implying that ordinarily we are less than that. *Sydney Morning Herald* music critic Bruce Elder, notoriously down on all things Tamworth, said of *True Believer*: "Cassar-Daley has crafted a marvellous hybrid. Here is music which is accessible and reflects both his Aboriginal heritage and his rural background."

Australian Rolling Stone was equivocal, however, describing Troy as "quickly outgrowing his roots. Maybe too quickly." Their review continued:

This is only the second album by an artist who's already one of the biggest acts in Australian country, and Sony have given it the full treatment. Recorded in Nashville with Troy going down songwriter's row in search of that elusive universal, somehow *True Believer* survives the process. Just. It's as if the plane that left Tamworth only got so far as Bakersfield. Which is to say, thankfully, there's still a modicum of earthiness about this album. Ironically, it's at its best when the songwriting credit belongs to Troy alone, when the material's attractive modesty cuts through the 'bigger' (blander) aspirations.

Reviews don't have a big impact on record sales in Australia, but bad ones, especially in an outlet like *Rolling Stone*, can cause their subjects distress. Troy, in typical fashion, tried to consider this one as just another opinion, and then got on with things.

In November 1996, not long after the album came out, Troy got married in Brisbane to 4KQ breakfast announcer Laurel Edwards, who, as befitting a member of one of Australian radio's stalwart major country stations, has been known to warble a hillbilly tune or two herself. Three months later, at the 1997 Golden Guitars, *True Believer* cleaned up, and Troy had effectively deposed Lee Kernaghan, at least for the moment. It was a nice wedding present.

"You could be protectionist about it," says Gina Mendello, "but when you compare the quality of the recording, it's so far beyond the first album. Troy acknowledges he could have done it in Australia, but it would have taken much longer."

True Believer established Troy as a major Australian country star, but at a price. Because despite the album's success in Australia, and despite the fact that Troy made reasonable inroads when he did go to Nashville, he hasn't returned there, but rather seems to have turned his back on the idea of cracking America.

"What you do here in Nashville is, you get in a queue," says Gina Mendello.

You might get signed, but then they say, okay, we've got a few other things to release first. Priorities. It's huge commitment of time, energy and money on behalf of a record company. And with that attitude, everybody's very careful, watching their budgets, and they have to have a success happening to fund everything else . . .

There's a whole drill you gotta do. You gotta have a manager, a publicist, you gotta get a bus, a staff, go on tour – and that's not something you can just pop into town and do. You gotta work on promotion, you gotta work on everything, you gotta do the job. You gotta want to do it.

And the thing is, you have to be here. And Troy's just had a baby. He can't get himself here for a long-term commitment right away. But if he did! . . .If he could stick around and get in his record company's face, and be willing to get in the queue . . .

What happened was that Troy realised what his true priorities were.

AFTER HE GOT MARRIED, Troy tried at first to a keep a base in Sydney. He was on the road all the time anyway. But it wasn't long before he moved to Brisbane. Country music's fabled lost highway becomes just that if you don't get off it after a certain point. Troy realised he didn't like living in such a big steaming city as Sydney anyway, when he wasn't living out of a suitcase – and he was losing the taste for that, too.

The following year, Troy's son Clay was born. Two years after that, in 1999, Troy finally slipped out his third album, *Dream Out Loud*, the follow-up to *True Believer*. *Dream Out Loud* didn't exactly set sales records, but it re-established Troy on the Australian scene.

People take my music for what it is, I guess. I hope that I've been able to say some things that are substantial enough to be remembered. I mean, all you ever want to do as an artist is be remembered for the volume of work you leave behind. But I really want to be, hopefully, remembered as an artist that has integrity and that has something to say that's important and I guess that, you know, Sony knew what they were signing. They understood it was going to be a hard thing to sell, I suppose, because there wasn't really a lot of other artists out there talking about that, but to their credit, Sony stuck their heels in, they sold a certain amount of *Beyond the Dancing*, they got a gold album with the second one, and then the third album's gone great and we are really proud of that too.

Oz country royalty, 90s-style: Troy and Lee Kernaghan shake, Tania Kernaghan and Gina Jeffries at back

Dream Out Loud yielded at least one classic track in 'One Big Land', which for some became the unofficial Republican anthem during the sadly unsuccessful 1999 referendum campaign.

"I've come across different sorts of equality and non-equality all through my life," says Troy.

I think going to Sydney really made me realise what a multicultural society it is. If people don't cope with that, it's going to be a really hard place to live in. I figure there's not many country artists beating the drum for equality, but because of my situation and my background, I feel that it's vitally important.

'One Big Land' tells about how much equality there is getting to be around now. I mean, we've got a big place here, there's enough room for everyone, and each of the verses in that song tells about: a Bundjalung man hunting, a bloke sailing out from Plymouth, you know, and a person that's run out of a war-torn country just looking for a happy life for their kids. I mean, that is what our Australian culture is made of, and those sorts of things are going to be forever in my music, I feel so strongly about and I love Australia so much that I want it to be the best place it can be for my kids too. I have my own agenda. I want my kids and my cousins and everyone else and my family and my friends to be happy, and I think that we don't have to work too much harder to make Australia happy.

Troy's priorities go way beyond just succeeding on the very rickety plane of American show business.

When we were in America, we got invited to play the Grand Ole Opry in Nashville, and that was like this mecca. But when we played some of the communities in the Western Desert regions, you know, it was the same high of highs that I got and that I find are the most rewarding experiences that I've ever had. Because, I mean, you get to an Aboriginal community, you start unpacking the gear, to go into the accommodation which might be the local hall where you'd lay your swag out and you'd stay there, and the little kids would come out and their little black hands are all around yours, they're lifting the guitars – and that to me meant more, sometimes, than playing some really big flash show because of the emotion that was around, it was just something, those sort of experiences, I'll never forget till the day I die.

The reality for Troy, however, having more or less turned his back on America, is that he's going to have to do doubly well in Australia. But it's clear also that after three albums, he regards that as just a start – when so few of his predecessors, with the conspicuous exception of Jimmy Little, made more than a couple of albums in their entire career.

❧❧❧

Dan Sultan, who in 2014 released his third album, Blackbird, named after the studio in which it was recorded in Nashville: "I am Aboriginal and I know where I'm from and I'm proud of that, but when we're sitting around talking about a new record that I've done, then it's none of your business where my mother's from. I was just seen as another bloody Australian in Nashville."

AFTERWORD

It was a beautifully sunny autumn morning in May 2012 when I made my way down to the Sydney Opera House to attend the state memorial service for Jimmy Little. Jimmy had died about a month earlier out west in Dubbo, where he'd lived for the previous few years, and there'd already been a funeral service there for family and friends. But the NSW government had decided, gratifyingly, to honor him officially.

I was touched by Jimmy's death, just as I had always been so touched by the man himself. Over the previous decade, I'd encountered him – and worked with him – on several occasions, and every time he lived up to the hype. He was one of the sweetest, most gentle, generous, and gifted individuals I have ever met.

I will never forget the night this book was originally launched, in tandem with the premiere of the accompanying documentary at the 2000 Sydney Film Festival. In a way I was unprepared for the impact it would have, on me and other people. At the magnificent old State Theatre, and then later at the Civic Hotel for the after-party, everybody was there: Jimmy, Bobby McLeod, Bob Randall, Auriel Andrew, Wilga Williams, Roger Knox, Kev Carmody. I was greatly flattered when Charlie Perkins spoke (he made a point I'd not fully grasped before, that it was listening to country music that helped him learn English). The whole event was one of the proudest moments of my life. All these amazing people had come out for a much-deserved celebration of . . . well, themselves – and I'd helped make it happen.

After the screening of the film, which won a standing ovation, there was a bit of speechifying, and then Jimmy got up and sang 'Shadow of the Boomerang'. After he finished the song he threw an imaginary boomerang from the lip of the stage out over the audience, and there was not an eye in the house that didn't follow that invisible thing as it flew over their heads, traced an arc around the room, and returned safely to Jimmy's hands. The crowd roared.

Jimmy had been unwell for a long time even back then. He was first diagnosed with kidney disease in 1990, and in 2004 his kidneys packed it in completely. He was hospitalised, and then went on to dialysis treatment. One of his typically selfless responses to all this was to form the Jimmy Little Foundation to promote indigenous health (which is still run by his latter-day manager, Buzz Bidstrup). In 2006 he got a kidney transplant, but then he developed diabetes and a heart condition. In 2009 he cut his last recording. Reunited with producer Martin Erdman, who'd overseen his 1978 *Live at the Opera House* album, Jimmy recorded a new version of 'Royal Telephone', which, in a perfect sign of the times, was released as a download as well as on CD. His wife and soulmate Marj died in 2011, and so it was perhaps understandable that after that, Jimmy started to fade too.

At the Opera House, the scene of previous triumphs, Jimmy's daughter Frances, an academic, spoke eloquently and lovingly, leaning on her walking stick. His grandson James Henry sang 'Yorta Yorta Man'; he's not a career musician, but James can certainly carry a tune. Even conservative NSW Premier Barry O'Farrell offered a tribute that seemed genuinely heartfelt. Jimmy was widely and deeply loved.

It seemed to be going round, this sorry business, as Aboriginal people call it. In May 2011, almost exactly a year before Jimmy's death, Lionel Rose died. In December 2012, eight months after Jimmy, Herb Laughton died. In March 2013 Ernie Bridge passed, then in July Mandawuy Yunupingu died.

I watched Lionel Rose's state funeral broadcast live on TV from Melbourne's Festival Hall, the scene of many of his great fights (I saw them on *TV Ringside*) and what he would doubtless have laughed off as some of his less great gigs. Lionel was perhaps even more widely and deeply loved than Jimmy. It was another memorable moment to have met Lionel, a boyhood hero of mine. Even my father, a died-in-the-wool racist, was impressed. What I couldn't tell him, of course, was that I was doubly delighted to have been able to enjoy a variation on the "Love to have a joint with Willie" idea, and actually share a joint with Lionel!

Lionel was 63 when he passed away, and for an ex-boxer and an Aborigine, who'd drunk and smoked for most of his life, that was a pretty good innings. Jimmy Little made it to 75, and even if he never smoked or drank that was a pretty good innings too.

Of course, it was inevitable that people would start passing. Gus Williams died a year before Lionel, up in the Territory, in 2010. He was 73, and he too was accorded a state funeral. Ruby Hunter died in 2010, too; she was only 55 and widely mourned.

It was perhaps especially sad when Bobby McLeod died suddenly the year before, in 2009. He was only 62, and his passing received none of the fanfare the others would enjoy. Bobby had recorded a couple more fine albums in the 2000s, *Paradox* and *Dumaradje*, was still a powerfully built man, still leading his Donooch Dance troupe, and seemed to have so much life ahead of him. But premature death is something Aboriginal people are all too accustomed to. Harry Williams was only 64 when he died in 1991, Dougie Young barely even 60 when he died at around the same time, Isaac Yamma only 50, Mandawuy Yunupingu only 56.

As I made my way down to the Opera House to pay my respects to Jimmy, I pondered the irony that despite all this posthumous acclaim, I was involved at the time in a campaign to help the still very much alive-and-kicking Roger Knox try and get a visa to tour the US. The more things change, it so often seems, the more they stay the same . . . (A further irony: at this same time, the mission where Roger grew up, Toomelah, was in the news for having become one of the most degraded Aboriginal settlements in all Australia.)

Roger had toured the US and Canada in 1990, but in 2009, when he was booked to play at the Old Town School of Folk Music in Chicago with expatriate Welshman Jon Langford and his neo-bluegrass collective the Pine Valley Cosmonauts, he was denied a visa only a week out from the gig, and had to cancel. The reason given by US immigration authorities was that Roger was not an "artist of international stature", or some such twaddle. Langford nonetheless persisted in his dream of getting Roger his due, having been turned on to Koori country generally by the first edition of this book and its accompanying 'soundtrack' CD.

"He come to Tamworth," Roger says of Langford, "and he performed a song that I recorded called 'Streets of Tamworth' – and I was shocked, because I'd never seen any whitefella singin' my songs before."

Roger is virtually the last man standing, and if it seems unlikely that a grizzled ex-art school punk rocker from Wales should seek him out in such a way, it makes perfect sense to me, since I too am a grizzled ex-art school punk rocker, only from *New South* Wales! This is the power of the music as it reaches further afield. Langford set to getting Roger back into the studio to record a new album. As a long-time fan of Jon's bands, the Mekons and the Waco Brothers, not to mention his paintings, I was delighted to meet him in Sydney and flattered that he so admired *Buried Country*. I gave him every assistance I could, even if that mainly amounted to feeding him sausages off my barbeque!

At a time when Kev Carmody, after being given an honorary doctorate by his alma mater, the University of South Queensland, in 2009, was being inducted into the ARIA Hall of Fame (joking in typically self-deprecating fashion, "I must be getting in with the lowest record sales in history!"), and Auriel Andrew received an Order of Australia medal, Roger Knox still couldn't get arrested in his home town. Nor could he convince the American authorities that he wasn't a terrorist, that he was in fact, not unlike Jimmy Little, as I wrote in a letter of support to the US Immigration Service, a sweet and gentle man and someone of inordinate, if admittedly not widely enough recognised, talent.

But then, Harry Williams and Dougie Young haven't been inducted into the ARIA Hall of Fame either, or even the Tamworth Hall of Fame, nor have any of their classic songs made it onto the National Film and Sound Archive's registry of great Australian sound recordings. The same goes for Bobby McLeod.

And so the struggle continues.

THIS AFTERWORD DOES NOT NEED TO BE all about injustice and death, though. Aboriginal music in Australia is in many ways a huge growth industry. When I read Ted Egan's little book *Due Inheritance* recently, I was struck by his observation that there are only four fields in which Aboriginal people might expect an even chance of success: the arts, music, sport and land management. Aboriginal people are plagued by appalling health and housing; they suffer intolerably high rates of incarceration, addiction, unemployment, domestic violence, sexual abuse and suicide – and yet they certainly have a better chance of succeeding in the notoriously volatile world of show business than they do of realising the dream of becoming a school teacher, a doctor, a fireman, even a labourer.

To repeat the oft-repeated quote from Archie Roach: "Thirty years ago we were marching for justice down the city streets, but now we're telling our stories in the concert halls." This is a symptom of liberal Australia's positive discrimination policies, and happily it has produced a whole slew of state-funded theatre companies. Yet when I attended a writers festival recently, I was somewhat bemused that in its associated bookshop there was a big stack of one and only one music CD for sale, namely Geoffrey Gurrumul's debut album.

Without wishing to take anything away from such a beautiful and haunting record, I couldn't help thinking: what about all the other good Aboriginal music, especially country music, that's at least as good as if not better than all the pretentious literary fiction and self-obsessed memoirs that clog up the elitist festival circuit? And what about all the other good white music, country or otherwise?

Arty Australia likes Aboriginal dance and theatre because it offers an exotic new twist on an old highbrow tradition that it can understand. It likes Aboriginal world music because it's apparently "authentic." The whole world loves Aboriginal painting for a similar reason, and doesn't seem to mind that the artists themselves are still being exploited by dealers and middlemen. But then, liberal-arty Australia puts career curators on the covers of weekend newspaper supplements ahead of the struggling artists themselves, and it fears and loathes Aboriginal country music because it fears and loathes country music and popular music in general – because it's lowbrow, the work of the underclass. Geoffrey Gurrumul is the latest token figure to be adopted by the chardonnay set; the greater body of contemporary music in this country is accustomed to having to bear up under the contempt, the cultural apartheid practised by Australia's cultural elites.

But just as Australian rock, pop and country have been broadly self-sufficient for a long time, Aboriginal music has also now established itself as a fact of life on the real-world live music circuit. It's just that it's no longer so predominantly country.

Certainly, the 'new corridos' of the 1990s kicked open the door for a whole generation of acoustic Aboriginal singer-songwriters. But this genre petered out somewhat, not least because it failed to produce any artists that even approached the stature of, say, Archie Roach. Perhaps only Toni Jenke came close. Gurrumul could arguably be seen as an extension of this tradition (at least sonically, to some extent), but his songs, in language, remain largely unintelligible to most listeners. Which of course, along with his blindness, only adds to his mystique.

The decline of the folk-country singer-songwriters was however happily offset by an explosion in soul or urban/R&B and hip-hop during the same period. The recent feature film *The Sapphires* is really just a nostalgic confection atop the real groundswell of popular Aboriginal music, which includes dancefloor divas from Christine Anu to the movie's star, Jessica Mauboy, and hip-hop acts, whether the Last Kinection or Sky'High. It's significant that when 'From Little Things, Big Things Grow' actually became a hit record in 2008, a Top Ten single in the wake of Prime Minister Kevin Rudd's 'Sorry' speech to Aboriginal Australia, it was in a remixed version courtesy of Sydney hip-hop renaissance man Urthboy.

Nevertheless, country music – Aboriginal country music – is still alive, if largely in the rural areas. In the Central Desert, the bloodlines carry on in the way the late Gus Williams's son Warren H. Williams has produced a string of fine (and successful) hard country albums in the 2000s, and the way the late Isaac Yamma's son, Frank Yamma, after taking his blistering electric guitar attack about as far as it could go, has more recently returned to his acoustic roots on 2010's *Countryman* album. At Tennant Creek, north of Alice Springs, the Benning Brothers are still twangin' after fifty years. And in the north-west too, the songlines refuse to die: Kevin Gunn may have retired – even his successor, Peter Brandy, has retired – but Geoffrey Fletcher carries on despite his advancing years, and so do Danny Marr and his Fitzroy Xpress, while a younger generation comes through in the form of the Pilbara's Theona Councillor and Derby's John Bennett. Bennett's single 'Wangkaja' was a beautiful song, and he recently cut his debut album in Perth with the assistance of former Asleep at the Wheel steel guitarist Lucky Oceans. And then there's Fitzroy Crossing's remarkable Olive Knight, who, already in her fifties, recently launched a career as a solo country-gospel-blues singer-songwriter-guitarist.

Tamworth is still big business, but like the bush ballad itself, it's becoming increasingly outmoded. Troy Cassar-Daley remains a favorite son, and Warren Williams now takes pride of place there too, but it's significant that the most recent young Aboriginal talent to emerge from the town, Loren Ryan, aims to succeed as a soul singer. This is a not uncommon scenario, especially among female artists: present-day black stars such as Emma Donovan and her cousin Casey, Kylie Auldist and Jessica Mauboy all readily admit that they started out singing country, only subsequently moving into soul-dance-pop. There is even one, Jacinta Price from Alice Springs, who actively embraces a sort of bipolar career: she's just cut her debut solo album, *Dry River*, with producer Bill Chambers, the veritable patriarch of Australian alt-country, but she also sings (under the name Sassy-J) in Alice hip-hop crew Catch the Fly, whose 2011 track 'Let It Rain' became something of a local anthem.

When I went to Tamworth on the *Buried Country* documentary shoot in 1999, we encountered a Nyungar fella from Western Australia by the name of Percy Hansen who'd lobbed into town in the hope of making it in country music. Hansen and his band made a couple of pretty good CDs, but then disappeared from view. More recently, another Western Australian Nyungar, Shelley Atkins, moved there with her father, didgeridooist Mark Atkins, and though she produced a fine album, *Shell*, for CAAMA, in 2005, she hasn't yet released a follow-up.

Of course, Tamworth still doesn't want to know about its prodigal son Roger Knox. Roger's son, Buddy, is another who carries on the bloodlines, but he has re-set his trajectory; he now plays a scorching, funky brand of blues with a power trio comprising two of his nephews, bassist Barega Knox and drummer Bareki.

Troy Cassar-Daley, as ever, continues to strike a satisfying balance between Tamworth and Byron Bay, between country and the alt-roots scene, for want of a better term – and this is perhaps the most promising ground for the extension of Aboriginal country music into the new century. 'Americana' is the generic tag in the US; it's much the same kind of music that's increasingly popular in Australia too, although it can hardly be dubbed Australiana because that tag has already been taken, more or less, by bush balladry.

Troy eventually parted ways with Sony, but like so many other artists of his ilk (Steve Earle, for example), this was the making of him, in a way. America can have Keith Urban! Troy went on to join forces with the new royal family of Australian alt-country, Kasey Chambers and her brother Nash, who ran the Essence label, and for Essence he produced a string of fine albums in the mid-2000s. When Essence folded, he joined Michael Gudinski's post-Mushroom label Liberation, which started life with a modest 'unplugged' agenda, and he's continued to release high-quality, successful albums.

The rise of Melbourne's Dan Sultan is another vote for the new roots revival. It's one thing for Gurrumul to find almost overnight success selling records to people who attend writers festivals and concerts at the Opera House but never go to pub gigs – echoing or rather surpassing the experience of TI's Seaman Dan, who in 2000 started his recording career at age 71 and promptly started collecting ARIA awards – but it's something else again to work your way up via the grass-roots live circuit the way Dan Sultan has, enjoying few of the benefits of positive discrimination that underwrite more respected Aboriginal cultural endeavors like 'legitimate' theatre and gallery art. Sultan, who is a direct descendent of Vincent Lingiari, is currently one of the hottest young properties in Australian music. He's perhaps less a great songwriter, more a great singer, a good guitarist and a great performer, but whatever he's already achieved, on the great leveller that is the pub circuit, has been on his merits alone.

Sultan describes his sound as "country-soul rock'n'roll", and he was indeed misplaced when the world music scene tried to claim him (as it does most Aboriginal artists who are not overtly country). But then he's slotted perfectly into the roots scene, where for a colour-blind hardcore music constituency all the genres like country, blues, soul, folk and jazz – black and white – meld together.

It's a bit like the way another new young act, Benny Walker, from Echuca, describes his influences. Walker, whose laid-back acoustic grooves could almost get him mistaken for a stoner surfer dude like Jack Johnson, told ABC-TV's *Message Stick*, "I write songs in a lot of different genres, anything from blues, you know, I've listened to a lot of country, there's country influences in there, reggae, rock, folk, everything . . ."

'A lot of country' – it provides most of the best new Aboriginal singer-songwriters with what Jimmy Little called "a solid base to work from." These new artists include a growing number of young women, whose development parallels that of their white sisters such as Missy Higgins, Sarah Blasko or Julia Stone, who've so revitalised the mainstream Australian scene. Leah Flanagan, Thelma Plum, Sue Ray, Nancy Bates, Jacinta Price and Naomi Pigram are all acoustic singer-songwriters whose blood is as mixed as their folk-country-blues influences.

The roots revival has also created the climate for an artist like Archie Roach to make a comeback to recording that was almost equally a homecoming. His 2002 album *Sensual Being* was perhaps a bit too much like its predecessors, and *Ruby* (2005) was simply a vast digression, but *Journey*, Archie's 2007 album for Liberation, was essentially a return to country. Co-produced by Nash Chambers and Shane Howard and featuring guests like Troy Cassar-Daley, some of the Pigrams and Paul Kelly, it was his perkiest album for some time. Sadly, however, Archie suffered a stroke in 2010, not long after Ruby Hunter died, and was subsequently diagnosed with lung cancer. And he wasn't even 60 yet. He said at the time that, having lost his soulmate, he hoped he hadn't lost his voice as well – and *Into the Bloodstream*, his 2012 follow-up to *Journey*, proved that he hadn't, finding him in fine form, delving deeper still into his true gospel, soul, blues and country roots.

Into the Bloodstream was produced by Craig Pilkington, a former member of 80s Melbourne indie pop outfit the Killjoys (which also spawned Gurrumul's producer and manager Michael Hohnen); Pilkington also had a hand in another stunning Aboriginal comeback album, Kutcha Edwards's *Blak & Blu*. Edwards is a veteran of the Melbourne Koori scene who'd touched on rock and reggae since starting out with his band Blackfire in the early 1990s, before emerging from illness and a crisis of faith with his third solo album and most convincing to date, with its rollicking acoustic country-blues sound and penetrating songs. The single 'Get Back Up Again' was a killer, with a message to anyone, black, white or brindle, who ever got knocked down by life.

South Australian Glenn Skuthorpe is a fine young country-rock singer-songwriter who's made four albums since 2001, and Tasmania's Dewayne Everettsmith is shaping up well too, but perhaps the best new Aboriginal songwriter is L.J. Hill. From the dusty plains of north-western NSW, Hill has Aboriginal, Cherokee and Irish blood, and before committing to music he had been a rodeo rider, a footballer, a shearer and a 'gentleman of the streets' in Melbourne and Sydney. He cites Springsteen, Merle Haggard and Tom T. Hall as his principal influences, but I can hear plenty of Kristofferson in him, and a bit of Townes van Zandt too; there's even a little Jimmy Little in his breathy intimacy. After a 2002 debut called *Inside the Universe*, Hill released his second album *Namoi Mud* through Sydney independent label Laughing Outlaw in 2009; produced by Brendan Gallagher, who helmed Jimmy's epochal *Messenger* (and who fronts his own alt-country band Karma County), and with Hill himself playing all the instruments (guitar, bouzouki, piano and organ), the album is a minor masterpiece.

"Rather than the social issues embraced by some of his fellow indigenous artists, Hill's themes approach the universal through the personal," said the *Australian*. "But it's not just the country feel that Hill brings to his songs," said the *Courier Mail*. "He has urban dislocation and alienation running through his tunes, heard clearly when he sings of a friend here and a relative there hit by the scourge of drink and drugs, in songs like '18th Day of May' and 'Pretty Bird Tree'."

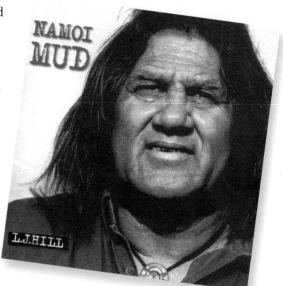

'Pretty Bird Tree' is as good a song as any written in Australia this century, and that includes hits by Gurrumul or Gotye. But as always seems to be the case in the music game, Hill is swamped in the marketplace by anything and everything louder, faster and less deep. For all the glowing reviews they garner, his albums sell only modestly. But his songs will last. If this book ever enjoys a third edition, I hope — and I'm willing to bet — that L.J. Hill will warrant a chapter in his own right, as will Dan Sultan. I hope too that Naomi Pigram, of the famous Broome dynasty, will deliver more fully on the promise of her swampy 2009 debut album *Other Side of*

Town; that John Bennett will do likewise; that the veteran Ali Mills will make another album as good as her belated 2010 solo debut; that Olive Knight can do something similar; that *Into the Bloodstream* won't be the ailing Archie Roach's last album; that the 68-year-old Vic Simms will finally get all the credit he's due following the release of a tribute album, *Painted Ladies*, produced by young Brisbane-Islander country-rocker Luke Peacock . . .

And that Roger Knox will no longer have to justify himself to bureaucrats.

Roger did get to America again, I'm glad to say. The efforts of Jon Langford and Sally Timms eventually paid off. The immigration authorities allowed him into the USA, and in October 2012 he played two shows in San Francisco and one each in Chicago and Madison, Wisconsin, as well as adding the finishing touches to the album Langford was putting together for indie roots label Bloodshot.

At the Hardly Strictly Bluegrass festival in San Francisco, Roger shared a stage with such giants as Earl Scruggs, Doc Watson, the Flatlanders, Guy Clark and Steve Earle among many others, and he was warmly received.

"It was huge!" said Roger after the show, talking to roving reporter Brian Wise from Melbourne radio station 3RRR's roots music program *Off the Record*. "Nothing like I've seen before . . . There was a couple of big huge eucalyptus trees . . . Just needed some koala bears!"

Roger was stung by his initial visa rejection in 2009, but it was just one in a long line of indignities he's suffered in his life as a black man, and now he was just pleased to finally get through. The album *Stranger in My Land* is a tribute to what Roger refers to as his peers and predecessors. It contains a dozen versions of Koori classics, and for producer Langford, at a time when most of this material was not generally available after the *Buried Country* CD compilation had been deleted, it was just a case of getting back out there again "these

Jon Langford and Roger Knox, San Francisco, October 2012

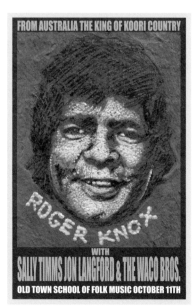

songs," as Langford put it, "that deserve to be heard." And indeed, until such time as the *Buried Country* CD returns to print, Roger's new album is the best introduction to the genre, alongside Enrec's *Koori Classics*, which was recently re-released as a download. Roger sings his heart out, as ever, and as he said, for international audiences it's "something different, the stories that I tell, and how I bring it across."

Indeed, response to the album in the US verged on astonishment, with such influential websites as PopMatters and No Depression giving it glowing reviews. Native Canadian writer Richard Wagamese hailed it as "the most important country release of 2013 . . . country music wrought bruised and aching from the dustbowl that is Australia's Outback."

Wagamese continued: "You can't hear 'Took The Children Away' without recalling Canada's history of residential schools, or the plaintive 'Blue Gums Calling Me Back Home' without recalling Whispering Pines, say, and in the end this is why this collection matters. Sure, there's nobody two-steppin' blonde-haired girls in tight jeans around a wooden dance floor, or roof-down-on-the-convertible faux-rock guitar solos makin' every night a Saturday night, but what there is is heart, a down-to-earth negotiation of pain, frustration, and heartbreak that fuses with hope and triumph and sheer élan to create a vibrant testimony to our human capacity to endure."

IT'S NOT UNUSUAL THAT THE REAL PROPHETS and innovators of Australian music are forced to make it overseas before being accepted at home. This is what happened in the 80s, for example, to post-punk/pre-alternative rock visionaries like Nick Cave, the Go-Betweens and the Triffids. But at a time in 2013 when the annual Vivid contemporary music festival at the Sydney Opera House can import an Alan Lomax tribute show from the US, how come a local living legend like Roger Knox has to go offshore to produce *Stranger in My Land*? Sadly the album's title still seems all too true. How come when Roger played a national tour to promote the album in April 2013, it amounted to a handful of gigs at tiny venues? How come the anointed have the red carpet rolled out for them at the Opera House when Roger Knox still has to scrabble around to find a couch to doss on for the night?

❥❥❥

The first Aborigine on wax – one of the very first Australians on wax – Fanny Cochrane Smith records her second session with Horace Watson at Sandy Bay, Tasmania, in 1903. From the settlement on Flinders Island, Smith was first recorded at the Tasmanian Museum in 1899. An unidentified voice on that recording said: "I feel very glad indeed that the Aboriginal language of this island, together with its songs, however fragmentary, have at last been permanently registered, and can be preserved and listened to in future years, when this and the remaining representatives have passed away."

DISCOGRAPHY

This discography covers indigenous artists in Australia who made their recorded debut prior to the early 1990s. This cut-off point was chosen not only because it aligns generally with the time frame of the book, but also because – not entirely coincidentally – it marks the point at which CDs superseded vinyl and cassettes.

It includes not just country artists but all indigenous artists in Australian pop. It does not include traditional or modern-traditional fusion music, which accounts for a fair swathe of didgeridoo music, nor does it include gospel choirs, though it does include country-gospel acts. It does not include performers without a standalone recording to their name (i.e., those who have only appeared on compilations). The Jimmy Little section, for a similar reason, includes only his original albums, not the many re-releases. Compilations are listed under 'Various Artists' at the end, and do not extend into the CD era.

Individual entries, however, extend up to the present day. The only acts included who did not make their debut on vinyl or cassette (or shellac for that matter) are Troy Cassar-Daley, TI's Mills Sisters, the Pigram Brothers, Tiddas, Danny Marr's Fitzroy Xpress and the Benning Brothers, but all of them have their roots in the pre-CD era, which I think justifies their inclusion.

A major starting point for this discography was obviously Peter Dunbar-Hall's ScreenSound publication, *Recordings by Australian Indigenous Artists 1899-1998*, but I have expanded on it considerably by drawing on other (largely label-based) discographies that are listed in the Sources and by referring to my own collection. Crate-digging is the anthropology of pop scholarship, and I remain an inveterate vinyl junkie.

In the decade since the first edition of this book was published, I have come across even more releases, and these are happily now included, most notably – incredibly! – Dempsey Knight's Polish single. Other (rumoured) releases whose existence I still can't confirm – like Clivie Kelly's 'My Home in the Valley', Mick and Aileen Donovan's 'Halfcaste Outcast', or an EP by Donna and Sandy Atkins – are still excluded.

Many of the items listed were only ever released regionally and in very limited quantities, and—in the 80s—only on cassette. Australia's National Film & Sound Archive, formerly ScreenSound, holds some, but by no means all of them. AIATSIS (Australian Institute of Aboriginal & Torres Strait Islander Studies) also holds some, but others, especially easily destructible cassettes, are all but lost. A *Buried Country* 2CD soundtrack set was released to coincide with the original publication of this book, but it had been deleted even before Larrikin-Festival was bought up by Warners; it is my hope that Warners may yet re-release it. At least, in the internet era, much of the music can easily be located online.

TREVOR ADAMSON
Trust in the Lord
(CC, Imparja, '85)
Godaku Walytja-Piti
(CC, Good God, '87)
Where I Belong
(CC, CAAMA, '89)
Waltzing Matilda
(CD, CAAMA, '95)
My Sunburnt Country
(CD, Pindaroo, '09)

AMUNDA
Better Late Than Never
(CC, '89)
Civilised World
(CC, CAAMA, '92)
'Pedlar Avenue'
(CDSP, Stunt, '93)

AURIEL ANDREW
Truck Driving Woman
(EP, Nationwide, '70)
Just For You
(LP, Nationwide, '71)
Chocolate Princess
(LP, Opal, '82)
Mbitjana
(CC, Imparja, '85)
Let's Get Together
(CC, Xtra, '94)

AREYONGA DESERT TIGERS
Light On (CC, Imparja, '88)

AROONA
Running Water
(CC, Imparja, '85)

ARTOOWARAPANA COUNTRY BAND
Artoowarapana Country
(CC, AIMS, '87)
Adnyamathanha Way
(CC, Dex, '88)

GEORGE ASSANG
[see also Vic Sabrino]
Daughter of Mona Lisa
(78, Mercury, '55)

ASSANG BROTHERS
[aka George & Ken,
aka the Colonials]
Just a Closer Walk
(LP, Philips, '65)
Songs from Down Under
(LP, Philips, '67)

DONNA ATKINS
Donna Atkins (CC, '86)

MOONIE ATKINSON
Hank, You're a Legend
(EP, Hydra, '81)
Moonie in Mildura
(CC, Enrec, '89)

BENNING BROTHERS
Kimberley Country
(CD, Pindaroo, '98)
King Sound
(CD, Pindaroo, '00)
Barry Benning and Friends
(CD, Pindaroo, '09)

BLACK ALLAN BARKER
Fire Burnin'
(CC, AbMusic, '83)

BLACK LACE
'Deaths In Custody'
(45, Maya, '88)

HAROLD BLAIR
Australian Aboriginal Songs (EP, Score, '56)
'How Great Thou Art'
(45, Crest, '61)
Music from the ABC-TV Documentary
(CD, ABC, '95)

BLEKBALA MUJIK
Midnait Mujik
(CC, CAAMA, '90)
Nitmiluk!
(CC, CAAMA, '90)
Come-n-Dance
(CD, CAAMA, '93)
Blekbala Mujik
(CD, CAAMA, '95)

CHARLES BOBONGIE
... and a Borrowed Guitar
(CC, LoveTale, '90)

JOSIE BOYLE
Warburton Mountains
(CC, '86)
Dinky Di Aussie (CC, '87)
Wongatha Gospel (CC)
Josie Boyle & Friends: Country Gospel (CC)

GEORGE BRACKEN
'Turn Me Loose'
(45, W&G, '59)
'Blue Jean Rock'
(45, W&G, '60)

ERNIE BRIDGE
Sings Kimberly Favorites
(LP, EMI Custom, '79)

'Helicopter Ringer'
(45, EMI Custom, '80)
Helicopter Ringer
(LP, EMI Custom, '80)
Live At The Concert Hall
(CC, EMI, '82)
Sings It Australian
(LP, EMI, '83)
Great Australian Dream
(LP, '90)
200 Years Ago (CD, '94)

BROWN BROTHERS
Cape Barren Island Dance Music
(EP, AWA Custom, c.'76)

KEV CARMODY
'Jack Deelin''
(45, Rutabagas, '88)
Pillars of Society
(LP, Rutabagas, '88)
'Thou Shalt Not Steal'
(45, Rutabagas '90)
'Eulogy' (45, Festival, '90)
Eulogy (for a Black Person)
(CD, Festival, '90)
'Cannot Buy My Soul'
(45, Festival, '91)
'Blood Red Rose'
(CDSP, Festival, '92)
Street Beat
(CDEP, Song Cycles, '93)
Bloodlines
(CD, Song Cycles, '93)
'Freedom'
(CDSP, Song Cycles, '93)
'On the Wire'
(CDSP, Song Cycles, '94)
Images & Illusions
(CD, Song Cycles, '95)
'The Young Dancer is Dead'
(CDSP, Song Cycles, '95)
Messages
(CD, Song Cycles, '00)
Mirrors
(CD, Song Cycles, '03)
Cannot Buy My Soul
(CD, EMI, '07)
'Children of Gurindji'
[with Sara Storer]
(CDSP, ABC, '11)

TROY CASSAR-DALEY
Dream Out Loud
(CDEP, Sony, '94)
Beyond The Dancing
(CD, Sony, '95)
True Believer
(CD, Sony, '96)

'Workin' for the Man'
[with Lee Kernaghan]
(CDSP, ABC, '96)
Big River (CD, Sony, '99)
Long Way Home
(CD, Essence, '02)
Borrowed and Blues
(CD, Essence, '04)
Brighter Day
(CD, Essence, '05)
Almost Home
(CD, Rajon, '06)
Love this Place
(CD, Liberation, '09)
Troy Cassar-Daley Live
(CD/DVD, Liberation, '10)
Home (CD, Liberation, '11)

CASSO & THE AXONS
Australia for Sale ·
(CC, Imparja, '87)

CASSO AND REGGAE DAVE
Love is the Only Drug
(CC, CAAMA, '90)

BARRY CEDRIC
'I'm an Aborigine'
(45, Huge, '87)
Where You From, My Brother? (CD, '93)
House of Prayer (CD)
Dreamtime (CD, '00)

VI CHITTY
'Awakening'
(45, Homegrown, '79)
Tall Trees
(CC, Homegrown, '84)

COLOURED STONE
Coloured Stone
(CC, Imparja, '83)
'Black Boy'
(45, Imparja, '84)
Koonibba Rock
(LP, Imparja, '85)
Island of Greed
(LP, Imparja, '85)
'Island of Greed'
(45, Imparja, '85)
Human Love
(LP, Powderworks, '86)
'Dancing in the Moonlight'
(45, Powderworks, '86)
Black Rock Red Centre
(LP, Powderworks, '86)
Wild Desert Rose
(LP, RCA, '88)

'Wild Desert Rose'
(45, RCA, '88)
'Stay Young'
(45, RCA, '88)
Crazy Mind (CC, RCA, '89)
Inma Juju (CD, RCA, '92)
'Love is the Medicine'
(CDEP, RCA, '92)
Songs from the Nullabor
(CC, '95)
Barefeet Dancing (CC, '95)
Best of Coloured Stone
(CD, CAAMA, '98)
Rhythm of Nature
(CD, CAAMA, '98)
'Australia'
(CDSP, CAAMA, '00)

**SLIM CONNOR WITH
THE ALDORARDOES**
Sing Country Music
(CC, Pioneer Sounds, c.'80s)

COUNTRY EBONY
Southern Cross
(CC, Ntjalka, '93)

COUNTRY LADS
Country Lads
(CC, CAAMA, '90)
Hermannsburg Mountain
(CC, CAAMA, '90)

COUNTRY SHADES
Shades of Country
(CC, RTC, '86)

FRANCIS COX
Beagle Bay (CC, c. 80s)
Just a Country Boy
(CC, c. 80s)
*Memories Will Last
Forever* (CD, '09)

KATHLEEN COX
Through My Eyes
(CC, Northlake, '85)

LUCY COX
Kimberley Legend
(CC, c. 80s)

CANDY DEVINE
Candy Devine Sings
(LP, Spin, '70)
'God Rest Ye Merry'
(45, Glen, '76)

DJAAMBI
Djaambi (CC, '90)

TIM EDWARDS
Today's the Day
(CC, Gospel Fire, '89)

FITZROY XPRESS
Live in Broome
(CD, Tube, '93)
*Little Bit of Country,
Little Bit of Rock'n'Roll*
(CD, '00)
Home Sweet Home
(CD, '04)

RICK FORD
'Nowadays'
(45, Enrec, '87)

JOE GEIA
Yil Lull (LP, Dex, '88)
Tribal Journey
(CD, Larrikin, '95)
Nunga, Koori & Murri Love
(CD, Across Borders, '05)

MERV GRAHAM
'150 On Down the Line'
(45, Homegrown, '79)
Life Puzzle (CD, '96)

TRACEY LEE GRAY
'Clicketty Clack'
(45, Enrec, '88)

ROBYN GREEN
He is the Answer
(CC, Alpha/Omega, '86)
Vol. 2: Good News
(CC, Focus, '88)
Shine On
(CC, Alpha/Omega, '92)

KEVIN GUNN
Travellin' Man
(LP, Matilda, '80)
Country Variety
(LP, Matilda, '82)
Best of Kevin Gunn
(CC, RTC)
Kimberley Roadtrain
(LP, Big Wheel, '91)
'Kimberley Roadtrain'
(45, Big Wheel, '91)

COL HARDY
Protest Protest
(EP, Opal, '71)
'(Land They Call) Down
Under' (45, Opal, '71)
Black Gold (LP, Opal, '73)
'Words' (45, Opal, '76)
Hardy Country
(LP, Opal, '78)
Black & White Tangle
(LP, Opal, '82)
Remember Me
(LP, Opal, '91)

JOHNNY HUCKLE
*Reflections of Johnny
Huckle* (CC, '87)
Wiradjuri Country
(CC, '90)
Koori Love (CD, '96)
Spiritman (CD, '07)

GEOFF HUNT
'Mum & Dad'
(45, EMI, '82)
... Sings Elvis (CC)
'Guitar Boogie'
(45, Stony Broke)

HUNTER, RUBY
Koorie (CC, VACHT, '89)
Thoughts Within
(CD, Aurora, '94)
Feeling Good
(CD, Mushroom, '00)
Ruby's Story
(CD, AAA/MGM, '05)

ILKARI MARU
Ilkari Maru
(CC, Imparja, '84)
*Wangangarangku
Rungkan: Lightning Strikes*
(CC, Imparja, '88)

DARYL KANTAWARA
My Country
(CC, Ntjalka, '92)
Finke River Blues
(CD, '00)

**KINTORE GOSPEL
BAND**
Western Desert Gospel
[with Mount Liebig Band]
(CC,Imparja, '88)

LEON 'TEX' KINCAID
'Let Us Walk in the Light'
(45, Blue Wren, '86)

JOSH KIRBY
... Plays Country Lovin'
(CC, '82)

DEMPSEY KNIGHT
'Annabelle'
(45, [Polskie] Nagrania
Muza, '69)

ROGER KNOX
Give It a Go
(LP, Enrec, '84)
The Gospel Album
(CC, Enrec, '86)
'Goulburn Jail'
(45, Enrec, '88)
Warrior in Chains
(CD, Enrec, '93)
Goin' On, Still Strong
(CD, Trailblazer, '04)
Stranger in My Land
(CD, Bloodshot, '12)

KUCKLES
'Traffic Lights'
(45, CASM, '82)
*Miliya Rumurra: Bran Nue
Dae* (CC, MRC, '85)
Songs From Bran Nue Dae
(CC, BND, '90)

HERBIE LAUGHTON
Herbie Laughton
(CC, CAAMA, '83)
Country from the Heart
(CD, Pindaroo, '98)

GEORGIA LEE
'Mean to Me'
[with Graeme Bell]
(78, EMI, '49)
'St. Louis Blues/
Blue Moon' [with the
Quintones]
(78, Jazzart, '51)
... Sings Blues Downunder
(LP, Crest, '62)

JIMMY LITTLE
'Mysteries of Life/
Heartbreak Waltz'
(78, Regal Zonophone, '56)
'Stolen Moments/
Someday You're Gonna Call'
(78, Regal Zonophone, '56)
'My Foot on the Stair/
Time to Pay'
(78, Regal Zonophone, '57)
'A Fool Such as I/
Sweet Mama'
(78, Regal Zonophone, '57)
'Golden Wristwatch/
Why Must There be a
Tomorrow'
(78, Regal Zonophone, '57)
'Grandest Show of All/
Silver City Comet'
(78, Regal Zonophone, '57)
Grandest Show of All
(EP, Columbia, '57)
'Waitin' for You/
Frances Claire'
(45, Columbia, '58)
'Oh, Lonely Heart/
The Coloured Lad'
(45, Columbia, '58)
Ballads with a Beat
(EP, Festival, '59)
'Danny Boy'
(45, Festival, '59)
'El Paso' (45, Festival, '59)

Whispering Hope
(EP, Festival, '60)
You'll Never Walk Alone
(LP, Festival, '60)
'Shadow of Boomerang'
(45, Festival, '60)
'Going My Way'
(45, Festival, '60)
'Somebody's Pushing Me'
(45, Festival, '60)
'Little Green Valley'
(45, Festival, '60)
*Too Many Parties -
and Too Many Pals*
(EP, Festival, '61)
'Kissing Someone New'
(45, Festival, '61)
'Christmas Roses'
(45, Festival, '61)
A Tree In The Meadow
(LP, Festival, '62)
The Way of the Cross
(EP, Festival, '62)
'Long Time to Forget'
(45, Festival, '63)
Sing To Glory
(LP, Festival, '63)
A Man Called Peter
(EP, Festival, '63)
'Royal Telephone'
(45, Festival, '63)
Royal Telephone
(LP, Festival, '64)
'One Road'
(45, Festival, '64)
Onward Christian Soldiers
(LP, Festival, '64)
'Eternally'
(45, Festival, '64)
Old Time Religion
(EP, Festival, '64)
Lifeline (EP, Festival, '64)
Royal Telephone
(EP, Festival, '64)

A Christmas Selection
(EP, Festival, '64)
'Secretly'
(45, Festival, '65)
'Ring, Bells, Ring'
(45, Festival, '65)
'His Faith in Me'
(45, Festival, '65)
*... Sings Country &
Western Greats*
(LP, Festival, '65)
'I Want to be Free'
(45, Festival, '66)
Ballads & Strings
(LP, Festival, '67)
'Too Many Times'
(45, Festival, '67)
New Songs From Jimmy
(LP, Festival, '67)
'Molly' (45, Festival, '68)
I Can't Stop Loving You
(LP, Festival, '69)
'I Can't Stop Loving You'
(45, Festival, '69)
Sing to Glory
(LP, Festival, '69)
'Goodbye Old Rolf'
(45, Festival, '70)
Goodbye Old Rolf
(LP, Festival, '70)
Winterwood
(LP, Festival, '72)
'Back in the Race'
(45, Festival, '73)
'Baby Blue'
(45, Festival, '74)
'Good to Feel This Way'
(45, Festival, '75)
'Goodbye Isn't Good At
All' (45, Festival, '75)
All For Love
(LP, Festival, '75)
'Good, Good Morning'
(45, Festival, '75)

Travellin' Minstrel Man
(LP, Festival, '76)
'Travellin' Minstrel Man'
(45, Festival, '76)
'May the Force Be With
You' (45, Festival, '78)
*An Evening with Jimmy
Little: Live at Sydney
Opera House*
(LP, Festival, '81)
'Beautiful Woman'
(45, Festival, '83)
'Ballad of Bobby White
& Billy Black'
(45, Bunyip, '88)
Yorta Yorta Man
(CD, Monitor, '95)
Messenger
(CD, Festival, '99)
'Randwick Bells'
(CDSP, Festival, '99)
'The Way I made You Feel'
(CDSP, Festival, '99)
'Bury Me Deep in Love'
[with Kylie Minogue]
(CDSP, Festival, '01)
Resonate (CD, Festival, '01)
Down the Road
(CD, ABC, '03)
Life's What You Make It
(CD, Festival, '04)
'Royal Telephone'
(CDSP, Du Monde, '09)

RONALD 'TONKY' LOGAN
Singing a Memory (CD,
Studio 19, '94)
Tonky's Country Country
(CC, '95)

MAGPIES
'Brisbane Blacks'
(45, Sunset, '82)

SHARON MANN
'Far Away'
(45, Enrec, '88)
Reach Out
(CC, Enrec, '90)
My Home in Joskeleigh
(CD, Enrec, '94)

CEDDY McGRADY
Culture Country
(CC, Enrec, '89)

BUCK McKENZIE
'Magpie & Crow'
(45, HBJ, '87)
Yura Udi (CC, SA Dept. Ed)

Yakarti Songs
(CC, SA Dept. Ed)
The Flag (CD, '08)

KEN McKENZIE
The Christian Bushman
(CC, Windwood, '84)

BOBBY McLEOD
'Friendship Road'
(45, Enrec, '87)
Culture Up Front
(CC, Larrikin, '87)
Spirit Mother
(CD, Larrikin, '93)
Paradox (CD, '01)
Dumaradje
(CD, ACMEC, '05)

MILLS SISTERS
[DARWIN]
Arafura Pearls
(CC, Capricorn, '87)
*Sing Along with the Mills
Sisters* (CD, '95)

MILLS SISTERS [TI]
Frangipani Land
(CD, Newmarket, '93)
Those Beautiful TI Girls
(CD, Newmarket, '96)

EVA AND PETER MORGAN
It's in My Heart (CC, '88)

PAT MORGAN
Never Give Up
(CC, Focus, '90)

MOUNT LIEBIG BAND
Western Desert Gospel
[with Kintore Gospel Band]
(CC, Imparja, '90)

JOHNNY NICOL
Touch of Blue
(LP, Phonogram, '72)
Traces (LP, Hunter, '79)
I Remember
(LP, Hunter, '83)
'What's the Use'
(45, Avan-Guard)
Where the Love Is
(LP, Larrikin, '89)
Moving Forward
(CD, La Brava, '97)
Music's Got a Hold on Me
(CD, '07)
Jazz at Home (DVD, '08)

NO FIXED ADDRESS
Wrong Side of the Road
[with Us Mob]
(LP, BAR, '81)
From My Eyes
(EEP, Rough Diamond, '81)
'We Have Survived'
(45, Rough Diamond, '82)

NORTH TANAMI BAND
Warlpiri, Warlpiri People
(CC, CAAMA, '90)
Travelling Warlpiri
(CC, CAAMA, '95)

OLIVE AND EVA
'Old Rugged Hills/
Rhythm of Corroboree'
(78, Prestophone, '55)
'When Homeland's
Calling/Maranoa Moon'
(78, Prestophone, '56)

DAVID PAGE
'Happy Birthday Sweet 16'
(45, Atlantic, '75)
'Dreamtime Lover'
(45, Atlantic, '75)

PIGRAM BROTHERS
Saltwater Country
(CD, Jigil, '98)
Jiir (CD, Pigram Music, '01)
Under the Mango Tree
(CD, Pigram Music, '06)
Live at the Pearl Luggers
(DVD, Pigram Music, '07)

BOB RANDALL
Ballads by Bob Randall
(CC, CAAMA, '83)
Tjilpi (CD, Axent, '00)

HEATHERMAE READING
'You Don't Need Me'
(45, Atlantic [NDR], '76)
'Keep on Dancin''
(45, Atlantic [NDR], '76)
'You're Really Something'
(45, Bovema-Negram
[NDR], '78)

WILMA READING
'Nature Boy' (45, Rex, '60)
'In My Little Corner of the
World' (45, Rex, '60)
'Only Came to Say
Goodbye' (45, Rex, '61)
'My Way'
(45, Vicor [PH], c.'71)

On Fire
(LP, CNR [NDR], '72)
'If You Hold My Hand'
(45, CNR [NDR], '72)
'One More Mountain'
(45, Pye [UK], '73)
'Down at Our Place'
(45, Pye [UK], '74)
'Something About You,
Baby' (45, Pye [UK], '74)
'Play it Again'
(45, Pye [UK], '74)
Take a Closer Look
(LP, Pye [UK], '74)
'Looking for Another Pure
Love'
(45, Pye [UK], '74)
Wilma Reading
(LP, Pye [UK], '76)
'It's Over'
(45, Pye [UK], '76)
Now You See Me (CD,
Australian Sun, '08)

JIM RIDGEWAY
'Ticket to Nowhere'
(45, CM Records, '80)

ARCHIE ROACH
Charcoal Lane
(LP, Aurora, '90)
'Took the Children Away'
(45, Aurora, '90)
'Down City Streets'
(45, Aurora, '90)
Jamu Dreaming
(CD, Mushroom, '93)
'From Paradise'
(CDSP, Mushroom, '93)
'Walking into Doors'
(CDSP, Mushroom, '93)
Looking for Butter Boy
(CD, Mushroom, '97)
'Hold On Tight'
(CDSP, Mushroom, '97)
Sensual Being
(CD, Mushroom, '02)
Definitive Collection
(CD, Festival, '04)
Journey
(CD, Liberation, '07)
Archie Roach: 1988
(CD, ABC, '09)

LIONEL ROSE
'I Thank You'
(45, Festival, '69)
I Thank You
(LP, Festival, '70)
'Please Remember Me'
(45, Festival, '70)

'Little Ol' You'
(45, Festival, '70)
Jackson's Track
(LP, Festival, '72)
'Had to Leave Her'
(45, RCA, '79)
Getting Sentimental
[with Howie Brothers]
(CD, Glenample, '93)

VIC SABRINO
[see also George Assang]
'The End Of The Affair'
(78, Pacific, '55)
'Merry-Go-Round'
(78, Pacific, '55)
'Rock Around the Clock'
(78, Pacific, '55)
'Blue Suede Shoes/
Heartbreak Hotel'
(78, Pacific, '56)
'Dust In The Sun'
(78, Festival, '57)
'Hitch Hiking Heart'
(45, Festival, '57)
'Painted Doll'
(45, Festival, '57)
'Sweet Georgia Brown/
Freight Train'
[this and following 45s
with Graeme Bell and his
Skiffle Gang]
(45, Columbia, '57)
'Don't You Rock Me,
Daddy-O/John Henry'
(45, Columbia, '57)
'Gospel Train/Come Skiffle
Chicken'
(45, Columbia, '57)
'Gamblin' Man/Skiffle
Board Blues'
(45, Columbia, '57)

SCRAP METAL
Just Looking (CC, '87)
Broken Down Man
(CC, Jigil, '88)
'Broken Down Man'
(45, Jigil, '88)
'Somewhere in the
Distance'
(45, Auralsect, '88)
'Nimunburr'
(45, Auralsect, '89)
Scrap Metal (LP, ABC, '90)
'Make It Work'
(45, ABC, '90)
'Howling at the Moon'
(45, ABC, '91)
Pub, Sweat & Tears
(CD, Jigil, '92)

FRANKIE SHOVELLER
Nulungu Songs (CC, c.'84)

MAC SILVA
'Malabar Mansion'
(45, Enrec, '88)

VIC SIMMS
'Yo-Yo Heart'
(45, Festival, '61)
'Counting Up My Love'
(45, Festival, '61)
Yo-Yo Heart
(EP, Festival, '62)
The Loner (LP, RCA, '73)
'Back into the Shadows'
(45, RCA, '73)
'Koala Bear'
(45, Enrec, '88)
From the Heart
(CD, Bunyip, '96)

ARNOLD 'PUDDING' SMITH
*Stop Ringing the
Submission Bells* (CC, '84)

SOFT SANDS
Soft Sands
(CC, Imparja, '85)
Soft Sands
(CD, TEABBA, '02)

SUBWAY
What Does It Mean?
(CC, '86)

LES SUMNER
Self-Portrait (CC, '86)

TABLELAND DRIFTERS
On the Road
(CC, CAAMA, '91)

MICK THAIDAY
Two Sides of Me
(CC, Imparja, '85)

TIDDAS
Inside my Kitchen
(CDEP, Blackheart, '92)
Sing About Life
(CD, PolyGram, '93)
'Waiting'/'Inanay'/'Long
Time Now'
(CDSP, PolyGram, '93)
'Real World'
(CDSP, PolyGram, '94)
Flat Notes and Bad Jokes
(CDEP, PolyGram, '94)
'Changing Times'
(CDSP, PolyGram, '95)

Tiddas (CD, PolyGram, '96)
Lethal by the Kilo
(CD, PolyGram, '98)
Show Us Ya Tiddas
(CD, PolyGram, '00)

TITJIKALA DESERT OAKS BAND
Titjikala Desert Oaks Band
(CC, CAAMA, '89)

UPK SPECIAL BAND
*Unwankara Palyanku
Kanyintjaku*
(CC, CAAMA, '89)

US MOB
Wrong Side of the Road
[with No Fixed Address]
(LP, BAR, '81)

WARUMPI BAND
Warumpi Band
(CC, CAAMA, '83)
'Jailanguru Pakarnu'
(45, Hot, '84)
Big Name, No Blankets
(LP, Yinura, '85)
'Breadline'
(45, Yinura, '85)
'Blackfella/Whitefella'
(45, Yinura, '85)
'Sit-down Money'
(45, Yinura, '85)
Go Bush (LP, Festival, '87)
'My Island Home'
(45, Festival, '87)
'Tjiluru, Tjiluru'
(45, Festival, '87)
'Stompin' Ground'
(CDSP, CAAMA, '96)
Too Much Humbug
(CD, CAAMA, '96)

WEDGETAIL EAGLE BAND
Wedgetail Eagle Band
(CC, CAAMA, '88)

BILL WELLINGTON
The Night Owl
(EP, Enrec, '85)
Rockin' on the Moon
(CC, CAAMA, c. '92)
Rainbow Song
(CCEP, Big Wheel)
Memories of Alice
(CC, CAAMA, '94)

MANNY WEST
Introducing…
(CC, Enrec, '87)

WESTERN DESERT BAND
Western Desert Band
(CC, CAAMA, '91)

CANDY WILLIAMS
'Tom Dooley' [with
Noeline Batley]
(45, Rex, '60)
'Five Brothers'
(45, Rex, '60)
'My Blue Heaven'
(45, Rex, '60)

GUS WILLIAMS & COUNTRY EBONY
Storm in my Heart
(CC, Ntjalka, '89)
I'm Not Trying to Forget
(CC, Ntjalka, '91)
Straight from the Heart
(CC, Ntjalka, '92)
My Kind of Heaven
(CC, Ntjalka, '93)
Through the Years
(CC, Hadley, '94)

HARRY AND WILGA WILLIAMS AND THE COUNTRY OUTCASTS
'Home-Made Didgeridoo'
(45, '74)
'Nullabor Prayer'
(45, Angelwood, '75)
*Harry Williams and
the Country Outcasts*
(LP, RCA, '79)
*Harry and Wilga Williams
and the Country Outcasts*
(LP, Hadley, '81)

WARREN H. WILLIAMS
Western Wind
(CD, CAAMA, '96)
Country Friends and Me
(CD, CAAMA, '98)
'Raining on the Rock'
[with John Williamson]
(CDSP, Emusic, '98)
Where My Heart Is
(CD, CAAMA, '01)
Places in Between
(CD, CAAMA, '02)
Mates on the Road [with
John Williamson and Pixie
Jenkins] (CD, EMI, '04)
Be Like Home
(CD, CAAMA, '05)
Looking Out
(CD, Heartland, '09)
Urna Marra
(CD, ABC, '11)

BILL WELLINGTON
RAINBOW SONG

MEMORIES ARE FOREVER
COUNTRY STYLE
YVONNE P. WINMAR

THROUGH THE YEARS
Gus Williams & Country Ebony

15 Australian Greats

YVONNE P. WINMAR
Memories Are Forever
(CC, Law, '93)

WIRRINYGA BAND
Dreamtime Shadow
(CC, CAAMA, '90)
Dreamtime Wisdom, Moderntime Vision
(CD, CAAMA, '95)

STEVE AND CAROL YARRAN
Hold His Healing Hand
(CC, '87)
My Jesus Cares (CC, '91)

FRANK YAMMA
Solid Eagle
(CD, CAAMA, '97)
Playing with Fire
(CD, CAAMA, '99)
Keep up the Pace
(CD, CAAMA, '06)
Countryman
(CD, Wantok/Planet, '10)

ISAAC YAMMA AND PITJANTATJARA COUNTRY BAND
#1 (CC, CAAMA, '83)
#2 (CC, Imparja, '87)

YIRARA PITJANTJATJARA GIRLS
'Alatjiringuna Jesunya Wanantjikitja' (45, 8HA)

YOTHU YINDI
Homeland Movement
(LP, Mushroom, '88)

'Mainstream'
(45, Mushroom, '89)
'Djapana'
(45, Mushroom, '89)
Tribal Voice
(LP, Mushroom, '91)
'Treaty' (Filthy Lucre Remix)
(12" 45, Mushroom, '91)
'Tribal Voice'
(CDSP, Mushroom, '92)
'Djapana'
(12" 45, Mushroom, '92)
'World Turning'
(CDSP, Mushroom, '93)
Freedom
(CDSP, Mushroom, '93)
'Dots on the Shells'
(CDSP, Mushroom, '94)
'Timeless Land'
(12" 45, Mushroom, '94)
'Superhighway'
(CDSP, Mushroom, '96)
Birrkuta: Wild Honey
(CDSP, Mushroom, '97)
One Blood
(CD, Mushroom, '98)
Garma
(CD, Mushroom, '00)
'Community Life'
(CDSP, Mushroom, '00)

DOUGIE YOUNG
Land Where the Crow Flies Backwards
(EP, Wattle, '65)
Songs of Dougie Young
(CD, AIATSIS, '93)

GALARRWUY YUNIPINGU
'Gurindji Blues'
(45, RCA, '71)

VARIOUS ARTISTS COMPILATIONS
4th National Aboriginal Country Music Festival
(CC, CMA, '79)
The First Australians
(LP, AAA, '79)
Desert Songs
(CC, CAAMA, '82)
Rebel Voices
(CC, CAAMA, '83)
Desert Songs 2
(CC, CAAMA, '83)
Koori Classics, Vol. 1
(CC, Enrec, '85)
Rock Against Racism
(CC, Aboriginal Radio Association, '85)
Fifteen Australian Greats
(CC, Josie Boyle Productions, c. '87)
Koori Classics, Vol. 2: Aboriginal Artists All-Australian Fifties Party
(CC, Enrec, '88)
Koori Classics, Vol. 3: The Girls (CC, Enrec, '88)
Koori Classics, Vol. 4: Aboriginal Prison Songs
(CC, Enrec, '88)
Papal Concert, Alice Springs (CC, Imparja, '88)
Beat the Grog
(CC, CAAMA, '88)
Building Bridges
(LP, CBS, '88)
Wama Wanti: Drink Little Bit (LP, CAAMA.'88)
From The Bush
(LP, CAAMA, '89)
AIDS: How Could I Know
(LP, CAAMA, '89)

Koori Classics, Vol. 7: Jump & Jive (CC, Enrec, '89)
Look at Us! Warlpiri Mix
(CC, CAAMA, '90)
Sing Loud, Play Strong
(CC, CAAMA, '90)
Croc Rock
(CC, Arafura, c. '91)
From The Bush II
(CC, CAAMA, '92)

Members of eighties black band Us Mob encounter, not uncommonly, a member of the constabulary (played by Chris Haywood) in a scene from Ned Landers's docu-drama Wrong Side of the Road, *which portrayed the realities of life for working, or rather non-working, Aboriginal musicians.*

SOURCES

Since this book is in such large part an oral history, the main sources were in every case the subjects themselves. All those with whom I conducted interviews are listed in the Acknowledgements. Additional sources are as follows:

BIBLIOGRAPHY

AMR/Quantam Harris. Australian National Country Music Survey (Country Music Association of Australian, '96, Tamworth)

Andrews, Shirley. 'The Co-Existing Folk Culture', article (*Australian Tradition*, July '65)

———. 'A Musical Mixed Marriage', article (*Australian Tradition*, June '66)

Baldwin, James. *Sonny's Blues* (Penguin, '95, UK)

Batty, J.D. *Namatjira* (Hodder & Stoughton, '63, Melbourne)

Beckett, Jeremy. 'Aborigines Make Music', article (*Quadrant*, Spring '58)

———. 'Where the Crow Flies Backwards', article (*Quadrant*, July '65)

Breen, Marcus (ed.). *Our Place, Our Music* (AIATSIS, '89, Canberra)

Brennan, Peter, and David Latta. *Australian Country Music* (Random House, '91, Sydney)

Bradley, Kevin. 'Leaf Music in Australia', article (*Australian Aboriginal Studies* #2, '95)

CAAMA. press kit ('83, Alice Springs)

Calvinist, John Henry. *The Dead Set*, liner notes (Shy-Tone Tapes, '98, Brisbane)

Cantwell, Alan. *When We Were Good* (Harvard University Press, '96, US)

Carr, Patrick (ed.). *The Illustrated History of Country Music* (Dolphin, '80, US)

Clare, John. *Bodgie Dada* (UNSWP, '95, Sydney)

Clark, Mavis. *Pastor Doug* (Rigby, '72, Melbourne)

Crocker, Andrew. *Papunya: Aboriginal Paintings from the Central Australian Desert* (AAA, '83, Sydney)

Davis, Jack (ed.). *Paperbark* (UQP, '90, Brisbane)

Dusty, Slim. *Walk a Country Mile* (Rigby, '84, Adelaide)

Edwards, Ron. *Overlander Song Book* (Rigby, '71, Sydney)

Egan, Ted. *Sitdown Up North* (Kerr, '97, Sydney)

Ellis, Catherine. *Aboriginal Music: Education for Living* (UQP, '85, Brisbane)

Gilbert, Kevin. *Because a White Man'll Never Do It* (A&R, '73, Sydney)

———. *Living Black* (Penguin, '78, Melbourne)

——— (ed.). *Inside Black Australia* (Penguin, '88, Melbourne)

Graham, Duncan. *Dying Inside* (Allen & Unwin, '89, Sydney)

Grissim, John. *Country Music: White Man's Blues* (Coronet, '70, US)

Gummow, Margaret. 'The Square Dance Song as an Aboriginal Performing Art', typescript ('87, Armidale)

Guralnick, Peter. *Lost Highway* (Penguin, '79, UK)

Harrison, K. *Dark Man, White World: Harold Blair* (Novalit, '75, Melbourne)

Hands, Ian. *Ambassadors of Country Music* (Queensland Country Style, '84, Brisbane)

Henson, Barbara. *A Straight-Out Man: FW Albrecht and Central Australian Aborigines* (MUP, '92, Melbourne)

Horton, David (ed.). *Encyclopaedia of Aboriginal Australia* (Aboriginal Studies Press, '94, Canberra)

Hoskyns, Barney. *Say It One Time for the Broken Hearted: The Country Side of Southern Soul* (Fontana, '87, UK)

Hume, Martha. *You're So Cold I'm Turnin' Blue* (Viking, '82, US)

Isaacs, Jennifer (ed.). *Australian Aboriginal Music* (AAA, '79, Sydney)

Ivey, Bill, et al. *From Where I Stand: The Black Experience in Country Music*, liner notes (Country Music Foundation/Warners, '98, US)

James, Darius. *That's Blaxploitation* (St. Martin's, '95, US)

Jackomos, Alick. 'Gumleaf Bands', article (*Identity*, July '71)

———, and Richard Broome. *Sideshow Alley* (Allen & Unwin, '98, Sydney)

Johnson, Colin. *Wildcat Falling* (Angus & Robertson, '65, Sydney)

Jones, Leroi. *Blues People* (Payback, '95, UK)

Langton, Marcia. *After the Tent Embassy* (Valadon, '83, Sydney)

Lemann, Simon. *The Promised Land* (Macmillan, '91, UK)

Lethbridge, Dr H.O.. *Australian Aboriginal Songs*, sheet music, (Allan & Co., '37, Sydney)

Lockwood, Douglas. *I, the Aboriginal* (Rigby, '62, Sydney)

Lomax, Alan. *Mister Jelly Roll* (Pan, '52, UK)

———. *Land Where the Blues Began* (Minerva, '94, UK)

———. *Alan Lomax Collection*, liner notes (Rounder Recs, '97, US)

Lowenstein, Wendy. 'Jabbi: The Aboriginal Contemporary Songs', article (*Australian Tradition*, December '69)

Lynch, Reg. personal correspondence, June '99

Marre, Jeremy, and Hannah Charlton. *Beats of the Heart: Popular Music of the World* (Pluto Press, '85, UK)

Moore, Carlos. *Fela, Fela: This Bitch of a Life* (Allison & Busby, '82, UK)

Morgan, Thomas, and William Barlow. *From Cakewalks to Concert Halls* (Elliott & Clark, '92, US)

McFarlane, Ian. *Encyclopedia of Australian Rock and Pop* (Allen & Unwin, '99, Sydney)

McGrath, Noel. *Australian Encyclopaedia of Rock & Pop* (Rigby, '84, Melbourne)

McMillan, Andrew. *Strict Rules* (Hodder & Stoughton, '88, Sydney)

McNally, Ward. *The Angry Australians* (Scope, '74, Melbourne)

Michaels, Eric. *Bad Aboriginal Art: Tradition, Media and Technological Horizons* (Allen & Unwin, '94, Sydney)

Miller, James Wilson. *Koori: A Will to Win* (A&R, '85, Sydney)

Murray, Neil. *Sing for Me, Countryman* (Sceptre, '93, Sydney)

Nettl, Bruno. *Western Impact on World Music* (Schirmer, '85, US)

O'Brien, Geoffrey. 'Recapturing the American Sound', article (*New York Review*, 9 April '98)

Oliver, Paul. *The Story of the Blues* (Penguin, '78, UK)

Onus, Bill. 'Corroboree Season', program notes (Wirth's Olympia Circus, April '49, Melbourne)

Oakley, Giles. *The Devil's Music: A History of the Blues* (Da Capo, '97, US)

Oram, James. *The Business of Pop* (Horwitz, '66, Sydney)

———. *The Last Showman* (Sun, '92, Sydney)

Perkins, Charlie. *A Bastard Like Me* (Ure Smith, '75, Sydney)

Reed-Gilbert, Kerry (ed.). *Message Stick* (Jukurrpa, '97, Alice Springs)

Riese, Randall. *Nashville Babylon* (Anaya, '89, UK)

Rintoul, Stuart. *The Wailing: A National Black Oral History* (William Heinemann, '93, Melbourne)

Roberts, John S.. *Black Music of Two Worlds* (Morrow, '74, US)

———. *The Latin Tinge* (Oxford University Press, '79, UK)

Rosengarten, Theodore. *All God's Dangers: The Life of Nate Shaw* (Avon, '74, US)

Rowley, Chip. *The Destruction of Aboriginal Society* (Penguin, '72, Melbourne)

Rutherford, Anna (ed.). *Aboriginal Culture Today* (Kangaroo Press, '88, Sydney)

Saunders, Keith. *Learning the Ropes* (Aboriginal Studies Press, '92, Canberra)

Schwerin, Jules. *Got to Tell It: Mahalia Jackson, Queen of Gospel* (Oxford University Press, '92, US)

Seale, Bobby. *Seize the Time: The Story of the Black Panther Party* (Arrow, '70, UK)

Shapiro, Nat, and Nat Hentoff. *Hear Me Talkin' to Ya* (Penguin, '62, UK)

Shaw, Bruce. *Banggaiyerri: The Story of Jack Sullivan* (AIATSIS, '83, Canberra)

Shestack, Melvin. *The Country Music Encyclopaedia* (Omnibus, '77, UK)

Sidran, Ben. *Black Talk* (Da Capo, '83, US)

Smith, Jazzer. *Book of Australian Country Music* (Berghouse Floyd Tuckey, '84, Sydney)

Spencer, Chris. *Who's Who of Australian Rock* (Five Mile Press, '89, Melbourne)

Stambler, Irwin. *Golden Guitars* (Four Winds, '71, US)

Stearns, Marshall. *The Story of Jazz* (Mentor, '58, US)

Sullivan, Chris. 'Non-tribal Dance Music and Song: from First Contact to Citizen Rights', article (*Australian Aboriginal Studies #1*, '88)

Sweeney, Philip. *Virgin Directory of World Music* (Virgin, '91, UK)

Sykes, Roberta. *Snake Dreaming* (Angus & Robertson, '97, Sydney)

——— (ed.). *Murseins: Australian Women of High Achievement* (Doubleday, '93, Sydney)

Taylor, Ken. *Rock Generation* (Sun, '70, Melbourne)

Tatz, Colin. *Obstacle Race* (UNSWP, '95, Sydney)

Toohey, Paul. 'The Story of Isaac', article (*God's Little Acre*, Duffy & Snellgrove, '96, Sydney)

———. personal correspondence, 26 March '97

Tonkin, Daryl, and Carolyn Landon. *Jackson's Track* (Viking, '99, Melbourne)

Toop, David. *Exotica: Fabricated Soundscapes in a Real World* (Serpent's Tail, '99, UK)

Tosches, Nick. *Country* (Dell, 1977, US)

Toyne, Phillip, and Daniel Vachon. *Growing Up the Country: The Pitjantjatjara Struggle for Their Land* (Penguin, '84, Melbourne)

Tucker, Margaret. *If Everyone Cared* (Ure Smith, '77, Sydney)

Ulman, Rick. *Hillbilly Jazz*, liner-notes (Flying Fish Recs, '74, US)

Ward, Russel. *Penguin Book of Australian Ballads* (Penguin, '64, Melbourne)

Walker, Clinton. 'The emergence of black music', article (*Rolling Stone*, June '84)

————. 'Aborigines express their hope in urban corroboree', article (*Age*, November 23 '84)

————. 'Black bop rocks Sydney and the bush', article (*Age*, '85)

————. 'Black Music: Roots, Rock & Reggae', article (*Age*, May 30 '86)

————. 'Archie Roach: His song cycles ...', article (*Rolling Stone*, March '93)

Watson, Eric. *Country Music in Australia, Volume 1* (Cornstalk, '75, Sydney)

————. *Country Music in Australia, Volume 2* (Cornstalk, '83, Sydney)

Watson, Sam. *The Kadaitcha Sung* (Penguin, '90, Melbourne)

Welch, James. *Winter in the Blood* (Penguin, '86, US)

Wiora, Walter. *The Four Ages of Music* (Norton, '65, US)

NEWSPAPERS & JOURNALS

Aboriginal News
ADC News
The Age
Australian Music Museum
Australian Tradition
Capital Country News
Dawn
Deadly Vibe
DEET News
Go-Set
Identity
Irabina
Koori Mail
Land Rights News
Music Maker
New Dawn
Pix
Rolling Stone
Spurs
Sydney Morning Herald
Tempo
Territory Digest
Tjungaringanyi

FILMOGRAPHY

The Squatter's Daughter (Cinesound, 1933)

'Hermannsburg Mission' (Arthur Murch, 1934)

'Aboriginal Girl Scores as Singer' (Cinesound Review, 1946)

'Billy Bargo: Champion Whip Cracker' (Pathé newsreel, 1947)

Tjilla Trail (BP, 1962)

In Song and Dance (Commonwealth Film Unit, 1964)

A Changing Race (ABC-TV, 1964)

Forgotten People (Aboriginal Advancement League, 1967)

Brown Skin Baby (ABC-TV, 1970)

Come Out Fighting (Nigel Buest, 1972)

Sister, If You Only Knew (Film Australia, 1975)

Malbangka Country (AIAS, 1975)

Country Outcasts (Film Australia, 1975)

My Survival as an Aborigine (AFI, 1979)

Lousy Little Sixpence (Ronin Films, 1983)

Aboriginal Video Magazine #4: Country Music Festival (NT Govt, 1983)

Aboriginal Video Magazine #5: Galwin'ku Music *Festival* (NT Govt, 1984)

The Slim Dusty Movie (Kent Chadwick, 1984)

Who Killed Malcolm Smith? (Film Australia)

Blood Brothers #2: Freedom Ride (Film Australia)

Sing it in the Music (ABC TV, 1987)

88.9: Radio Redfern (Film Australia, 1989)

Night Cries (Ronin Films, 1989)

Sing Loud, Play Strong (CAAMA, 1989)

DISCOGRAPHIES

Crotty, George. 'Festival Singles, 1961-1969', typescript

de Looper, Michael. 'The Australian W&G Catalogue', typescript

————. 'Australian EMI 45's and 12" Singles, 1968-1979', typescript

Dunbar-Hall, Peter. *Recordings by Australian Indigenous Artists 1899-1998* (ScreenSound Australia, '99, Canberra)

Spencer, Chris. *An Australian Discography of Folk & Associated Artists* (Moonlight Publications, '95, Bendigo)

Kelly, Aidan. *Floods, Sweat & Beers: Rockin' Round the Northern Territory* (Moonlight Publications, '95, Bendigo)

Laird, Ross. *The First Wave: Australian Rock & Pop Recordings, 1955 to 1963* (ScreenSound Australia, '98, Canberra)

That petrol emotion: Central desert (surf) instrumental outfit the Black Shadows, unashamed petrol-sniffers, winning the Mount Liebig Battle of the Bands, July 1999. "Petrol helps me play music," said 21-year-old Barnabas, the band's leader. "When I sniff, brain inside is working. I sniff petrol and play music. Sometimes I think it's bad, but I think two ways. Sometimes it's good. But that's why I want to stop, so my son doesn't start."

NOTES & PICTURE CREDITS

FRONT MATTER

Purfleet church band – photo courtesy Patricia Davis-Hurst; Billy Craigie – photo by Bruce McGuinness, courtesy Gary Foley; Kelly Gang – courtesy *Northern Daily Leader*; Vince Quayle – photo by Chris McGuigan.

CHAPTER ONE

REFERENCES: Jimmy Little's amazing two-foot-thick scrapbook was the source of practically every article referred to and quoted, and image reproduced. Wallaga Lake Vaudeville – photo courtesy AIATSIS.

SIDEBARS: Hermannsburg Choir album cover – by permission of the Lutheran Church, Australia. WA gospel boys – photo courtesy the State Library of Western Australia, from the Battye Library collection. Billy Bargo – illustrations courtesy Ian Hands.

CHAPTER TWO

REFERENCES: Debra Jopson, 'The Baby Snatchers', article (*Sydney Morning Herald*, 30 June '97); Robert Manne, 'The Whitening Australia Policy', article (*Sydney Morning Herald*, 27 February '99).

PICTURES: Courtesy Herb Laughton, except Warrabri Festival – photo by Chris McGuigan.

SIDEBARS: **References**. Phillip Hayward, 'From the Top', article (*Perfect Beat*, v. 8 #1 July 2006); Jeff Corfield, 'String Bands and Shake Hands: Days of Old Darwin Town', paper (2002), and 'Keep Him My Heart', paper (2005 Folklore Conference, Canberra); Graham Seal and Rob Willis (eds.), *Verandah Music: Roots of Australian Tradition* (Curtin University Books, 2003); Ronnie Summers, *Ronnie: Tasmanian Songman* (Magabala Books, 2009). **Pictures**. Purfleet string band – photo courtesy Patricia Davis-Hurst; Cherbourg – from the John Oxley Library, Queensland; servicemen – from the *Argus* collection at the State Library of Victoria; Paddy Rowe and Wendy Lowenstein – photo by permission of Wendy Lowenstein, courtesy the Milne family.

CHAPTER THREE

REFERENCES: Graeme Bell, *Australian Jazzman* (Childs & Associates, '88, Sydney); Andrew Bisset, *Black Roots, White Flowers* (ABC, '87, Sydney); Bruce Conway, 'Wilma's Flying High', article (*TV Week*, 22 June '74); Mary Haugh, 'How Bettie Fisher forced Black Theatre on the map', article (*National Times*, 12 January '76); Bruce Johnson, *Oxford Companion to Australian Jazz* (OUP, '87, Melbourne); Jack Mitchell, *Australian Jazz on Record* (NFSA/AGPS, '88, Canberra); Steve Waldon,

'Rock'n'roll's Scratchy Start', article (*Age*, 4 June 2005); Clinton Walker, 'Before the Big Bang: On the Origins of Oz Rock', article (*Meanjin* #65, 2006); Darcy Niland with Leslie Raphael, *Travelling Songs of Old Australia* (Horwitz, '66, Sydney); George Assang obituary, unattributed (*Sydney Morning Herald*, 18 August 1997). Additional information from Dulcie Flower, Nancia Guivarra, Brett Assang and Jordie Kilbey.

PICTURES: Pitt Sisters – courtesy ScreenSound/Unilever' Georgia Lee with Nat King Cole – courtesy NFSA; Wilma Reading – photos courtesy Wilma Reading; 1978 Georgia Lee photo – courtesy Marcus Herman; George Assang photos – courtesy Brett Assang; Johnny Nicol photo – courtesy Johnny Nicol; Heathermae Reading photo by Les Allen, from the Les Allen Collection at the Gosford City Library, courtesy the library with special thanks to Geoff Potter.

SIDEBARS: **Pictures**. Songbook cover – courtesy Allan & Co./EMI Music; FAA photo – courtesy Col Hardy; Candy Williams photo – courtesy Jimmy Little. **References**. Richard Shears, 'Rolf Harris says sorry for racist song lyrics', article, *Daily Mail* (UK), 29 November 2008.

CHAPTER FOUR

REFERENCES: Jeremy Beckett, 'Aboriginal Balladeer', article (*Australian*, 3 July 1965); Black Allan Barker article, untitled and unattributed (*Go-Set*, 4 April 1970); 'Youthful native sings, composes', article, unattributed (*Young Modern*, 24 March 1965).

PICTURES: Dougie Young – courtesy the Young family; Bill Riley photo – courtesy *Quadrant*/NSW State Library; folknik Allan photo – with thanks to Phil Jarratt, from his Ted Noffs biography *Man of the Cross* (Macmillan, 1997); hippie Allan – photo by Philip Morris.

SIDEBARS: Gary Shearston photo – courtesy *Dawn*/NSW State Library.

CHAPTER FIVE

REFERENCES: Gary Tippet, 'A Country Rose', article (*Age*, 19 December '93); Tony Squires, 'The Game of the Rose', article (*Sydney Morning Herald*, 20 May '95).

PICTURES: Lead photo by Chris McGuigan; Lionel Rose and Slim Dusty – courtesy *Northern Daily Leader*; other photos – courtesy Lionel Rose, George Bracken.

SIDEBAR: Dempsey Knight photo – courtesy *Dawn*/NSW State Library.

CHAPTER SIX

REFERENCES: John Byrell, *Bandstand... and all that* (Kangaroo Press, '95, Sydney); Royal Commission into NSW Prisons Report (Government Printers, '78, Sydney).

PICTURES: Courtesy Vic Simms, John Fairfax.

SIDEBAR: 'Gurindji Blues' clipping courtesy *Identity/* NSW State Library.

CHAPTER SEVEN

REFERENCES: Abart Productions, press release (Dec. '86, Sydney); Deborah Jopson, 'Healer back from the brink', article (*Sydney Morning Herald*, 26 November '94); Christopher Keating, *On the Frontier: A Social History of Liverpool* (Hale & Iremonger, '95, Sydney).

PICTURES: At Parliament House – courtesy *Identity/* NSW State Library; family portrait – courtesy *Dawn/* NSW State Library; *7:30 Report* – still courtesy ABC-TV; Kooriers –photo by John Ellis, courtesy the John Ellis Collection at the University of Melbourne Archives, with thanks to Jane Beattie. Clipping – courtesy John Fairfax.

SIDEBAR: Pictures courtesy Col Hardy.

CHAPTER EIGHT

REFERENCES: Eric Myers, 'The musical emergence of outcasts', article (*Nation Review*, 25 January '79); Keith Richard, 'Beside Black Mountain', article (*Men's Vogue*, June/July '77); John Stokes, program notes (NACMF, Adelaide '79); Angela Wales, 'Australia's Great Black Hope: country and western music', article (*National Times*, 21 March '77).

PICTURES: Photos by Chris McGuigan. Posters courtesy Chris McGuigan.

SIDEBAR: *Reference*. Liner notes to Buddy Williams's album *Under Western Skies* (Axis, 1991), by Andrew Smith. *Picture*. Jimmy Little and Brian Young – courtesy Evelyn Silk.

CHAPTER NINE

PICTURES: Lead photo by Chris McGuigan. Poster – courtesy Chris McGuigan. On the street at Tamworth – courtesy *Northern Daily Leader*.

CHAPTER TEN

REFERENCES: Chris Butler, 'She's the Evonne Goolagong of Song', article (*Adelaide Advertiser*, 7 July '73); Mike Hughes, 'One-Way Ticket from the Never-Never', article (*TV Times*, 3 February '71); Elizabeth Johnswood, 'My People are a Singing People', article (*Women's World*, 16 August '72).

PICTURES: Courtesy Auriel Andrew. Outcasts – photo by Chris McGuigan.

CHAPTER ELEVEN

PICTURES: Lead photo by the author, courtesy Film Australia. Other photos courtesy ABC-TV, Bob Randall.

SIDEBAR: Darwin's Mills Sisters – photo courtesy *Northern Daily Leader*; other photo – courtesy Bumma Bippera Media.

CHAPTER TWELVE

PICTURES: Lead image from the *NT News*; 'Jam in Alice' photos – courtesy Herb Laughton; cassette cover by Redback Grafix, design by Michael Callaghan and/ or Ray Young, courtesy Bronwyn Barwell.

SIDEBAR: Photos of No Fixed Address, Coloured Stone and Warumpi Band – courtesy *Rolling Stone* (Warumpi Band photo by Frank Hinder).

CHAPTER THIRTEEN

REFERENCES: Eddie Greenaway, 'King of Koori Country', article (*Eddie* #8, '94); Carolyn Osterhaus, 'We Call It Koori Music', article (*Aboriginal Culture Today*, ibid.); Heather Perryman, *Koori Kountry Music: Set to Go in January*, press release (TKKMA, '86); Royal Commission into Aboriginal Deaths in Custody, National Report (Australian Government Publishing Service, '91, Canberra); Margaret Scheikowski, 'Horror Story of a Not So Lucky Country', article (*Northern Daily Leader*, 8 January '88).

PICTURES: Photos courtesy Roger Knox, Heather Perryman, and Evelyn Silk; 'Mop' Conlon and James Wilson-Miller – photo courtesy *Northern Daily Leader*; Jimmy Knox – photo courtesy Rick Carey.

SIDEBARS: 'Moonie' Atkinson and Mop and the Drop-Outs – photos courtesy *Northern Daily Leader*; Mac Silva – photo by Chris McGuigan; Ed Matzenik – photo courtesy Ed Matzenik.

CHAPTER FOURTEEN

PICTURES: Courtesy Rick Carey.

SIDEBARS: *References*. Raymond Conder, *Ernie Bridge Biography*, booklet (Ernie Bridge Promotions, '85, Perth); Chris Havercroft's Pigram Brothers interview in *X-Press*. *Pictures*. Ernie Bridge – photo courtesy *Northern Daily Leader*; Pigram Brothers – photo by Helene Jedwab, with thanks.

CHAPTER FIFTEEN

REFERENCES: Andrew Stafford, *Pig City* (UQP, 2004, Brisbane); One Louder Entertainment, Kev Carmody bio (c. 2009, Sydney); Richard Flanagan, liner notes to *Cannot Buy My Soul* (EMI, 2005); Noel Mengle, 'Why Kev Carmody Rules, OK', article (*Courier Mail*, 16

February 2007); Richard Guilliatt, 'Two of Us', article (*Good Weekend*, 14 November '98); John O'Donnell, 'The Black & the Blues', article (*Rolling Stone*, January '89); interviews with Kev Carmody and with Archie Roach and Ruby Hunter (together), from ABC-TV's *Talking Heads*, respectively 21 May 2007 and 12 May 2008; Paul Kelly, *How to Make Gravy* (Penguin, 2010, Melbourne); Michael Dwyer, 'Ruby's River Song', article (Age, 15 October 2004); concluding Archie Roach quote from *Art of Healing*, vol. 1 no. 22.

PICTURES: Lead photo by Liisa Hannus; Archie Roach trophy photo by Chris McGuigan; Archie Roach and Ruby Hunter – photos courtesy Jacqueline Mitelman and Mushroom Records.

SIDEBAR: Tiddas photo – courtesy PolyGram/UMA.

CHAPTER SIXTEEN

REFERENCES: Jon Farkas, 'From Grafton to Golden Guitars', article (*Capital Country News*, April '97); Sony Music artist biography (March '97).

PICTURES: Courtesy *Northern Daily Leader*.

COLOUR PLATES

Dougie Young photo – courtesy the Young family; all record sleeves and labels from the author's collection. Fantales box image – authorized by Sweetacres trademark owner, Societé des Produits Nestlé S.A., Vevey, Switzerland; Warrabri Country Bluegrass Band live in Alice – photo courtesy Herb Laughton; Mac Silva – still from the film *Country Outcasts*; Herb Laughton artwork and Isaac Yamma portrait – by Redback Grafix, design by Michael Callaghan and/or Ray Young, courtesy Bronwyn Barwell; Billy Bargo and

Jim Ridgeway – artwork by Jon Langford, courtesy the artist; Roger Knox – photo courtesy Heather Perryman; Wilga Williams – photo by Chris McGuigan; Euraba Band – photo by Peter Brennan; TV stills by the author; Kev Carmody – photo by Stephen Booth; dual portrait of Archie Roach and Ruby Hunter by Jandamarra Cadd, courtesy the artist (prints of this and other works by the artist available for purchase from the website http://jandamarrasart.com).

END MATTER

Dan Sultan – photo by Rachel Raymen, courtesy Buzz Thompson; Roger Knox and Jon Langford – photo by Jean Cook; Roger Knox poster by Jon Langford, courtesy the artist; Fanny Cochrane Smith – picture courtesy Museum of Tasmania; cassette covers from the author's collection; *Wrong Side of the Road* – still courtesy *Rolling Stone*; Black Shadows – photo by Paul Toohey, courtesy the *Australian*; Herb Laughton in front of the Ghan train – photo by Andy Nehl or the author, courtesy Film Australia; photo of the author with Lionel Rose by Andy Nehl.

NOTE

The author and the publisher would like to thank all those who supplied photographs and gave permission to reproduce copyright material in this book. Every effort has been made to contact all copyright holders; in the rare instances where our efforts proved unsuccessful, we offer our apologies and urge the copyright holder to contact the publisher. In such cases, we will be pleased to obtain appropriate permission and provide suitable acknowledgment in future printings.

ACKNOWLEDGMENTS

It's a statement of the obvious to say this book would not have been possible without the artists who are its subject, and so my biggest thanks go to these amazing people: Jimmy Little, John Nicol, George Bracken, Wilma Reading, Herb Laughton, Bill Riley, Lionel Rose, Vic Simms, Bobby McLeod, Paul Meredith, Col Hardy, Wilga Williams, Gus Williams, Warren Williams, Auriel Andrew, Bob Randall, June Mills, Tiga Bayles, Galarrwuy Yunupingu, Roger Knox, Denis Conlon, Kevin Gunn, Ernie Bridge, Troy Cassar-Dalcy, Les Collins, Wally Pitt, Archie Roach, Ruby Hunter, Tiddas and Kev Carmody. I interviewed all of them first-hand at least once, some of them more than once. And some of them, to my great delight and edification, I got to know, and could call my friends.

Whitefellas I interviewed include Ted Egan, Coral Dasey, Kenny Kitching, Gina Mendello, Bill Davis, Slim Dusty, Ed Matzenik, Heather Perryman, Brian Young, Jeremy Beckett, Ron Wills, Geoff Brown, Graeme Bell, Randall Wilson and Rick Carey. They were also very generous with their personal collections of memorabilia, and I'm very grateful to them.

I also drew on interviews I had previously conducted in the 80s with the Warumpi Band, Coloured Stone's Bunna Lawrie and Bart Willoughby. James Wilson-Miller, author of *Koori: A Will To Win*, was another fella with whom I had illuminating, informal conversations.

Thanks too to the book's original publisher, Pluto Press. Pluto's then-boss, Tony Moore, took a punt when no-one else was game, and it was a delight to work on the first edition with such an open, capable team: Kate Florance, Chris Mikul, Michael Wall, Colin Hood, Brendan O'Dwyer, Colette Hoeben, designer Wendy Farley and everyone else at Social Change Media.

I owe a special thank-you to Dave Studdert for giving me the title. His former band Tactics was a favorite of mine in the early 80s, and I never forgot their song 'Buried Country' ("Memories of baited flour/From the small bush birds fly up/Carried away by the sacred hour . . . Black blood on frozen ground"). I am also grateful to Paul Kelly, not just for writing the foreword but for his help, inspiration and example.

It was really only in the process of getting *Buried Country* up as a documentary film that I was able to complete the research for the book (the shoot took me to farther flung reaches of the continent I hadn't been able to get to before), and there are many people associated with the film to whom I also owe thanks. Courtney Gibson was the first to share my vision of a film's potential; Andy Nehl then took up the reins to direct the film, and I can't begin to express my appreciation for his true heart and bottomless patience (Andy also conducted a number of preliminary interviews which I draw on in the book). Mark Hamlyn and Sharon Connolly at Film Australia picked up on the project, so thanks to them and everyone else at Lindfield, and to John Hughes at SBS. The crew we went out and shot the film with, cameraman Warwick Thornton and sound recordist Leo Sullivan, made it an even more pleasurable experience.

Special thanks must also go to Simon Drake, at the Sydney office of the National Film & Sound Archive, formerly ScreenSound; Chris McGuigan, formerly of the Aboriginal Arts Board, for his extraordinary personal archive and generosity; and James Cockington, a fellow traveller.

Thanks to Anna Rose and the *Northern Daily Leader* for allowing me such open access; thanks also for photographs to Evelyn Silk, Patricia Davis-Hurst, Rick Carey and Heather Perryman (full photo credits are listed with the sources). Ed Matzenik's Enrec scrapbook was another goldmine. And Jimmy Little's scrapbook, I trust, is now held by an appropriate library or museum.

The following people all helped in different ways: Crispin Till (*Centralian Advocate*), David Cooke, Anthony Wallis, Stuart Coupe, Paul Toohey, Peter Doyle, Richard Guilliatt, Sophie Cunningham, Martin Delaney, Geoff Mac, Doug Trevor, Dulcie Flower, Jim Paton, Steve Newton, Barry Cundy (AIATSIS Library), Eric Watson, Eric and Hilary Scott (Hadley Records), Ross Murphy (Opal Records), Marek Urbanski, Ian McFarlane, Marcus Herman, Keith Glass, and, at Festival Records, Warren Fahey, Warren Barnett and Jeremy Fabinyi. Not to mention my own family, Debbie, Lewanna and Earl, as well as my mother.

For this new edition, my thanks go first to Steve Connell and Verse Chorus Press, and to Louise Cornwall for the wonderful new design. Thanks also to Damien Minton and Bronwyn Barwell, Donat Tahiraj, Jordie Kilbey, Buzz Thompson, Buzz Bidstrup, Jandamurra Cadd, Jon Langford, Sally Timms, Geoff Potter, Stephen Booth, Philip Morris, Peter Brennan and James Scanlon. Props to Jon Langford for *Stranger in My Land*, and to Luke Peacock, Leanne de Souza and the whole Halfway/Plus One crew up in Brisbane for the Painted Ladies project.

❧❧❧

Ghan to the Alice: In front of the train of that name, Herb Laughton performs one of his greatest hits for the Buried Country *film crew, 1999.*

INDEX

Hailed by Sydney's *Sun-Herald* as "our best chronicler of Australian grass-roots culture," Clinton Walker was born in Bendigo in rural Victoria in 1957. He is an art school dropout and recovering rock critic, and the author of nine books, including *Inner City Sound,* his 1981 debut on the Australian punk uprising; *Highway to Hell: The Life and Death of AC/DC Legend Bon Scott* (1994); *Football Life* (1998); *Golden Miles: Sex, Speed and the Australian Muscle Car* (2005); *The Wizard of Oz: Speed, Modernism and the Last Ride of Norman 'Wizard' Smith* (2012); and *History is Made at Night* (2012), an extended essay on the endangered Australian live music circuit published in Currency House's prestigious Platform Papers series.

For ABC-TV, Walker was the presenter of late-night live music show *Studio 22* and co-writer of the hit 2001 Oz-rockumentary series *Long Way to the Top*, and for SBS-TV he wrote the documentary film version of *Buried Country*. In addition, he produced soundtrack CDs for all three shows, and for the expanded current edition of *Inner City Sound*, and he co-produced the 2013 anthology of 70s Australian country-rock and singer-songwriters, *Silver Roads*. His hillbilly-grunge band the Killer Sheep, after being run out of the Tamworth festival in 1987, released the single 'Wild Down Home' on Au-Go-Go Records.

Walker lives with his family in Sydney's inner-west and is currently working on a companion book to *Buried Country*, a graphic history of black women in Australian music with the title *Deadly Woman Blues*, and on a PhD called 'Reverse Crossover.'

clintonwalker.com.au